THE ROYAL HORTICULTURAL SOCIETY
PLANT ⅋ GUIDES
SHRUBS
&CLIMBERS

DORLING KINDERSLEY
London • New York • Stuttgart • Moscow

A DORLING KINDERSLEY BOOK

Produced for Dorling Kindersley by
Cooling Brown (*Book Packaging*)
9-11 High Street, Hampton, Middlesex TW12 2SA

MANAGING EDITOR Francis Ritter
MANAGING ART EDITOR Derek Coombes

Copyright © 1996
Dorling Kindersley Limited, London

First published in Great Britain in 1996
by Dorling Kindersley Limited
9 Henrietta Street, London WC2E 8PS

A CIP catalogue record for this book
is available from the British Library

ISBN 0-7513-017-44

Colour reproduction by Colourscan, Singapore
Printed and bound by Star Standard Industries, Singapore

The Library
Hadlow College
Spring Lane
Canterbury
Kent CT1 1TB
Tel: **01227 829340**

Hadlow
college

Date of Return	Date of Return	Date of Return
11 MAY 2012		
30 MAY 2013		
3 DEC 2013		
14 MAY 2014		
20 MAY 2014		
15 SEP 2014		
9.2.18		

Please note that fines will be charged if this book is returned late

THE ROYAL HORTICULTURAL SOCIETY
PLANT ❦ GUIDES
SHRUBS
&CLIMBERS

CONTENTS

CLIMBERS

CONTRIBUTORS

SUSYN ANDREWS
Hollies

KENNETH A. BECKETT
Tender Shrubs and Climbers

ALLEN J. COOMBES
*Hardy Shrubs, Hydrangeas,
Lilacs, Magnolias*

RAYMOND EVISON
Clematis

VICTORIA MATTHEWS
Hardy Climbers

CHARLES PUDDLE
Camellias

PETER Q. ROSE
Ivies

TONY SCHILLING
Rhododendrons

JOHN WRIGHT
Fuchsias

HOW TO USE THIS BOOK

THIS BOOK PROVIDES the ideal quick reference guide to selecting and identifying shrubs and climbers.

The **Shrubs and Climbers in the Garden** section is a helpful introduction and gives advice on choosing a suitable plant for a particular site or purpose, such as for a container, as a screen, or simply as a specimen plant.

To choose or identify your plant, turn to the **Catalogue of Shrubs and Climbers** where photographs are accompanied by concise plant descriptions. The entries are grouped by size and season of interest. In addition, if you have a colour preference, the plants are also grouped by colour (see the Colour Wheel below) for easy selection. Clear descriptions and cultivation requirements are to be found under each plant entry.

To gain additional information on cultivation, routine care, and propagation, turn to the **Guide to Shrub and Climber Care**, where comprehensive information on all aspects of caring for your plant can be found.

The Colour Wheel
All the plants featured in the book are grouped according to the colour of their main feature of interest.

They are always arranged in the same order, indicated by the Colour Wheel below, from white through reds and blues, to yellows and oranges. Variegated plants are categorized by the colour of their variegation, that is, white or yellow.

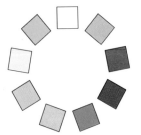

THE SYMBOLS

The symbols below are used throughout the **Catalogue of Shrubs and Climbers** to indicate a plant's preferred growing conditions and hardiness. However, both the climate and soil conditions of your particular site should also be taken into account, as they may affect a plant's growth.

☀ Prefers full sun ◖ Prefers well-drained soil

◐ Prefers partial shade ◖ Prefers moist soil

☀ Tolerates full shade ● Prefers wet soil

pH Needs acid soil

❄ Half-hardy – can withstand temperatures down to 0°C (32°F)

❄❄ Frost hardy – can withstand temperatures down to -5°C (23°F)

❄❄❄ Fully hardy – can withstand temperatures down to -15°C (5°F)

♈ RHS Award of Garden Merit. The symbol is shown for those plants deemed by the Royal Horticultural Society to be of exceptional quality and reliability. They must be of good constitution and not susceptible to any pest or disease, as well as not requiring any highly specialized care.

Plant size categories
The plants featured in the Catalogue are divided according to the average height they attain. However, heights may vary from the ones given, according to site, climate, and age.

The categories are as follows:

LARGE
Over 3m (10ft)
MEDIUM
1.5–3m (5–10ft)
SMALL
Up to 1.5m (5ft)

HOW TO USE THE CATALOGUE OF SHRUBS AND CLIMBERS

HEADINGS
Each chapter is subdivided into sections, according to the average size of the plants and their main season of interest.

The plant's *family name* appears here.

The plant's *common name(s)* appear here.

The plant's *botanical name* appears here.

PLANT PORTRAITS
The colour photographs show the main features of the plant (see THE COLOUR WHEEL on previous page).

ENTRIES
Each plant's growing habit, flowers, fruits, and leaves are described. Details of the plant's native habitat, cultivation, and propagation, together with any other botanical names, is also provided.

SYMBOLS
The symbols indicate the sun, soil, and temperature requirements (see THE SYMBOLS on previous page). Ideal temperatures are given for plants that cannot withstand below 0°C (32°F).

SMALL/Spring

| Leguminosae | HOLLY FLAME PEA |

CHORIZEMA ILICIFOLIUM
Habit Upright to sprawling. **Flowers** Pea-like, in loose racemes in spring and summer. Standard petal orange-yellow; keel rosy-mauve.
Leaves Evergreen, spiny-toothed, holly-like. Dark green.
• NATIVE HABITAT By the coast and on riverbanks in gravelly soils of W. Australia.
• CULTIVATION Grow in a conservatory in fertile, neutral to acid soil or compost, with additional sharp sand. Water moderately in growth, then sparingly.
• PROPAGATION By seed in spring.

Min. 7°C (45°F)

HEIGHT 50cm–1m (20–36in)

SPREAD 75cm (30in)

| Gesneriaceae | CLOG PLANT |

NEMATANTHUS GREGARIUS
Habit Climbing or sprawling. **Flowers** Inflated, tubular, 1–3 in loose clusters, from spring to autumn. Bright orange and yellow. **Leaves** Evergreen, elliptic to oval, fleshy. Dark green.
• NATIVE HABITAT Eastern S. America.
• CULTIVATION Grow in the home or conservatory in a humus-rich soil or compost. Water moderately in full growth; allow to almost dry out in between.
• PROPAGATION By softwood or greenwood cuttings in summer.
• OTHER NAMES *N. radicans, Hypocyrta radicans.*

Min. 13–15°C (55–59°F)

HEIGHT To 80cm (32in)

SPREAD 80cm (32in)

| Hydrangeaceae | |

DEUTZIA MONBEIGII
Habit Arching, with slender branches.
Flowers Small, star-shaped, in profuse clusters from early to mid-summer. Glistening white.
Leaves Deciduous, small, oval to lance-shaped. Dark green.
• NATIVE HABITAT In scrub at high altitudes of Yunnan, China.
• CULTIVATION Tolerates partial shade and almost any fertile, well-drained soil, but grows best in humus-rich soils that do not dry out in summer.
• PROPAGATION By softwood cuttings in summer.

HEIGHT 1–1.5m (3–5ft)

SPREAD 1.5m (5ft)

| Scrophulariaceae | |

HEBE BRACHYSIPHON 'White Gem'
Habit Low-growing, dense, rounded.
Flowers Small, 4-lobed, in tight racemes in early summer. White. **Leaves** Evergreen, small, oval to lance-shaped, smooth. Bright green.
• NATIVE HABITAT Garden origin.
• CULTIVATION Thrives in seaside gardens. Grow in any fertile, freely draining soil, with shelter from cold winter winds. Growth may be restricted on leggy plants tidied by cutting back in spring. Useful for contrasts of form and texture in the shrub border.
• PROPAGATION By semi-ripe cuttings in summer.

HEIGHT 75cm–1m (30–36in)

SPREAD 1m (3ft)

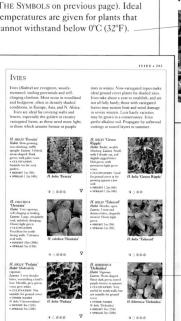

IVIES • 283

IVIES

Ivies (*Hedera*) are evergreen, woody-stemmed, trailing perennials and self-clinging climbers. Most occur in woodland and hedgerow, often in densely shaded conditions, in Europe, Asia, and N. Africa.
Ivies are ideal for covering walls and fences, especially the golden or creamy variegated forms, as these need more light, or those which assume bronze or purple tints in winter. Non-variegated types make ideal ground cover plants for shaded sites. Ivies take about a year to establish, and are not all fully hardy; those with variegated leaves may sustain frost and wind damage in severe winters. Less hardy varieties may be grown in a conservatory. Ivies prefer alkaline soil. Propagate by softwood cuttings or rooted layers in summer.

H. HELIX 'Erecta'
Habit Slow-growing, non-climbing, stiffly upright. *Leaves* 5-lobed, arrow-shaped. Dark green, with pale veins.
• CULTIVATION Suitable for the rock garden.
• HEIGHT 1m (3ft).
• SPREAD 1.2m (4ft).

H. helix 'Erecta'

H. COLCHICA 'Dentata'
Habit Very vigorous, self-clinging or trailing. *Leaves* Large, unregularly oval, unlobed, drooping. Glossy light green.
• CULTIVATION Excellent for north-facing walls. Tolerates acid soils.
• HEIGHT 10m (30ft).
• SPREAD 5m (15ft).

H. colchica 'Dentata'

H. HELIX 'Pedata'
Habit Moderately vigorous.
Leaves 5 very slender lobes, resembling a bird's foot. Metallic grey-green, with grey-white veins.
• CULTIVATION Not suitable for ground cover
• OTHER NAMES *H. helix 'Caenwoodiana'*
• HEIGHT 4m (12ft).
• SPREAD 3m (10ft).

H. helix 'Pedata'

H. HELIX 'Green Ripple'
Habit Bushy, weakly climbing. *Leaves* Small, with 5 deeply cut, and slightly jagged lobes. Mid-green, with prominent light green veins.
• CULTIVATION Good for ground cover or for growing against a low wall.
• HEIGHT 1.2m (4ft).
• SPREAD 1.2m (4ft).

H. helix 'Green Ripple'

H. HELIX 'Telecurl'
Habit Slender, open. *Leaves* 5 neat and distinct lobes, elegantly twisted. Glossy light green.
• HEIGHT 1m (3ft).
• SPREAD 1m (3ft).

H. helix 'Telecurl'

H. HIBERNICA 'Deltoidea'
Habit Vigorous.
Leaves Heart-shaped. Shiny dark green, tinted purple-bronze in autumn.
• CULTIVATION Very useful for north walls, but not suitable for ground cover.
• OTHER NAMES *H. helix 'Deltoidea'*
• HEIGHT 5m (15ft).
• SPREAD 5m (10ft).

H. hibernica 'Deltoidea'

SILHOUETTES
The shape and proportions of shrubs are indicated by silhouettes.

SIZES
The average height and spread of the plant are given, although these may vary according to site, climate, and age.

FEATURE BOXES
Plant groups or genera of special interest to the gardener are presented in separate feature boxes.

SHRUBS AND CLIMBERS IN THE GARDEN

SHRUBS FORM THE BACKBONE of a planting design, offering a rich palette of form, colour, and texture with a diversity of ornamental features including foliage, flowers, and fruits. They can also provide a substantial and contrasting framework for the softer, more transient glories of herbaceous plants, or may be used to create effective year-round interest by combining evergreen and deciduous species.

Climbers, too, are almost infinitely versatile, either when grown with support or allowed to sprawl gracefully among other plants. They are invaluable as linking elements in the garden as they can add height, colour, texture, or strong horizontal or vertical lines to a planting scheme. Climbers are unsurpassed as a means of screening or camouflaging

Combining climbers and shrubs
Climbers can be used to clothe other plants. Here the delicately coloured pink flowers of Clematis viticella *'Abundance' are shown scrambling through* Weigela florida *'Variegata'.*

otherwise unsightly garden features. Most buildings are enhanced by the softening effect of a climber grown up them. In the same way, garden walls and fences become decorative features when clothed with flowering plants.

Choosing shrubs and climbers
There are several factors to consider when selecting shrubs and climbers for the garden. One of the most vital is that the plants should grow well in the climatic and growing conditions of each particular garden. Other considerations are a plant's eventual height, spread, and rate of growth. These factors are essential for the success of all garden designs, not just for those small gardens where space is at a premium.

Overplanting is not only wasteful but expensive, and overcrowded plants will seldom grow well or achieve the full beauty or form for which they were originally selected. A plant's vigour and habit are also important: for example, *Vinca major* makes an excellent groundcover plant, but it does need careful siting if it is not to overwhelm its less vigorous neighbours.

While shrubs and climbers are invaluable as a structural framework in a design, they are far from being merely functional keystones. They are, of course, also chosen for the range of ornamental qualities that they offer, which with thoughtful planning, can provide a long succession of interest.

Site, aspect, and microclimate
One of the key factors in successful design is the selection of plants that will thrive in the particular conditions in your garden. Matching plants to soil type is a primary consideration (see p.290). A plant's preference for sun or shade should also be borne in mind. Select species to suit the temperature range and degree of shelter that pertain in the

garden. Plants of borderline hardiness are more likely to thrive in the microclimates provided by a warm, sunny wall or sheltered niche. Distance from the sea may also be a consideration. Coastal gardens are often warmer, but plants grown in such sites must be able to tolerate salt-laden winds.

Planning for successional interest
With careful planning, shrubs and climbers can offer a continuity of interest throughout the seasons. There is a huge diversity of shrubs and climbers to provide fragrance, colour, and vitality during the warmer months. Many also produce ornamental fruits or berries, or vibrant foliage colour in autumn.

Planning for the duller months is more challenging but the colours and textures of evergreen foliage make invaluable contributions to the winter garden. In winter, plants with an interesting branch form, such as the corkscrew hazel *Corylus avellana* 'Contorta', come into their own, as do those with coloured stems, such as *Rubus*

Covering a wall as a backdrop
Climbers used on this wall are (left to right) Vitis vinifera, Clematis *'Perle d'Azur' and* C. viticella *'Etoile Violette'.*

biflorus or *Cornus alba* 'Sibirica', which provide brilliant effects when caught in the low rays of the winter sun. *Garrya elliptica*, a dark-leaved evergreen, is at its elegant best when bearing swags of grey catkins in winter. Winter flowers are especially welcome when they also offer fragrance, such as the blooms of many *Hamamelis* species, *Sarcococca* var. *humilis*, and *Lonicera* × *purpusii*. Winter-flowering climbers such as the evergreen *Clematis cirrhosa* are also much valued, but climbers also show great versatility when woven through other shrubs, especially if they bloom before or after their host.

Shrubs as structural plantings
Shrubs range in size from low, dome-forming plants such as *Buxus microphylla* 'Green Pillow', to almost tree-like rhododendrons. They offer a variety of forms and habits, including rounded,

arching, and strongly vertical. One of their primary contributions in gardens is that they can be used to impart shape, structure, and substance to a design. Their forms can link house and garden, softening the transition between the rigid lines of buildings and the gentler shapes of borders and lawn. Structural plantings can be invaluable in marking an entrance, flanking a drive, or forming a boundary between one part of the garden and another. Consider how the shape, form, colour, and texture of a particular shrub mix with other plants, and elements such as walls and paving.

Shrubs in borders

Making a shrub border is the simplest way of using shrubs. Some very successful schemes rely almost entirely on foliage interest. Aim to create a balance of mass, texture, colour, and form. Avoid the temptation to plant for flowers alone; even when plants are selected to give continuity of interest their blooms are transient. Consider the height and spread of each shrub, as well as its ornamental qualities and seasonal changes of appearance.

Some shrubs may be regarded as long-term, while others tend to mature and fade quickly. When planning a border, space out the long-term plants so that they will not need drastic pruning to keep them in check once mature. Fast-growing shrubs may also be included, but they should be thinned as soon as they threaten to crowd out the core plant.

Allow space for each plant to develop to its natural form and size, in-filling if necessary with shorter-lived species.

Mixed borders combine the individual beauties of shrubs with those of other types of plants, the former making a foil and framework for the latter. Herbaceous perennials, annuals,

Autumn interest in the garden
In autumn, Acer palmatum, *as with many of the maples, helps provide a brilliant display of vibrant colour to liven up the garden when summer flowers are over.*

Unusual flowers in winter
The dwarf evergreen Daphne laureola **subsp.** philippi *will bear its lightly fragrant, pale green flowers in late winter and early spring, followed by spherical black fruits.*

and bulbs may be interplanted to provide contrasts and successional interest when the shrubs are not in flower. Dense ground cover planting will help to keep down weeds. Mulching is advisable not only to keep down weeds but to reduce water loss while the shrubs are becoming established.

Designing with climbers

Climbing plants constitute one of the most versatile of plant groups and provide enormous scope for imaginative design. They can be selected for strong colour, in flower or foliage, or to provide a more diffuse and subtle backdrop.

Many, especially twining species such as *Wisteria*, *Celastrus*, and *Vitis* species, also provide interesting architectural forms when leafless in winter. Climbers can complement or camouflage their support, whether wall, fence, trellis,

Evergreens in summer and winter
The small, white summer flowers of the evergreen Cotoneaster lacteus *give way to attractive red berries in autumn and winter.*

pillar, or pergola, creating vertical impact in a scheme. They can bring out the warm tones of stone or brickwork and soften their hard lines. Those with dense foliage and vigorous growth can disguise the most unsightly of garden buildings. When grown on supports such as trellis they can make dense visual screens, or provide wind-filtering shelter. If allowed to sprawl, those with a trailing or scrambling habit, such as *Jasminum mesnyi*, can make very effective ground cover and they look especially beautiful when clothing banks or sprawling over terrace edges. Climbers also have a place in mixed borders, either grown on pyramidal trellis or used to extend the

Climbers of similar habit combined
Several climbers have been combined together to provide a subtle range of flower colours. This mixed planting includes species of clematis, honeysuckle, solanum, passionflower and an ipomoea.

season of interest when allowed to scramble through other plants. When used in this way they can be invaluable as linking, toning, or contrasting elements in the colour scheme. Where the border backs onto a wall, climbers will provide the dimension of height, as well as being able to enhance or disguise fixed elements in the garden.

Climbing methods and supports
Climbers use a variety of techniques to scramble and climb through host plants in search of light. In gardens, both natural and purpose-built supports should be matched to suit the climbing method of the selected plant.

Some are self-clinging climbers that attach themselves by aerial roots, such as ivies (*Hedera* species), or by adhesive tendril tips, as with Virginia creeper (*Parthenocissus quinquefolia*). They will scramble up any surface that offers

purchase, but need the support of canes, string, or wires until they establish secure contact. Twining species coil around their supports in a clockwise or anti-clockwise motion. They need the permanent support of trellis or wire, or can be grown through host plants that have a sturdy branch framework.

Climbers such as clematis and some nasturtiums use curling leaf stalks to spread and gain height. Tendril climbers attach themselves with contact-sensitive tendrils which may be modified leaves, as with sweet peas; side shoots, as with passion flower (*Passiflora*); or terminal shoots, as with vines.

Trailing or scrambling climbers attach themselves only loosely – if at all – to their support. However, they can be tied in to a framework or trellis in order to control their growth habit, or allowed to sprawl unsupported, so that they cascade over walls and down banks.

PLANTER'S GUIDE TO SHRUBS AND CLIMBERS

SHRUBS FOR EXPOSED SITES

Calluna vulgaris (and cvs)
Cornus alba (and cvs)
  C. stolonifera (and cvs)
Cotoneaster horizontalis
Erica carnea (and cvs)
Euonymus fortunei (and cvs)
Hippophäe rhamnoides
Hydrangea paniculata (and cvs)
Ilex aquifolium (and cvs)
Kerria japonica (and vars)
Lonicera pileata
Mahonia aquifolium
Prunus spinosa 'Purpurea'
Pyracantha (most)
Rhamnus alaternus
Spartium junceum
Spiraea (most)
Tamarix ramosissima
Viburnum opulus (and cvs)

CLIMBERS FOR NORTH AND EAST-FACING WALLS

Akebia quinata
Celastrus orbiculatus
Clematis montana (and cvs)
Hedera colchica (and cvs)
  H. helix (and cvs)
Humulus lupulus
Hydrangea anomala subsp.
  petiolaris
Lathyrus latifolius
Lonicera × *americana*
  L. × *brownii* (and cvs)
  L. × *heckrottii* (and cvs)

L. sempervirens
  L. × *tellmanniana*
Pileostegia viburnoïdes
Schizophragma integrifolium
Tropaeolum speciosum
Vitis coignetiae

AIR POLLUTION-TOLERANT

CLIMBERS
Campsis radicans
Fallopia baldschuanicum
Hydrangea anomala subsp.
  petiolaris

SHRUBS
Aucuba japonica
Berberis (most)
Buddleja davidii (and cvs)
Cornus stolonifera 'Flaviramea'
Cotoneaster (most)
Euonymus japonicus
  'Macrophyllus Albus'
Fatsia japonica
Fuchsia magellanica (and cvs)
Garrya elliptica
Ilex × *altaclerensis* (and cvs)
  I. aquifolium (and cvs)
Leycesteria formosa
Ligustrum (all)
Lonicera pileata
Mahonia aquifolium
Philadelphus (most)
Spiraea (most)
Viburnum (most)

SHRUBS TOLERANT OF HEAVY SHADE

Aucuba japonica (and cvs)
Buxus sempervirens
  'Suffruticosa'
Daphne laureola subsp.
  philippi
Euonymus fortunei (and cvs)
  E. japonicus (and cvs)
  × *Fatshedera lizei*
Fatsia japonica
Ilex × *altaclerensis* (and

green-leaved cvs)
  I. aquifolium (and green-
  leaved cvs)
Hypericum calycinum
Leucothöe fontanesiana
Prunus laurocerasus (and cvs)
  P. lusitanica
  (and cvs)
Rhodotypos
  scandens
Ruscus (all)
Sarcococca
  (all)
Skimmia (all)
Vinca (all)

SHRUBS FOR SEASIDE GARDENS

Choisya (all)
Colutea (all)
Corokia cotoneaster
Cytisus (many)
Escallonia (most)
Genista (most)
Hebe (all)

SHRUBS FOR ACID SOILS

Camellia
Corylopsis (most)
Enkianthus (all)
Fothergilla major
Kalmia (all)
Pieris (all)
Rhododendron
  Vaccinium (all)

FOR ALKALINE SOILS

CLIMBERS
Akebia quinata
Jasminum officinale
Wisteria sinensis

SHRUBS
Cotoneaster (all)
Deutzia (all)
Forsythia (all)
Philadelphus (all)

CATALOGUE OF
SHRUBS &
CLIMBERS

Rosaceae	SARGENT CRAB APPLE

MALUS SARGENTII

Habit Spreading, thorny, sometimes tree-like with age. **Flowers** Shallowly cup-shaped, in profuse clusters in late spring. Brilliant white.
Fruits Long-lasting, globose, berry-like. Deep red.
Leaves Deciduous, oval, sometimes lobed. Dark green.
• NATIVE HABITAT Scrub and woodland of Japan.
• CULTIVATION Tolerates semi-shade and any but waterlogged soil. In winter, cut out dead and diseased wood, if necessary. Can be susceptible to fireblight. It is a beautiful shrub with a long season of interest, being densely clothed in flowers during spring and offering a profusion of small, cherry-like fruits in autumn. It is suitable for small gardens and can be grown in the shrub border or as a free-standing lawn specimen.
• PROPAGATION By budding in late summer or by grafting in winter.

HEIGHT
5m (15ft)

SPREAD
5m (15ft)

Oleaceae	

OSMANTHUS DELAVAYI

Habit Rounded, bushy, with arching branches.
Flowers Fragrant, tubular, in profusion from mid-
to late spring. White. **Leaves** Evergreen, small,
oval, finely toothed. Glossy dark green.
• NATIVE HABITAT Dry hillsides, often on
limestone, in scrub or forest of Yunnan, China.
• CULTIVATION Tolerates partial shade and lime-
rich soils. Prune after flowering, to restrict growth.
• PROPAGATION By semi-ripe cuttings in summer.
• OTHER NAMES *Siphonosmanthus delavayi.*

HEIGHT
4m (12ft)

SPREAD
4m (12ft)

Rosaceae	

AMELANCHIER LAMARCKII

Habit Bushy, wide-spreading. **Flowers** Small,
star-shaped, opening with the leaves, in sprays from
mid- to late spring. White. **Fruits** Small, berry-
like. Black. **Leaves** Deciduous, elliptic to oblong-
oval. Bronze when young, later dark green, turning
brilliant red and orange in autumn.
• NATIVE HABITAT Probably E. North America.
• CULTIVATION Grow in neutral to acid, humus-
rich soil. Tolerates semi-shade.
• PROPAGATION By seed or layering in autumn.

HEIGHT
6m (20ft)

SPREAD
4m (12ft)

Ericaceae	LILY-OF-THE-VALLEY BUSH

PIERIS JAPONICA

Habit Rounded, bushy, dense. **Flowers** Small,
urn-shaped, waxy, in drooping panicles in spring.
White. **Leaves** Evergreen, lance-shaped. Glossy
dark green, bronze when young.
• NATIVE HABITAT Open mountain forests of
Japan, Taiwan, and E. China.
• CULTIVATION Grow in moist, peaty soil, in a
sheltered site. Young tips are susceptible to frost;
cut back to healthy wood as soon as possible.
• PROPAGATION By soft tip or semi-ripe cuttings
in summer.

HEIGHT
2.5–4m
(8–12ft)

SPREAD
2.5–4m
(8–12ft)

Escalloniaceae	TASMANIAN LAUREL

ANOPTERUS GLANDULOSUS

Habit Bushy, tree-like with age. **Flowers** Cup-
shaped, waxy, in clusters from mid- to late spring.
White or pink. **Leaves** Evergreen, oval to lance-
shaped, leathery. Glossy dark green.
• NATIVE HABITAT Temperate rainforests of
Tasmania.
• CULTIVATION Grow in well-drained, humus-rich,
acid soil or compost. Water plentifully when in growth,
less in low temperatures. Prune after flowering to
restrict size. Suitable for a cool conservatory.
• PROPAGATION By semi-ripe cuttings in summer.

HEIGHT
5m (15ft)

SPREAD
5m (15ft)

Caprifoliaceae	

VIBURNUM PLICATUM 'Mariesii' ♟

Habit Bushy, spreading, with horizontally tiered branches. **Flowers** Large, flattened heads, with 'lace-cap'-type florets, in late spring and early summer. White. **Leaves** Deciduous, oval to elliptic. Bright green, then bronze-purple in autumn.
• NATIVE HABITAT Garden origin. Species occurs in mountain scrub of Japan.
• CULTIVATION Grow in deep, fertile, not too dry soil, in sun or semi-shade. Requires little pruning, other than to remove dead wood.
• PROPAGATION By softwood cuttings in summer.

HEIGHT
3m (10ft) or more

SPREAD
4m (12ft)

Oleaceae	

OSMANTHUS × BURKWOODII ♟

Habit Dense, rounded. **Flowers** Small, very fragrant, tubular with spreading lobes, in clusters from mid- to late spring. White. **Leaves** Evergreen, small, oval to elliptic, leathery. Dark green.
• NATIVE HABITAT Garden origin.
• CULTIVATION Tolerates semi-shade. Grows in any moderately fertile, well-drained soil, including chalky soils. Good for hedging.
• PROPAGATION By semi-ripe cuttings in summer.
• OTHER NAMES × Osmarea burkwoodii.

HEIGHT
3m (10ft) or more

SPREAD
3m (10ft)

Rosaceae	ALLEGHENY SERVICEBERRY

AMELANCHIER LAEVIS

Habit Spreading, tree-like with maturity.
Flowers Star-shaped, fragrant, in profusion in spring. White. **Fruits** Rounded, fleshy, berry-like. Purple. **Leaves** Deciduous, oval. Bronze, then dark green, turning rich red and orange in autumn.
• NATIVE HABITAT Damp woods and riversides in the Allegheny mountains of North America.
• CULTIVATION Grow in neutral to acid, humus-rich soil.
• PROPAGATION By fresh seed or by layering in autumn.

HEIGHT
8m (25ft) or more

SPREAD
8m (25ft)

Caprifoliaceae	

DIPELTA YUNNANENSIS

Habit Multi-stemmed, upright, then arching.
Flowers Tubular, in clusters in late spring. Creamy-white with orange throats. **Fruits** Conspicuous, with papery wings. **Leaves** Deciduous, oval to lance-shaped. Mid-green.
• NATIVE HABITAT Scrub and pine forest in the high hills of N.W. Yunnan.
• CULTIVATION Tolerates semi-shade. Grow in any moderately fertile, humus-rich soil. Prune only to thin crowded branches after flowering.
• PROPAGATION By softwood cuttings in summer.

HEIGHT
3.5m (11ft)

SPREAD
3m (10ft)

Staphyleaceae	EUROPEAN BLADDERNUT

STAPHYLEA PINNATA

Habit Vigorous, upright. *Flowers* Small, in clusters in late spring. White, ageing to pink. *Fruits* Papery, bladder-like. Green. *Leaves* Deciduous, divided into 3–7 oval-oblong leaflets. Bright green.
• NATIVE HABITAT Moist scrub and woodlands from Europe to Asia Minor.
• CULTIVATION Grow in any fertile soil, in sun or semi-shade. Prune after flowering, if necessary.
• PROPAGATION By seed or by softwood or greenwood cuttings in summer.

HEIGHT
5m (15ft)

SPREAD
5m (15ft)

Caprifoliaceae	

DIPELTA FLORIBUNDA

Habit Vigorous, upright. *Flowers* Funnel-shaped, fragrant, in clusters in late spring and early summer. White, flushed pale pink, marked yellow inside. *Fruits* Conspicuous, with papery wings. *Leaves* Deciduous, elliptic to lance-shaped. Pale green. *Bark* Peeling. Pale yellow-brown.
• NATIVE HABITAT Woodland and open scrub in the hills of C. and W. China.
• CULTIVATION Tolerates semi-shade. Grow in any fertile soil.
• PROPAGATION By softwood cuttings in summer.

HEIGHT
4m (12ft)

SPREAD
4m (12ft)

Ericaceae	FURIN-TSUTSUJI, REDVEIN ENKIANTHUS

ENKIANTHUS CAMPANULATUS ♛

Habit Bushy, spreading. *Flowers* Small, bell-shaped, in pendent clusters in late spring. Creamy-yellow, veined red. *Leaves* Deciduous, oval to elliptic, in clusters at ends of shoots. Dull green, turning orange-red in autumn.
• NATIVE HABITAT Mountain scrub and woodland of Japan.
• CULTIVATION Tolerates semi-shade. Grow in peaty or humus-rich, acid soils.
• PROPAGATION By seed in autumn or by semi-ripe cuttings in summer.

HEIGHT
4m (12ft)

SPREAD
4m (12ft)

Caprifoliaceae	

VIBURNUM × *CARLCEPHALUM* 🏆

Habit Vigorous, rounded, bushy.
Flowers Small, fragrant, in large, rounded heads in late spring. White, pink in bud.
Leaves Deciduous, broadly oval, heart-shaped at the base. Dull green above, paler beneath, tinted red in autumn.
• NATIVE HABITAT Garden origin.
• CULTIVATION Tolerates semi-shade. Grow in deep, fertile, moisture-retentive soil.
• PROPAGATION By softwood cuttings in early summer.

HEIGHT
3.5m (11ft)

SPREAD
3.5m (11ft)

Staphyleaceae	

STAPHYLEA HOLOCARPA 'Rosea'

Habit Upright, spreading. Tree-like with age.
Flowers Small, in drooping clusters from mid- to late spring. Soft pink. *Fruits* Bladder-like. Pale green. *Leaves* Deciduous, divided into 3 elliptic to oblong leaflets. Bronze, turning blue-green.
• NATIVE HABITAT Scrub and woodland edge in China.
• CULTIVATION Tolerates semi-shade and any moist, fertile soil.
• PROPAGATION By softwood or greenwood cuttings in summer.

HEIGHT
6m (20ft)

SPREAD
6m (20ft)

Rosaceae	

MALUS × *ARNOLDIANA*

Habit Dense, with arching branches.
Flowers Fragrant. Shallowly cup-shaped, in mid- to late spring. Pale pink, fading to white. *Fruits* Small, pea-shaped. Red-flushed, yellow, in autumn.
Leaves Deciduous, oval, deeply serrated. Mid-green.
• NATIVE HABITAT Garden origin.
• CULTIVATION Tolerates semi-shade, but flowers and fruits best in sun. Grow in any but waterlogged soil.
• PROPAGATION By budding in late summer or grafting in mid-winter.

HEIGHT
3m (10ft) or more

SPREAD
3m (10ft) or more

Rosaceae	JAPANESE CRAB

MALUS FLORIBUNDA

Habit Dense, spreading shrub or small tree.
Flowers Shallowly cup-shaped, appearing along the branches from mid- to late spring. Pale pink, red in bud. **Fruits** Tiny, pea-shaped, crab apples. Yellow. **Leaves** Deciduous, oval to elliptic, deeply serrated. Mid-green.
• NATIVE HABITAT Scrub and woodland of Japan.
• CULTIVATION Grow in any but waterlogged soil. Tolerates semi-shade but flowers and fruits best in sun. Prune in winter to remove dead or misplaced wood. *M. floribunda* is one of the earliest-flowering of the crab apples and is an exceptionally beautiful species when in full bloom. It is also valued for its gracefully arching branches and its long season of interest. The tiny crab apples often persist into winter and can provide a valuable food source for wildlife in the garden.
• PROPAGATION By seed in autumn, by budding in late summer, or by grafting in late winter.

HEIGHT
4–10m
(12–30ft)

SPREAD
To 10m
(30ft)

Rosaceae	

PHOTINIA × FRASERI 'Birmingham'

Habit Bushy, dense, upright. **Flowers** Small, 5-petalled, in broad clusters in late spring. White. **Leaves** Evergreen, oval, leathery. Dark green, bright purple-red when young.
• NATIVE HABITAT Garden origin.
• CULTIVATION Tolerates dappled shade. Grow in any moderately fertile and freely draining soil. Provide a sheltered site with protection from cold, dry, winter winds. Grown mainly for its leaves rather than its flowers.
• PROPAGATION By semi-ripe cuttings in summer.

HEIGHT
5m (15ft) or more

SPREAD
5m (15ft)

Magnoliaceae	BANANA SHRUB

MICHELIA FIGO

Habit Dense, rounded, much branched. **Flowers** Small, banana-scented, cup-shaped, in spring-summer. Creamy-yellow, petals edged maroon. **Leaves** Evergreen, oval. Glossy rich green.
• NATIVE HABITAT China.
• CULTIVATION Best grown in a conservatory. Tolerates partial shade. Grow in humus-rich, neutral to acid soil or compost.
• PROPAGATION By fresh seed in autumn or by semi-ripe cuttings in summer. Seldom needs pruning.
• OTHER NAMES M. fuscata.

Min. 5°C (41°F)

HEIGHT
4m (12ft) or more

SPREAD
4m (12ft)

Daphniphyllaceae	

DAPHNIPHYLLUM MACROPODUM

Habit Dense, bushy with stout shoots. **Flowers** Small green flowers with pungent scent on female plants, red-purple flowers on males. **Fruits** Small. Blue-black. **Leaves** Evergreen, oblong. Glossy dark green; red midrib and petiole.
• NATIVE HABITAT Japan, China, and Korea.
• CULTIVATION Tolerates semi-shade and some lime. Grow in deep, fertile, moist but well-drained soil. Provide shelter from cold wind.
• PROPAGATION By semi-ripe cuttings in summer.
• OTHER NAMES D. glaucescens.

HEIGHT
6m (20ft)

SPREAD
6m (20ft)

Hamamelidaceae	

CORYLOPSIS GLABRESCENS

Habit Open, spreading, with slender twigs. **Flowers** Small, fragrant, in pendent tassels, on bare branches in mid-spring. Pale yellow. **Fruits** Small berries. Blue-black. **Leaves** Deciduous, oval, with bristle-like teeth at margins. Dark green above, blue-green beneath.
• NATIVE HABITAT Kirishima mountains, Japan.
• CULTIVATION Grow in neutral to acid soil. Provide shelter from wind and late frost. Prune to shape.
• PROPAGATION By seed in autumn or by softwood cuttings in early summer.

HEIGHT
4m (12ft)

SPREAD
4m (12ft)

Berberidaceae	DARWIN BARBERRY

BERBERIS DARWINII

Habit Vigorous, arching. *Flowers* Small, rounded, in profusion from mid- to late spring. Deep golden-orange. *Fruits* Small, globose berries. Blue-bloomed. *Leaves* Evergreen, small, oval, with spiny teeth. Glossy dark green.
• NATIVE HABITAT Mountains of Patagonia and Chile.
• CULTIVATION Grow in any but waterlogged soils. Provide shelter from cold wind. It often produces dense thickets of growth from the base and is good for hedging. Trim after flowering,

otherwise no regular pruning required. It will also grow well in partial shade. This species is often considered one of the finest and most reliable of early flowering shrubs. It has the additional interest of being named after Charles Darwin, who discovered it in 1835 during the voyage of the *Beagle*.
• PROPAGATION By semi-ripe cuttings in summer.

HEIGHT
3m (10ft) or
more

SPREAD
3m (10ft)

LILACS

Lilacs (*Syringa*) are deciduous trees and shrubs grown for their small, tubular, and usually intensely fragrant flowers, which are carried in dense or open pyramidal panicles in spring and early summer.

The best known – and loved – are the many cultivars of *Syringa vulgaris*, with a colour range from pure and creamy-whites, to the deepest of claret-purples.

A number of the smaller species, often bearing very delicate but beautifully scented blooms, are particularly well suited to smaller gardens, where the tree lilacs may be unsuitable.

All lilacs are fully hardy and the larger species and cultivars make fine screens or informal hedges, or may be used as a backdrop for the shrub and mixed border.

The flowers of lilacs are suitable for cutting and make a bold contribution to arrangements. Cut them in the early morning so they do not wilt prematurely.

Grow lilacs in full sun, in deep, fertile, moisture-retentive and, preferably, alkaline soils. Remove flowerheads from newly planted lilacs and dead-head for the first few years until well established, taking care not to damage new growth. Prune out weak and damaged growth in winter and tip back strong-growing plants in summer to shape and encourage bushiness. Old trees can be rejuvenated by hard pruning in winter. Cut back to the base and select strong shoots to form a new framework. Feed and mulch. Flowers will be lost in the following season but blooming will resume within 2 to 3 years. If possible, buy plants on their own roots, as grafted plants sucker freely and vigorous suckers may eventually overtake the grafted cultivar. Propagate species by seed or suckers in spring and cultivars by softwood cuttings in summer. Leaf miners, leaf spot, and lilac blight may cause problems.

S. 'Mme Florent Stepman'
Habit Upright, spreading with age. ***Flowers*** Fragrant, single, in dense panicles in mid- to late spring. Soft white, opening from creamy-yellow buds. ***Leaves*** Heart-shaped. Dark green.
- HEIGHT 4m (12ft).
- SPREAD 4m (12ft).

S. 'Mme Florent Stepman'

☼ ◊ ❄❄❄

S. 'Cora Brandt'
Habit Open, upright, spreading with age. ***Flowers*** Fragrant, double, in very large, loose panicles in mid- to late spring. Pure white. ***Leaves*** Broadly heart-shaped. Mid-green.
- HEIGHT 3–4m (10–12ft).
- SPREAD 3–4m (10–12ft).

S. 'Cora Brandt'

☼ ◊ ❄❄❄

S. 'Jan van Tol'
Habit Upright, spreading with age. ***Flowers*** Fragrant, single, in long panicles from mid- to late spring. Pure white. ***Leaves*** Heart-shaped. Dark green.
- HEIGHT 4m (12ft).
- SPREAD 4m (12ft).

S. 'Jan van Tol'

☼ ◊ ❄❄❄

S. 'Mme Lemoine'
Habit Bushy, upright, spreading with age. ***Flowers*** Large, fragrant, double, in compact panicles in late spring and early summer. Creamy-yellow in bud, opening pure white. ***Leaves*** Heart-shaped. Dull mid-green.
- HEIGHT 4m (12ft).
- SPREAD 4m (12ft).

S. 'Mme Lemoine'

☼ ◊ ❄❄❄ 🏆

S. × CORRELATA
Habit Dense, bushy, with arching stems.
Flowers Fragrant, tubular, single, in long, arching panicles in late spring. Very pale lilac, almost white.
Leaves Oval. Dark green.
• HEIGHT 4m (12ft).
• SPREAD 4m (12ft).

S. × correlata
Rouen lilac

☼ ◊ ✿✿✿

S. 'Michel Buchner'
Habit Upright, spreading with age.
Flowers Large, fragrant, double, in long, dense, narrow panicles from mid- to late spring. Clear rose-lilac. **Leaves** Heart-shaped. Dark green.
• HEIGHT 4m (12ft).
• SPREAD 4m (12ft).

S. 'Michel Buchner'

☼ ◊ ✿✿✿

S. YUNNANENSIS
Habit Upright, open.
Flowers Fragrant, in slender panicles in early summer. Shell-pink, fading to white.
Leaves Large, elliptic to oblong-lance-shaped. Olive green, bluish beneath.
• HEIGHT 3–4m (10–12ft).
• SPREAD 2.5m (8ft).

S. yunnanensis
Yunnan lilac

☼ ◊ ✿✿✿

S. 'Maréchal Foch'
Habit Bushy, upright, spreading with age.
Flowers Large, fragrant, single, in broad, open panicles in late spring to early summer. Carmine-pink. **Leaves** Heart-shaped. Mid-green.
• HEIGHT 4m (12ft).
• SPREAD 3m (10ft).

S. 'Maréchal Foch'

☼ ◊ ✿✿✿

S. MICROPHYLLA
'Superba'
Habit Bushy, rounded, floriferous. **Flowers** Very fragrant, in small, open panicles in spring, and also intermittently until early autumn. Rose-pink.
Leaves Small, oval, pointed. Mid-green.
• HEIGHT 1.5–2m (5–6ft).
• SPREAD 1.5–2m (5–6ft).

S. microphylla
'Superba'

☼ ◊ ✿✿✿   ▽

S. 'Mme F. Morel'
Habit Strongly upright.
Flowers Large, fragrant, single, in dense, very large panicles in mid- to late spring. Mauve-pink.
Leaves Heart-shaped. Dark green.
• HEIGHT 5m (15ft).
• SPREAD 5m (15ft).

S. 'Mme F. Morel'

☼ ◊ ✿✿✿

S. 'Mrs Edward Harding'

Habit Vigorous, upright, loose, spreading with age, very floriferous.
Flowers Large, fragrant, double, in long, widely spreading panicles in late spring. Deep claret in bud, opening to claret pink and fading with age.
Leaves Heart-shaped. Dark green.
• HEIGHT 4m (12ft).
• SPREAD 4m (12ft).

S. 'Mrs Edward Harding'

☼ ◊ ✿✿✿   ♛

S. 'Congo'

Habit Upright, spreading with age.
Flowers Fragrant, single, in large, dense, branching clusters in late spring. Deep lilac-red, darker in bud and fading with age.
Leaves Heart-shaped. Dark green.
• HEIGHT 5m (15ft).
• SPREAD 5m (15ft).

S. 'Congo'

☼ ◊ ✿✿✿

S. 'Monge'

Habit Vigorous, upright.
Flowers Large, fragrant, single, in dense panicles in mid- to late spring. Deep purple.
Leaves Heart-shaped. Dark green.
• HEIGHT 5m (15ft).
• SPREAD 5m (15ft).

S. 'Monge'

☼ ◊ ✿✿✿

S. 'Masséna'

Habit Dense, upright, spreading with age.
Flowers Large, fragrant, single, in loose, broad panicles in late spring. Dark red-purple.
Leaves Heart-shaped. Dark green.
• HEIGHT 5m (15ft).
• SPREAD 5m (15ft).

S. 'Masséna'

☼ ◊ ✿✿✿

S. 'Paul Thirion'

Habit Upright, spreading with age.
Flowers Fragrant, double, in broad, dense panicles in late spring. Deep carmine-pink in bud, opening to rich rosy red and fading to lilac-pink.
Leaves Heart-shaped. Dark green.
• HEIGHT 4m (12ft).
• SPREAD 4m (12ft).

S. 'Paul Thirion'

☼ ◊ ✿✿✿

S. 'Decaisne'

Habit Upright, spreading with age.
Flowers Fragrant, single, in large panicles in mid- to late spring. Clear blue-lilac.
Leaves Heart-shaped. Dark green.
• HEIGHT 4m (12ft).
• SPREAD 4m (12ft).

S. 'Decaisne'

☼ ◊ ✿✿✿

S. 'Clarke's Giant'

Habit Vigorous, upright, spreading with age.
Flowers Large, fragrant, single, in large, pyramidal panicles from mid- to late spring. Lilac-blue, mauve-pink within, opening from rosy-mauve buds.
Leaves Large, heart-shaped. Dark green.
• HEIGHT 5m (15ft).
• SPREAD 5m (15ft).

S. 'Clarke's Giant'

☼ ◊ ✿✿✿

S. 'Charles Joly'

Habit Bushy, upright.
Flowers Large, fragrant, double, in dense panicles from mid-spring to early summer. Purple-red.
Leaves Heart-shaped. Dark green.
• HEIGHT 3.5m (11ft).
• SPREAD 3m (10ft).

S. 'Charles Joly'

☼ ◊ ✿✿✿   ♛

S. *MEYERI* 'Palibin'
Habit Dense, bushy,
slow-growing.
Flowers Fragrant, single,
in dense panicles, in
profusion in late spring
and early summer. Pale
lilac-pink. *Leaves* Small,
oval. Dark green.
• OTHER NAMES
S. palibiniana of gardens,
S. velutina of gardens.
• HEIGHT 1.5m (5ft).
• SPREAD 1.5m (5ft).

S. meyeri 'Palibin'

☼ ◊ ❁❁❁   ♚

S. 'Président Grévy'
Habit Upright,
spreading with age.
Flowers Fragrant, semi-
double to double, in very
large, open, pyramidal
panicles in mid- to late
spring. Clear lilac-blue.
Leaves Heart-shaped.
Dark green.
• HEIGHT 4m (12ft).
• SPREAD 4m (12ft).

S. 'Président Grévy'

☼ ◊ ❁❁❁

**S. 'Mme Antoine
Buchner'**
Habit Bushy, upright,
spreading with age.
Flowers Fragrant,
double, in loose, narrow
panicles in late spring to
early summer. Pink-
mauve, red-purple in
bud. *Leaves* Heart-
shaped. Dark green.
• HEIGHT 3.5m (11ft).
• SPREAD 3m (10ft).

*S. 'Mme Antoine
Buchner'*

☼ ◊ ❁❁❁   ♚

S. 'Blue Hyacinth'
Habit Open, upright,
spreading with age.
Flowers Fragrant, single,
in large, loose panicles in
mid- to late spring. Lilac
to powder blue.
Leaves Broadly heart-
shaped. Mid-green.
• HEIGHT 3m (10ft).
• SPREAD 3m (10ft).

S. 'Blue Hyacinth'

☼ ◊ ❁❁❁

S. × *PERSICA*
Habit Bushy, dense,
rounded, with slender
branches.
Flowers Fragrant, in
small, dense panicles in
late spring. Lilac.
Leaves Narrowly lance-
shaped, pointed. Dark
green.
• HEIGHT 2m (6ft) or
more.
• SPREAD 2m (6ft) or
more.

S. × persica
Persian lilac

☼ ◊ ❁❁❁   ♚

**S. × *HYACINTHIFLORA*
'Esther Staley'**
Habit Bushy, upright,
very floriferous.
Flowers Fragrant, single,
in broadly conical
panicles from mid-spring
to early summer. Lilac-
pink, red in bud.
Leaves Broadly heart-
shaped. Mid-green.
• HEIGHT 3.5m (11ft).
• SPREAD 3m (10ft).

S. × hyacinthiflora
'Esther Staley'

☼ ◊ ❁❁❁

S. 'Primrose'
Habit Bushy, upright.
Flowers Slightly
fragrant, in small, dense
panicles in late spring
and early summer. Pale
yellow. *Leaves* Heart-
shaped. Mid-green.
• HEIGHT 3.5m (11ft).
• SPREAD 3m (10ft).

S. 'Primrose'

☼ ◊ ❁❁❁

Escalloniaceae	

ESCALLONIA LEUCANTHA

Habit Upright. **Flowers** Small, shallowly cup-shaped, in large racemes in mid-summer. White. **Leaves** Evergreen, narrow, oval. Glossy dark green.
• NATIVE HABITAT Mountain scrub of Chile and Argentina.
• CULTIVATION Good for coastal gardens if not exposed to very cold winds. In cool areas provide the shelter of a warm, south-facing wall. Tolerates a range of soils, including lime, if deep and fertile. The flowers are produced on the previous season's wood, and if pruning is necessary to shape or restrict growth, it should be done immediately after flowering. Most escallonias regenerate freely from old wood and overgrown specimens can be rejuvenated by hard pruning. This is best done in spring, followed by feeding with general purpose fertilizer and the application of a mulch of well-rotted organic matter. Flowering will resume in the following year.
• PROPAGATION By softwood cuttings in summer.

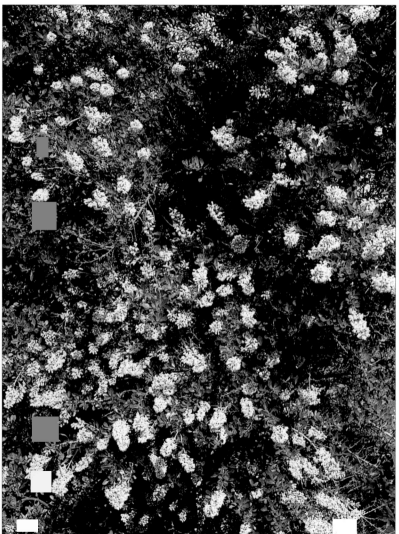

HEIGHT
3.5m (11ft)

SPREAD
3m (10ft)

Oleaceae	CHINESE PRIVET

LIGUSTRUM SINENSE

Habit Upright, bushy. *Flowers* Fragrant, tubular, in large panicles in mid-summer. White. *Fruits* Small. Purple-black. *Leaves* Deciduous or semi-evergreen, oval. Pale green.
• NATIVE HABITAT In scrub of Central China.
• CULTIVATION A choice specimen which flowers profusely in sunny, sheltered sites where fragrance can best be appreciated. Grow in any well-drained soil, including chalk. Mulch to conserve moisture. Trim lightly in mid-spring to maintain bushiness.
• PROPAGATION By semi-ripe cuttings in summer.

☀ ◊
❁ ❁ ❁

HEIGHT
4m (12ft)

SPREAD
3m (10ft)

Buddlejaceae	

BUDDLEJA DAVIDII 'Peace'

Habit Vigorous, arching. *Flowers* Fragrant, in long plumes from mid-summer to autumn. Pure white. *Leaves* Deciduous, long, pointed. Dark green, white-felted beneath.
• NATIVE HABITAT Garden origin.
• CULTIVATION Thrives on chalky and lime-rich soils. Cut back hard in spring to ground, or to a permanent woody framework, as the best flowers are borne on young growth. Attractive to butterflies.
• PROPAGATION By semi-ripe cuttings in summer or hardwood cuttings in autumn.

☀ ◊
❁ ❁ ❁

HEIGHT
To 3.5m
(11ft)

SPREAD
3m (10ft)

Compositae	DAISY BUSH

OLEARIA VIRGATA

Habit Dense, with long, graceful, arching stems. *Flowers* Small, star-shaped, carried along the length of stem, in early summer. White. *Leaves* Evergreen, very narrow. Dark grey-green, white beneath.
• NATIVE HABITAT Sub-alpine scrub of New Zealand.
• CULTIVATION Tolerant of salt-laden winds, providing good, wind-resistant shelter in seaside gardens. Cut out dead wood in spring.
• PROPAGATION By semi-ripe cuttings in summer.

☀ ◊
❁ ❁

HEIGHT
4–5m
(12–15ft)

SPREAD
4–5m
(12–15ft)

Styraceae	STORAX, SNOWBELL

STYRAX OFFICINALIS

Habit Slow-growing, loose to dense, sometimes tree-like. *Flowers* Bell-shaped, fragrant, in pendent clusters at branch tips in early summer. White. *Leaves* Deciduous, oval. Dark green, grey-white beneath.
• NATIVE HABITAT Rocky slopes, often on limestone, of the Mediterranean and California.
• CULTIVATION Grow in lime-free soil. Unlike most *Styrax*, *S. officinalis* tolerates dry conditions.
• PROPAGATION By softwood cuttings in summer.

☀ ◊ pH
❁ ❁

HEIGHT
4m (12ft)

SPREAD
2.5m (8ft)

Escalloniaceae	

ESCALLONIA 'Iveyi'

Habit Vigorous, upright. **Flowers** Fragrant, tubular, in large racemes, from mid- to late summer. Pure white. **Leaves** Evergreen, large, rounded. Glossy dark green.
• NATIVE HABITAT Garden origin.
• CULTIVATION Thrives in mild areas. Useful for hedging in coastal gardens. Inland, provide a warm, sheltered, site. Tolerant of lime-rich soils and drought.
• PROPAGATION By softwood or semi-ripe cuttings in summer.

HEIGHT
3m (10ft) or more

SPREAD
2.5–3m
(8–10ft)

Caprifoliaceae	LEATHERLEAF VIBURNUM

VIBURNUM RHYTIDOPHYLLUM

Habit Vigorous, open. **Flowers** Small, in dense heads in late spring and early summer. Creamy-white. **Fruits** Berry-like. Red, black when ripe. **Leaves** Evergreen, long, narrow, corrugated. Dark green, greyish and woolly beneath.
• NATIVE HABITAT Woodlands of C. and W. China.
• CULTIVATION Thrives on chalk. Best foliage is produced on deep, fertile soil. A good screening plant. Prune after flowering to restrict growth.
• PROPAGATION By semi-ripe cuttings in summer.

HEIGHT
4m (12ft)

SPREAD
4m (12ft)

Eucryphiaceae	

EUCRYPHIA × NYMANSENSIS

Habit Erect, columnar, tree-like with age. **Flowers** Large, cup-shaped, in late summer to early autumn. Glistening white. **Leaves** Evergreen, oval, serrated, simple, or divided into 3 leaflets. Glossy dark green.
• NATIVE HABITAT Garden origin.
• CULTIVATION Tolerates lime. Provide shelter from wind, which will scorch the leaves. Ideally, prefers roots in moist shade and crown in sun.
• PROPAGATION By semi-ripe cuttings in late summer.

HEIGHT
12–15m
(40–50ft)

SPREAD
7m (22ft)

Tiliaceae	AFRICAN HEMP

SPARMANNIA AFRICANA

Habit Erect, sometimes tree-like. **Flowers** In clusters in late spring and summer. White, with yellow and red-purple stamens. **Leaves** Evergreen, large, shallowly lobed. Bright green.
• NATIVE HABITAT S. Africa.
• CULTIVATION Best grown in a conservatory. Will also grow in partial shade. Water freely when in full growth, otherwise moderately. Cut back after flowering to keep compact. Susceptible to whitefly.
• PROPAGATION By greenwood cuttings in late spring.

Min. 7°C
(45°F)

HEIGHT
To 3.5m
(11ft)

SPREAD
To 3m
(10ft)

Sapindaceae	

XANTHOCERAS SORBIFOLIUM

Habit Vigorous, upright. **Flowers** Large, fragrant, in long, erect panicles, in late spring and early summer. White, with carmine patches at petal base. **Fruit** Walnut-like. **Leaves** Deciduous, divided into many slender, toothed leaflets. Bright green.
• NATIVE HABITAT N. China.
• CULTIVATION Tolerates chalky soils. Needs a warm, dry, sheltered position to flower well. Prune to shape after flowering. Susceptible to coral spot.
• PROPAGATION By stratified seed in spring or by root cuttings or suckers in winter.

HEIGHT
4m (12ft)

SPREAD
2m (6ft)

Solanaceae	ANGEL'S TRUMPET

BRUGMANSIA × CANDIDA

Habit Rounded. **Flowers** Large, fragrant, trumpet-shaped, from summer to autumn. White, sometimes cream or pink. **Leaves** Semi-evergreen, oval, downy. Dark green. All parts are poisonous.
• NATIVE HABITAT Andes of Ecuador.
• CULTIVATION Water potted specimens freely only when in growth, otherwise moderately. Prune hard in early spring. Will tolerate partial shade.
• PROPAGATION By heeled semi-ripe cuttings in summer.
• OTHER NAMES Datura × candida.

Min.7°C
(45°F)

HEIGHT
To 3.5m
(11ft)

SPREAD
3m (10ft)

Oleaceae	WHITE FRINGE TREE

CHIONANTHUS VIRGINICUS

Habit Bushy shrub, sometimes tree-like.
Flowers Fragrant, in drooping sprays, from late spring to early summer. White. **Fruits** Damson-like. Dark blue. **Leaves** Deciduous, oval. Glossy dark green, turning clear yellow in autumn.
• NATIVE HABITAT Damp woods, E. United States.
• CULTIVATION Grow in fertile, neutral to slightly acid, moist but well-drained soil. Needs a warm position in full sun to flower well.
• PROPAGATION By seed or layering in autumn.

HEIGHT
4–5m
(12–15ft)

SPREAD
3.5m (11ft)

Winteraceae	WINTER'S BARK

DRIMYS WINTERI

Habit Conical, shrubby when young.
Flowers Star-shaped, fragrant, in clusters in early summer. White. **Leaves** Evergreen, elliptic to lance-shaped, leathery. Dark green, bluish-white beneath.
• NATIVE HABITAT Dense thickets, in damp ground of Chile.
• CULTIVATION Tolerates light shade. Grow in a warm, sheltered site, protected from cold, dry winds.
• PROPAGATION By semi-ripe cuttings in summer or by seed in autumn.

HEIGHT
To 15m
(50ft)

SPREAD
8m (25ft)

Cornaceae	

CORNUS MACROPHYLLA

Habit Spreading, shrubby, making a small tree at maturity. **Flowers** Small, in broad clusters in summer. Creamy-white. **Leaves** Deciduous, large, oval, pointed. Glossy bright green.
• NATIVE HABITAT Mountain forests from the Himalaya to Japan.
• CULTIVATION Grow in any moderately fertile, well-drained soil.
• PROPAGATION By seed in autumn or by softwood cuttings in summer.

HEIGHT
12m (40ft)
or more

SPREAD
7m (21ft)

Cornaceae	VARIEGATED CORNELIAN CHERRY

CORNUS MAS 'Variegata'

Habit Bushy, dense. **Flowers** Small, star-shaped, carried on bare branches in early spring. Yellow. **Fruits** Cherry-like. Bright red. **Leaves** Deciduous, oval. Dark green, edged with white.
• NATIVE HABITAT Species occurs in scrub and woodland of Europe and W. Asia.
• CULTIVATION Undemanding, thriving in acid and alkaline soils and in sun or semi-shade. Seldom requires pruning.
• PROPAGATION By softwood cuttings in summer.

HEIGHT
3.5m (11ft)

SPREAD
3.5m (11ft)

Ericaceae	SORREL TREE, SOURWOOD

OXYDENDRUM ARBOREUM

Habit Broadly conical. **Flowers** Tiny, fragrant, urn-shaped, in large, erect clusters at branch tips, in late summer and autumn. Creamy-white.
Leaves Deciduous, elliptic to oblong, pointed, finely toothed. Glossy dark green, crimson in autumn.
• NATIVE HABITAT E. North America.
• CULTIVATION Tolerates semi-shade but autumn colour is best in sun. Grow in humus-rich, lime-free soil.
• PROPAGATION By softwood cuttings in summer, or by seed in autumn.

HEIGHT
To 20m
(65ft)

SPREAD
12m (40ft)

Myrtaceae	

LUMA APICULATA

Habit Vigorous, upright, then arching.
Flowers Small, cup-shaped, from mid-summer to mid-autumn. White. **Leaves** Evergreen, aromatic. Dark green. **Bark** Cinnamon, creamy-grey below.
• NATIVE HABITAT By lakes and riverbanks in cool, humid areas of Argentina and Chile.
• CULTIVATION Grow against a warm wall in cool areas.
• PROPAGATION By semi-ripe cuttings in late summer.
• OTHER NAMES *Myrtus luma.*

HEIGHT
5–6m
(15–20ft)
or more

SPREAD
4m (12ft)

Rosaceae	OCEAN SPRAY, CREAM BUSH

HOLODISCUS DISCOLOR

Habit Fast-growing, arching. *Flowers* Small, in large, pendent sprays in mid-summer. Creamy-white. *Leaves* Deciduous, lobed, toothed. Dark green, grey-white beneath.
• NATIVE HABITAT Open woodlands of W. North America.
• CULTIVATION Tolerates semi-shade and any but very dry soil. Prune, if necessary, after flowering to remove old or overcrowded wood. It is a very hardy shrub and is suitable for specimen planting or as a background plant in the shrub border, where its light, airy panicles of bloom can provide a foil for stronger, brighter colours. *H. discolor* is also useful for plantings in open glades in woodland gardens where conditions will be similar to those of its natural habitat.
• PROPAGATION By softwood cuttings in summer or by layering in spring.
• OTHER NAMES *Spiraea discolor.*

HEIGHT
3.5–5m
(11–15ft)

SPREAD
3.5–4m
(11–12ft)

Malvaceae	

ABUTILON VITIFOLIUM var. *ALBUM*

Habit Fast-growing, upright. ***Flowers*** Large, bowl-shaped, borne in profusion in late spring and early summer. White. ***Leaves*** Deciduous, deeply lobed, sharply toothed, downy. Grey-green.
• NATIVE HABITAT Dry areas and mountain valleys of Chile.
• CULTIVATION Grow in a sheltered position with very well-drained soil. Tip prune when young. Cut mature specimens back hard in spring.
• PROPAGATION By softwood, greenwood, or semi-ripe cuttings in summer.

☀ ◊
❀ ❀

HEIGHT
To 5m
(15ft)

SPREAD
3m (10ft)

Caprifoliaceae	

ABELIA TRIFLORA

Habit Vigorous, upright. ***Flowers*** Small, very fragrant, in dense clusters in summer. Rose-tinted, white. ***Leaves*** Deciduous or semi-evergreen, oval to lance-shaped, pointed. Dull dark green.
• NATIVE HABITAT Rocky slopes and dry scrub of the N.W. Himalaya.
• CULTIVATION Provide the shelter of a warm, sunny wall in cold areas.
• PROPAGATION By softwood or semi-ripe cuttings in summer.

☀ ◊
❀ ❀

HEIGHT
To 3.5m
(11ft)

SPREAD
3.5m (11ft)

Hippocastanaceae	BUCKEYE

AESCULUS PARVIFLORA ♛

Habit Vigorous, bushy, suckering.
Flowers Slender, erect panicles from mid- to late summer. White, with long, red-pink anthers.
Leaves Deciduous, large, palmate. Bronze, turning dark green in summer, then yellow in autumn.
• NATIVE HABITAT Streamsides in woodlands of S.E. United States.
• CULTIVATION Tolerates semi-shade and thrives in any but very dry soil. Prune only to restrict spread. Damaged wood is susceptible to coral spot.
• PROPAGATION By seed in autumn or by suckers.

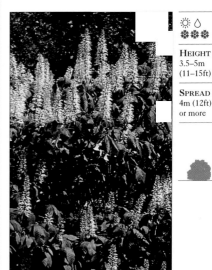

☀ ◊
❀ ❀ ❀

HEIGHT
3.5–5m
(11–15ft)

SPREAD
4m (12ft)
or more

Clethraceae

CLETHRA DELAVAYI

Habit Upright, open shrub, sometimes tree-like.
Flowers Cup-shaped, very fragrant, in long, dense clusters in mid-summer. White, pink in bud.
Leaves Deciduous, lance-shaped, toothed. Rich green above and pale, softly hairy beneath.
• NATIVE HABITAT Coniferous woods in the mountains of W. China.
• CULTIVATION Grow in a moist but well-drained, peaty acid soil, in a semi-shaded site, and with shelter from cold, drying winds. A beautiful specimen for a shady shrub border, and ideal for a woodland garden, *Clethra delavayi* is best planted with ample space so that it can achieve its natural habit and display its horizontally-held racemes of flowers to best advantage. It needs little regular pruning but congested growth can be thinned out by cutting out at the base after flowering.
• PROPAGATION By softwood cuttings in summer or by seed in autumn.

HEIGHT
To 5m
(15ft) or
more

SPREAD
3m (10ft)

Caprifoliaceae | BEAUTY BUSH

KOLKWITZIA AMABILIS 'Pink Cloud'

Habit Vigorous, upright then arching.
Flowers Bell-shaped, in profusion from late spring to early summer. Clear pink. *Leaves* Deciduous, small, oval. Dull dark green.
• NATIVE HABITAT Garden origin. Species occurs on rocky mountain slopes of W. China.
• CULTIVATION Tolerant of a range of soils, including chalk. Although mature plants are very hardy, young growth may be damaged by late frost. Prune out old, damaged or weak growth from the base after flowering. This cultivar makes a beautiful and floriferous specimen for the shrub border. Despite its eventual height, its upright, then arching habit permits placement quite close to the front of the shrub border, where its flowers can be appreciated at close quarters. The original seedling was selected and raised at Wisley in 1946.
• PROPAGATION By softwood cuttings in summer.

HEIGHT
3–3.5m
(10–11ft)

SPREAD
2.5–3m
(8–10ft)

Tamaricaceae	TAMARISK

TAMARIX RAMOSISSIMA

Habit Arching shrub, sometimes tree-like.
Flowers Small, carried in large, upright plumes, in late summer and early autumn. Pink.
Leaves Deciduous, tiny, narrow. Blue-green.
• NATIVE HABITAT Coastal habitats from E. Europe to C. and E. Asia.
• CULTIVATION Tolerant of salt-laden winds and any soil except shallow chalk. Good for hedging by the sea. Prune in early spring to maintain bushiness.
• PROPAGATION By semi-ripe cuttings in summer or by hardwood cuttings in winter.

HEIGHT
4m (12ft)

SPREAD
3.5m (11ft)

Apocynaceae	OLEANDER, ROSE BAY

NERIUM OLEANDER

Habit Bushy, upright. *Flowers* Periwinkle-like, in clusters from spring to autumn. Pink, white, red, apricot, or yellow. *Leaves* Evergreen, in whorls, lance-shaped, leathery. Dark green. Poisonous.
• NATIVE HABITAT Stony soils in seasonally dry water courses or river valleys from the Mediterranean to W. China.
• CULTIVATION Grow in a warm, sunny, sheltered site. In cool areas grow in a cool conservatory.
• PROPAGATION By seed in spring or by semi-ripe cuttings in summer.

Min. 10°C
(50°F)

HEIGHT
To 4m
(12ft)

SPREAD
3m (10ft)

Lythraceae	CRAPE MYRTLE, CREPE FLOWER

LAGERSTROEMIA INDICA

Habit Rounded, tree-like with age.
Flowers Small, with round, crinkled petals, in dense, pyramidal panicles in summer to early autumn. White, pink, or purple. *Leaves* Deciduous, oval to oblong. Glossy dark green.
• NATIVE HABITAT In grassland and open forest in the foothills of the Himalaya, China, and Japan.
• CULTIVATION Grow in fertile soil, in a warm, sunny site. Needs long, hot summers to bloom well.
• PROPAGATION By seed in spring or by semi-ripe cuttings in summer.

HEIGHT
To 6m
(20ft)

SPREAD
5m (15ft)

Buddlejaceae	

BUDDLEJA DAVIDII 'Royal Red'

Habit Vigorous, arching. *Flowers* Fragrant, very large panicles, from mid-summer to autumn. Rich purple-red. *Leaves* Deciduous, long, pointed. Dark green above, white-felted beneath.
• NATIVE HABITAT Garden origin.
• CULTIVATION Thrives on chalk and lime-rich soils. Cut back hard in spring, to ground or to a permanent woody framework. Attractive to butterflies.
• PROPAGATION By semi-ripe cuttings in summer or by hardwood cuttings in autumn.

HEIGHT
To 4.5m
(14ft)

SPREAD
3.5–4m
(11–12ft)

Buddlejaceae	

BUDDLEJA DAVIDII 'Harlequin'

Habit Vigorous, arching. *Flowers* Fragrant, in long plumes, from mid-summer to autumn. Red-purple. *Leaves* Deciduous, long, pointed. Dark green with creamy-white margins.
• NATIVE HABITAT Garden origin.
• CULTIVATION Thrives on chalk and lime-rich soils. Cut back hard in spring, to the ground or to a permanent woody framework. Attractive to butterflies.
• PROPAGATION By semi-ripe cuttings in summer or by hardwood cuttings in autumn.

HEIGHT
To 4.5m
(14ft)

SPREAD
3.5–4m
(11–12ft)

Aceraceae	

ACER PALMATUM f. *ATROPURPUREUM*

Habit Bushy-headed, sometimes tree-like.
Flowers Tiny, in drooping clusters, in spring. Red-purple. *Fruits* Sycamore-like, with red wings.
Leaves Deciduous, lobed. Rich coppery-red, turning brilliant red in autumn.
• NATIVE HABITAT Species grows in hill and mountainside thickets of China, Japan, and Korea.
• CULTIVATION Tolerates light shade, but colours best in sun. Needs moist but well-drained soil. Provide shelter from cold wind to avoid leaf scorch.
• PROPAGATION By softwood cuttings in spring.

HEIGHT
4m (12ft)
or more

SPREAD
4m (12ft)

Malvaceae	SLEEPY MALLOW, WAX MALLOW

MALVAVISCUS ARBOREUS

Habit Vigorous, rounded. *Flowers* Closed bell-shape, with protruding stamens, in summer and autumn. Brilliant red. *Leaves* Evergreen, broadly oval to heart-shaped, softly hairy. Bright green.
• NATIVE HABITAT Mexico to Brazil.
• CULTIVATION Suitable for a warm conservatory. Water potted plants freely when in growth, otherwise moderately. Cut flowered stems back hard in late winter to maintain shape.
• PROPAGATION By seed in spring or by semi-ripe cuttings in summer.

Min.
13–16°C
(55–61°F)

HEIGHT
4m (12ft)

SPREAD
3m (10ft)

Buddlejaceae	

BUDDLEJA COLVILEI

Habit Vigorous, arching, sometimes tree-like with age. *Flowers* Large, bell-shaped, borne in drooping clusters, in early summer. Deep pink to red-purple, with white centres. *Leaves* Deciduous, lance-shaped, pointed, softly hairy. Dark green.
• NATIVE HABITAT Scrubland of the Himalaya.
• CULTIVATION Provide a warm, sheltered position. Flowers are borne on the previous season's wood. If necessary, cut back lightly after flowering to maintain bushiness.
• PROPAGATION By semi-ripe cuttings in summer.

HEIGHT
To 6m
(20ft)

SPREAD
3.5m (11ft)

Hippocastanaceae	RED BUCKEYE

AESCULUS PAVIA 'Atrosanguinea'

Habit Bushy, rounded, tree-like with age.
Flowers Tubular, in loose, upright panicles in
summer. Deep red. **Leaves** Deciduous, divided
into 5–7 narrowly oval leaflets. Glossy dark green.
• NATIVE HABITAT Species occurs in rich
woodland soils and by streambanks in N. America.
• CULTIVATION Tolerates dappled shade. Grow
in any well-drained soil that remains reliably moist
in the growing season.
• PROPAGATION By budding in late summer or by
grafting in winter.

HEIGHT
5m (15ft) or
more

SPREAD
To 3m
(10ft)

Aceraceae	

ACER PALMATUM 'Rubrum'

Habit Bushy-headed, becoming tree-like with
age. **Flowers** Small, in drooping clusters in spring.
Red-purple. **Fruits** Sycamore-like, with red wings.
Leaves Deciduous, lobed. Red when young,
bronze in summer, turning red or orange in autumn.
• NATIVE HABITAT Garden origin.
• CULTIVATION Tolerates light shade, but colours
best in sun. Provide shelter from cold wind.
• PROPAGATION By grafting in late winter or early
spring or by budding in summer.

HEIGHT
6m (20ft)

SPREAD
6m (20ft)

Anacardiaceae	SMOKE BUSH

COTINUS COGGYGRIA 'Notcutt's Variety'

Habit Bushy. **Flowers** Tiny, in feathery plumes
in late summer. Pink-purple. **Leaves** Deciduous,
rounded, broadly oval. Deep red-purple, turning
bright red in autumn.
• NATIVE HABITAT Garden origin. Species occurs
on rocky hillsides, often on limestone, from
S. Europe to C. China.
• CULTIVATION Tolerates dry soils. Autumn
colour is best on soils that are not too rich.
• PROPAGATION By softwood or greenwood
cuttings in summer or by layering in late winter.

HEIGHT
3.5–4m
(10–12ft)

SPREAD
3.5m (10ft)

Rosaceae	BLACKTHORN, SLOE

PRUNUS SPINOSA 'Purpurea'

Habit Dense, spiny. **Flowers** Saucer-shaped,
from early to mid-spring. Pale pink. **Fruits** Black
sloes. Blue-bloomed. **Leaves** Deciduous, elliptic
to oval. Red when young, then dark red-purple.
• NATIVE HABITAT Garden origin. Species occurs
in hedgerows and woodland edges from Europe to
W. Asia.
• CULTIVATION Grow in any but waterlogged
soils. Good for hedging, especially in coastal and
exposed sites. Trim after flowering.
• PROPAGATION By softwood cuttings in summer.

HEIGHT
To 4m
(12ft)

SPREAD
3m (10ft)

Corylaceae	PURPLE FILBERT

CORYLUS MAXIMA 'Purpurea'

Habit Vigorous, open, tree-like with age.
Flowers Pendulous catkins, on bare branches in late winter. Purplish, with yellow anthers.
Fruits Edible nuts (filberts). Brown.
Leaves Deciduous, rounded, heart-shaped. Purple.
• NATIVE HABITAT Woodland, S.E. Europe to Asia Minor.
• CULTIVATION Tolerates semi-shade and any fertile soil, including chalk.
• PROPAGATION By suckers or by layering from late autumn to early spring.

HEIGHT
To 6m
(20ft)

SPREAD
4m (12ft)

Melastomataceae	GLORY BUSH, LENT TREE

TIBOUCHINA URVILLEANA

Habit Vigorous, erect to spreading, with slender branches. **Flowers** Large, saucer-shaped, satiny, from summer to early winter. Rich purple.
Leaves Evergreen, velvety, veined. Mid-green.
• NATIVE HABITAT Forests of tropical S. America.
• CULTIVATION Best grown in a conservatory. Water freely in growth, less in winter. Cut flowered stems back hard in late winter.
• PROPAGATION By greenwood or semi-ripe cuttings in late spring or summer.
• OTHER NAMES *T. semidecandra.*

Min. 7°C
(45°F)

HEIGHT
3m (10ft) or
more

SPREAD
3m (10ft)

Buddlejaceae	

BUDDLEJA ALTERNIFOLIA

Habit Dense, with slender, arching branches.
Flowers Small, fragrant, in neat clusters in early summer. Lilac-purple. **Leaves** Deciduous, long, narrow. Grey-green.
• NATIVE HABITAT Hedgerows and dry slopes of China.
• CULTIVATION Grow in any well-drained soil; especially good on chalk. Prune immediately after flowering. This species is very effective if trained as a weeping tree.
• PROPAGATION By semi-ripe cuttings in summer.

HEIGHT
To 4m
(12ft)

SPREAD
4m (12ft)

Aceraceae	

ACER PALMATUM 'Lutescens'

Habit Bushy-headed, becoming tree-like with age. **Flowers** Small, in drooping clusters, in mid-spring. Red-purple. **Fruits** Sycamore-like, winged.
Leaves Deciduous, lobed. Glossy mid-green, turning clear butter-yellow in autumn.
• NATIVE HABITAT Garden origin.
• CULTIVATION Tolerates light shade, but colours best in autumn with sun. Shelter from wind.
• PROPAGATION By grafting in late winter or early spring or by budding in summer.

HEIGHT
6m (20ft)

SPREAD
6m (20ft)

Moraceae	PAPER MULBERRY

BROUSSONETIA PAPYRIFERA

Habit Bushy when young, a small tree with
maturity. *Flowers* Small, in globose clusters on
female plants, in early summer. Purple. Male plants
have creamy catkins. Needs both sexes for fruits.
Fruits Fleshy, in tight, globular clusters. Orange-
red. *Leaves* Deciduous, large, broadly oval,
toothed. Dull green, velvety beneath.
• NATIVE HABITAT Forests of E. Asia.
• CULTIVATION Tolerant of poor, dry soils.
• PROPAGATION By softwood cuttings in summer
or by seed in autumn.

HEIGHT
8m (25ft) or
more

SPREAD
8m (25ft)

Lardizabalaceae	

DECAISNEA FARGESII

Habit Upright, semi-arching. *Flowers* Delicate,
bell-shaped, in slender racemes in early summer.
Greenish-white. *Fruits* Large, pendent, sausage-
shaped pod. Metallic blue, bloomed.
Leaves Deciduous, divided into paired leaflets.
Mid-green.
• NATIVE HABITAT Woodland thickets, W. China.
• CULTIVATION Grow in fertile, moisture-
retentive soil, in a sheltered site. Tolerates semi-
shade, but fruits best in sun.
• PROPAGATION By seed in autumn.

HEIGHT
6m (20ft)

SPREAD
6m (20ft)

Caprifoliaceae	FERN-LEAVED ELDER

SAMBUCUS NIGRA f. *LACINIATA*

Habit Dense, bushy. *Flowers* Small, fragrant, in
broad, flat heads in early summer. Creamy-white.
Fruits Small, spherical berries. Black.
Leaves Deciduous, very finely divided leaflets.
Rich green.
• NATIVE HABITAT Riverbanks, in woods and
scrub, from Europe to N. Africa and W. Asia.
• CULTIVATION Grow in any fertile soil. Cut back
in early spring for best foliage effects.
• PROPAGATION By softwood cuttings in summer
or by hardwood cuttings in winter.

HEIGHT
6m (20ft)

SPREAD
6m (20ft)

Caprifoliaceae	GOLDEN ELDER

SAMBUCUS NIGRA 'Aurea'

Habit Dense, bushy. *Flowers* Small, fragrant, in
broad, flat heads in early summer. Creamy-white.
Fruits Small, spherical berries. Black.
Leaves Deciduous, divided into 5–7 oval leaflets.
Golden-yellow.
• NATIVE HABITAT Species occurs in woods and
scrub from Europe to N. Africa and W. Asia.
• CULTIVATION Grow in any reasonably moist,
fertile soil. Cut back in early spring for best foliage.
• PROPAGATION By softwood cuttings in summer
or by hardwood cuttings in winter.

HEIGHT
6m (20ft)

SPREAD
6m (20ft)

| Rhamnaceae | CHRIST'S THORN, JERUSALEM THORN |

PALIURUS SPINA-CHRISTI

Habit Bushy, with slender, crooked, thorny shoots.
Flowers Small, in clusters along the current year's
growth in late summer. Yellow. **Fruits** Woody,
winged, disc-shaped in autumn.
Leaves Deciduous, oval. Glossy bright green, clear
yellow in autumn.
• NATIVE HABITAT Dry hills from the
Mediterranean to N. China.
• CULTIVATION Grow in any very well-drained
soil. Drought tolerant. Good for informal hedging.
Prune in winter, if necessary, to thin overcrowded
growth. Trim hedging also in winter, when the
plant is fully dormant. Pruning of specimens is best
kept to a minimum, but if necessary to restrict size,
cut out overgrown branches from within the bush
to hide pruning cuts. Old and overgrown
specimens respond well to hard pruning and will
regenerate, even if cut back almost to ground level.
• PROPAGATION By softwood cuttings in summer
or by seed in autumn.

HEIGHT
3–7m
(10–22ft)

SPREAD
3.5m (11ft)

Elaeagnaceae	OLEASTER

ELAEAGNUS ANGUSTIFOLIA ♀

Habit Bushy, spreading. **Flowers** Small, fragrant, in clusters in early summer. Creamy-yellow.
Fruits Small, edible berries. Silvery-amber.
Leaves Deciduous, long, narrow. Silver-grey.
• NATIVE HABITAT W. Asia.
• CULTIVATION Grow in any well-drained soil. No regular pruning required unless grown as hedge. Wind-resistant and good for shelter belts, especially in coastal gardens.
• PROPAGATION By seed in autumn or by hardwood cuttings in winter.

☀ ◊
❀ ❀ ❀

HEIGHT
To 7m
(22ft)

SPREAD
6m (20ft)

Solanaceae	ANGEL'S TRUMPET

BRUGMANSIA × *CANDIDA* ♀
'Grand Marnier'

Habit Vigorous, bushy. **Flowers** Large, pendent, trumpet-shaped, in summer. Peach-coloured.
Leaves Semi-evergreen, large, oval to elliptic. Mid-green. All parts are poisonous.
• NATIVE HABITAT Garden origin.
• CULTIVATION Water potted specimens freely only when in growth. Cut back hard in early spring.
• PROPAGATION By heeled semi-ripe cuttings in summer.

☀ ◊

Min 7–10°C
(45–50°F)

HEIGHT
To 3.5m
(11ft)

SPREAD
3m (10ft)

Solanaceae	RED ANGEL'S TRUMPET

BRUGMANSIA SANGUINEA ♀

Habit Erect to rounded, often tree-like.
Flowers Large, pendent, trumpet-shaped, from late summer to winter. Orange-red, yellow at the base, veined yellow. **Leaves** Semi-evergreen, large, lobed when young, softly hairy. Poisonous.
• NATIVE HABITAT Scrubland, Colombia, Chile.
• CULTIVATION Needs a protected site, or grow under cover. Cut back in early spring.
• PROPAGATION By heeled semi-ripe cuttings in summer.
• OTHER NAMES *Datura sanguinea*.

☀ ◊

Min. 10°C
(50°F)

HEIGHT
3m (10ft)
or more

SPREAD
3m (10ft)
or more

Leguminosae	BIRD-OF-PARADISE, POINCIANA

CAESALPINIA GILLIESII

Habit Open, spreading, often tree-like.
Flowers Many, borne in short, erect, rigid racemes, from mid- to late summer. Golden-yellow, with long, bright scarlet stamens.
Leaves Deciduous, long, finely divided. Dark green.
• NATIVE HABITAT Dry, open scrub of Argentina.
• CULTIVATION Tolerant of dry soils. Provide the shelter of a warm, sunny wall. Flowers best in areas with long, hot summers.
• PROPAGATION By seed in autumn or spring or by softwood cuttings in summer.

☀ ◊
❀ ❀

HEIGHT
To 3.5m
(11ft)

SPREAD
6m (20ft)

Leguminosae	CANARY-BIRD BUSH

CROTALARIA AGATIFLORA

Habit Vigorous, sprawling. **Flowers** Pea-like, in long racemes, in several flushes, mainly in summer. Greenish-yellow. **Leaves** Evergreen, divided, with 3 elliptic to oval leaflets. Grey-green.
• NATIVE HABITAT E. and N.E. Africa.
• CULTIVATION Suitable for a warm conservatory. Water freely when in full growth, otherwise moderately. Cut back old stems by half after flowering to keep compact.
• PROPAGATION By pre-soaked seed in spring or by semi-ripe cuttings in summer.

Min. 15°C (59°F)

HEIGHT 3.5m (11ft) or more

SPREAD 3.5m (11ft)

Buddlejaceae	ORANGE BALL TREE

BUDDLEJA GLOBOSA ♈

Habit Erect, open. **Flowers** Tiny, in dense, round clusters in early summer. Orange-yellow. **Leaves** Deciduous or semi-evergreen, lance-shaped. Dark green, brown and woolly beneath.
• NATIVE HABITAT Scrub in the foothills of the Andes of Argentina, Chile, and Peru.
• CULTIVATION Thrives on chalky and lime-rich soils. Flowers best in a sunny site, sheltered from cold wind. Prune after flowering to remove crowded wood.
• PROPAGATION By semi-ripe cuttings in summer.

HEIGHT 5m (15ft) or more

SPREAD 5m (15ft)

Leguminosae	BROOM

GENISTA CINEREA

Habit Erect, with silky, semi-arching shoots. **Flowers** Pea-like, fragrant, in profusion from early to mid-summer. Bright yellow. **Leaves** Deciduous, tiny. Grey-green, silky-hairy beneath.
• NATIVE HABITAT Woods and scrub on the hillsides of S.W. Europe and N. Africa.
• CULTIVATION Thrives in a range of soils, if not too rich. Tip back when young and trim lightly after flowering to maintain bushiness.
• PROPAGATION By softwood or semi-ripe cuttings in summer or by seed in autumn.

HEIGHT To 3.5 m (11ft)

SPREAD 3.5m (11ft)

Sterculiaceae	FLANNEL FLOWER

FREMONTODENDRON 'California Glory' ♈

Habit Vigorous, upright. **Flowers** Large, cup-shaped, from late spring to mid-autumn. Golden-yellow. **Leaves** Evergreen or semi-evergreen, rounded, lobed. Dark green above, tawny beneath.
• NATIVE HABITAT Species occur in scrub of Mexico and California. Garden origin.
• CULTIVATION Tolerant of chalky and dry soils. Prefers light, not too fertile soils; will not bloom well on rich soils. Flowers best against a warm sunny wall, with shelter from cold, winter winds.
• PROPAGATION By semi-ripe cuttings in summer.

HEIGHT To 6m (20ft)

SPREAD 5m (15ft)

| Leguminosae | MOROCCAN BROOM, PINEAPPLE BROOM |

CYTISUS BATTANDIERI

Habit Loose, open. **Flowers** Pineapple-scented, in dense racemes from early to mid-summer. Bright yellow. **Leaves** Semi-evergreen, laburnum-like, divided, with 3 leaflets. Silvery-grey.
• NATIVE HABITAT Sandy soils in cedar and oak forests of the Rif and Atlas mountains of Morocco.
• CULTIVATION Thrives on a range of well-drained soils, provided they are not too rich. Flowers best when given the shelter of a warm, sunny wall. When sited as a wall shrub it is invaluable as a backdrop to herbaceous and mixed plantings, as even when not in flower its beautiful foliage provides an elegant foil for plants with strongly coloured flowers. It blooms on wood produced during the previous season and frequently produces strong, new growth from the base. Cut out old flowered wood immediately after flowering. Resents transplanting.
• PROPAGATION By pre-soaked seed in spring.
• OTHER NAMES *Argyrocytisus battandieri.*

HEIGHT
To 4m
(12ft)

SPREAD
4m (12ft)

Leguminosae	MOUNT ETNA BROOM

GENISTA AETNENSIS

Habit Shrubby when young, rounded, with weeping branches. **Flowers** Pea-like, fragrant, in loose racemes in mid-summer. Golden-yellow. **Leaves** Deciduous. Very few, tiny, linear, carried on bright green, rush-like shoots.
• NATIVE HABITAT Slopes of Mount Etna in Sicily and on dry hills of Sardinia.
• CULTIVATION Grow in light, fertile but not too rich soil, in a warm, sunny, sheltered site.
• PROPAGATION By seed in autumn or by softwood or semi-ripe cuttings in summer.

HEIGHT
8–10m
(25–30ft)

SPREAD
8m (25ft)

Proteaceae	CHILEAN FIREBUSH

EMBOTHRIUM COCCINEUM

Habit Upright, suckering. **Flowers** Narrowly tubular, with twisted lobes, in crowded racemes in late spring and early summer. Brilliant orange-scarlet. **Leaves** Evergreen or semi-evergreen, lance-shaped. Glossy, pale or deep green.
• NATIVE HABITAT Low-altitude forests of the Chilean Andes.
• CULTIVATION Grow in freely draining, lime-free soil, with shelter from cold, dry winds.
• PROPAGATION By suckers in spring or autumn or by seed in autumn.

HEIGHT
10m (30ft)

SPREAD
5m (15ft)

Rosaceae	

COTONEASTER FRIGIDUS 'Cornubia'

Habit Vigorous, arching. **Flowers** Small, in dense clusters in early summer. White. **Fruits** Large, in pendent clusters, from autumn to winter. Brilliant red. **Leaves** Semi-evergreen, oval. Glossy dark green.
• NATIVE HABITAT Garden origin.
• CULTIVATION Tolerates some shade. Thrives on most soils, especially dry ones. Overgrown specimens will respond well to hard pruning. Useful for screens. Susceptible to fireblight.
• PROPAGATION By semi-ripe cuttings in summer.

HEIGHT
6.5–7m
(21–22ft)

SPREAD
6.5–7m
(21–22ft)

Aceraceae	

ACER PALMATUM var. *HEPTALOBUM*

Habit Bushy-headed shrub or small tree.
Flowers Small, red-purple, in mid-spring.
Leaves Deciduous, large, lobed. Green, turning brilliant red, orange, and yellow in autumn.
• NATIVE HABITAT Woodland in the hills and mountains of Japan.
• CULTIVATION Grow in well-drained soil. Thrives in light shade but colours better in sun. Provide shelter from cold wind to avoid leaf scorch. *A. palmatum* and its varieties and cultivars generally need little pruning, but any major pruning cuts should be made when the plant is fully dormant in winter as maples will 'bleed' if pruned in spring when the sap is rising. They are best allowed to develop naturally, but young specimens may need to have any crossing, rubbing, or badly placed shoots removed. Minor pruning cuts can be made in late summer or early autumn when no bleeding should occur.
• PROPAGATION By seed in autumn or by grafting in late winter or early spring.

HEIGHT
6m (20ft)

SPREAD
6m (20ft)

Anacardiaceae	STAGHORN SUMACH

RHUS TYPHINA 'Dissecta' ♈

Habit Open, spreading shrub or small tree.
Flowers Small, in conical panicles in summer.
Greenish-yellow. **Fruits** Erect clusters. Dark red.
Leaves Deciduous, fern-like. Dark green, turning
brilliant orange-red in autumn.
• NATIVE HABITAT Garden origin.
• CULTIVATION Grow in any well-drained soil. A
good specimen for autumn colour and winter outline.
• PROPAGATION By semi-ripe cuttings in summer
or by suckers or root cuttings in winter.
• OTHER NAMES *Rhus hirta* 'Laciniata'.

HEIGHT
3.5m (8ft)

SPREAD
5m (15ft)

Anacardiaceae	SMOKE BUSH

COTINUS 'Flame' ♈

Habit Bushy, tree-like. **Flowers** Showy, plume-
like, carried above the foliage from late summer.
Pink-purple. **Leaves** Deciduous, oval. Dark green,
turning brilliant orange-red in autumn.
• NATIVE HABITAT Garden origin.
• CULTIVATION Tolerates dry soils. Autumn
colour is best in full sun and on soils that are not too
rich. Prune only to cut out dead wood or to tidy
weak growth in spring.
• PROPAGATION By softwood or greenwood
cuttings in summer or by layering in late winter.

HEIGHT
3–3.5m
(10–11ft)

SPREAD
3–3.5m
(10–11ft)

Hamamelidaceae	

HAMAMELIS VERNALIS 'Sandra' ♈

Habit Upright, open. **Flowers** Small, strongly
scented, spidery, in late winter and early spring.
Yellow. **Leaves** Deciduous, oval. Purple when
young, then green, turning red, yellow, and orange
in autumn.
• NATIVE HABITAT Garden origin.
• CULTIVATION Flowers are frost-resistant.
Tolerates light shade and deep soil over chalk, but
prefers peaty, acid and well-drained soil.
• PROPAGATION By softwood cuttings in summer,
by budding in late summer, or by grafting in winter.

HEIGHT
5m (15ft)

SPREAD
5.5m (17ft)

Aceraceae	CORAL-BARK MAPLE

ACER PALMATUM 'Sango-kaku' ♈

Habit Bushy-headed, tree-like with age.
Leaves Deciduous, palmate. Orange-yellow in
spring, green in summer, turning pink and yellow in
autumn. **Bark** Young shoots bright coral-pink.
• NATIVE HABITAT Garden origin.
• CULTIVATION Tolerates light shade. Provide
shelter from cold winds. Needs moist but well-
drained soil.
• PROPAGATION By softwood cuttings in early
summer, or by grafting in spring.
• OTHER NAMES *A. palmatum* 'Senkaki'.

HEIGHT
To 6m
(20 ft)

SPREAD
6m (20ft)

Elaeagnaceae	SEA BUCKTHORN

HIPPOPHAË RHAMNOIDES 🏆

Habit Bushy, arching, spiny. **Flowers** Small, either male or female, in spring. Yellow. **Fruits** Small berries from autumn to winter. Orange. **Leaves** Deciduous, narrow. Silvery-grey.
• NATIVE HABITAT Coasts, riverbanks, and shady woods of Asia and Europe, including Britain.
• CULTIVATION Grows in almost any soil. Plant male and female plants together for good fruiting. Makes good hedging, especially in coastal gardens.
• PROPAGATION By seed in autumn, semi-ripe cuttings in summer or by hardwood cuttings in winter.

HEIGHT
3–6m
(10–20ft)

SPREAD
To 6m
(20ft)

Celastraceae	

EUONYMUS MYRIANTHUS

Habit Bushy, slow-growing. **Flowers** Small, yellow-green, in dense clusters in summer. **Fruits** 4-sided, yellow capsule, splits to reveal orange seeds. **Leaves** Evergreen, lance-shaped to oval, leathery. Mid-green.
• NATIVE HABITAT Cliffs, scrubland of W. China.
• CULTIVATION Tolerates semi-shade and almost any soil that is well-drained but reliably moist.
• PROPAGATION By seed in autumn or by semi-ripe cuttings in summer.
• OTHER NAMES *E. sargentianus*.

HEIGHT
To 3.5m
(11ft)

SPREAD
3.5m (11ft)

Rosaceae	

PYRACANTHA ATALANTIOIDES 'Aurea'

Habit Vigorous, upright, spiny, arching with age. **Flowers** Small, in clusters, in summer. White. **Fruits** Small berries, in dense clusters, in autumn and winter. Yellow. **Leaves** Evergreen, narrowly oval. Glossy dark green.
• NATIVE HABITAT Garden origin.
• CULTIVATION Needs a sheltered site and fertile soil. Suitable for north-facing, sheltered walls. Train and cut back wall-grown plants after flowering.
• PROPAGATION By semi-ripe cuttings in summer.

HEIGHT
5–6m
(15–20ft)

SPREAD
4m (12ft) or more

Berberidaceae	

MAHONIA × MEDIA 'Charity' 🏆

Habit Vigorous, dense, upright. **Flowers** Slender, fragrant, upright spikes from late autumn to early spring. Yellow. **Leaves** Evergreen, large, comprising many spiny leaflets. Dark green.
• NATIVE HABITAT Garden origin.
• CULTIVATION Prefers shade or semi-shade, although will become leggy in deep shade. Grow in fertile, moisture-retentive soil.
• PROPAGATION By leaf bud or semi-ripe cuttings in summer.

HEIGHT
4m (12ft)

SPREAD
3.5m (11ft)

Berberidaceae	

MAHONIA × *MEDIA* 'Buckland'

Habit Vigorous, dense, upright.
Flowers Fragrant, in clustered, branched spikes from late autumn to early spring. Yellow.
Leaves Evergreen, large, comprising many spiny leaflets. Dark green.
• NATIVE HABITAT Garden origin.
• CULTIVATION Prefers shade or semi-shade, although will become leggy in deep shade. Grow in fertile, moisture-retentive soil.
• PROPAGATION By leaf bud or semi-ripe cuttings in summer.

HEIGHT
4m (12ft)

SPREAD
3.5m (11ft)

Hamamelidaceae	COMMON WITCH HAZEL

HAMAMELIS VIRGINIANA

Habit Upright, open. ***Flowers*** Small, fragrant, spidery, opening in autumn as leaves fall. Yellow.
Leaves Deciduous, broadly oval. Green, turning clear yellow in autumn.
• NATIVE HABITAT Understorey of deciduous forests of E. North America.
• CULTIVATION Tolerates shade and deep soil over chalk, but prefers peaty, acid, well-drained soil.
• PROPAGATION By seed in autumn or by softwood cuttings in summer.

☼ ◊ pH

HEIGHT
3.5–5m
(11–15ft)

SPREAD
3.5–5m
(11–15ft)

Hamamelidaceae	WITCH HAZEL

HAMAMELIS × *INTERMEDIA* 'Diane'

Habit Open, spreading. ***Flowers*** Small, fragrant, spidery, carried on bare branches, in mid- to late winter. Deep red. ***Leaves*** Deciduous, broadly oval. Mid-green, turning brilliant red and yellow in autumn.
• NATIVE HABITAT Garden origin.
• CULTIVATION Thrives in sun or semi-shade, in fertile, well-drained, peaty soil. Provide shelter from cold winter winds.
• PROPAGATION By softwood cuttings in summer, by budding in late summer, or by grafting in winter.

HEIGHT
3.5m (11ft)

SPREAD
3.5m (11ft)

Solanaceae	TREE TOMATO, TAMARILLO

CYPHOMANDRA CRASSICAULIS

Habit Open, upright, tree-like with age.
Flowers Small, fragrant, in early summer. White-pink. ***Fruits*** Tomato-like, from summer to winter. Bright red. ***Leaves*** Evergreen, large, heart-shaped. Rich green.
• NATIVE HABITAT Dry forests of Peru and Brazil.
• CULTIVATION Best grown in a conservatory. Shade from hot summer sun. Water freely when in full growth, otherwise sparingly. Tip prune when young.
• PROPAGATION By seed in spring.
• OTHER NAMES *C. betacea*.

☼ ◊

Min. 10°C
(50°F)

HEIGHT
3–5m
(10–15ft)

SPREAD
3m (10ft)

Rosaceae	

COTONEASTER LACTEUS

Habit Arching. *Flowers* Small, cup-shaped, in clusters, from early to mid-summer. Milky-white. *Fruits* Small berries in broad, dense clusters, from autumn to winter. Red. *Leaves* Evergreen, oval, leathery. Dark green, grey-woolly beneath.
• NATIVE HABITAT In scrub of Yunnan, China.
• CULTIVATION Tolerates some shade. Thrives on most soils, including dry soils, but will not tolerate waterlogging. Needs no regular pruning. Useful for windbreaks and informal hedges. Can be susceptible to fireblight. As with other *Cotoneaster*

species, *C. lacteus* is not only ornamental but also useful for wildlife. The flowers in summer provide a valuable nectar source for honey bees and other beneficial insects, while the long-persistent clusters of berries are valued by garden birds in winter.
• PROPAGATION By semi-ripe cuttings in summer.

HEIGHT
3.5–5m
(11–15ft)

SPREAD
4m (12ft)
or more

Trochodendraceae	

TROCHODENDRON ARALIOIDES

Habit Shrubby, or broadly conical tree.
Flowers Small, without petals, stamens radiating from central disc, in clusters in late spring and early summer. Bright green. *Leaves* Evergreen, narrowly elliptic. Glossy dark green above, paler beneath.
• NATIVE HABITAT Mountain woodland of Japan, Korea, and Taiwan.
• CULTIVATION Tolerates semi-shade. Grow in moist, well-drained soil. Shelter from cold, dry winds.
• PROPAGATION By semi-ripe cuttings in summer or by seed in autumn.

HEIGHT
12m (40ft)
or more

SPREAD
7m (21ft)

Fagaceae	CALIFORNIA LIVE OAK

QUERCUS AGRIFOLIA

Habit Broad-crowned, spreading, often shrubby.
Fruits Cone-shaped acorns, with a silky-haired cup. *Leaves* Evergreen, oval-elliptic to broadly oval, with rigid, spiny teeth. Glossy dark green.
Bark Corky and fissured with age. Grey to black.
• NATIVE HABITAT Valleys and foothills of coastal mountains of California.
• CULTIVATION Tolerates lime-rich soils, but not shallow, chalky ones. Grow in deep, fertile soil. Shelter from cold, dry winds.
• PROPAGATION By seed in autumn.

HEIGHT
To 12m
(40ft)

SPREAD
7m (21ft)

Garryaceae	SILK-TASSEL BUSH

GARRYA ELLIPTICA

Habit Dense, bushy, tree-like with age.
Flowers Catkins, which are longer on male plants, from mid-winter to early spring. Silver-grey.
Leaves Evergreen, wavy-edged. Glossy dark green.
• NATIVE HABITAT Chaparral and forest, in coastal mountain foothills of W. North America.
• CULTIVATION Tolerates poor, dry soil and coastal conditions. Resents transplanting. Provide shelter from cold winds to avoid leaf scorch. Thrives on west- or north-facing walls.
• PROPAGATION By semi-ripe cuttings in summer.

HEIGHT
To 4m
(12ft)

SPREAD
3.5–4m
(11–12ft)

Flacourtiaceae	

AZARA MICROPHYLLA

Habit Elegant, open, often tree-like.
Flowers Tiny, vanilla-scented, in small clusters in late winter and early spring. Deep yellow.
Leaves Evergreen, small, round to broadly oval. Glossy dark green.
• NATIVE HABITAT In forests with *Nothofagus obliqua* in Chile and S. Argentina.
• CULTIVATION Tolerates partial shade, but in cool areas needs the shelter of a warm, south-facing wall to thrive and bloom.
• PROPAGATION By semi-ripe cuttings in summer.

HEIGHT
6m (20ft)

SPREAD
6m (20ft)

Leguminosae	OVENS WATTLE

ACACIA PRAVISSIMA

Habit Bushy, arching, a small tree with maturity.
Flowers Small, globose, in loose racemes in late
winter or early spring. Bright yellow.
Leaves Evergreen, triangular, spine-tipped,
flattened leaf-stalks. Silver-grey.
• NATIVE HABITAT S.E. Australia.
• CULTIVATION Grow in well-drained, humus-
rich soil, in a warm, sunny, sheltered site. Prune
after flowering to restrict growth. In cold areas, it
may also be pot grown in a cool conservatory.
• PROPAGATION By pre-soaked seed in spring.

HEIGHT
To 6m
(20ft)

SPREAD
5m (15ft)
or more

Leguminosae	COOTAMUNDRA WATTLE, GOLDEN MIMOSA

ACACIA BAILEYANA ♀

Habit Spreading, arching, tree-like with maturity.
Flowers Small, globose, in dense racemes from
winter to spring. Golden-yellow.
Leaves Evergreen, finely divided into leaflets.
Grey-green.
• NATIVE HABITAT S.E. Australia.
• CULTIVATION Grow in well-drained, humus-
rich soil, in a warm, sunny, sheltered site. Prune
after flowering to restrict growth. In cold areas, may
also be pot grown in a cool conservatory.
• PROPAGATION By pre-soaked seed in spring.

HEIGHT
To 8m
(25ft)

SPREAD
5m (15ft)

Corylaceae	CORKSCREW HAZEL, HARRY LAUDER'S WALKING STICK

CORYLUS AVELLANA 'Contorta' ♀

Habit Bushy, with spirally twisted shoots.
Flowers Pendent catkins, in late winter. Pale
yellow. *Leaves* Deciduous, almost circular,
pointed, sharply toothed. Mid-green.
• NATIVE HABITAT This cultivar was discovered
in Gloucestershire in 1863.
• CULTIVATION Tolerates semi-shade and any
fertile soil, including chalk. Has a beautiful winter
outline and is useful for flower arrangements.
• PROPAGATION By grafting in late summer or by
layering in late autumn to early spring.

HEIGHT
To 6m
(20ft)

SPREAD
To 6m
(20ft)

Hamamelidaceae	WITCH HAZEL

HAMAMELIS × *INTERMEDIA* 'Arnold Promise' ♀

Habit Open, spreading. *Flowers* Large, fragrant,
with 4 crimped petals, on bare branches in mid- to
late winter. Pale yellow. *Leaves* Deciduous,
broadly oval. Mid-green, yellow in autumn.
• NATIVE HABITAT Garden origin.
• CULTIVATION Thrives in sun or semi-shade, in
fertile, well-drained, peaty soil. Provide shelter
from cold winter winds.
• PROPAGATION By softwood cuttings in summer,
by budding in late summer, or by grafting in winter.

HEIGHT
3.5m (11ft)

SPREAD
3.5m (11ft)

Hamamelidaceae	

HAMAMELIS JAPONICA 'Sulphurea'

Habit Open, upright, later spreading.
Flowers Fragrant, spidery, with 4 crimped, soft petals, on bare branches in winter. Yellow.
Leaves Deciduous, broadly oval. Dark green, turning yellow in autumn.
• NATIVE HABITAT Garden origin.
• CULTIVATION Thrives in sun or semi-shade, in fertile, well-drained, peaty soil. Provide shelter from cold winter winds.
• PROPAGATION By softwood cuttings in summer, by budding in late summer or by grafting in winter.

HEIGHT
3.5m (11ft)

SPREAD
6m (20ft)

Hamamelidaceae	

HAMAMELIS MOLLIS 'Coombe Wood'

Habit Open, spreading. **Flowers** Fragrant, spidery, with narrow petals, on bare branches from mid- to late winter. Golden-yellow.
Leaves Deciduous, broadly oval. Dark green, turning yellow in autumn.
• NATIVE HABITAT Garden origin.
• CULTIVATION Thrives in sun or semi-shade, in fertile, well-drained, peaty soil. Provide shelter from cold winter winds.
• PROPAGATION By softwood cuttings in summer, by budding in late summer, or by grafting in winter.

HEIGHT
3.5m (11ft)

SPREAD
6m (20ft)

Dracaenaceae	

DRACAENA DEREMENSIS 'Warnecki' ♀

Habit Slow-growing, erect, sparsely branched.
Leaves Evergreen, upright to arching, lance-shaped. Banded grey-green and cream.
• NATIVE HABITAT Garden origin.
• CULTIVATION Suitable for a warm conservatory. Water moderately in growth, otherwise sparingly. If leggy, cut back near to soil level in spring.
• PROPAGATION By air-layering in spring or by tip or stem cuttings in summer.
• OTHER NAMES *D. deremensis* 'Souvenir de Schriever', *D. fragrans* 'Warneckii'.

Min.
15–18°C
(59–64°F)

HEIGHT
To 3.5m
(11ft)

SPREAD
3m (10ft)

Oleaceae	PRIVET, OVAL-LEAF PRIVET

LIGUSTRUM OVALIFOLIUM

Habit Vigorous, dense, upright. **Flowers** Small, malodorous, in compact panicles in mid-summer. White. **Fruits** Small, spherical, berry-like. Black. **Leaves** Evergreen or semi-evergreen, oval. Glossy mid-green.
• NATIVE HABITAT Scrub and forest of Japan.
• CULTIVATION Grows in any well-drained, fertile soil, including chalk. Cut hedging plants back to 30cm (12in) on planting and prune hard in the first two years. Trim as necessary during summer.
• PROPAGATION By semi-ripe cuttings in summer.

HEIGHT
4m (12ft)

SPREAD
3m (10ft)

Rosaceae	VARIEGATED PORTUGAL LAUREL

PRUNUS LUSITANICA 'Variegata'

Habit Slow-growing, bushy. *Flowers* Small, fragrant, in slender racemes in summer. Creamy-white. *Fruits* Small berries. Red then dark purple. *Leaves* Evergreen, oval. Glossy dark green and white-edged. May be flushed pink in winter.
• NATIVE HABITAT Garden origin.
• CULTIVATION Wind-resistant, tolerant of semi-shade and any but waterlogged soil. Cut back informal hedges in late summer, preferably with secateurs, and formal hedges in spring.
• PROPAGATION By semi-ripe cuttings in summer.

HEIGHT
To 4m
(12ft)

SPREAD
4m (12ft)

Araliaceae	RICE-PAPER PLANT, CHINESE RICE-PAPER PLANT

TETRAPANAX PAPYRIFER ♥

Habit Upright, suckering. *Flowers* Small, in bold sprays in summer. Creamy-white. *Fruits* Small, fleshy. Black. *Leaves* Evergreen, circular, and deeply lobed. Dull green, felted beneath.
• NATIVE HABITAT Humid forests of Taiwan.
• CULTIVATION Suitable for a warm conservatory. Tolerates semi-shade. Water potted specimens freely when in growth, less in winter.
• PROPAGATION By seed in autumn or spring or by suckers in spring.
• OTHER NAMES *Fatsia papyrifera.*

HEIGHT
4m (12ft)
or more

SPREAD
5m (15ft)
or more

Rosaceae	AZORES CHERRY LAUREL

PRUNUS LUSITANICA subsp. *AZORICA* ♥

Habit Slow-growing, bushy. *Flowers* Small, fragrant, in slender spikes in summer. White. *Fruits* Small berries. Purple. *Leaves* Evergreen, oval. Glossy bright green, red when young.
• NATIVE HABITAT Forests of the Azores.
• CULTIVATION Wind-resistant, tolerant of semi-shade and any but waterlogged soil. Grows well on shallow chalk. Makes excellent wind break or informal hedging. Cut back informal hedges in spring, preferably with secateurs.
• PROPAGATION By semi-ripe cuttings in summer.

HEIGHT
To 6m
(20ft)

SPREAD
6m (20ft)

Griseliniaceae	BROADLEAF

GRISELINIA LITTORALIS 'Variegata'

Habit Upright, dense, bushy.
Flowers Inconspicuous, in late spring. Yellow-green. **Leaves** Evergreen, rounded, leathery. Grey-green, marked bright green and creamy-white.
• NATIVE HABITAT Lowland and mountain forest of New Zealand.
• CULTIVATION Grow in moist but well-drained soil, in sun or semi-shade. Shelter from cold, drying winds. Makes good salt-resistant hedging.
• PROPAGATION By semi-ripe cuttings in summer.

HEIGHT
4m (12ft)
or more

SPREAD
3m (10ft)
or more

Pittosporaceae	

PITTOSPORUM 'Garnettii' ♟

Habit Columnar or conical, dense, bushy.
Flowers Tiny, honey-scented, in summer, but not reliable. Red-purple. **Leaves** Evergreen, oval-elliptic. Grey-green, irregularly edged creamy-white, flushed pink in cold areas in winter.
• NATIVE HABITAT Garden origin.
• CULTIVATION Thrives in mild areas, especially on the coast. In cold areas, site against a south- or west-facing wall. Provide shelter from cold winds.
• PROPAGATION By semi-ripe cuttings in summer.

HEIGHT
3.5m (11ft)
or more

SPREAD
2m (6ft)

Araliaceae	LACE ARALIA

POLYSCIAS GUILFOYLEI 'Victoriae'

Habit Slow-growing, rounded, tree-like with age.
Leaves Evergreen, deeply divided, oval to rounded, irregularly toothed leaflets. Deep green, with white margins.
• NATIVE HABITAT Garden origin.
• CULTIVATION Suitable for a warm conservatory. Water plentifully when in growth, otherwise moderately. Cut out straggly stems in spring. Draughts will cause foliage drop.
• PROPAGATION By stem tip or leafless stem-section cuttings in summer.

Min.
15–18°C
(59–64°F)

HEIGHT
To 4m
(12ft)

SPREAD
3m (10ft)

Araliaceae	FALSE ARALIA

SCHEFFLERA ELEGANTISSIMA ♟

Habit Upright, open. **Leaves** Evergreen, large, divided into 7–10 coarsely toothed leaflets. Lustrous grey-green, sometimes bronze-tinted.
• NATIVE HABITAT Forests of New Caledonia.
• CULTIVATION Good for a warm conservatory. Water plentifully when in growth, then moderately. Provide humidity. If leggy, cut back hard in spring.
• PROPAGATION By seed or by air-layering in spring or by stem tip or stem-section cuttings in summer.
• OTHER NAMES *Aralia elegantissima, Dizygotheca elegantissima.*

Min. 13°C
(55°F)

HEIGHT
To 3.5m
(11ft)

SPREAD
3m (10ft)

Compositae	

BRACHYGLOTTIS REPANDA 'Purpurea'

Habit Bushy, upright when young, tree-like with age. *Flowers* Small, fragrant, in clusters in summer. White. *Leaves* Evergreen, oblong to broadly oval. Soft green, white-downy beneath, turning purplish-tinged with purple veins.
Bark White-downy on young shoots.
• NATIVE HABITAT Lowland forest and coastal scrub of New Zealand.
• CULTIVATION Tolerates partial shade. Water potted specimens freely in summer, otherwise moderately. Prune to shape or restrict size after flowering. This variety makes a beautiful addition to shrub or mixed borders in mild, frost-free gardens, lending a lush sub-tropical effect to plantings. In cooler areas it can be grown in tubs in a conservatory where the mignonette-like fragrance of its flowers and its soft, downy foliage can be fully appreciated at close quarters.
• PROPAGATION By semi-ripe cuttings in late summer.

Min. 3°C
(37°F)

HEIGHT
To 6m
(20ft)

SPREAD
6m (20ft)

Pittosporaceae	TAWHIWHI, KOHUHU

PITTOSPORUM TENUIFOLIUM ♈

Habit Columnar, later rounded, becoming tree-like. **Flowers** Tiny, honey-scented, in late spring. Purple. **Leaves** Evergreen, oval with wavy edges. Glossy mid-green. **Bark** Young shoots dark purple.
• NATIVE HABITAT Lowland and coastal forest of New Zealand.
• CULTIVATION Thrives in mild areas, especially on the coast. In cold areas, site against a south- or west-facing wall. Provide shelter from cold winds.
• PROPAGATION By seed in autumn or spring or by semi-ripe cuttings in summer.

☀ ◊
❀ ❀

HEIGHT
6m (20ft)
or more

SPREAD
3.5m (11ft)

Oleaceae	

LIGUSTRUM LUCIDUM 'Excelsum Superbum' ♈

Habit Vigorous, upright, tree-like with age. **Flowers** Small, tubular, in panicles in late summer. White. **Leaves** Evergreen, large, oval. Glossy bright green, marked pale green and edged with yellow.
• NATIVE HABITAT Garden origin.
• CULTIVATION Thrives on any well-drained soil, including chalk. Requires little pruning, but will regenerate freely from old wood, if cut in mid-spring.
• PROPAGATION By semi-ripe cuttings in summer.

☀ ◊
❀ ❀

HEIGHT
6m (20ft)

SPREAD
6m (20ft)

Oleaceae	

OSMANTHUS HETEROPHYLLUS 'Aureomarginatus'

Habit Slow-growing, upright, dense. **Flowers** Small, fragrant, in clusters in autumn. White. **Leaves** Evergreen, toothed. Glossy bright green, margined yellow.
• NATIVE HABITAT Garden origin. Species occurs in scrub of Japan and Taiwan.
• CULTIVATION Tolerates sun or semi-shade and most well-drained soils. Re-grows freely from old wood. Makes an attractive informal hedge or screen.
• PROPAGATION By semi-ripe cuttings in summer.

☀ ◊
❀ ❀

HEIGHT
To 5m
(15ft)

SPREAD
3.5m (11ft)

Elaeagnaceae	

ELAEAGNUS PUNGENS 'Maculata' ♈

Habit Bushy, slightly spiny. **Flowers** Small, very fragrant, urn-shaped, from mid- to late autumn. Creamy-white. **Leaves** Evergreen, oval to oblong. Lustrous dark green, with deep yellow central patch.
• NATIVE HABITAT Garden origin.
• CULTIVATION Thrives in most well-drained, fertile soils, except shallow chalk. Tolerates semi-shade. Prune out branches with all-green leaves. Good for hedging, especially in coastal gardens.
• PROPAGATION By semi-ripe cuttings in summer.

☀ ◊
❀ ❀

HEIGHT
To 4m
(15ft)

SPREAD
4m (12ft)

CAMELLIAS

Camellias are a genus of evergreen shrubs and trees originating mainly in the forests of warm-temperate Asia. They are much valued for their dark, lustrous foliage and for the unsurpassed elegance of their flowers, which range from pure white to deepest crimson.

Camellias make handsome and floriferous specimens for a cool conservatory or when planted in a shrub border. They also grow well against walls or in containers. In areas with hard spring frosts, a north or north-west facing wall will provide additional frost protection and reduce risk of damage to flowers. They should be grown in moisture-retentive, well-drained, acid to neutral, and lime-free soils. Most prefer semi-shade, and if grown outdoors all must have shelter from cold, dry winds and frost. Flowers may be damaged by rain.

Generally, camellias need little pruning but if young plants have a very open framework or are leggy they should be pruned back to encourage bushiness. After flowering, cut leggy shoots back by up to one-third of their length before new buds break in spring. Old and neglected specimens respond well to hard pruning, and can be rejuvenated by cutting back all shoots by at least one-third. After pruning, feed and mulch well with leaf mould or well-rotted organic matter.

Propagate camellias by taking semi-ripe or hardwood cuttings from mid-summer to early winter, or by grafting in late winter or early spring. Camellias may be infested with aphids, thrips, or scale insects when grown under glass and should be treated with a suitable insecticide.

Flowers are classified according to the following types:

SINGLE – shallowly cup-shaped or flat, with a single row of no more than 8 petals, arranged around a central boss of conspicuous stamens.

SEMI-DOUBLE – cup-shaped or flat, with 9–21 regular or irregular petals, arranged in 2 or more rows around a central boss of conspicuous stamens.

ANEMONE – rounded, with one or more rows of large, flat or undulating outer petals, surrounding a domed centre of massed petaloids and stamens.

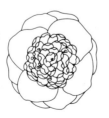

PEONY-FORM – domed, rounded, the usually irregular petals intermingled with petaloids and stamens.

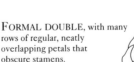

ROSE-FORM – cup-shaped, with several rows of overlapping petals, opening to reveal the stamens.

FORMAL DOUBLE, with many rows of regular, neatly overlapping petals that obscure stamens.

IRREGULAR DOUBLE, with many rows of loosely arranged, irregular petals that obscure stamens.

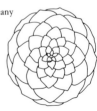

C. JAPONICA 'Lady Vansittart'
Habit Slow-growing, dense, upright.
Flowers Medium-sized, saucer-shaped, semi-double. White, flushed or striped rose-pink.
Leaves Holly-like, twisted, with wavy margins. Dark green.
• CULTIVATION Ideal for pot or tub cultivation.
• HEIGHT 3m (10ft).
• SPREAD 3m (10ft).

C. japonica 'Lady Vansittart'
SEMI-DOUBLE

☀ ◊ pH ✿✿✿

C. 'Cornish Snow'
Habit Open, upright, very free-flowering.
Flowers Small, single, carried in profusion from early spring. White, occasionally flushed pink, with a cluster of golden stamens. *Leaves* Narrow, taper-pointed. Very dark green, flushed purple in summer.
• HEIGHT 4–5m (12–15ft).
• SPREAD 4m (12ft).

C. 'Cornish Snow'
SINGLE

☀ ◊ pH ✿✿✿   ♔

C. SASANQUA 'Narumigata'
Habit Fast-growing, dense, upright.
Flowers Large, fragrant, single, cup-shaped, in autumn. White, sometimes pink-flushed.
Leaves Lance-shaped. Glossy bright green.
• CULTIVATION Needs a hot, sunny, and sheltered site to flower well.
• HEIGHT 3m (10ft).
• SPREAD 1.5m (5ft).

C. sasanqua 'Narumigata'
SINGLE

☀ ◊ pH ✿✿   ♔

C. JAPONICA 'Alba Simplex'
Habit Vigorous, bushy, upright. *Flowers* Cup-shaped, single, in early spring. White.
Leaves Broadly lance-shaped. Mid- to pale green.
• HEIGHT 5m (15ft).
• SPREAD 3m (10ft).

C. japonica 'Alba Simplex'
SINGLE

☀ ◊ pH ✿✿✿

C. 'Shiro-wabisuke'
Habit Compact, upright.
Flowers Small, single cup-shaped, in spring. Pure white. *Leaves* Small, lance-shaped. Dull green.
• HEIGHT 2.5m (8ft).
• SPREAD 1.5m (5ft).

C. 'Shiro-wabisuke'
SINGLE

☀ ◊ pH ✿✿✿

C. JAPONICA 'Janet Waterhouse'
Habit Slow-growing, bushy.
Flowers Medium-sized, formal double, in spring. Pure white.
Leaves Lance-shaped. Very glossy dark green.
• CULTIVATION Flowers are very weather-resistant. Excellent for containers.
• HEIGHT To 3m (10ft).
• SPREAD 3m (10ft).

C. japonica 'Janet Waterhouse'
FORMAL DOUBLE

☀ ◊ pH ✿✿

CAMELLIA X WILLIAMSII 'Francis Hanger'
Habit Upright, later spreading.
Flowers Single, from late winter to spring. White, with a brush of golden stamens. *Leaves* Lance-shaped, undulate. Glossy dark green.
• CULTIVATION Suffers sun scald in full sun.
• HEIGHT 4m (12ft).
• SPREAD 3m (10ft).

C. x *williamsii* 'Francis Hanger'
SINGLE

☀ ◊ pH ✿✿✿

C. TSAII
Habit Bushy, delicate, graceful. *Flowers* Small, cup-shaped, single, carried in profusion in spring. White, with golden stamens.
Leaves Small, narrowly lance-shaped. Light green, coppery when young.
• HEIGHT 4m (12ft).
• SPREAD 3m (10ft).

C. tsaii
SINGLE

☀ ◊ pH ✿✿   ♔

C. × WILLIAMSII
'Jury's Yellow'
Habit Compact, upright.
Flowers Medium-sized,
anemone-form, with
waved petals, in spring.
White, with creamy-
yellow central petaloids.
Leaves Small, lance-
shaped. Glossy dark
green.
• HEIGHT 4m (12ft).
• SPREAD 2.5m (8ft).

C. × williamsii
'Jury's Yellow'
ANEMONE

☀ ◊ pH ❋ ❋ ❋

C. JAPONICA
'Mrs D. W. Davis'
Habit Vigorous,
compact, spreading.
Flowers Very large,
pendulous, cup-shaped,
semi-double. Delicate
pink. *Leaves* Oval to
lance-shaped. Glossy
dark green.
• HEIGHT 3m (10ft).
• SPREAD 3m (10ft).

C. japonica
'Mrs D. W. Davis'
SEMI-DOUBLE

☀ ◊ pH ❋ ❋   ♛

C. JAPONICA
'Tomorrow's Dawn'
Habit Vigorous, open,
upright. *Flowers* Very
large, semi-double, with
irregular petals, and large
petaloids, in spring. Soft
pink, fading to white at
margins, often red-
streaked. *Leaves* Lance-
shaped. Mid-green.
• HEIGHT 5m (15ft).
• SPREAD 4m (12ft).

C. japonica
'Tomorrow's Dawn'
IRREGULAR DOUBLE

☀ ◊ pH ❋ ❋

C. JAPONICA
'Berenice Boddy'
Habit Vigorous, upright.
Flowers Medium-sized,
semi-double, in spring.
Light pink, with a deeper
colour on reverse.
Leaves Oval to lance-
shaped. Glossy dark
green.
• CULTIVATION Flowers
are frost-resistant.
• HEIGHT 4m (12ft).
• SPREAD 3m (10ft).

C. japonica
'Berenice Boddy'
SEMI-DOUBLE

☀ ◊ pH ❋ ❋ ❋   ♛

C. JAPONICA
'Ave Maria'
Habit Vigorous, bushy,
mound-forming.
Flowers Small, formal
double, from late winter
to early spring. Soft pink.
Leaves Broadly lance-
shaped. Glossy dark
green.
• HEIGHT 2.5–3m
(8–10ft).
• SPREAD 2.5–3m
(8–10ft).

C. japonica
'Ave Maria'
FORMAL DOUBLE

☀ ◊ pH ❋ ❋

C. × WILLIAMSII
'J. C. Williams'
Habit Vigorous,
horizontally branching,
long-flowering.
Flowers Single, cup-
shaped, from early winter
to late spring. Pink.
Leaves Small, lance-
shaped. Glossy dark green.
• CULTIVATION Has an
exceptionally long
flowering period.
• HEIGHT 4m (12ft).
• SPREAD 2.5m (8ft).

C. × williamsii **'J.C.
Williams'**
SINGLE

☀ ◊ pH ❋ ❋ ❋

C. × WILLIAMSII
'Clarrie Fawcett'
Habit Upright.
Flowers Semi-double,
cup-shaped, in early
spring. Rose-pink.
Leaves Small, lance-
shaped. Glossy mid-
green.
• HEIGHT 4m (12ft).
• SPREAD 2.5m (8ft).

C. × williamsii
'Clarrie Fawcett'
SEMI-DOUBLE

☀ ◊ pH ❋ ❋ ❋

C. × WILLIAMSII
'Donation'
Habit Vigorous,
compact, upright, very
free-flowering.
Flowers Large, semi-
double, cup-shaped, in
early spring. Delicate
silvery-pink, with darker
veins. *Leaves* Small,
lance-shaped. Glossy
dark green.
• HEIGHT 4m (12ft).
• SPREAD 2.5m (8ft).

C. × williamsii
'Donation'
SEMI-DOUBLE

☀ ◊ pH ❋ ❋ ❋   ♛

C. JAPONICA 'Margaret Davis Picotee'

Habit Compact, spreading.
Flowers Medium-sized, irregular double, with ruffled petals. Creamy-white, often lined with pink, and edged bright rose-red. **Leaves** Oval to lance-shaped. Dark green.
• HEIGHT 3m (10ft).
• SPREAD 3m (15ft).

C. japonica
'Margaret Davis Picotee'
IRREGULAR DOUBLE

C. JAPONICA 'Tricolor'

Habit Compact.
Flowers Large, single, in late winter and early spring. White, striped red and carmine pink.
Leaves Broadly lance-shaped, toothed, crinkled. Glossy dark green.
• OTHER NAMES
C. japonica 'Sieboldii'.
• HEIGHT 3m (10ft)
• SPREAD 3m (10ft)

C. japonica **'Tricolor'**
SINGLE

C. JAPONICA 'Lavinia Maggi'

Habit Vigorous, upright.
Flowers Large, formal double, in spring. White or pale pink, striped rose-cerise. **Leaves** Broadly lance-shaped, tapering. Glossy dark green.
• OTHER NAMES
C. japonica 'Contessa Lavinia Maggi'.
• HEIGHT 4m (12ft).
• SPREAD 3m (10ft).

C. japonica
'Lavinia Maggi'
FORMAL DOUBLE

C. × WILLIAMSII 'Mary Larcom'

Habit Spreading, free-flowering.
Flowers Fragrant, single, cup-shaped, from mid-winter to late spring. Cerise-pink.
Leaves Small, lance-shaped. Glossy dark green.
• HEIGHT 4m (12ft).
• SPREAD 2.5m (8ft).

C. × *williamsii* **'Mary Larcom'**
SINGLE

C. × WILLIAMSII 'E. G. Waterhouse'

Habit Upright, free-flowering.
Flowers Formal double, in early spring. Pale pink.
Leaves Small, lance-shaped. Pale green.
• HEIGHT 4m (12ft).
• SPREAD 2.5m (8ft).

C. × *williamsii*
'E. G. Waterhouse'
FORMAL DOUBLE

C. SALUENENSIS

Habit Vigorous, fast-growing, bushy, free-flowering.
Flowers Fragrant, single, cup-shaped, from early to late spring. White to rose-red. **Leaves** Lance-shaped, stiff. Dull green.
• CULTIVATION Does best in a warm, sunny site with part-day shade.
• HEIGHT 4m (12ft).
• SPREAD 2.5m (8ft).

C. saluenensis
SINGLE

C. × WILLIAMSII 'Joan Trehane'

Habit Vigorous, open.
Flowers Large, double, rose-form, in mid- to late spring. Clear rose-pink.
Leaves Small, lance-shaped. Glossy dark green.
• HEIGHT 4m (12ft).
• SPREAD 2.5m (8ft).

C. × *williamsii*
'Joan Trehane'
ROSE-FORM

C. JAPONICA 'Betty Sheffield Supreme'

Habit Compact, upright.
Flowers Large, semi-double with irregular petals. White, each petal bordered with several shades of rose-pink.
Leaves Lance-shaped. Mid-green.
• HEIGHT 3m (10ft).
• SPREAD 3m (10ft).

C. japonica
'Betty Sheffield Supreme'
IRREGULAR DOUBLE

C. × *WILLIAMSII*
'Bow Bells'
Habit Upright,
spreading, pendulous.
Flowers Single, cup-
shaped, pendulous, in
early spring or sometimes
from mid-winter. Rose-
pink, darker at the
centre, and with deep
pink veins. *Leaves* Small,
lance-shaped. Mid-green.
• HEIGHT 4m (12ft).
• SPREAD 2.5m (8ft).

C. × *williamsii*
'Bow Bells'
SINGLE

☀ ◊ pH ❀ ❀ ❀

C. **'Inspiration'**
Habit Dense, upright,
free-flowering.
Flowers Saucer-shaped,
semi-double, in
abundance in spring.
phlox-pink.
Leaves Oval, leathery.
Dark green.
• HEIGHT 4m (12ft).
• SPREAD 3m (10ft).

C. **'Inspiration'**
SEMI-DOUBLE

☀ ◊ pH ❀ ❀ ❀   ♈

C. × *WILLIAMSII*
'Brigadoon'
Habit Upright, bushy,
compact.
Flowers Medium-sized,
semi-double, in
succession from late
winter to spring. Rose-
pink. *Leaves* Small,
lance-shaped. Glossy
dark green.
• CULTIVATION
Excellent for containers.
• HEIGHT 3m (10ft).
• SPREAD 2.5m (8ft).

C. × *williamsii*
'Brigadoon'
SEMI-DOUBLE

☀ ◊ pH ❀ ❀ ❀   ♈

C. × *WILLIAMSII*
'Mary Christian'
Habit Vigorous, open,
upright, free-flowering.
Flowers Small, single,
cup-shaped, in late
winter-early spring.
Phlox-pink, with darker
veins. *Leaves* Small,
broadly elliptic. Glossy
dark green.
• HEIGHT 4m (12ft).
• SPREAD 2.5m (8ft).

C. × *williamsii*
'Mary Christian'
SINGLE

☀ ◊ pH ❀ ❀ ❀   ♈

C. RETICULATA
'Mudan Cha'
Habit Open, tree-like.
Flowers Very large, cup-
shaped, semi- to irregular
double, with curled
petals, in spring. Deep
pink. *Leaves* Large, oval,
leathery. Dark green.
• OTHER NAMES
C. reticulata 'Moutancha',
C. reticulata 'Peony
Camellia'.
• HEIGHT 10m (30ft).
• SPREAD 5m (15ft).

C. reticulata
'Mudan Cha'
SEMI- TO IRREGULAR
DOUBLE

☀ ◊ pH ❀ ❀

C. × *WILLIAMSII*
'George Blandford'
Habit Low, spreading.
Flowers Large, fully
double, anemone to
peony form, in late
winter to early spring.
Purplish-mauve.
Leaves Lance-shaped,
conspicuously veined.
Dark green.
• HEIGHT 2.5m (8ft).
• SPREAD 3m (10ft).

C. × *williamsii*
'George Blandford'
ANEMONE TO PEONY-FORM

☀ ◊ pH ❀ ❀ ❀   ♈

C. × *WILLIAMSII*
'St. Ewe'
Habit Upright, free-
flowering.
Flowers Large, single,
funnel-shaped, from mid-
winter to late spring.
Deep pink.
Leaves Small, lance-
shaped. Glossy light
green.
• HEIGHT 4m (12ft).
• SPREAD 2.5m (8ft).

C. × *williamsii*
'St. Ewe'
SINGLE

☀ ◊ pH ❀ ❀ ❀   ♈

C. JAPONICA **'Elegans'**
Habit Slow-growing,
dense, spreading, free-
flowering. *Flowers* Very
large, anemone-form,
early to mid-spring. Deep
rose-pink, with central
twisted petaloids often
variegated white.
Leaves Broadly lance-
shaped, wavy. Dark green.
• OTHER NAMES
C. 'Chandleri Elegans'.
• HEIGHT 4m (12ft).
• SPREAD 3m (10ft).

C. japonica **'Elegans'**
ANEMONE

☀ ◊ pH ❀ ❀ ❀   ♈

C. × *WILLIAMSII*
'Water Lily'
Habit Vigorous,
compact, upright.
Flowers Medium-sized,
formal double, from late
winter to early spring.
Bright rose-pink.
Leaves Lance-shaped.
Glossy dark green.
• HEIGHT 3m (10ft).
• SPREAD 3m (10ft).

C. × *williamsii*
'Water Lily'
FORMAL DOUBLE

☀ ◊ 凹 ❀❀❀   ♗

C. 'Leonard Messel'
Habit Open.
Flowers Large, flattish
to cup-shaped, semi-
double, in profusion in
spring. Rose-pink.
Leaves Large, oval,
leathery. Dark green.
• HEIGHT 4m (12ft).
• SPREAD 2.5m (8ft).

C. 'Leonard Messel'
SEMI-DOUBLE

☀ ◊ 凹 ❀❀❀   ♗

C. × *WILLIAMSII*
'Golden Spangles'
Habit Vigorous, open,
upright. *Flowers* Small,
single, cup-shaped, in
late winter-early spring.
Phlox-pink, with darker
veins. *Leaves* Small,
broadly elliptic. Glossy
dark green, variegated
yellow-green.
• HEIGHT 4m (12ft).
• SPREAD 2.5m (8ft).

C. × *williamsii*
'Golden Spangles'
SINGLE

☀ ◊ 凹 ❀❀❀

C. JAPONICA
'Jupiter'
Habit Vigorous, upright.
Flowers Medium-sized,
saucer-shaped, single, in
spring. Carmine-red, with
golden stamens.
Leaves Lance-shaped.
Dark green.
• HEIGHT 5m (15ft).
• SPREAD 3m (10ft).

C. japonica
'Jupiter'
SINGLE

☀ ◊ 凹 ❀❀❀   ♗

C. JAPONICA
'Elegans Supreme'
Habit Slow-growing,
spreading, free-flowering.
Flowers Large,
anemone-form, from
early to late-spring.
Deep, glowing rose-pink.
Leaves Broadly lance-
shaped, wavy. Dark
green.
• HEIGHT 4m (12ft).
• SPREAD 3m (10ft).

C. japonica
'Elegans Supreme'
ANEMONE

☀ ◊ 凹 ❀❀

C. JAPONICA
'Rubescens Major'
Habit Compact, upright,
bushy with age, free-
flowering.
Flowers Large, formal
double. Rose red, veined
crimson. *Leaves* Oval to
lance-shaped. Dark
green.
• HEIGHT 3m (10ft).
• SPREAD 3m (10ft).

C. japonica
'Rubescens Major'
FORMAL DOUBLE

☀ ◊ 凹 ❀❀❀   ♗

C. 'Innovation'
Habit Open, spreading.
Flowers Large, peony-
form, with twisted petals,
in spring. Claret red,
shaded lavender.
Leaves Large, oval,
leathery. Dark green.
• HEIGHT 5m (15ft).
• SPREAD 3m (10ft).

C. 'Innovation'
PEONY-FORM

☀ ◊ 凹 ❀❀

C. JAPONICA
'Gloire de Nantes'
Habit Upright, compact,
bushy with age.
Flowers Large, flattish,
semi-double, over a long
period from late winter to
early spring. Bright rose-
pink. *Leaves* Oval to
lance-shaped, lustrous.
Very glossy dark green.
• HEIGHT 4m (12ft).
• SPREAD 3m (10ft).

C. japonica
'Gloire de Nantes'
SEMI-DOUBLE

☀ ◊ 凹 ❀❀❀   ♗

C. RETICULATA 'William Hertrich'

Habit Strong-growing, open. **Flowers** Large, flattish to cup-shaped, semi-double with irregular petals, often tightly clustered in the centre, in mid-spring. Bright cherry red. **Leaves** Large, oval. Deep green.
• HEIGHT 5m (15ft).
• SPREAD 3m (10ft).

C. reticulata 'William Hertrich'
SEMI-DOUBLE

☀ ◊ pH ❀❀

C. x *WILLIAMSIII* 'Anticipation'

Habit Robust, compact, upright. **Flowers** Large, peony-form, in abundance in spring. Deep rose pink. **Leaves** Lance-shaped. Glossy dark green.
• CULTIVATION Suitable for pot cultivation, and ideal for small gardens.
• HEIGHT 3m (10ft).
• SPREAD 1.5m (5ft).

C. x *williamsii* 'Anticipation'
PEONY-FORM

☀ ◊ pH ❀❀❀   ♔

C. RETICULATA 'Zaotaohong'

Habit Open, tree-like. **Flowers** Large, cup-shaped, semi- to formal double, in spring. Crimson. **Leaves** Large, oval, leathery. Dark green.
• CULTIVATION Needs a sheltered site.
• OTHER NAMES *C. reticulata* 'Early Crimson'.
• HEIGHT 10m (30ft).
• SPREAD 5m (15ft).

C. reticulata 'Zaotaohong'
SEMI- TO FORMAL DOUBLE

☀ ◊ pH ❀❀

C. RETICULATA 'Zaomudan'

Habit Open, tree-like. **Flowers** Large, irregular double, inner petals forming a peony centre, in spring. Rose-pink. **Leaves** Large, oval, leathery. Dark green.
• CULTIVATION Needs a sheltered site.
• OTHER NAMES *C. reticulata* 'Early Peony'.
• HEIGHT 10m (30ft).
• SPREAD 5m (15ft).

C. reticulata 'Zaomudan'
IRREGULAR DOUBLE

☀ ◊ pH ❀❀

C. x *WILLIAMSII* 'Caerhays'

Habit Arching, spreading. **Flowers** Large, anemone to peony-form, in early spring. Crimson-pink; purplish with age. **Leaves** Large, long, tapering, elliptic, often puckered. Glossy dark green.
• CULTIVATION Good for wall-training.
• HEIGHT 4m (12ft).
• SPREAD 2.5m (8ft).

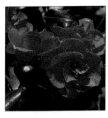

C. x *williamsii* 'Caerhays'
VARIABLE

☀ ◊ pH ❀❀❀

C. JAPONICA 'Julia Drayton'

Habit Upright. **Flowers** Large, variable, from formal double to rose-form, in spring. Crimson. **Leaves** Oval to lance-shaped, slightly twisted. Dark green.
• HEIGHT 4m (12ft).
• SPREAD 3m (10ft).

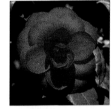

C. japonica 'Julia Drayton'
VARIABLE

☀ ◊ pH ❀❀

C. RETICULATA 'Houye Diechi'

Habit Open, tree-like, free-flowering. **Flowers** Very large, flat to cup-shaped, semi-double, with wavy central petals, in spring. Rose-pink. **Leaves** Large, oval, leathery. Dark green.
OTHER NAMES *C. reticulata* 'Butterfly Wings'.
• HEIGHT 10m (30ft).
• SPREAD 5m (15ft).

C. reticulata 'Houye Diechi'
SEMI-DOUBLE

☀ ◊ pH ❀❀

C. 'Dr Clifford Parks'

Habit Compact, spreading. **Flowers** Large, semi-double, peony- and anemone-form on same plant, in mid-spring. Flame-red. **Leaves** Large, oval. Dark green.
• CULTIVATION Tolerates full sun. Good for wall cultivation.
• HEIGHT 4m (12ft).
• SPREAD 2.5m (8ft).

C. 'Dr Clifford Parks'
VARIABLE

☀ ◊ pH ❀❀❀   ♔

C. JAPONICA 'Giulio Nuccio'

Habit Vigorous, upright, spreading with age.
Flowers Very large, cup-shaped, semi-double, with wavy, velvety petals, and tight clusters of stamens and petaloids, in mid- to late spring. Rose-red.
Leaves Lance-shaped, long-tapering, sometimes with 'fish-tail' tips.
• HEIGHT 4m (12ft).
• SPREAD 3m (10ft).

C. japonica
'Giulio Nuccio'
SEMI-DOUBLE

C. JAPONICA 'Althaeiflora'

Habit Vigorous, bushy, upright, free-flowering.
Flowers Large, peony-form, in spring; very frost-resistant. Dark red.
Leaves Broadly oval. Very dark green.
• HEIGHT 4m (12ft).
• SPREAD 3m (10ft).

C. japonica
'Althaeiflora'
PEONY-FORM

C. JAPONICA 'R. L. Wheeler'

Habit Robust, upright.
Flowers Very large, flattish, anemone-form to semi-double, often with petaloids, in late winter-early spring. Rose-pink, with golden stamens.
Leaves Large, broadly oval, puckered and recurved at margins, leathery. Very dark green.
• HEIGHT 5m (15ft).
• SPREAD 3m (10ft).

C. japonica
'R. L. Wheeler'
VARIABLE

C. RETICULATA 'Captain Rawes'

Habit Open, tree-like,
Flowers Very large, semi-double, in profusion in late winter-early spring. Carmine-rose.
Leaves Broadly elliptic to oblong-elliptic, rigid, leathery. Dark green.
• OTHER NAMES
C. reticulata 'Semi-plena', *C. reticulata* 'Guixia'.
• HEIGHT To 5m (15ft).
• SPREAD 2.5–3m (8–10ft).

C. reticulata
'Captain Rawes'
SEMI-DOUBLE

C. JAPONICA 'Adolphe Audusson'

Habit Vigorous, compact, open, upright.
Flowers Large, saucer-shaped, semi-double, in spring. Rich dark red, with prominent yellow stamens. **Leaves** Broadly lance-shaped, curved downwards at margins, thick-textured. Dark green.
• HEIGHT 5m (15ft).
• SPREAD 3m (25ft).

C. japonica
'Adolphe Audusson'
SEMI-DOUBLE

C. JAPONICA 'Apollo'

Habit Vigorous, open, free-flowering.
Flowers Medium-sized, semi-double, in spring; fairly frost-resistant. Rose-red, sometimes blotched white.
Leaves Long, narrow, pointed, twisted at the tip. Dark green.
• HEIGHT 4m (12ft).
• SPREAD 3m (10ft).

C. japonica 'Apollo'
SEMI-DOUBLE

C. JAPONICA 'Alexander Hunter'

Habit Vigorous, compact, upright.
Flowers Flattish, single, in mid-spring. Deep crimson, with a central boss of yellow stamens.
Leaves Lance-shaped. Dark green.
• HEIGHT 3m (10ft).
• SPREAD 3m (10ft).

C. japonica
'Alexander Hunter'
SINGLE

C. JAPONICA 'Mathotiana'

Habit Bushy, compact, upright. **Flowers** Very large, formal double to rose-form, velvety, in mid- to late spring. Dark crimson; purplish with age. **Leaves** Lance-shaped to oval, pointed, slightly twisted. Glossy rich green.
• HEIGHT 3m (10ft).
• SPREAD 3m (10ft).

C. japonica
'Mathotiana'
FORMAL DOUBLE TO ROSE-FORM

Ericaceae	FETTERBUSH

PIERIS FLORIBUNDA

Habit Bushy, compact, rounded. *Flowers* Small, pitcher-shaped, in slender, erect racemes, from early to mid-spring. White. *Leaves* Evergreen, oval. Glossy dark green.
• NATIVE HABITAT In moist woodland on mountain foothills in S.E. United States.
• CULTIVATION Grows in any acid soil. Provide shelter from cold, drying winds. Dead-heading after flowering improves growth.
• PROPAGATION By softwood or semi-ripe cuttings in summer, or by seed in spring.

HEIGHT
To 2m (6ft)

SPREAD
3m (10ft)

Hamamelidaceae	WITCH ALDER

FOTHERGILLA MAJOR

Habit Slow-growing, erect. *Flowers* Fragrant, in bottlebrush spikes, in late spring. White.
Leaves Deciduous, broadly oval. Glossy dark green, turning orange, red, and yellow in autumn.
• NATIVE HABITAT Woodland in the Alleghany mountains of S.E. United States.
• CULTIVATION Thrives in semi-shade, but for best autumn colour requires sun. Needs peaty or humus-rich soil.
• PROPAGATION By softwood cuttings in summer.
• OTHER NAMES *F. monticola.*

HEIGHT
2.5m (8ft)

SPREAD
2m (6ft)

Rutaceae	MEXICAN ORANGE BLOSSOM

CHOISYA TERNATA

Habit Rounded, dense. *Flowers* Fragrant, in clusters, in late spring, sometimes with a second flush in autumn. White. *Leaves* Evergreen, aromatic, divided into 3 leaflets. Bright green.
• NATIVE HABITAT Mexico.
• CULTIVATION Provide a warm site, with shelter from cold winds. *Choisya ternata* is tolerant of clipping, drought, and urban pollution but it may be scorched by frost. It may also defoliate in cold weather, but will usually re-sprout from the base. Both the flowers and foliage of the plant are useful

for arrangements, although when in a confined space the fragrance can be somewhat overpowering. The cultivar *C. ternata* 'Sundance' has bright yellow leaves but is slower growing, and reaches only 2.5m (8ft).
• PROPAGATION By semi-ripe cuttings in late summer.

HEIGHT
2.5–3m
(8–10ft)

SPREAD
2.5m (8ft)

Ericaceae	LILY-OF-THE-VALLEY BUSH

PIERIS JAPONICA 'Scarlett O'Hara'

Habit Bushy, dense, rounded. *Flowers* Small, pendent, urn-shaped, waxy, in profusion in mid-spring. White, sometimes splashed with red.
Leaves Evergreen, oval to lance-shaped. Lustrous dark green, bronze when young.
• NATIVE HABITAT Garden origin.
• CULTIVATION Grow in peaty or humus-rich, acid soil in a sheltered position. Young tips are susceptible to frost; cut back to undamaged wood as soon as possible. *Pieris japonica* and its cultivars make beautiful specimens for the peat bed and thrive in the sheltered conditions provided by a woodland garden. The flowers are often sweetly fragrant, although subtly so. In gardens with alkaline soil, *Pieris* can be grown in pots or tubs of ericaceous compost, but it will need additional protection at the roots to prevent freezing in winter.
• PROPAGATION By soft tip or semi-ripe cuttings in summer.

HEIGHT
2.5m (8ft)

SPREAD
2.5m (8ft)

Ericaceae	DODAN-TSUTSUJI

ENKIANTHUS PERULATUS

Habit Slow-growing, compact, dense.
Flowers Small, pendent, urn-shaped, appearing
with or before the leaves, in mid-spring. White.
Leaves Deciduous, oval or elliptic-oval. Mid-
green, scarlet in autumn.
• NATIVE HABITAT Mountain scrub and
woodland of Japan.
• CULTIVATION Requires humus-rich or peaty
soil. Mulch to conserve moisture.
• PROPAGATION By seed in autumn or by semi-
ripe cuttings in summer.

HEIGHT
2–2.5m
(6–8ft)

SPREAD
1.5–2m
(5–6ft)

Rosaceae	RED CHOKEBERRY

ARONIA ARBUTIFOLIA

Habit Upright, arching with age. **Flowers** Small,
in late spring. White, with red anthers. **Fruits** Small
berries. Red. **Leaves** Deciduous, elliptic to oval.
Dull green, grey beneath, red in autumn.
• NATIVE HABITAT Scrub and woodlands of
E. North America.
• CULTIVATION Tolerates most fertile soils,
except shallow chalk. Grows in semi-shade, but
autumn colour is best in sun.
• PROPAGATION By suckers or by seed in autumn
or by softwood or semi-ripe cuttings in summer.

HEIGHT
To 3m
(10ft)

SPREAD
3m (10ft)

Caprifoliaceae	

LONICERA FRAGRANTISSIMA

Habit Bushy, spreading. **Flowers** Small, very
fragrant, short-tubed with spreading lobes, in winter
and early spring. Creamy-white. **Leaves** Semi-
evergreen, oval. Dark green.
• NATIVE HABITAT China.
• CULTIVATION Tolerates semi-shade, although
flowers best in sun. Grow in any fertile soil. Prune
after flowering only to remove dead wood or to
restrict size.
• PROPAGATION By semi-ripe cuttings in summer
or by hardwood cuttings in autumn.

HEIGHT
2m (6ft)

SPREAD
4m (12ft)

Magnoliaceae	STAR MAGNOLIA

MAGNOLIA STELLATA 🏆

Habit Slow-growing, compact, rounded, tree-like with age. **Flowers** Star-shaped, fragrant, with many strap-shaped petals, opening from silky buds, in early to mid-spring. White. **Leaves** Deciduous, narrowly oblong. Deep green.
• NATIVE HABITAT Mountain woodland of Japan.
• CULTIVATION Tolerates some shade. Prefers neutral to acid, humus-rich soil. Provide shelter from cold winds.
• PROPAGATION By seed in autumn or by semi-ripe cuttings in summer.

HEIGHT
3m (10ft)

SPREAD
4m (12ft)

Magnoliaceae	

MAGNOLIA STELLATA 'Waterlily' 🏆

Habit Slow-growing, compact, rounded. **Flowers** Star-shaped, fragrant, with many strap-shaped petals, opening from silky buds, in early to mid-spring. White. Free-flowering, with larger flowers and more petals than the species.
Leaves Deciduous, narrowly oblong. Deep green.
• NATIVE HABITAT Garden origin.
• CULTIVATION Tolerates some shade. Prefers neutral to acid, humus-rich soil. Shelter from cold winds.
• PROPAGATION By semi-ripe cuttings in summer.

HEIGHT
3m (10ft)

SPREAD
4m (12ft)

Myrtaceae	COMMON MYRTLE

MYRTUS COMMUNIS 🏆

Habit Dense, bushy, rounded. **Flowers** Small, fragrant, borne in profusion from mid-spring to early summer. White. **Fruits** Small berries. Purple-black. **Leaves** Evergreen, aromatic, small, oval to lance-shaped. Glossy mid-green.
• NATIVE HABITAT Maquis and dry scrub from the Mediterranean and S.W. Europe to W. Asia.
• CULTIVATION Provide the shelter of a warm wall in cold areas. Trim back in spring; withstands close clipping.
• PROPAGATION By semi-ripe cuttings in summer.

HEIGHT
Up to 3m
(10ft)

SPREAD
3m (10ft)

Rosaceae	JAPANESE CRAB APPLE

MALUS TORINGO

Habit Dense, spreading, with arching branches. **Flowers** In mid-spring. Pink, fading to white, deep pink in bud. **Fruits** Small, round. Red or yellow. **Leaves** Deciduous, oval-elliptic, often lobed. Dark green; red or yellow in autumn.
• NATIVE HABITAT Scrub and woodland of Japan.
• CULTIVATION Grows in any but waterlogged soil.
• PROPAGATION By budding in late summer, by grafting in winter, or by seed in autumn (seed raised plants variable).
• OTHER NAMES *M. sieboldii*.

HEIGHT
3m (10ft)

SPREAD
3m (10ft)

Rosaceae	

PRUNUS MUME 'Omoi-no-mama'

Habit Rounded, spreading. **Flowers** Fragrant, semi-double, cup-shaped, in spring, before the leaves. White, pink-flushed. **Leaves** Deciduous, broadly oval, toothed. Bright green on emergence.
• NATIVE HABITAT Garden origin.
• CULTIVATION Grows in any but waterlogged soil. Flowers profusely if sited on a warm wall and sheltered from cold winds. Susceptible to silver leaf.
• PROPAGATION By softwood cuttings in summer.
• OTHER NAMES *P. mume* 'Omoi-no-wae'.

HEIGHT
2.5m (8ft)
or more

SPREAD
2m (6ft)

Rosaceae	

CHAENOMELES SPECIOSA 'Moerloosei' ♥

Habit Vigorous, bushy. **Flowers** Large, cup-shaped, in early spring. White, flushed pink and carmine. **Fruits** Apple-like, aromatic. Yellow-green. **Leaves** Deciduous, oval, Glossy dark green.
• NATIVE HABITAT Garden origin.
• CULTIVATION Grows in any but waterlogged soil. Tolerates shade but flowers best in sun. If wall-trained, shorten side-shoots to 2–3 buds after flowering.
• PROPAGATION By softwood or greenwood cuttings in summer.

HEIGHT
To 3m
(10ft)

SPREAD
3m (10ft)

Caprifoliaceae	

VIBURNUM PLICATUM 'Pink Beauty' ♥

Habit Slow-growing, bushy. **Flowers** Small, 'lace-cap' type, in late spring and early summer. White, flushed soft pink with age. **Fruits** Small, berry-like. Red to black. **Leaves** Deciduous, broadly oval to elliptic. Dark green, bronze-purple in autumn.
• NATIVE HABITAT Garden origin.
• CULTIVATION Tolerates semi-shade. Grow in any deep, fertile, and well-drained soil that is not too dry. A freely fruiting cultivar.
• PROPAGATION By softwood cuttings in early summer.

HEIGHT
To 2m (6ft)

SPREAD
2m (6ft)

Rosaceae	

COTONEASTER DIVARICATUS

Habit Bushy, spreading. **Flowers** Small, shallowly cupped, in late spring to early summer. White, flushed pink. **Fruits** Small berries, in autumn and winter. Dark red. **Leaves** Deciduous, oval to elliptic. Glossy dark green, red in autumn.
• NATIVE HABITAT Scrubland of W. China.
• CULTIVATION Thrives on most soils, including dry ones, but will not tolerate waterlogging. Useful for informal hedging. Susceptible to fireblight.
• PROPAGATION By seed in autumn or by softwood cuttings in summer.

HEIGHT
To 2m (6ft)

SPREAD
3m (10ft)

Grossulariaceae	

RIBES SANGUINEUM ♧
'Pulborough Scarlet'
Habit Upright, bushy. *Flowers* Small, tubular, in pendent clusters in spring. Deep red.
Fruits Berries. Black, bloomed white.
Leaves Aromatic, deciduous, 3–5 lobed. Dark green.
• NATIVE HABITAT Garden origin.
• CULTIVATION Grow in any moderately fertile, well-drained soil. Cut out some older shoots after flowering and cut back overgrown specimens hard in winter or early spring.
• PROPAGATION By hardwood cuttings in winter.

☼ ◌
❀ ❀ ❀

HEIGHT
To 3m
(10ft)

SPREAD
2.5m (8ft)

Aceraceae	

ACER PALMATUM 'Corallinum'
Habit Slow-growing, bushy-headed, tree-like with age. *Flowers* Small, in clusters, in spring. Red-purple. *Fruits* Sycamore-like, winged. *Leaves* Deciduous, lobed. Bright red-pink when young, then green; brilliant red, yellow, or orange in autumn.
• NATIVE HABITAT Garden origin.
• CULTIVATION Needs moist but well-drained soil. Colours best in sun. Provide shelter from cold winds.
• PROPAGATION By grafting in late winter or early spring or by softwood cuttings in early summer.

☼ ◌
❀ ❀ ❀

HEIGHT
1.5m (5ft)
or more

SPREAD
1.5m (5ft)

Rosaceae	

PRUNUS MUME 'Beni-chidori'
Habit Rounded, spreading. *Flowers* Fragrant, single, cup-shaped, in spring before the leaves. Carmine pink. *Leaves* Deciduous, broadly oval, pointed, toothed. Bright green on emergence, then dark green.
• NATIVE HABITAT Garden origin.
• CULTIVATION Grows in any but waterlogged soil. Flowers profusely if sited on a warm wall and sheltered from cold winds.
• PROPAGATION By softwood cuttings in summer.
• OTHER NAMES *P. mume* 'Beni-shidori'.

☼ ◌
❀ ❀ ❀

HEIGHT
To 2m (6ft)
or more

SPREAD
2m (6ft)

Ericaceae	

ENKIANTHUS CERNUUS f. *RUBENS* ♧
Habit Bushy, much branched. *Flowers* Small, bell-shaped, fringed, in drooping racemes in late spring. Deep red. *Leaves* Deciduous, in dense clusters. Dark green, turning dark red-purple in autumn.
• NATIVE HABITAT Mountain woodland of Japan.
• CULTIVATION Grow in peaty, humus-rich soil. Tolerates part-day full sun where soils are reliably moist. Cut back hard in spring if overgrown.
• PROPAGATION By seed in autumn or by semi-ripe cuttings in summer.

☼ ◌ pH
❀ ❀ ❀

HEIGHT
To 3m
(10ft)

SPREAD
3m (10ft)

Proteaceae	SCARLET BANKSIA

BANKSIA COCCINEA

Habit Upright, open. *Flowers* Tightly clustered in large heads in late winter and spring. Bright red. *Leaves* Evergreen, oblong, toothed. Dark green, silver-downy beneath; pink-velvety when young.
• NATIVE HABITAT W. Australia.
• CULTIVATION Best grown in a conservatory or greenhouse with good ventilation. Needs a sandy, well-drained soil that is low in nitrates and phosphates. Water potted specimens moderately when in growth, otherwise sparingly.
• PROPAGATION By seed in spring.

Min. 10°C
(50°F)

HEIGHT
1.5m (5ft)

SPREAD
1.5m (5ft)

Proteaceae	

LEUCOSPERMUM REFLEXUM

Habit Erect, with ascending branchlets. *Flowers* Slender, tubular, in tight rounded heads, with long styles in spring to summer. Crimson. *Leaves* Evergreen, small, oblong to lance-shaped. Blue-grey.
• NATIVE HABITAT Cape province, S. Africa.
• CULTIVATION Best grown in a conservatory or greenhouse with good ventilation. Needs sandy, well-drained soil, low in nitrates and phosphates. Water potted plants moderately when in growth.
• PROPAGATION By seed in spring.

Min 7°C
(45°F)

HEIGHT
To 3m
(10ft)

SPREAD
2m (6ft)

Proteaceae	TASMANIAN WARATAH

TELOPEA TRUNCATA

Habit Upright, bushy with age. *Flowers* Small, tubular, in dense, rounded heads, in late spring and summer. Brilliant crimson. *Leaves* Evergreen, narrow, pointed, thick and leathery. Dark green.
• NATIVE HABITAT Mountains of Tasmania.
• CULTIVATION Grow in moist, humus-rich, well-drained soil, in a warm, sunny position with shelter from cold winds. Once established, prune lightly after flowering to maintain bushiness.
• PROPAGATION By seed in spring or by layering in winter.

HEIGHT
3m (10ft)

SPREAD
3m (10ft)

Greyiaceae	NATAL BOTTLEBRUSH

GREYIA SUTHERLANDII

Habit Rounded. **Flowers** Small, in dense spikes in spring. Scarlet-red. **Leaves** Deciduous or semi-evergreen, nearly circular, coarsely serrated, leathery. Green, turning red in autumn.
• NATIVE HABITAT Dry, grassy hills of S. Africa.
• CULTIVATION Grow in a conservatory in sandy, well-drained soil. Water potted specimens moderately when in growth, otherwise sparingly. Provide good ventilation. Dead-head after flowering.
• PROPAGATION By seed in spring or by semi-ripe cuttings in summer.

Min. 7–10°C (45–50°F)

HEIGHT To 3m (10ft)

SPREAD 3m (10ft)

Myrtaceae	

LEPTOSPERMUM SCOPARIUM
'Red Damask'

Habit Upright, bushy. **Flowers** Small, double, carried along the length of shoots in late spring and summer. Dark red. **Leaves** Aromatic, evergreen, narrow but variable in shape. Dark green.
• NATIVE HABITAT Species occurs in Tasmania, New Zealand, and New South Wales. Garden origin.
• CULTIVATION Grow in a humus-rich, neutral to acid soil. Provide the shelter of a warm wall in cold areas. Resents root disturbance.
• PROPAGATION By semi-ripe cuttings in summer.

HEIGHT 3m (10ft)

SPREAD 3m (10ft)

Berberidaceae	

BERBERIS THUNBERGII f. ATROPURPUREA

Habit Low-growing, dense, arching, spiny. **Flowers** Globose to cup-shaped, in mid-spring. Pale yellow, red-tinged. **Fruits** Small, elliptic berries. Red. **Leaves** Deciduous, oval. Red-purple, turning bright red in autumn.
• NATIVE HABITAT Light woodland of Japan.
• CULTIVATION Grows in any but waterlogged soils. Tolerates semi-shade but flowers and autumn leaf colour are better in sun.
• PROPAGATION By softwood or semi-ripe cuttings in summer.

HEIGHT 1.5m (5ft) or more

SPREAD 3m (10ft)

Hamamelidaceae	

CORYLOPSIS PAUCIFLORA

Habit Dense, bushy, spreading.
Flowers Small, fragrant, tubular- to bell-shaped, on bare branches from early to mid-spring. Pale yellow. **Leaves** Deciduous, oval. Bright green, bronze when young.
• NATIVE HABITAT Mountain scrub and forest of Japan and Taiwan.
• CULTIVATION Grow in humus-rich, well-drained acid to neutral soil. Provide shelter from cold winds. Space should be allowed for the plant to spread. Pruning should be avoided as it may spoil

its graceful habit. *Corylopsis pauciflora* makes a beautiful specimen for the woodland garden and other sheltered sites in dappled shade. Although the plant is fully hardy, the flowers may be damaged by frost.
• PROPAGATION By seed in autumn or by softwood cuttings in early summer.

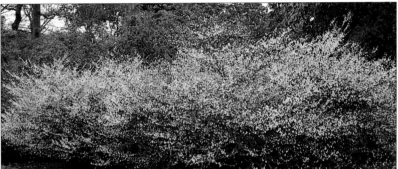

HEIGHT
1.5–2m
(5–6ft)

SPREAD
2m (6ft)

Berberidaceae	

BERBERIS GAGNEPAINII

Habit Upright, compact, dense, spiny.
Flowers Small, globose to cup-shaped, in profusion in late spring. Yellow. **Fruits** Small, egg-shaped berries. Black, blue-bloomed.
Leaves Evergreen, narrowly lance-shaped, pointed. Grey-green.
• NATIVE HABITAT Mountain thickets, W. China.
• CULTIVATION Tolerates any but waterlogged soil, but prefers a humus-rich and fertile soil. Makes excellent hedging; trim after flowering.
• PROPAGATION By semi-ripe cuttings in summer.

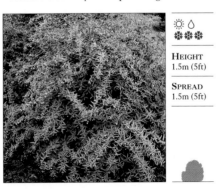

HEIGHT
1.5m (5ft)

SPREAD
1.5m (5ft)

Lauraceae	BENJAMIN BUSH, SPICE BUSH

LINDERA BENZOIN

Habit Rounded, open, with slender branches.
Flowers Tiny, in small clusters, in mid-spring. Pale yellow-green. **Fruits** Small berries on female plants. Red. **Leaves** Deciduous, aromatic, oblong to oval. Bright green, turning clear yellow in autumn.
• NATIVE HABITAT Damp woodland and streamsides in E. North America.
• CULTIVATION Needs a peaty or humus-rich soil.
• PROPAGATION By fresh seed in autumn or by semi-ripe cuttings in summer.

HEIGHT
To 3m
(10ft)

SPREAD
3m (10ft)

Rosaceae	

KERRIA JAPONICA 'Pleniflora'   ♛

Habit Upright, then arching, suckering.
Flowers Pompon-like, from mid- to late spring.
Bright golden-yellow. **Leaves** Deciduous, oval,
long-pointed, toothed and veined. Bright green.
• NATIVE HABITAT Garden origin. Species occurs
by rivers and in rocky mountain gorges of China.
• CULTIVATION Tolerates semi-shade and most
soils, if not dry in summer.
• PROPAGATION By softwood or semi-ripe
cuttings in summer or by suckers in autumn.
• OTHER NAMES *K. japonica* 'Flore Pleno'.

HEIGHT
2m (6ft) or
more

SPREAD
3m (10ft)

Oleaceae	

FORSYTHIA SUSPENSA   ♛

Habit Erect, then arching, with slender shoots.
Flowers Nodding, narrowly trumpet-shaped, from
early to mid-spring before the leaves. Bright yellow.
Leaves Deciduous, oval, often divided with 3
leaflets. Mid-green.
• NATIVE HABITAT On rocky cliffs and in scrub of
China.
• CULTIVATION Grow in any moderately fertile
soil. Tolerates shade but flowers best in sun.
• PROPAGATION By softwood cuttings in summer
or by hardwood cuttings in autumn or winter.

HEIGHT
2–3m
(6–10ft)

SPREAD
2m (6ft)

Berberidaceae	

BERBERIS VERRUCULOSA   ♛

Habit Slow-growing, compact, bushy.
Flowers Small, cup-shaped, in spring. Bright
yellow. **Fruits** Oval to pear-shaped berries. Black,
blue-bloomed. **Leaves** Evergreen, oval-elliptic.
Glossy dark green, blue-white beneath.
• NATIVE HABITAT Mountain thickets and rocky
places of W. Sichuan, China.
• CULTIVATION Tolerates light shade and any but
waterlogged soils. Prefers humus-rich, fertile soil
and blooms best in sun.
• PROPAGATION By semi-ripe cuttings in summer.

HEIGHT
1.5m (5ft)

SPREAD
1.5m (5ft)

Berberidaceae	

BERBERIS JULIANAE

Habit Bushy, very spiny. **Flowers** Small, slightly
fragrant, in dense clusters in late spring and early
summer. Yellow. **Fruits** Oblong berries. Blue-
black, grey-bloomed. **Leaves** Evergreen, stiff,
narrow, leathery, spine-toothed. Dark green.
• NATIVE HABITAT Mountain scrub of China.
• CULTIVATION Tolerates light shade and any but
waterlogged soils. Prefers humus-rich, fertile soil.
Blooms best in sun. Good for screens or hedges.
Trim after flowering.
• PROPAGATION By semi-ripe cuttings in summer.

HEIGHT
To 3m
(10ft)

SPREAD
3m (10ft)

RHODODENDRONS

Rhododendrons and azaleas both belong to the enormous genus of *Rhododendron*, which comprises some 700–800 evergreen, semi-evergreen and deciduous shrubs, ranging from those with a dwarf habit to those of tree-like stature. They are grown primarily for their flowers, but the genus includes many with beautiful foliage clothed in golden, silver or bronze felt-like hairs, especially when young.

Rhododendrons occur mainly in the humid, mountainous regions of the world. The smallest, dwarf species usually grow in open, alpine meadows. The large-leaved, tree-like species are generally found in the sheltered conditions of moist, temperate forests. The azaleas (the common name for deciduous species and hybrids, and the compact evergreens derived mainly from Japanese species) are valued for their profusion of small but wonderfully coloured blooms in spring.

Many of the deciduous azaleas have leaves which colour well in autumn, in rich shades of orange, scarlet, crimson, and gold. They may be grown as specimens in shrub borders and are also used in mass-plantings. The smaller species may be grown in tubs or raised beds.

Most rhododendrons prefer dappled shade, although many, notably the dwarf species and deciduous azaleas, will tolerate full sun, especially in cool, moist climates. All are surface rooting, and need shallow planting. Grow in a humus-rich, moisture-retentive but well-drained, acid soil. Shelter large-leaved species and hybrids from cold, dry winds. Deep planting, poor drainage, and lime will cause the leaves to yellow. Propagate by semi-ripe cuttings or layering in late summer. Adult and larval stages of weevils can cause problems, and powdery mildew may do serious damage.

R. AURICULATUM
Habit Bushy, widely branching.
Flowers Large, heavily scented, tubular to funnel-shaped, in large trusses in mid- to late summer. White, green-tinted at base.
Leaves Evergreen, large, oblong, with ear-like lobes at the base. Dark green, paler beneath, with long thread-like hairs.
• CULTIVATION Thrives in the dappled shade of woodland.
• HEIGHT To 6m (20ft)
• SPREAD 6m (20ft)

R. auriculatum
RHODODENDRON

☀ ◖ pH ✽ ✽ ✽

R. REX subsp.
FICTOLACTEUM
Habit Open or upright, rounded, spreading tree.
Flowers Bell-shaped, in large trusses in spring. White, with dark blotch.
Leaves Evergreen, large, oblong-oval. Dark green above, red-brown beneath.
• OTHER NAMES
R. fictolacteum.
• HEIGHT 6m (20ft) or more.
• SPREAD 6m (20ft).

R. rex subsp.
fictolacteum
RHODODENDRON

☀ ◖ pH ✽ ✽

R. 'Beauty of Littleworth'
Habit Open, shrubby, upright. **Flowers** Large, fragrant, funnel-shaped, in huge trusses in late spring. White, crimson-spotted.
Leaves Evergreen, large, slightly glossy. Dark green.
• HEIGHT 4m (12ft).
• SPREAD 1.8m (6ft).

R. 'Beauty of Littleworth'
RHODODENDRON

☀ ◖ pH ✽ ✽ ✽ ♈

R. 'Silver Moon'

Habit Broadly spreading.
Flowers Funnel-shaped,
petal edges frilled, in
spring. White, with pale
green blotched throats.
Leaves Evergreen,
small, broadly oval.
Bright green.
• HEIGHT 1.5m (5ft).
• SPREAD 1.5m (5ft).

R. 'Silver Moon'
AZALEA

☀ ◊ pH ❀❀

R. 'Palestrina'

Habit Compact, free-
flowering. **Flowers** Small,
open funnel-shaped, in
late spring. White, with
faint green rays within.
Leaves Evergreen,
oblong-oval. Pale green.
• CULTIVATION
Tolerates sun where soils
are reliably moist but
prefers light, dappled
shade.
• HEIGHT 1.2m (4ft).
• SPREAD 1.2m (4ft).

R. 'Palestrina'
AZALEA

☀ ◊ pH ❀❀❀ ♆

R. OCCIDENTALE

Habit Very variable.
Flowers Fragrant, widely
funnel-shaped, from early
to mid-summer. Creamy-
white or pale pink, with a
basal golden blotch.
Leaves Deciduous, oval.
Glossy green, turning
yellow, orange, and
crimson in autumn.
• HEIGHT 1.5–2.5m
(5–8ft).
• SPREAD 1.5–2.5m
(5–8ft).

R. occidentale
AZALEA

☀ ◊ pH ❀❀❀ ♆

R. YAKUSHIMANUM

Habit Neat, compact,
dome-shaped.
Flowers Open funnel-
shaped, in rounded
trusses in late spring.
Pink, fading to white,
flecked green within.
Leaves Evergreen,
broadly oval. Silvery
when young, later dark
green, brown-felted
beneath.
• HEIGHT 1.2m (4ft).
• SPREAD 1.5m (5ft).

R. yakushimanum
RHODODENDRON

☀ ◊ pH ❀❀❀

R. FULVUM

Habit Rounded to
spreading, sometimes
tree-like. **Flowers** Bell-
shaped, in loose trusses
in early spring. Pink,
fading to white, with dark
basal blotch.
Leaves Evergreen,
oblong to oval. Shining
dark green, rich brown
felted beneath.
• HEIGHT 5m (15ft).
• SPREAD 3m (10ft).

R. fulvum
RHODODENDRON

☀ ◊ pH ❀❀ ♆

R. CALOPHYTUM

Habit Dense, tier-
forming, widely
branched.
Flowers Fragrant, bell-
shaped, in huge clusters
in early spring. White or
pink, with crimson spots
and basal blotch.
Leaves Evergreen, large,
lance-shaped. Rich,
glossy green, paler
beneath.
• HEIGHT 6m (20ft).
• SPREAD 6m (20ft).

R. calophytum
RHODODENDRON

☀ ◊ pH ❀❀❀ ♆

R. RACEMOSUM

Habit Upright, stiffly
branched, compact, free-
flowering.
Flowers Small, widely
funnel-shaped, along the
stems in spring. Bright
pink. **Leaves** Evergreen,
aromatic, small, broadly
oval. Dull green above,
grey-green beneath.
• HEIGHT 2m (6ft).
• SPREAD 2m (6ft).

R. racemosum
RHODODENDRON

☀ ◊ pH ❀❀❀

R. SCHLIPPENBACHII

Habit Open, rounded.
Flowers Saucer-shaped,
in loose clusters of 3–6, in
mid-spring. Pink.
Leaves Deciduous,
spoon-shaped, thin-
textured. Bright green in
whorls at branch tips.
• CULTIVATION Prefers
dappled shade. Needs
protection from late
frosts.
• HEIGHT 2.5m (8ft).
• SPREAD 2.5m (8ft).

R. schlippenbachii
AZALEA

☀ ◊ pH ❀❀❀ ♆

R. 'Seven Stars'
Habit Vigorous, dense, upright. *Flowers* Bell-shaped, petals with wavy margins, in a profusion of small, dense clusters in spring. White flushed apple-blossom pink, opening from pink buds. *Leaves* Evergreen, narrowly oval. Dull dark green.
• HEIGHT 2–3m (6–10ft).
• SPREAD 2–3m (6–10ft).

R. 'Seven Stars'
RHODODENDRON

☀ ◊ ᵖᴴ ❀ ❀ ❀

R. SOULIEI
Habit Slow-growing, open, pyramidal. *Flowers* Saucer-shaped, in loose, flat-topped clusters in late spring. Soft pink to white. *Leaves* Evergreen, rounded, heart-shaped at the base. Glossy rich green, blue-tinted.
• HEIGHT 1.5–4m (5–12ft).
• SPREAD 1.5–4m (5–12ft).

R. souliei
RHODODENDRON

☀ ◊ ᵖᴴ ❀ ❀ ❀

R. ARGYROPHYLLUM
Habit Upright or rounded, dense, spreading. *Flowers* Bell-shaped, in loose umbels in spring. Rose-pink, sometimes with darker spots. *Leaves* Evergreen, oblong. Dark or olive-green, silvery-white beneath.
• CULTIVATION Shelter from cold, dry winds.
• HEIGHT To 5m (15ft).
• SPREAD 5m (15ft).

R. argyrophyllum
RHODODENDRON

☀ ◊ ᵖᴴ ❀ ❀ ❀

R. SUTCHUENENSE
Habit Rounded, spreading, tree-like with age. *Flowers* Broadly bell-shaped, in large clusters in early spring. Pale to deep rose-pink, with crimson spots. *Leaves* Evergreen, large, drooping, long, oblong-oval. Dark green, paler beneath.
• HEIGHT To 5m (16ft).
• SPREAD 5m (16ft).

R. sutchuenense
RHODODENDRON

☀ ◊ ᵖᴴ ❀ ❀ ❀

R. 'Nobleanum'
Habit Slow-growing, upright, tree-like with age. *Flowers* Large, broadly funnel-shaped, in compact trusses in winter or early spring. Brilliant rose-red, white within. *Leaves* Evergreen. Dull dark green, buff-felted beneath.
• HEIGHT To 5m (15ft).
• SPREAD 5m (15ft).

R. 'Nobleanum'
RHODODENDRON

☀ ◊ ᵖᴴ ❀ ❀ ❀

R. WILLIAMSIANUM
Habit Compact, spreading. *Flowers* Bell-shaped, loosely clustered, in spring. Pale pink. *Leaves* Evergreen, rounded oval to almost circular, pointed. Bronze when young, later mid-green.
• CULTIVATION Tolerates sun.
• HEIGHT 1.5m (5ft).
• SPREAD 1.5m (5ft).

R. williamsianum
RHODODENDRON

☀ ◊ ᵖᴴ ❀ ❀ ❀   ♈

R. ORBICULARE
Habit Slow-growing, compact, rounded-dome-shaped. *Flowers* Bell-shaped, in loose clusters in late spring. Bright rose-pink. *Leaves* Evergreen, almost circular, heart-shaped at base, smooth. Matt green.
• HEIGHT To 3m (10ft).
• SPREAD 3m (10ft).

R. orbiculare
RHODODENDRON

☀ ◊ ᵖᴴ ❀ ❀ ❀

R. 'Mrs G. W. Leak'

Habit Vigorous, dense.
Flowers Large, funnel-shaped, in compact, conical trusses in late spring. Clear pale pink, with brown blotch, and crimson markings.
Leaves Evergreen, broadly oval to elliptic, smooth. Olive green.
• CULTIVATION Thrives in sun or dappled shade, and strikes easily from cuttings.
• HEIGHT To 4m (16ft).
• SPREAD 4m (16 ft).

R. 'Mrs G. W. Leak'
RHODODENDRON

☼ ◊ pH ❀ ❀ ❀

R. 'Percy Wiseman'

Habit Compact, dome-forming, free-flowering.
Flowers Large, open funnel-shaped, in spherical trusses in late spring. Creamy, flushed peach-pink, fading with maturity.
Leaves Evergreen. Glossy dark green.
• CULTIVATION Tolerates full sun.
• HEIGHT 2m (6ft).
• SPREAD 2m (6ft).

R. 'Percy Wiseman'
RHODODENDRON

☼ ◊ pH ❀ ❀ ❀

R. YUNNANENSE

Habit Open, free-flowering.
Flowers Butterfly-like, in profusion in spring. Pale pink or white, spotted or blotched darker within.
Leaves Semi-evergreen or deciduous, narrowly elliptic. Grey-green.
• HEIGHT 1.5–4m (5–12ft).
• SPREAD 1.5–4m (5–12ft).

R. yunnanense
RHODODENDRON

☼ ◊ pH ❀ ❀ ❀

R. 'Corneille'

Habit Bushy.
Flowers Small, scented, double, honeysuckle-like, in early summer. Cream, flushed pale pink. *Leaves* Deciduous, small, oblong to lance-shaped. Bright green, colouring well in autumn.
• HEIGHT 1.5–2.5m (5–8ft).
• SPREAD 1.5–2.5m (5–8ft).

R. 'Corneille'
AZALEA

☼ ◊ pH ❀ ❀ ❀   ♛

R. 'Seta'

Habit Upright.
Flowers Small, tubular, glossy, in loose umbels in early spring. Pale pink, with darker pink stripes, fading to white at the base. *Leaves* Evergreen, small, narrowly oval. Dark green.
• CULTIVATION Best given a sheltered site to protect flowers from frost.
• HEIGHT 1.5m (5ft).
• SPREAD 1.5m (5ft).

R. 'Seta'
RHODODENDRON

☼ ◊ pH ❀ ❀

R. 'Azuma-kagami'

Habit Compact, free-flowering, slow-growing.
Flowers Small, hose-in-hose, in mid-spring. Deep salmon-pink, with chestnut-brown spots.
Leaves Evergreen, small. Glossy bright green.
• CULTIVATION Tolerates sun where soils are reliably moist.
• HEIGHT To 1.5m (5ft).
• SPREAD 1.2m (4ft).

R. 'Azuma-kagami'
KURUME AZALEA

☼ ◊ pH ❀ ❀ ❀   ♛

R. 'Strawberry Ice'

Habit Bushy, dense. ***Flowers*** Trumpet-shaped, in late spring. Flesh-pink, mottled darker pink at petal edges, deep yellow at the throat; deep pink in bud. ***Leaves*** Deciduous, oval-elliptic. Bright green, colouring well in autumn.
- HEIGHT 1.5–2.5m (5–8ft).
- SPREAD 1.5–2.5m (5–8ft).

R. 'Strawberry Ice'
AZALEA

R. 'Kirin'

Habit Compact, dense. ***Flowers*** Small, hose-in-hose, carried in profusion in spring. Deep rose-pink with delicate, silvery-rose shading. ***Leaves*** Evergreen, small. Glossy bright green.
- CULTIVATION Will grow in sun where soils are reliably moist.
- HEIGHT To 1.5m (5ft).
- SPREAD 1.5m (5ft).

R. 'Kirin'
AZALEA

R. 'Rosalind'

Habit Vigorous, open. ***Flowers*** Broadly funnel-shaped, in loose trusses in spring. Pink. ***Leaves*** Evergreen, rounded-oval. Dull green with a faint blue cast.
- HEIGHT 4m (12ft).
- SPREAD 4m (12ft).

R. 'Rosalind'
RHODODENDRON

R. 'Pink Pearl'

Habit Vigorous, open, upright. ***Flowers*** Large, open funnel-shaped, in dense, upright trusses in late spring. Blush-pink, deep pink in bud. ***Leaves*** Evergreen, long, elliptic to lance-shaped. Dark green.
- HEIGHT 4m (12ft).
- SPREAD 4m (12ft).

R. 'Pink Pearl'
RHODODENDRON

R. CALOSTROTUM

Habit Neat, compact. ***Flowers*** Small, delicate, saucer- to butterfly-shaped, in clusters of 2–5 in spring. Rich rose-purple, with brownish spots. ***Leaves*** Evergreen, aromatic, small, oblong-oval. Silvery blue-green, with fawn, felt-like hairs beneath.
- HEIGHT 1m (3ft).
- SPREAD 1m (3ft).

R. calostrotum
RHODODENDRON

R. 'Hino-mayo'

Habit Compact, dense. ***Flowers*** Small, funnel-shaped, in great abundance in spring. Clear pink. ***Leaves*** Evergreen, small. Glossy bright green.
- CULTIVATION Tolerates sun where soils are reliably moist. Prefers dappled shade.
- HEIGHT 1.5m (5ft).
- SPREAD 1.5m (5ft).

R. 'Hino-mayo'
KURUME AZALEA

R. 'Hatsugiri'

Habit Compact, low-growing, free-flowering.
Flowers Small, funnel-shaped, in profusion in spring. Brilliant magenta.
Leaves Evergreen, small. Glossy bright green.
• CULTIVATION
Tolerates sun where soils are reliably moist. Prefers light, dappled shade.
• HEIGHT 60cm (2ft).
• SPREAD 60cm (2ft).

R. 'Hatsugiri'
AZALEA

☼ ◐ ◌ pH ✽✽✽   ♛

R. 'President Roosevelt'

Habit Slow-growing, open, weakly branched.
Flowers Open bell-shaped, petals frilled at the margins, in almost spherical clusters from mid- to late spring. Bright red, fading to pale pink at the centre.
Leaves Evergreen. Dark green, variegated yellow. Have a tendency to revert.
• HEIGHT 2m (6ft).
• SPREAD 2m (6ft).

R. 'President Roosevelt'
RHODODENDRON

☼ ◐ ◌ pH ✽✽✽

R. 'Cynthia'

Habit Vigorous, dome-shaped. *Flowers* Bell-shaped, in large, conical trusses in late spring. Rose-crimson, with very dark crimson markings.
Leaves Evergreen, long-oval. Dark green.
• CULTIVATION
Tolerates sun or shade.
• OTHER NAMES
R. 'Lord Palmerston'.
• HEIGHT To 6m (20ft).
• SPREAD To 6m (20ft).

R. 'Cynthia'
RHODODENDRON

☼ ◐ ◌ pH ✽✽✽   ♛

R. ARBOREUM

Habit Shrubby when young, increasingly tree-like with age.
Flowers Bell-shaped, in dense trusses in spring. Pink to scarlet; sometimes white.
Leaves Evergreen, broadly lance-shaped. Dark or olive green, felted silver, fawn or cinnamon beneath.
• HEIGHT To 12m (40ft).
• SPREAD 3m (10ft).

R. arboreum
RHODODENDRON

☼ ◐ ◌ pH ✽✽

R. 'Hinode-giri'

Habit Compact, dense.
Flowers Small, funnel-shaped, in profusion in late spring. Bright crimson.
Leaves Evergreen, small. Glossy bright green.
• CULTIVATION
Tolerates sun where soils are reliably moist. Prefers dappled shade.
• HEIGHT 1.5m (5ft).
• SPREAD 1.5m (5ft).

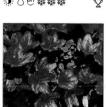

R. 'Hinode-giri'
AZALEA

☼ ◐ ◌ pH ✽✽✽   ♛

R. 'Vuyk's Scarlet'

Habit Compact, dense.
Flowers Large, open funnel-shaped, with wavy petals, in great profusion in spring. Brilliant red.
Leaves Evergreen, small, oval-elliptic, very glossy. Bright green.
• CULTIVATION
Tolerates sun where soils are reliably moist. Best in light, dappled shade.
• HEIGHT 60cm (2ft).
• SPREAD 60cm (2ft).

R. 'Vuyk's Scarlet'
AZALEA

☼ ◐ ◌ pH ✽✽✽   ♛

R. 'Elizabeth'
Habit Dense, dome-shaped. **Flowers** Large, bell- to trumpet-shaped, in loose trusses in late spring. Brilliant red. **Leaves** Evergreen, oblong. Glossy dark green.
• CULTIVATION
Thrives in sun or partial shade.
• HEIGHT 1.5m (5ft).
• SPREAD 2m (6ft).

R. 'Elizabeth'
RHODODENDRON

R. 'John Cairns'
Habit Compact, upright. **Flowers** Funnel-shaped, in great profusion in spring. Deep orange-red. **Leaves** Evergreen, small, oval. Bright green.
• CULTIVATION
Thrives equally well in sun and semi-shade, but flowers tend to fade in bright sun.
• HEIGHT 1.5–2m (5–6ft).
• SPREAD 2m (6ft).

R. 'John Cairns'
AZALEA

R. 'May Day'
Habit Vigorous, fast-growing, spreading. **Flowers** Large, funnel-shaped, long-lasting, waxy, in loose trusses in late spring. Brilliant orange-scarlet. **Leaves** Evergreen, lance-shaped. Dark green, felted pale tan beneath.
• HEIGHT 1.5m (5ft).
• SPREAD 2m (6ft).

R. 'May Day'
RHODODENDRON

R. KAEMPFERI
Habit Erect, loosely branched. **Flowers** Delicate, funnel-shaped, in late spring to early summer. Shades of orange and red. **Leaves** Semi-evergreen or deciduous, lance-shaped. Bright to mid-green.
• OTHER NAMES
R. obtusum var. kaempferi.
• HEIGHT 1.5–2.5m (5–8ft).
• SPREAD 1.5–2.5m (5–8ft).

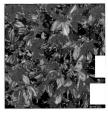

R. kaempferi
AZALEA

R. THOMSONII
Habit Rounded, open, tree-like with age. **Flowers** Bell-shaped, in loose clusters in early spring. Rich blood-red. **Leaves** Evergreen, rounded oval, waxy. Dark green above, paler beneath. **Bark** Peeling. Cinnamon, fawn, and plum.
• HEIGHT To 5.5m (18ft).
• SPREAD 5.5m (18ft).

R. thomsonii
RHODODENDRON

R. CINNABARINUM
Habit Upright, open, sometimes straggling. **Flowers** Tubular, waxy, in loose, drooping clusters in spring. Deep golden-orange to plum-red. **Leaves** Evergreen, narrowly or broadly elliptic. Rich blue-green, paler beneath.
• HEIGHT 1.5–4m (5–12ft).
• SPREAD 1.5–4m (5–12ft).

R. cinnabarinum
RHODODENDRON

R. 'Homebush'
Habit Compact.
Flowers Small, semi-double, in tight, rounded heads in late spring. Rose-purple, with paler shading.
Leaves Deciduous, broadly oval. Bright green, colouring well in autumn.
• CULTIVATION Thrives in sun or dappled shade.
• HEIGHT 1.5m (5ft).
• SPREAD 1.5m (5ft).

R. 'Homebush'
AZALEA

☀ ◊ pH ❀ ❀ ❀   ♗

R. 'Irohayama'
Habit Compact, dense.
Flowers Small, funnel-shaped, carried in great abundance in spring. White, with pale lavender margins and pale chestnut brown eye.
Leaves Evergreen, small. Glossy bright green.
• HEIGHT 1.5m (5ft).
• SPREAD 1.5m (5ft).

R. 'Irohayama'
KURUME AZALEA

☀ ◊ pH ❀ ❀ ❀   ♗

R. DAVIDSONIANUM
Habit Upright.
Flowers Small, funnel- to butterfly-shaped, in profusion in late spring. Pale pink to lilac-mauve, sometimes with olive spots. *Leaves* Evergreen, aromatic, lance-shaped to oblong. Dark or light green.
• HEIGHT 1.5–4m (5–12ft).
• SPREAD 1.5–4m (5–12ft).

R. davidsonianum
RHODODENDRON

☀ ◊ pH ❀ ❀   ♗

R. OREOTREPHES
Habit Upright, tree-like with age, free-flowering.
Flowers Broadly funnel-shaped, variable, in loose clusters in spring. Mauve to purple or rose, sometimes with crimson spots. *Leaves* Evergreen or semi-evergreen, oblong-elliptic. Blue-green, scaly, blue-white beneath.
• HEIGHT To 5m (15ft).
• SPREAD 5m (15ft).

R. oreotrephes
RHODODENDRON

☀ ◊ pH ❀ ❀ ❀

R. 'Blue Peter'
Habit Bushy, slightly spreading.
Flowers Open funnel-shaped, petal edges frilled, in tight conical trusses in early summer. Lavender-blue, with a purple flare.
Leaves Evergreen, large, slightly rolled at the edge. Glossy dark green.
• HEIGHT 1.5m (5ft).
• SPREAD To 2m (6ft) or more.

R. 'Blue Peter'
RHODODENDRON

☀ ◊ pH ❀ ❀ ❀   ♗

R. 'Susan'
Habit Bushy, dense.
Flowers Open funnel-shaped, in large, open trusses in spring. Clear lilac-blue, paler at the centre, spotted maroon within.
Leaves Evergreen, long, broadly elliptic. Rich, glossy dark green.
• HEIGHT 1.5–4m (5–12ft).
• SPREAD 1.5–4m (5–12ft).

R. 'Susan'
RHODODENDRON

☀ ◊ pH ❀ ❀ ❀   ♗

R. HIPPOPHAËOÏDES
Habit Dense, compact, neat. **Flowers** Small, funnel-shaped, in compact clusters in spring. Lilac to lilac-blue. **Leaves** Small, aromatic, narrowly lance-shaped. Grey-green.
• CULTIVATION Tolerates sun, and very moist, but not stagnant soils.
• HEIGHT 1.5m (5ft).
• SPREAD 1.5m (5ft).

R. hippophaëoïdes
RHODODENDRON

☀ ◐ pH ✿ ✿ ✿

R. AUGUSTINII
Habit Fast-growing, bushy, sometimes tree-like with age. **Flowers** Widely funnel-shaped, in abundance in spring. Pale to deep blue or lavender, spotted green or brown inside. **Leaves** Evergreen, lance-shaped to oblong. Light green.
• HEIGHT To 4m (12ft).
• SPREAD 4m (12ft).

R. augustinii
RHODODENDRON

☀ ◐ pH ✿ ✿

R. 'Queen Elizabeth II'
Habit Bushy. **Flowers** Funnel-shaped, in loose, open trusses in late spring. Pale chartreuse-green. **Leaves** Evergreen, lance-shaped to narrowly elliptic. Glossy mid-green above, paler beneath.
• HEIGHT 1.5–4m (5–12ft).
• SPREAD 1.5–4m (5–12ft).

R. 'Queen Elizabeth II'
RHODODENDRON

☀ ◐ pH ✿ ✿ ✿   ♛

R. WARDII
Habit Compact. **Flowers** Open funnel-shaped or saucer- to bell-shaped, in loose trusses in late spring. Pale clear yellow, sometimes with crimson basal blotch. **Leaves** Evergreen, narrowly to broadly oval. Dark green, paler beneath.
• HEIGHT 1.5–4m (5–12ft).
• SPREAD 1.5–4m (5–12ft).

R. wardii
RHODODENDRON

☀ ◐ pH ✿ ✿ ✿

R. LUTESCENS
Habit Upright, slender. **Flowers** Small, funnel-shaped, in early spring. Primrose-yellow. **Leaves** Evergreen or semi-deciduous, oval to narrowly lance-shaped. Red-bronze when young.
• CULTIVATION Tolerates sun where soils are reliably moist during the growing season. Exceptionally elegant.
• HEIGHT 1.5–3m (5–10ft).
• SPREAD 1.5–3m (5–10ft).

R. lutescens
RHODODENDRON

☀ ◐ pH ✿ ✿ ✿

R. CINNABARINUM subsp. XANTHOCODON
Habit Open, upright. **Flowers** Bell-shaped, waxy, in loose trusses in late spring. Yellow. **Leaves** Evergreen, elliptic-oblong. Blue-green, turning mid-green.
• OTHER NAMES R. xanthocodon.
• HEIGHT 1.5–4m (5–12ft).
• SPREAD 1.5–4m (5–12ft).

R. cinnabarinum subsp. **xanthocodon**
RHODODENDRON

☀ ◐ pH ✿ ✿ ✿   ♛

R. 'Crest'
Habit Open, upright. **Flowers** Large, bell-shaped, in large, loose, dome-shaped clusters in late spring. Creamy primrose yellow. **Leaves** Evergreen, oval. Glossy dark green.
• OTHER NAMES R. 'Hawk'.
• HEIGHT 1.5–4m (5–12ft).
• SPREAD 1.5–4m (5–12ft).

R. 'Crest'
RHODODENDRON

☀ ◐ pH ✿ ✿ ✿   ♛

R. 'Narcissiflorum'

Habit Vigorous, compact, upright. *Flowers* Sweetly fragrant, hose-in-hose, in late spring or early summer. Delicate pale yellow, darker on outside and in the centre. *Leaves* Deciduous, lance-shaped. Bright green, bronze in autumn.
• CULTIVATION Tolerates sun.
• HEIGHT 1.5–2m (5–6ft).
• SPREAD 1.5–2m (5–6ft).

R. 'Narcissiflorum'
AZALEA

R. 'Moonshine Crescent'

Habit Rounded to upright. *Flowers* Large, bell-shaped, in compact, dome-shaped trusses, in late spring. Soft primrose yellow. *Leaves* Evergreen, oblong to oval. Dull dark green.
• HEIGHT 2–2.5m (6–8ft).
• SPREAD 2–2.5m (6–8ft).

R. 'Moonshine Crescent'
RHODODENDRON

R. 'Curlew'

Habit Compact, spreading, free-flowering. *Flowers* Large, widely funnel-shaped, in profusion in late spring. Pale yellow, marked greenish brown. *Leaves* Evergreen, rounded-oval. Dull green.
• CULTIVATION Best in a cool site.
• HEIGHT 30cm (12in).
• SPREAD 30cm (12in).

R. 'Curlew'
RHODODENDRON

R. MACABEANUM

Habit Rounded, becoming tree-like with age. *Flowers* Bell-shaped, in dense clusters, in early spring. Pale yellow, with purple blotch. *Leaves* Evergreen, very large, broadly oval. Shiny dark green, with yellow midrib and dense grey felt beneath.
• HEIGHT 10m (30ft).
• SPREAD 10m (30ft).

R. macabeanum
RHODODENDRON

R. 'Yellow Hammer'

Habit Bushy, open, slender, upright. *Flowers* Small, tubular to narrowly bell-shaped, in a profusion of small clusters, in spring, often again in autumn. Bright yellow. *Leaves* Evergreen, small, oblong to narrowly elliptic, pale green.
• HEIGHT 2m (6ft).
• SPREAD 2m (6ft).

R. 'Yellow Hammer'
RHODODENDRON

R. LUTEUM

Habit Open. *Flowers* Large, fragrant, funnel-shaped, sticky outside, in rounded trusses, in late spring. Yellow. *Leaves* Deciduous, oblong to lance-shaped, sticky. Dark green, turning red, orange and purple in autumn.
• HEIGHT 1.5–2.5m (5–8ft).
• SPREAD 1.5–2.5m (5–8ft).

R. luteum
AZALEA

R. 'George Reynolds'
Habit Bushy.
Flowers Large, scented, funnel-shaped, with or before the leaves in spring. Rich butter-yellow, flushed pink, especially in bud.
Leaves Deciduous, broadly oval. Bright green, colouring well in autumn.
• HEIGHT 2m (6ft).
• SPREAD 2m (6ft).

R. 'George Reynolds'
AZALEA

☼ ◊ pH ❀❀❀

R. 'Glory of Littleworth'
Habit Bushy, stiff, upright.
Flowers Fragrant, bell-shaped, in compact clusters, in late spring–early summer. White, with orange blotch.
Leaves Evergreen or semi-evergreen, oblong to lance-shaped, often wavy. Grey-blue.
• HEIGHT 1.5m (5ft).
• SPREAD 1.5m (5ft).

R. 'Glory of Littleworth'
AZALEODENDRON

☼ ◊ pH ❀❀❀

R. 'Medway'
Habit Bushy, open.
Flowers Large, trumpet-shaped, petal margins frilled, carried in late spring. Pale pink with darker edges, and orange flash at the throat.
Leaves Deciduous.
• HEIGHT 1.2–2.5m (5–8ft).
• SPREAD 1.2–2.5m (5–8ft).

R. 'Medway'
AZALEA

☼ ◊ pH ❀❀❀

R. 'Freya'
Habit Bushy, compact.
Flowers Small, double, fragrant, funnel-shaped, from late spring to early summer. Pale orange-salmon, flushed pink.
Leaves Deciduous, narrowly oval. Bright green.
• CULTIVATION Thrives in sun, and dappled shade.
• HEIGHT 1.5m (5ft).
• SPREAD 1.5m (5ft).

R. 'Freya'
AZALEA

☼ ◊ pH ❀❀❀

R. 'Gloria Mundi'
Habit Bushy, twiggy.
Flowers Small, fragrant, honeysuckle-like, petal margins frilled, in early summer. Orange with a yellow flare.
Leaves Deciduous, oval. Bright green.
• CULTIVATION Tolerates sun; enjoys moist but well-drained soil.
• HEIGHT 2m (6ft) or more.
• SPREAD 2m (6ft).

R. 'Gloria Mundi'
AZALEA

☼ ◊ pH ❀❀❀

R. 'Fabia'
Habit Neat, compact, dome-shaped.
Flowers Funnel-shaped, in loose, flat, slightly pendent trusses in early summer. Scarlet-orange, with brown speckles.
Leaves Evergreen, lance-shaped. Dark green.
• HEIGHT To 2m (6ft).
• SPREAD To 2m (6ft).

R. 'Fabia'
RHODODENDRON

☼ ◊ pH ❀❀❀ ♔

R. 'Frome'
Habit Compact, shrubby.
Flowers Trumpet-shaped, petal margins waved and frilled, in spring. Saffron-yellow, overlaid with red at the throat.
Leaves Deciduous, broadly oval. Bright green, colouring well in autumn.
• HEIGHT 1.5m (5ft).
• SPREAD 1.5m (5ft).

R. 'Frome'
AZALEA

☼ ◊ pH ❀❀❀

Oleaceae

FORSYTHIA × *INTERMEDIA* 'Spectabilis'

Habit Vigorous, spreading, with stout shoots.
Flowers Large, in densely packed clusters all along the shoots, in early to mid-spring before the leaves emerge. Deep yellow. *Leaves* Deciduous, oval to lance-shaped, sharply toothed. Dark green. *Bark* Many conspicuous pores. Green-gold.
• NATIVE HABITAT Garden origin. The plant is a cultivar derived from the hybrid *F. suspensa* × *F. viridissima.*
• CULTIVATION Tolerates light shade and most soils but grows and flowers best in a fertile, well-drained soil, in full sun. The flowers are carried at joints on the previous year's wood. Thin out the oldest shoots immediately after flowering, cutting back to a strong bud near the base. Feed and mulch after pruning.
• PROPAGATION By softwood cuttings in summer or by hardwood cuttings in autumn or winter.

HEIGHT
2.5m (8ft)

SPREAD
2.5m (8ft)

Flacourtiaceae	

AZARA SERRATA

Habit Upright, sometimes tree-like with age.
Flowers Slightly fragrant, in dense, rounded clusters, in spring or early summer. Bright yellow.
Leaves Evergreen, oblong or elliptic. Glossy green.
• NATIVE HABITAT Cool, humid areas of the Chilean Andes.
• CULTIVATION Grow in deep, humus-rich soil. In cold areas, plant against a warm wall. Provide shelter from cold winds.
• PROPAGATION By semi-ripe cuttings in summer or by simple layering in spring.

☼ ◊
❀ ❀

HEIGHT
To 3m
(10ft)

SPREAD
2m (6ft)

Leguminosae	KNIFE-LEAF WATTLE

ACACIA CULTRIFORMIS

Habit Upright, then arching. *Flowers* Small, in dense, round heads, in early spring. Bright yellow.
Leaves Evergreen, triangular phyllodes (flattened leaf-like stalks). Silver-grey.
• NATIVE HABITAT Understorey of eucalyptus forest of New South Wales.
• CULTIVATION Grow in a well-ventilated conservatory or greenhouse in sandy, humus-rich soil or compost. Water moderately when in growth, then sparingly. Prune after flowering to restrict growth.
• PROPAGATION By pre-soaked seed in spring.

☼ ◊
❀

HEIGHT
To 3m
(10ft)

SPREAD
2m (6ft)

Oleaceae	

FORSYTHIA × *INTERMEDIA*
'Beatrix Farrand'

Habit Vigorous, erect then arching.
Flowers Large, single, in profusion from early to mid-spring. Golden-yellow. *Leaves* Deciduous, oval, coarsely toothed. Mid-green.
• NATIVE HABITAT Garden origin.
• CULTIVATION Tolerates light shade, but grows and flowers best in fertile, well-drained soil in sun. Thin out old shoots after flowering.
• PROPAGATION By softwood cuttings in summer or by hardwood cuttings in autumn or winter.

☼ ◊
❀ ❀ ❀

HEIGHT
2m (6ft)

SPREAD
2m (6ft)

Berberidaceae	

BERBERIS × *STENOPHYLLA*   ♔

Habit Vigorous, arching. *Flowers* Dense racemes all along the shoots in mid- to late spring. Golden-yellow. *Fruits* Small, round berries. Blue-black.
Leaves Evergreen, narrowly lance-shaped, spine-tipped. Deep green; blue-grey beneath.
• NATIVE HABITAT Garden origin.
• CULTIVATION. Prefers humus-rich, fertile soil and blooms best in sun. Tolerates light shade and any but waterlogged soils. Good for informal hedges. Trim after flowering.
• PROPAGATION By semi-ripe cuttings in summer.

☼ ◊
❀ ❀ ❀

HEIGHT
3m (10ft)

SPREAD
3m 10ft)

Berberidaceae	

BERBERIS X *LOLOGENSIS* 'Stapehill'

Habit Vigorous, arching. *Flowers* Globose to cup-shaped, in profuse racemes, from mid- to late spring. Orange-yellow, tinted red. *Fruits* Egg-shaped berries. Blue, bloomed. *Leaves* Evergreen, spatula-shaped. Glossy dark green.
• NATIVE HABITAT Garden origin.
• CULTIVATION Can be grown in light shade, but blooms best in sun. Tolerates any but waterlogged soil, including chalk, but prefers humus-rich, fertile soil. Needs no regular pruning.
• PROPAGATION By semi-ripe cuttings in summer.

Apocynaceae	

CARISSA MACROCARPA 'Tuttlei'

Habit Very compact, spreading, thorny.
Flowers Fragrant, in spring and summer. White.
Fruits Plum-like, edible, in autumn. Red.
Leaves Evergreen, oval. Lustrous dark green.
• NATIVE HABITAT Garden origin. Species occurs in tropical and sub-tropical S. Africa.
• CULTIVATION Best grown in a warm conservatory. Water moderately when in growth, then sparingly. Cut back flowered stems by half in early spring.
• PROPAGATION By semi-ripe cuttings in summer.
• OTHER NAMES *C. grandiflora* 'Tuttlei'.

HEIGHT
3m (10ft)

SPREAD
3m (10ft)

Min.13°C
(55°F)

HEIGHT
2m (6ft)

SPREAD
2m (6ft)

Berberidaceae	

BERBERIS LINEARIFOLIA 'Orange King'

Habit Upright, stiff-branched. *Flowers* Large, globose to cup-shaped, in late spring. Brilliant deep orange. *Fruits* Egg-shaped berries. Black, blue-bloomed. *Leaves* Evergreen, oval to lance-shaped. Glossy dark green.
• NATIVE HABITAT Garden origin.
• CULTIVATION Can be grown in light shade, but blooms best in sun. Tolerates any but waterlogged soil, including chalk, but prefers humus-rich, fertile soil.
• PROPAGATION By semi-ripe cuttings in summer.

Hydrangeaceae	

PHILADELPHUS 'Beauclerk'

Habit Slightly arching, spreading.
Flowers Large, fragrant, from early to mid-summer. White, with a pale cerise petal base.
Leaves Deciduous, broadly oval. Dark green.
• NATIVE HABITAT Garden origin.
• CULTIVATION Tolerant of a range of soils, including shallow chalk, and of part-shade, although flowers better in sun. Cut back some older shoots to new young growth after flowering, leaving young shoots to flower in the following year.
• PROPAGATION By softwood cuttings in summer.

HEIGHT
3m (10ft)

SPREAD
1.5m (5ft)

HEIGHT
2–2.5m
(6–8ft)

SPREAD
2m (6ft)

Rosaceae	

EXOCHORDA × *MACRANTHA* 'The Bride'

Habit Compact, dense, arching. **Flowers** Large, fragrant, in racemes, borne in profusion in late spring and early summer. Paper-white.
Leaves Deciduous, narrowly oval, tapering at the base. Fresh green, especially when young.
• NATIVE HABITAT Garden origin.
• CULTIVATION Tolerant of a range of well-drained soils, except chalk. Grow in sun or part-shade, although flowering is more profuse in sun. Old flowered shoots may be thinned after flowering to improve vigour. This hybrid, which is noted for its abundant flowers, may be trained as a small standard to display its beautiful, pendulous branches. It is very attractive when used in shrub or mixed borders, as even after flowering its graceful habit and fresh foliage make a beautiful foil for other plants.
• PROPAGATION By softwood or semi-ripe cuttings in summer or by layering in spring or autumn.

HEIGHT
To 2m (6ft)

SPREAD
2.5m (8ft)

Hydrangeaceae	

DEUTZIA SCABRA

Habit Upright. **Flowers** Small, honey-scented, in dense, erect clusters in early to mid-summer. White. **Leaves** Deciduous, oval, coarsely toothed. Dark green.
• NATIVE HABITAT Scrub and woodland edge of China and Japan.
• CULTIVATION Grow in fertile, well-drained soil in sun. Thin out old, flowered shoots after flowering.
• PROPAGATION By softwood cuttings in summer.
• OTHER NAMES *D. sieboldiana*.

HEIGHT
2.5–3m
(8–10ft)

SPREAD
1.5m (5ft)

Rosaceae	APACHE PLUME

FALLUGIA PARADOXA

Habit Bushy, with slender branches.
Flowers Large, in summer. Paper-white.
Fruits Clustered seedheads, with long, silky, styles. Purplish. **Leaves** Deciduous, finely cut. Dark green. **Bark** Peeling. White and buff.
• NATIVE HABITAT Dry, rocky hills of S.W. North America.
• CULTIVATION Needs perfect drainage and a hot, sunny, sheltered wall. Dislikes cold, wet winters.
• PROPAGATION By softwood cuttings in summer or by seed in autumn.

HEIGHT
2m (6ft)

SPREAD
3m (10ft)

Hydrangeaceae	

DEUTZIA × MAGNIFICA 'Staphyleoides'

Habit Vigorous, upright. **Flowers** Large, with 5 recurved petals, in dense clusters in early summer. Pure white. **Leaves** Deciduous, oval to oblong, finely toothed. Bright green.
• NATIVE HABITAT Garden origin.
• CULTIVATION Tolerates almost any fertile, well-drained soil, but grows best in humus-rich soils that do not dry out in summer. Thin out old, flowered shoots, cutting back to the base after flowering; flowers are more abundant on young wood.
• PROPAGATION By softwood cuttings in summer.

HEIGHT
2.5m (8ft)

SPREAD
1.5–2m
(5–6ft)

Hydrangeaceae	

PHILADELPHUS 'Belle Etoile'

Habit Compact, arching. **Flowers** Large, very fragrant, in profusion in late spring and early summer. White, with a pale purple mark at the base. **Leaves** Deciduous, broadly oval. Dark green.
• NATIVE HABITAT Garden origin.
• CULTIVATION Tolerant of a range of soils, including shallow chalk, and of part-shade, although flowers better in sun. Cut back some older shoots to new young growth after flowering, leaving young shoots to flower in the following year.
• PROPAGATION By softwood cuttings in summer.

HEIGHT
2m (6ft)

SPREAD
2m (6ft)

Papaveraceae	CALIFORNIAN POPPY, TREE POPPY

ROMNEYA COULTERI ♔

Habit Vigorous, bushy. *Flowers* Large, fragrant, in late summer. White, with a central boss of golden stamens. *Leaves* Deeply cut, smooth. Blue-grey.
• NATIVE HABITAT Dry canyons of S. California.
• CULTIVATION Grow in deep, moderately fertile soil in a warm, sunny, sheltered position. Provide a deep winter mulch in cool areas.
• PROPAGATION By softwood cuttings of basal shoots in spring, by seed in autumn, or by root cuttings in winter.

HEIGHT
2m (6ft)

SPREAD
2m (6ft)

Rosaceae	BLACK CHOKEBERRY

ARONIA MELANOCARPA

Habit Bushy, suckering. *Flowers* Small, in loose clusters in late spring and early summer. White. *Fruits* Shiny, berry-like, in autumn. Black. *Leaves* Deciduous, elliptic to oval. Glossy dark green, turning red in autumn.
• NATIVE HABITAT Woodlands of E. North America.
• CULTIVATION Grows in most fertile soils, except shallow chalk. Tolerates dry soils.
• PROPAGATION By seed in autumn or by suckers from autumn to spring.

HEIGHT
1–1.5m
(3–5ft)

SPREAD
3m (10ft)

Rosaceae	

RUBUS 'Benenden' ♔

Habit Upright then arching, thornless.
Flowers Large, in late spring and early summer. Glistening pure white with boss of yellow stamens. *Leaves* Deciduous, 3–5 lobed. Dark green.
• NATIVE HABITAT Garden origin.
• CULTIVATION Grow in any rich, fertile soil in sun or partial shade. Remove old, flowered stems occasionally after flowering to relieve overcrowding.
• PROPAGATION By division or layering in spring.
• OTHER NAMES *R.* 'Tridel'.

HEIGHT
3m (10ft)

SPREAD
3m (10ft)

Rosaceae	

PYRACANTHA X *WATERERI* ♔

Habit Vigorous, upright, dense. *Flowers* Small, shallowly cup-shaped, in clusters in early summer. White. *Fruits* Berries, in profusion in autumn. Bright orange-red. *Leaves* Evergreen, narrowly oval. Glossy dark green.
• NATIVE HABITAT Garden origin.
• CULTIVATION Provide a fertile soil or compost. Shelter from cold winds.
• PROPAGATION By semi-ripe cuttings in summer.
• OTHER NAMES *P.* 'Watereri', *P.* 'Waterer's Orange'.

HEIGHT
2.5m (8ft)

SPREAD
2.5m (8ft)

Compositae	HARD-LEAVED DAISY BUSH

OLEARIA NUMMULARIIFOLIA

Habit Rounded, dense, with upright shoots.
Flowers Small, fragrant, in clusters in mid-summer. Creamy-white. **Leaves** Evergreen, small, oval to almost circular, thick. Olive green.
Bark Stems golden-green.
• NATIVE HABITAT Sub-alpine scrub of New Zealand.
• CULTIVATION Grow in any fertile, well-drained soil, including chalk. It is tolerant of salt-laden winds and so is suitable for informal hedging in seaside gardens. However, it does best with shelter from cold, dry, winter winds. In regions at the limit of its hardiness, grow against a warm, sunny wall. Prune to remove dead wood in spring. Responds well to hard pruning if necessary. The bush makes a neat and attractive specimen due to both its flowers and foliage. The thick, leathery leaves make a beautiful contrast to the golden stems.
• PROPAGATION By semi-ripe cuttings in summer.

HEIGHT
To 3m
(10ft)

SPREAD
3m (10ft)

Rosaceae	

PRINSEPIA UNIFLORA

Habit Arching, spiny. **Flowers** Small, fragrant, all
along the stems in late spring to summer. White.
Fruits Cherry-like, edible. Deep red.
Leaves Deciduous, narrow, linear. Glossy dark
green.
• NATIVE HABITAT Dry scrub in mountain valleys
of N.W. China.
• CULTIVATION Grow in any fertile soil or
compost. Needs a hot, sunny site to fruit well.
• PROPAGATION By softwood cuttings in summer
or by seed in autumn.

HEIGHT
1.5–2m
(5–6ft)

SPREAD
3m (10ft)

Rosaceae	

SPIRAEA CANESCENS

Habit Rounded with upright, then arching, stems.
Flowers Small, in compact clusters in early to mid-
summer. Creamy-white. **Leaves** Deciduous,
narrowly oval. Dull green above, grey-green beneath.
• NATIVE HABITAT Hedges and scrub of the
Himalaya.
• CULTIVATION Grows in most fertile soils, if not
too dry. Cut out a proportion of older wood after
flowering.
• PROPAGATION By softwood or semi-ripe
cuttings in summer.

HEIGHT
2.5m (8ft)
or more

SPREAD
2m (6ft)

Rosaceae	

SORBARIA SORBIFOLIA

Habit Upright, suckering. **Flowers** Small, in
large, soft, erect panicles in mid- to late summer.
White. **Leaves** Deciduous, divided, with many
sharply toothed leaflets. Mid-green.
• NATIVE HABITAT Scrub and forest of N. Asia.
• CULTIVATION Grow in deep, fertile, humus-rich
soil. In late winter cut out some older stems and
shorten the remainder to growing points.
• PROPAGATION By softwood cuttings in summer,
by division in autumn, or by root cuttings in winter.
• OTHER NAMES Spiraea sorbifolia.

HEIGHT
2m (6ft)

SPREAD
3m (10ft)

Agavaceae	SPANISH DAGGER, ROMAN CANDLE

Yucca gloriosa

Habit Stout-stemmed, tree-like. **Flowers** Large, bell-shaped, in long, dense, erect panicles in summer and autumn. Creamy-white. **Leaves** Evergreen, long, narrow, lance-shaped, stiff. Blue-green.
• NATIVE HABITAT Arid areas of S.E. United States.
• CULTIVATION Needs a hot, dry, sunny position to bloom well. Grows well in seaside gardens and on sandy soils. Remove spent flowering stems.
• PROPAGATION By root cuttings in winter.

HEIGHT
1.2–2.5m
(4–8ft)

SPREAD
1.5m (5ft)

Hydrangeaceae	

Philadelphus 'Boule d'Argent'

Habit Compact, bushy, arching. **Flowers** Large, slightly fragrant, semi-double to double, in profusion from early to mid-summer. Pure white. **Leaves** Deciduous, broadly oval. Dark green.
• NATIVE HABITAT Garden origin.
• CULTIVATION Tolerant of a range of soils, including shallow chalk, and of part-shade, although flowers better in sun. Cut back some older shoots to new young growth after flowering, leaving young shoots to flower the following year.
• PROPAGATION By softwood cuttings in summer.

HEIGHT
1.5–2m
(5–6ft)

SPREAD
1.5–2m
(5–6ft)

Escalloniaceae	

Escallonia virgata

Habit Arching, graceful, spreading.
Flowers Small, open cup-shaped, in racemes from early to mid-summer. White or pale pink.
Leaves Deciduous, small, lance-head shaped to oval. Glossy dark green.
• NATIVE HABITAT Mountain scrub of S. Chile and Argentina.
• CULTIVATION Tolerates a range of soils, except chalky ones, provided they are deep and fertile.
E. virgata is one of the hardier species, growing up to the tree line in its native mountains, and thrives in both coastal and inland gardens but grows best when sheltered from cold, dry winds. Cut back older, flowered wood immediately after flowering. May be rejuvenated by hard pruning and feeding. It makes an elegant and graceful specimen in the shrub border and is valued for its long flowering period.
• PROPAGATION By softwood cuttings in summer.

HEIGHT
2m (6ft)

SPREAD
2.5m (8ft)

Hydrangeaceae	

PHILADELPHUS 'Dame Blanche'

Habit Compact, bushy, arching. **Flowers** Large, slightly fragrant, semi-double to loosely double, in profusion from early to mid-summer. Pure white. **Leaves** Deciduous, broadly oval. Dark green. **Bark** Peeling with age.
• NATIVE HABITAT Garden origin.
• CULTIVATION Tolerant of a range of soils, including shallow chalk, and of part-shade, although flowers better in sun. Cut back some older shoots to new young growth after flowering, leaving young shoots to flower in the following year. As with other

Philadelphus, the flowers are good for arrangements, and the less heavily scented cultivars will not be overpowering indoors. 'Dame Blanche' makes a beautiful addition to the shrub border and provides a good backdrop for old roses, especially in sheltered sites.
• PROPAGATION By softwood cuttings in summer.

HEIGHT
1.5–2m
(5–6ft)

SPREAD
1.5–2m
(5–6ft)

Eucryphiaceae	

EUCRYPHIA MILLIGANII

Habit Erect, narrow, columnar. *Flowers* Small, cup-shaped, in mid-summer. Glistening white. *Leaves* Evergreen, tiny, oval to oblong. Dark green, bluish-white beneath.
• NATIVE HABITAT Mountains of Tasmania.
• CULTIVATION Grow in acid soil in a semi-shaded position with shelter from wind; withstands more exposure in mild, damp climates. Ideally, it prefers roots in moist shade and crown in sun.
• PROPAGATION By semi-ripe cuttings in late summer.

HEIGHT
To 3m
(10ft)

SPREAD
1m (3ft)

Rosaceae	

OSTEOMELES SCHWERINIAE

Habit Arching, with long, slender shoots. *Flowers* Small, in clusters in early summer. White, with prominent stamens. *Fruits* Oval to rounded, small, berry-like. Black. *Leaves* Evergreen, divided into many small leaflets. Dark green.
• NATIVE HABITAT Hot, dry valleys of Yunnan, S.W. China.
• CULTIVATION Grow in any well-drained soil. In all but the mildest areas, grow against a sunny south- or west-facing wall.
• PROPAGATION By semi-ripe cuttings in summer.

HEIGHT
1.5m (5ft)

SPREAD
3m (10ft)

Hydrangeaceae	TREE ANEMONE

CARPENTERIA CALIFORNICA

Habit Bushy, rounded, sometimes sprawling. *Flowers* Large, fragrant, in summer. Pure white, with a boss of yellow stamens. *Leaves* Evergreen, narrowly oval to oblong. Glossy dark green.
• NATIVE HABITAT Chaparral of C. California.
• CULTIVATION Grow in moderately fertile, moist but well-drained soil. Flowers best against a warm, south- or west-facing wall, with shelter from cold winds. Prune after flowering if necessary.
• PROPAGATION By greenwood cuttings in summer or by seed in autumn.

HEIGHT
1.5–2m
(5–6ft)

SPREAD
2m (6ft)

Styraceae	STORAX, SILVERBELL

STYRAX WILSONII

Habit Slow-growing, bushy, with slender shoots.
Flowers Bell-shaped, in pendent racemes in early summer. White with yellow centres.
Leaves Deciduous, small, oval to elliptic. Dark green.
• NATIVE HABITAT Scrub and rocky hills, W. China.
• CULTIVATION Grow in a neutral to acid, moist but well-drained soil, with shelter from cold winds. Tolerates semi-shade. Seldom requires pruning.
• PROPAGATION By softwood cuttings in summer or by seed in autumn.

HEIGHT
To 3m
(10ft)

SPREAD
2m (6ft)

Hydrangeaceae	

PHILADELPHUS × LEMOINEI

Habit Upright, then slightly arching.
Flowers Small, very fragrant, in profuse racemes from early to mid-summer. Pure white.
Leaves Deciduous, broadly oval. Dark green.
• NATIVE HABITAT Garden origin.
• CULTIVATION Tolerant of a range of soils, including shallow chalk, and of part-shade, although flowers best in sun. Cut back some older shoots to new young growth after flowering, leaving young shoots to flower in the following year.
• PROPAGATION By softwood cuttings in summer.

HEIGHT
2m (6ft)

SPREAD
2m (6ft)

Compositae	

OZOTHAMNUS ROSMARINIFOLIUS

Habit Upright, dense. *Flowers* Small, honey-scented, in dense clusters in early summer. White, opening from red buds. *Leaves* Evergreen, small, narrow. Deep green.
• NATIVE HABITAT Moist mountain heathlands of Tasmania and S.E. Australia.
• CULTIVATION Will produce dense growth on soils that remain reliably moist during the growing season. Provide a warm, sheltered site in cold areas.
• PROPAGATION By semi-ripe cuttings in summer.
• OTHER NAMES *Helichrysum rosmarinifolium.*

HEIGHT
2.5–3m
(8–10ft)

SPREAD
1.5m (5ft)

Symplocaceae	SAPPHIRE BERRY, ASIATIC SWEETLEAF

SYMPLOCOS PANICULATA

Habit Bushy, sometimes tree-like.
Flowers Small, fragrant, in small panicles in late spring and early summer. White. **Fruits** Small, berry-like. Metallic blue. **Leaves** Deciduous, variable, oval to broadly oval. Dark green.
• NATIVE HABITAT Scrub and woodland of the Himalaya and E. Asia.
• CULTIVATION Grow in a fertile, neutral to acid soil. Needs a warm, sunny site. Several individual shrubs must be planted together to fruit well.
• PROPAGATION By seed in autumn.

HEIGHT
3m (10ft) or more

SPREAD
3m (10ft)

Rhamnaceae	COAST WHITETHORN

CEANOTHUS INCANUS

Habit Erect, bushy, with spiny shoots.
Flowers Small, in dense racemes in late spring and early summer. White. **Leaves** Evergreen, broadly oval. Grey-green.
• NATIVE HABITAT In forest in the foothills of coastal mountains of N. California.
• CULTIVATION Grow in light soil in a sunny and sheltered site. In cold areas site against a south- or west-facing wall. Cut out dead wood in spring and trim side-shoots after flowering.
• PROPAGATION By semi-ripe cuttings in summer.

HEIGHT
To 3m (10ft)

SPREAD
3m (10ft)

Clethraceae	WHITE ALDER, SUMMER-SWEET

CLETHRA BARBINERVIS

Habit Upright, bushy. **Flowers** Small, fragrant, in racemes in late summer and early autumn. White. **Leaves** Deciduous, oval, toothed. Dark green, turning red and yellow in autumn. **Bark** Peeling. Orange.
• NATIVE HABITAT In mountain woodland from E. China to Japan.
• CULTIVATION Grow in humus-rich, acid soil. Requires no regular pruning.
• PROPAGATION By softwood cuttings in summer or by seed in autumn.

HEIGHT
3m (10ft)

SPREAD
3m (10ft)

Ericaceae	

ZENOBIA PULVERULENTA

Habit Bushy, suckering. **Flowers** Anise-scented, bell-shaped, waxy, in erect clusters from early to mid-summer. White. **Leaves** Deciduous or semi-evergreen, oval to oblong. Glossy green, blue-white beneath. **Bark** Shoots bloomed blue-white.
• NATIVE HABITAT Heathland and pine barrens of E. United States.
• CULTIVATION Grow in humus-rich, acid soil. Prune lightly after flowering to keep compact.
• PROPAGATION By semi-ripe cuttings in summer or by seed in late winter.

HEIGHT
1.5–2m (5–6ft) or more

SPREAD
1.5–2m (5–6ft)

Cornaceae	

CORNUS ALBA 'Elegantissima' ♥

Habit Vigorous, upright. **Flowers** In small clusters in late spring and early summer. Creamy-white. **Fruits** Small, berry-like. White. **Leaves** Deciduous, oval to elliptic. Grey-green, edged and mottled with white. **Bark** Young stems bright red in winter.
• **NATIVE HABITAT** Garden origin.
• **CULTIVATION** For bright winter stems, cut back almost to ground level each year in early spring.
• **PROPAGATION** By softwood cuttings in summer or by hardwood cuttings in autumn or winter.

☼ ◊
❀ ❀ ❀

HEIGHT
To 2m (6ft)

SPREAD
2–2.5m
(6–8ft)

Compositae	DAISY BUSH

OLEARIA × HAASTII

Habit Rounded, bushy, dense. **Flowers** Small, fragrant, daisy-like, in clusters from mid- to late summer. Creamy-white. **Leaves** Evergreen, small, oval. Glossy dark green, white-felted beneath.
• **NATIVE HABITAT** Sub-alpine scrub of New Zealand.
• **CULTIVATION** Grow in any fertile, well-drained soil, including chalk. Tolerant of salt-laden winds. Good for hedging, especially in seaside gardens. Prune to remove dead wood.
• **PROPAGATION** By semi-ripe cuttings in summer.

☼ ◊
❀ ❀

HEIGHT
1.5m (5ft)

SPREAD
1.5m (5ft)

Caprifoliaceae	

VIBURNUM DILATATUM 'Catskill'

Habit Compact, low, spreading. **Flowers** Small, in flat trusses in late spring and early summer. Creamy-white. **Fruits** Berry-like, in clusters from autumn to winter. Bright red. **Leaves** Deciduous, broadly oval, sharply toothed. Dark green, turning yellow, orange, and red in autumn.
• **NATIVE HABITAT** Garden origin.
• **CULTIVATION** Grow in deep, moisture retentive but well-drained fertile soil, in sun or semi-shade.
• **PROPAGATION** By softwood cuttings in early summer.

☼ ◊
❀ ❀ ❀

HEIGHT
2m (6ft)

SPREAD
To 3m
(10ft)

Hydrangeaceae	MOCK ORANGE

PHILADELPHUS CORONARIUS ♥
'Variegatus'

Habit Vigorous, bushy. **Flowers** Small, very fragrant, in late spring and early summer. Creamy-white. **Leaves** Deciduous, oval. Mid-green, broadly edged with white.
• **NATIVE HABITAT** Garden origin.
• **CULTIVATION** Tolerant of many soils, including shallow chalk and very dry soils. Cut back some older shoots to new young growth after flowering.
• **PROPAGATION** By softwood cuttings in summer.

☼ ◊
❀ ❀ ❀

HEIGHT
2m (6ft)

SPREAD
2m (6ft)

Rosaceae

SPIRAEA NIPPONICA 'Snowmound'

Habit Vigorous, bushy, mound-forming, with stout, arching stems. **Flowers** Small, in dense clusters along the stems in early summer. Pure white. **Leaves** Deciduous, oblong to lance-shaped. Fresh bright green when young, later dark green and blue-tinted. **Bark** Young shoots red-brown.
• NATIVE HABITAT Garden origin.
• CULTIVATION. Grow in any moderately fertile soil that does not dry out too much during the growing season. Flowers are carried on wood made in the previous season. Prune after flowering to remove older, flowered wood, leaving space for new growth which will flower in the following year. Mulch and feed after pruning. This is one of the most generous of *Spiraea* in bloom, and makes a beautiful specimen for the shrub border.
• PROPAGATION By softwood cuttings in summer.
• OTHER NAMES *S. nipponica* var. *tosaensis* of gardens.

HEIGHT
2m (6ft)

SPREAD
2m (6ft)

Polygonaceae	ST CATHERINE'S LACE

ERIOGONUM GIGANTEUM

Habit Rounded, branching. **Flowers** Tiny, in large, branching clusters, to 30cm (12in) across, in summer. White. **Leaves** Evergreen, oblong to oval, leathery. Grey-white woolly above, white beneath.
• NATIVE HABITAT Coastal islands, S. California.
• CULTIVATION Prefers very well-drained, low fertility soil or compost. Water moderately when in growth, otherwise sparingly. Provide good ventilation if under cover. Prune to shape in early spring and deadhead after flowering.
• PROPAGATION By seed in spring or autumn.

☼ ◊

Min. 5°C (41°F)

HEIGHT
To 2.5m (8ft)

SPREAD
2m (6ft)

Rhamnaceae	

RHAMNUS ALATERNUS 'Argenteovariegatus'

Habit Fast-growing, bushy. **Flowers** Tiny, in early to mid-summer. Yellowish-green.
Fruits Spherical, berry-like. Red then black.
Leaves Evergreen, oval, leathery. Grey-green, edged with creamy-white.
• NATIVE HABITAT Garden origin.
• CULTIVATION Tolerates semi-shade. Grow in any fertile soil in a warm position. Shelter from cold winds.
• PROPAGATION By semi-ripe cuttings in summer.

☼ ◊
❀ ❀

HEIGHT
3m (10ft)

SPREAD
3m (10ft)

Caprifoliaceae	

VIBURNUM 'Pragense' ♥

Habit Rounded, bushy. **Flowers** Small, in domed heads from late spring to early summer. Creamy-white, pink in bud. **Leaves** Evergreen, elliptic to lance-shaped, corrugated. Shining green, white-felted beneath.
• NATIVE HABITAT Garden origin.
• CULTIVATION Tolerates a range of soils, including chalk. Best foliage is obtained on deep, fertile soils.
• PROPAGATION By semi-ripe cuttings in summer.
• OTHER NAMES *V. x pragense.*

☼ ◊
❀ ❀ ❀

HEIGHT
2.5–3m (8–10ft)

SPREAD
2.5–3m (8–10ft)

Myrtaceae	TANTOON

LEPTOSPERMUM POLYGALIFOLIUM

Habit Arching, graceful, tree-like with age.
Flowers Small, in mid-summer. White, tinted pink. **Leaves** Evergreen, aromatic, small, lance-shaped. Glossy bright green.
• NATIVE HABITAT Sandy heaths and forests of E. Australia and Lord Howe Island.
• CULTIVATION Grow in humus-rich, neutral to acid soil. Provide the shelter of a warm wall in cold areas.
• PROPAGATION By semi-ripe cuttings in summer.
• OTHER NAMES *L. flavescens.*

☼ ◊
❀ ❀

HEIGHT
To 3m (10ft)

SPREAD
3m (10ft)

Hydrangeaceae	

PHILADELPHUS DELAVAYI f. MELANOCALYX

Habit Vigorous, upright. *Flowers* Large, extremely fragrant, from early to mid-summer. Pure white, with deep purple sepals. *Leaves* Deciduous, large, oval. Dark green.
• NATIVE HABITAT Garden origin. Species occurs by streams and in scrub of S.W. China.
• CULTIVATION Tolerant of a range of soils, including shallow chalk, and of part-shade, although flowers better in sun.
• PROPAGATION By softwood cuttings in summer.

HEIGHT
2m (6ft)

SPREAD
2m (6ft)

Malvaceae	

HIBISCUS SYRIACUS 'Red Heart' ♥

Habit Vigorous, upright. *Flowers* Large, mallow-like, in profusion from late summer to mid-autumn. White, with conspicuous red centres. *Leaves* Deciduous, lobed. Deep green.
• NATIVE HABITAT Garden origin.
• CULTIVATION Prefers humus-rich, fertile soil. Flowers more freely in a warm, sunny site, such as on a south- or west-facing wall. Restrict size if necessary by cutting back hard in spring.
• PROPAGATION By greenwood or semi-ripe cuttings in summer.

HEIGHT
2.5m (8ft)

SPREAD
2.5m (8ft)

Caprifoliaceae	FLY HONEYSUCKLE

LONICERA XYLOSTEUM

Habit Erect, bushy, dense. *Flowers* Delicate, in late spring and early summer. Creamy-white. *Fruits* Small, round berries. Bright red. *Leaves* Deciduous, elliptic to oval. Grey-green.
• NATIVE HABITAT Woodland and hedgerow, often on limestone, from Europe to N. Asia.
• CULTIVATION Grows in any fertile soil in sun or semi-shade.
• PROPAGATION By seed in autumn or spring, by semi-ripe cuttings in summer, or by hardwood cuttings in autumn.

HEIGHT
3m (10ft)

SPREAD
3m (10ft)

Paeoniaceae	MOUTAN PEONY

PAEONIA SUFFRUTICOSA subsp. ROCKII

Habit Upright, branching. *Flowers* Large, cup-shaped, semi-double, in summer. White, with deep maroon basal blotch. *Leaves* Deciduous, divided into 3–5 lobed leaflets. Dark green, tinged purple.
• NATIVE HABITAT Garden origin.
• CULTIVATION Tolerates light shade. Grow in fertile, neutral to alkaline soil.
• PROPAGATION By semi-ripe cuttings in late summer or by grafting in winter.
• OTHER NAMES *P. suffruticosa* 'Joseph Rock', *P. suffruticosa* 'Rock's Variety'.

HEIGHT
2m (6ft)

SPREAD
2m (6ft)

Rosaceae	

STEPHANANDRA TANAKAE

Habit Graceful, rounded, with arching, slender shoots. **Flowers** Tiny, in soft, airy panicles from early to mid-summer. White. **Leaves** Deciduous, lobed, sharply toothed. Mid-green, turning orange and yellow in autumn. **Bark** Shoots are rich brown.
• NATIVE HABITAT Mountain scrub of Japan.
• CULTIVATION Tolerates semi-shade and any fertile soil that is not too dry. Cut out some of the oldest shoots after flowering.
• PROPAGATION By softwood cuttings in summer or by division in autumn.

☼ ◐ ◊
❀❀❀

HEIGHT
3m (10ft)

SPREAD
2m (6ft)

Aceraceae	

ACER PALMATUM 'Butterfly' ♛

Habit Slow-growing, mounded, tree-like with age. **Flowers** Small, in pendent clusters in spring. Red-purple. **Fruits** Sycamore-like. **Leaves** Deciduous, lobed. Grey-green, edged with cream and pink.
• NATIVE HABITAT Garden origin.
• CULTIVATION Provide shelter from cold winds to avoid leaf scorch. Needs moist but well-drained soil.
• PROPAGATION By softwood cuttings in summer or by grafting in late winter or early spring.

☼ ◐ ◊
❀❀❀

HEIGHT
2m (6ft)

SPREAD
3m (10ft)

Caprifoliaceae	

LONICERA TATARICA

Habit Erect, bushy. **Flowers** Tubular, 5-lobed, in spring and early summer. White, pink, or red. **Fruits** Small, round berries. Bright red. **Leaves** Deciduous, oval to lance-shaped. Dark green.
• NATIVE HABITAT On dry hills and in scrub from S. Russia to C. Asia.
• CULTIVATION Grow in any fertile soil.
• PROPAGATION By seed in autumn or spring, by semi-ripe cuttings in summer, or by hardwood cuttings in autumn.

☼ ◊
❀❀❀

HEIGHT
To 2.5m
(8ft)

SPREAD
To 3m
(10ft)

Escalloniaceae	

ESCALLONIA 'Donard Seedling'

Habit Vigorous, arching. *Flowers* Funnel-shaped, from early to mid-summer. White, flushed pink, opening from pink buds. *Leaves* Evergreen, oval. Glossy dark green.
• NATIVE HABITAT Garden origin.
• CULTIVATION Tolerant of lime-rich soils and drought. Thrives in coastal gardens and is one of the hardiest of *Escallonia* hybrids for inland gardens.
• PROPAGATION By softwood or semi-ripe cuttings in summer.

HEIGHT
2–3m
(6–10ft)

SPREAD
2.5m (8ft)

Hydrangeaceae	

DEUTZIA LONGIFOLIA 'Veitchii' ♛

Habit Vigorous, upright then arching.
Flowers 5-petalled, in large clusters from early to mid-summer. Deep pink, paler within.
Leaves Deciduous, narrow, lance-shaped, pointed. Dull green. *Bark* Shoots are purple.
• NATIVE HABITAT Garden origin. Species grows in scrub of Sichuan and Yunnan, China.
• CULTIVATION Tolerates almost any fertile, well-drained soil but grows best in soils that are not too dry. Also suitable for a cool conservatory.
• PROPAGATION By softwood cuttings in summer.

HEIGHT
1.5–2m
(5–6ft)

SPREAD
1.5–2m
(5–6ft)

Paeoniaceae	MOUTAN PEONY

PAEONIA SUFFRUTICOSA 'Reine Elizabeth'

Habit Upright, branching. *Flowers* Large, cup-shaped, fully double. Salmon pink, with ruffled petals flushed bright copper-red at margins.
Leaves Deciduous, deeply divided into 3–5 lobed, lance-shaped to oval leaflets. Pale green.
• NATIVE HABITAT Garden origin.
• CULTIVATION Tolerates chalk and light shade. Grow in a fertile, neutral to alkaline soil.
• PROPAGATION By semi-ripe cuttings in late summer or by grafting in winter.

HEIGHT
2m (6ft)

SPREAD
2m (6ft)

Proteaceae	

PROTEA NERIIFOLIA

Habit Upright, bushy. *Flowers* Large heads, in spring-summer. Red, pink, or white; bracts have tufts of black hair. *Leaves* Evergreen, narrowly oblong. Dark or bright green.
• NATIVE HABITAT Cape Province, S. Africa.
• CULTIVATION Grow in a conservatory in a neutral to acid medium that is low in phosphates and nitrates. Water moderately when in growth, otherwise sparingly. Provide good ventilation.
• PROPAGATION By seed in spring or by semi-ripe cuttings in summer.

Min. 5–7°C
(41–45°F)

HEIGHT
To 3m
(10ft)

SPREAD
2.5–3m
(8–10ft)

Rosaceae	

NEILLIA THIBETICA

Habit Upright, then arching. *Flowers* Small, tubular, in dense, slender panicles in late spring and early summer. Rose-pink. *Leaves* Deciduous, narrowly oval, pointed and sharply toothed. Mid-green.
• NATIVE HABITAT In scrub and by rocky streambanks of W. China.
• CULTIVATION Tolerates most soils if not too dry, and semi-shade, although it blooms best in sun. *Neillia thibetica* is suitable for the shrub border. It is an uncommon but very graceful plant, which is

beautiful in both foliage and flower, and deserves to be more widely grown. Cut out the oldest, flowered wood immediately after flowering to rejuvenate the plant. It will produce new canes freely from the base.
• PROPAGATION By softwood cuttings in summer or by suckers in autumn.

HEIGHT
2m (6ft)

SPREAD
2m (6ft)

Escalloniaceae	

ESCALLONIA 'Apple Blossom'

Habit Dense, bushy, compact. *Flowers* Small, chalice-shaped, in profusion from early to mid-summer. White, flushed apple-blossom pink. *Leaves* Evergreen, oval. Glossy dark green.
• NATIVE HABITAT Garden origin.
• CULTIVATION Thrives in mild and coastal areas. Inland, provide a warm site and shelter from wind. Tolerant of lime-rich soils and drought. Prune after flowering to remove old or weak growth.
• PROPAGATION By softwood or semi-ripe cuttings in summer.

HEIGHT
2m (6ft)

SPREAD
2.5m (8ft)

Leguminosae	ROSE ACACIA, BRISTLY LOCUST

ROBINIA HISPIDA

Habit Upright then arching, loose, suckering. *Flowers* Large, pea-like, in short racemes in late spring and early summer. Deep rose-pink. *Leaves* Deciduous, 13–17 leaflets. Dark green.
• NATIVE HABITAT Hillside scrub and dry woodland of S.E. United States.
• CULTIVATION Tolerates any but waterlogged soil and is useful on poor, dry soils. Shelter from wind to avoid damage to the brittle branches.
• PROPAGATION By seed or by suckers in autumn or by root cuttings in winter.

HEIGHT
To 3m
(10ft)

SPREAD
3m (10ft)

Leguminosae	

INDIGOFERA HETERANTHA

Habit Upright, then arching. *Flowers* Small, in racemes, from early summer to autumn. Bright rosy-purple. *Leaves* Deciduous, finely divided into 13–21 leaflets. Grey-green.
• NATIVE HABITAT Dry scrub of N.W. Himalaya.
• CULTIVATION Tolerates any but waterlogged soil and is very useful on poor, dry soils. Grows from the base if cut back by frost.
• PROPAGATION By softwood cuttings in summer or by seed in autumn.
• OTHER NAMES *I. gerardiana*.

HEIGHT
1.5–2m
(5–6ft)
or more

SPREAD
1.5–2m
(5–6ft)

Melastomataceae	

MEDINILLA MAGNIFICA

Habit Epiphytic, upright with stout branches. *Flowers* Long, pendant trusses in spring to summer. Pink to coral-red, with large pink bracts. *Leaves* Evergreen, large, broadly oval, veined. Glossy dark green.
• NATIVE HABITAT Tropical forest of Philippines.
• CULTIVATION Grow in a warm glasshouse or conservatory. Needs a fertile, humus-rich soil. Water freely in growth, then moderately. Mist often and feed monthly from spring to autumn.
• PROPAGATION By greenwood cuttings in summer.

Min.
16°C (61°F)

HEIGHT
1.5–2m
(5–6ft)
or more

SPREAD
1.5–2m
(5–6ft)

Ericaceae	CALICO BUSH, MOUNTAIN LAUREL

KALMIA LATIFOLIA

Habit Dense, bushy, rounded. **Flowers** Saucer-shaped, opening from distinctive, tightly crimped buds. Pink. **Leaves** Evergreen, elliptic to lance-shaped. Glossy rich green.
• NATIVE HABITAT Dry, rocky sites in mixed oak and pine woods of E. United States.
• CULTIVATION Grow in humus-rich, peaty, or sandy, acid soil. Tolerates semi-shade. No regular pruning is needed but plants regenerate very slowly if cut back. The calico bush makes a beautiful specimen for woodland gardens and other sites in light, dappled shade, thriving in conditions similar to those needed for rhododendrons. It is very attractive when in full bloom as well as when in bud. The buds are very distinctive: dark pink, symmetrically formed, and neatly crimped.
• PROPAGATION By seed in autumn, by softwood cuttings in summer, or by layering in autumn.

HEIGHT
3m (10ft)

SPREAD
3m (10ft)

Malvaceae	

HIBISCUS ROSA-SINENSIS 'The President'

Habit Bushy. *Flowers* Large, funnel-shaped, in summer. Bright pink with a magenta centre and prominent yellow anthers. *Leaves* Evergreen, oval. Glossy dark green.
• NATIVE HABITAT Garden origin.
• CULTIVATION Grow in a warm greenhouse or conservatory. Water freely when in growth, then moderately. Cut established plants back in spring.
• PROPAGATION By greenwood cuttings in late spring or by semi-ripe cuttings in summer.

Min. 15°C (59°F)

HEIGHT 2.5–3m (8–10ft)

SPREAD 2m (6ft)

Malvaceae	

LAVATERA 'Rosea'

Habit Vigorous, upright. *Flowers* Large, hollyhock-like, in profusion throughout summer. Deep pink. *Leaves* Semi-evergreen, lobed, downy. Sage-green.
• NATIVE HABITAT Garden origin. Species occurs in rocky areas of C. and S.E. Europe.
• CULTIVATION Tolerates seaside conditions and a range of soils.
• PROPAGATION By softwood cuttings in early spring or summer.
• OTHER NAMES *L. olbia* 'Rosea'.

HEIGHT 1.5–2m (5–6ft)

SPREAD 1.5m (5ft)

Malvaceae	

HIBISCUS SYRIACUS 'Woodbridge'

Habit Vigorous, upright. *Flowers* Large, single, mallow-like, from late summer to mid-autumn. Deep rose-pink, with a darker blotch at the petal base. *Leaves* Deciduous, lobed. Dark green.
• NATIVE HABITAT Garden origin.
• CULTIVATION Prefers humus-rich soils. Flowers more freely in a warm, sunny site, such as on a south-facing wall. Old plants may be cut back hard in spring to rejuvenate.
• PROPAGATION By greenwood cuttings in late spring or by semi-ripe cuttings in summer.

HEIGHT 2.5m (8ft)

SPREAD 2m (6ft)

Malvaceae	MALVA ROSA

LAVATERA ASSURGENTIFLORA

Habit Upright, with twisted branches.
Flowers Hollyhock-like, in clusters in mid-summer. Deep cerise with darker veins.
Leaves Semi-evergreen, with 5–7 triangular lobes. Mid-green, white-hairy beneath.
• NATIVE HABITAT Coastal islands of California.
• CULTIVATION Tolerates seaside conditions and a range of soils. Cut back to a permanent woody framework in spring when hard frosts have passed.
• PROPAGATION By softwood cuttings in early spring or summer.

HEIGHT 2.5m (8ft)

SPREAD 2m (6ft)

Escalloniaceae	

ESCALLONIA 'Langleyensis'

Habit Vigorous, arching. **Flowers** Small, funnel-shaped, in profusion from early to mid-summer. Rose-pink. **Leaves** Evergreen or semi-evergreen, small, oval. Glossy bright green.

• NATIVE HABITAT Garden origin.

• CULTIVATION Thrives in mild areas and is useful for seaside gardens where it may be used for hedging. In inland gardens, provide a warm site, sheltered from cold, drying winter winds. Tolerant of lime-rich soils and drought. Prune after flowering to remove old or weak growth. Old or overgrown specimens may be rejuvenated by hard pruning followed by feeding and mulching. It is best to do this in late spring to give new growth time to ripen before winter, although plants may not flower in the same season. This hybrid, between *Escallonia punctata* and *E. virgata*, makes an elegant and free-flowering specimen for the shrub border.

• PROPAGATION By softwood or semi-ripe cuttings in summer.

HEIGHT
2–3m
(6–10ft)

SPREAD
3m (10ft)

Myrtaceae	GRANITE BOTTLEBRUSH

MELALEUCA ELLIPTICA

Habit Bushy, rounded. *Flowers* Brush-like,
comprising many red stamens, in dense, cylindrical
spikes in spring to summer. *Leaves* Evergreen,
oval to almost circular, leathery. Grey-green.
• NATIVE HABITAT W. Australia.
• CULTIVATION Grow in a well-ventilated
greenhouse or conservatory in a humus-rich compost
that is low in nitrates. Water moderately when in
growth, otherwise sparingly. Tip back when young.
• PROPAGATION By seed in spring or by semi-ripe
cuttings in summer.

HEIGHT
3m (10ft)

SPREAD
2m (6ft)

Solanaceae	

CESTRUM ELEGANS ♥

Habit Vigorous, arching, tree-like with age.
Flowers Small, tubular, in dense racemes in late
spring and summer. Red-purple. *Fruits* Small,
fleshy berries. Dark red-purple.
Leaves Evergreen, oval-oblong to lance-shaped,
downy. Olive green.
• NATIVE HABITAT Evergreen tropical forests of
Mexico.
• CULTIVATION In cold areas provide the shelter
of a south- or west-facing wall.
• PROPAGATION By softwood cuttings in summer.

HEIGHT
To 3m
(10ft)

SPREAD
2m (6ft)

Ericaceae	

PIERIS FORMOSA var. FORRESTII ♥
'Wakehurst'

Habit Bushy, dense. *Flowers* Small, fragrant,
urn-shaped, in dense, drooping panicles in spring or
early summer. White. *Leaves* Evergreen, elliptic
to lance-shaped. Brilliant red in early summer,
turning pink, creamy-yellow, and then deep green.
• NATIVE HABITAT Garden origin.
• CULTIVATION Grow in a sheltered site. Young
growth is susceptible to frost; cut back frost-damaged
growth to healthy wood as soon as possible.
• PROPAGATION By semi-ripe cuttings in summer.

HEIGHT
2.5m (8ft)
or more

SPREAD
2.5m (8ft)

Malvaceae	

ABUTILON MEGAPOTAMICUM

Habit Arching, with slender stems.
Flowers Pendent, bell-shaped, from late spring to autumn. Red calyx, purple anthers, and golden-yellow petals. *Leaves* Evergreen, oval, heart-shaped at base. Dark green.
• NATIVE HABITAT Dry areas in mountain valleys of Brazil.
• CULTIVATION Prefers a light soil and needs a warm, sunny site on a south- or west-facing wall.
• PROPAGATION By seed in spring or by softwood, greenwood, or semi-ripe cuttings in summer.

☀ ◊
❀❀

HEIGHT
To 3m
(10ft)

SPREAD
3m (10ft)

Calycanthaceae	CALIFORNIA ALLSPICE

CALYCANTHUS OCCIDENTALIS

Habit Rounded, bushy. *Flowers* Fragrant, with many strap-shaped petals, in summer. Purplish-red.
Leaves Aromatic, deciduous, oval-oblong to lance-shaped. Dark green.
• NATIVE HABITAT Damp places in the foothills of coastal mountains of California.
• CULTIVATION Tolerates light shade. Grow in a deep, fertile, moist but well-drained soil.
• PROPAGATION By softwood cuttings in summer or by seed in autumn.

☀ ◖
❀❀❀

HEIGHT
3m (10ft)

SPREAD
3m (10ft)

Elaeocarpaceae	CHILE LANTERN TREE

CRINODENDRON HOOKERIANUM

Habit Upright. *Flowers* Large, lantern-like, fleshy, in late spring and early summer. Scarlet to carmine. *Leaves* Evergreen, narrowly oblong to lance-shaped. Glossy dark green.
• NATIVE HABITAT By water courses and in marshland in cool, very humid areas of Chile.
• CULTIVATION Grow in a fertile, acid, moist, well-drained soil. Shelter from cold winds.
• PROPAGATION By softwood cuttings in summer or by seed in autumn.
• OTHER NAMES *Tricuspidaria lanceolata.*

☀ ◖ pH
❀❀

HEIGHT
2.5m (8ft)
or more

SPREAD
2.5–3m
(8–10ft)

Caprifoliaceae	

LONICERA INVOLUCRATA var. LEDEBOURII

Habit Vigorous, erect, bushy. **Flowers** Small, tubular, in late spring and early summer. Yellow, with orange bracts. **Fruits** Small, shining berries. Black, with red bracts. **Leaves** Deciduous, oval to oblong. Dark green.
• NATIVE HABITAT Coastal areas of California.
• CULTIVATION Tolerant of seaside conditions and urban pollution. Grows in any fertile soil.
• PROPAGATION By semi-ripe cuttings in summer or by hardwood cuttings in autumn.

HEIGHT
3m (10ft)

SPREAD
3m (10ft)

Leguminosae	ORCHID TREE

BAUHINIA GALPINII

Habit Spreading, sometimes semi-climbing. **Flowers** Fragrant, in short racemes in summer. Bright brick-red. **Leaves** Evergreen, 2-lobed. Mid-green.
• NATIVE HABITAT Mountain scrub of S. Africa.
• CULTIVATION Grow in a fertile soil or compost. Water freely when in growth, otherwise moderately. A beautiful specimen for the cool conservatory.
• PROPAGATION By seed in spring.
• OTHER NAMES *B. punctata.*

Min. 5°C
(41°F)

HEIGHT
3m (10ft)

SPREAD
2m (6ft)

Proteaceae	WARATAH

TELOPEA SPECIOSISSIMA

Habit Upright, bushy, becoming straggling with age. **Flowers** Small, tubular, in dense, globose heads in spring and summer. Red, with bright red bracts. **Leaves** Evergreen, narrowly oval, toothed, leathery. Dark green.
• NATIVE HABITAT Mountains of E. Australia.
• CULTIVATION Grow in moist, humus-rich, well-drained, acid soil in a warm, sunny position. Shelter from cold winds.
• PROPAGATION By seed in spring or by layering in winter.

HEIGHT
2.5–3m
(8–10ft)

SPREAD
2m (6ft)

Leguminosae	COCKSPUR CORAL-TREE

ERYTHRINA CRISTA-GALLI

Habit Upright, becoming tree-like with age. **Flowers** Large, pea-like, waxy, in leafy racemes in summer to autumn. Scarlet. **Leaves** Deciduous, divided, with 3 oval leaflets. Mid-green.
• NATIVE HABITAT Brazil.
• CULTIVATION Needs a warm, sunny position with well-drained soil and shelter from cold winds. Is cut to the base by frost but will re-sprout if mulched thickly in winter.
• PROPAGATION By seed in spring or by semi-ripe cuttings in summer.

HEIGHT
3m (10ft)

SPREAD
2m (6ft)

Loganiaceae	

DESFONTAINIA SPINOSA ♀

Habit Slow-growing, bushy, dense.
Flowers Long, tubular, drooping, from mid-summer to late autumn. Red, with a yellow mouth.
Leaves Evergreen, small, spiny, holly-like. Glossy dark green.
• NATIVE HABITAT Cool, damp areas of coastal zones and Andean foothills of S. America.
• CULTIVATION Grow in deep, fertile, humus-rich, and well-drained soil. Shelter from cold wind. Mulch with leafmould or similar.
• PROPAGATION By semi-ripe cuttings in summer.

HEIGHT
2–3m
(6–10ft)

SPREAD
2.5m (8ft)

Myrtaceae	STIFF BOTTLEBRUSH

CALLISTEMON RIGIDUS

Habit Bushy, slightly arching. *Flowers* In dense, bottlebrush spikes in late spring and early summer. Deep red. *Leaves* Evergreen, long, narrow, sharply pointed. Dull green.
• NATIVE HABITAT Mainly damp areas in E. Australia.
• CULTIVATION Requires the shelter of a warm, south- or west-facing wall. Grow in a fertile, well-drained, preferably neutral to acid soil.
• PROPAGATION By semi-ripe cuttings in summer or by seed in autumn or spring.

HEIGHT
2m (6ft)

SPREAD
2m (6ft)

Leguminosae	CORAL TREE

ERYTHRINA × BIDWILLII

Habit Upright sub-shrub. *Flowers* Small, sweet pea-like, in long racemes in late summer or autumn. Brilliant red. *Leaves* Deciduous, divided into 3 leaflets. Pale to mid-green.
• NATIVE HABITAT Garden origin.
• CULTIVATION Needs a warm, sunny position with well-drained soil and shelter from cold winds. Will be cut to the base by frost but will re-sprout from the base if mulched thickly in winter.
• PROPAGATION By semi-ripe cuttings in summer.

HEIGHT
To 3m
(10ft)

SPREAD
2m (6ft)

Myrtaceae	

CALLISTEMON CITRINUS 'Splendens' ♀

Habit Bushy, slightly arching, graceful.
Flowers In dense, bottlebrush spikes in summer. Brilliant red. *Leaves* Evergreen, lemon-scented, long. Grey-green, bronze-red when young.
• NATIVE HABITAT Garden origin. Species occurs mainly in damp areas in E. Australia.
• CULTIVATION Requires the shelter of a warm, south- or west-facing wall. Grow in a fertile, well-drained, and preferably neutral to acid soil. Tip prune when young to encourage bushiness.
• PROPAGATION By semi-ripe cuttings in summer.

HEIGHT
2m (6ft)

SPREAD
2m (6ft)

Anacardiaceae	SMOOTH SUMACH, SCARLET SUMACH

RHUS GLABRA

Habit Bushy, wide-spreading. **Flowers** Small, in long, dense panicles in summer. Greenish-red. **Fruits** Minutely downy, in upright clusters on female plants. Scarlet. **Leaves** Deciduous, divided into leaflets. Deep blue-green, turning red in autumn.
• NATIVE HABITAT North America.
• CULTIVATION Thrives on any fertile soil in full sun.
• PROPAGATION By semi-ripe cuttings in summer or by root cuttings in winter.

HEIGHT
2.5m (8ft)

SPREAD
2m (6ft)

Paeoniaceae	

PAEONIA DELAVAYI

Habit Upright, open. **Flowers** Small, single, bowl-shaped, surrounded by leafy bracts in summer. Rich dark red. **Leaves** Deciduous, divided into oval leaflets. Dark green above, blue-green beneath.
• NATIVE HABITAT In scrub on limestone in Yunnan, China.
• CULTIVATION Tolerates light shade. Grow in a fertile soil in a sunny, sheltered position. Will re-sprout from the base if cut down by frost.
• PROPAGATION By seed in autumn or by semi-ripe cuttings in late summer.

HEIGHT
2m (6ft)

SPREAD
1.2m (4ft)

Myrtaceae	PINEAPPLE GUAVA

ACCA SELLOWIANA

Habit Bushy, tree-like with age. **Flowers** Large, fleshy, in mid-summer. Dark red, white beneath. Stamens bright red and prominent.
Fruits Large, egg-shaped, edible.
Leaves Evergreen, elliptic to oblong. Grey-green, white-felted beneath.
• NATIVE HABITAT Brazil and Argentina.
• CULTIVATION Needs a south- or west-facing wall. Tolerates drought and coastal conditions.
• PROPAGATION By softwood cuttings in summer.
• OTHER NAMES *Feijoa sellowiana.*

HEIGHT
To 3m
(10ft)

SPREAD
3m (10ft)

Aceraceae	

ACER PALMATUM 'Bloodgood'

Habit Bushy-headed, tree-like with age.
Flowers Small, in pendent clusters in spring. Red-purple. **Fruits** Sycamore-like. Red.
Leaves Deciduous, lobed. Very dark red-purple, turning red in autumn.
• NATIVE HABITAT Garden origin.
• CULTIVATION Tolerates light shade, but colours best in sun. Provide shelter from cold winds. Needs moisture-retentive but well-drained soil.
• PROPAGATION By softwood cuttings in early summer or by grafting in late winter or early spring.

HEIGHT
To 3m
(10ft)

SPREAD
3m (10ft)

Berberidaceae	

BERBERIS THUNBERGII 'Rose Glow'

Habit Compact, spiny. *Flowers* Globose to cup-shaped, in mid-spring. Pale yellow, red-tinged.
Fruits Small, elliptic berries. Red.
Leaves Deciduous, oval. Reddish-purple, marbled with pink and silvery-white in young shoots.
• NATIVE HABITAT Garden origin.
• CULTIVATION Grow in any but waterlogged soil. Tolerates semi-shade. Remove dead wood in summer when it is most easily distinguished.
• PROPAGATION By softwood or semi-ripe cuttings in summer.

☀ ◊
❀ ❀ ❀

HEIGHT
2m (6ft) or more

SPREAD
2m (6ft)

Euphorbiaceae	COPPERLEAF, JACOB'S COAT

ACALYPHA WILKESIANA

Habit Bushy. *Flowers* Small, in slender spikes. Red. *Leaves* Evergreen, large, oval, serrated. Rich coppery-green, splashed with red and crimson.
• NATIVE HABITAT Tropical islands of the Pacific.
• CULTIVATION Grow in a warm conservatory in a coarse, humus-rich soil or compost. Prefers partial shade. Water freely when in full growth, otherwise sparingly. Pinch out stem tips of young plants to encourage branching.
• PROPAGATION By softwood, greenwood, or semi-ripe cuttings in summer.

☀◑ ◊

Min. 16°C (61°F)

HEIGHT
2.5m (8ft)

SPREAD
2.5m (8ft)

Verbenaceae	LEMON VERBENA

ALOYSIA TRIPHYLLA

Habit Erect, bushy. *Flowers* Tiny, in slender racemes in summer. White, lilac-tinted.
Leaves Deciduous, strongly lemon-scented, lance-shaped, pointed. Pale green.
• NATIVE HABITAT Dry areas of Chile and Argentina.
• CULTIVATION Provide the shelter of a warm, south- or west-facing wall in cold areas and mulch in winter.
• PROPAGATION By softwood cuttings in summer.
• OTHER NAMES *Lippia citriodora*.

☀ ◊
❀ ❀

HEIGHT
3m (10ft)

SPREAD
2.5m (8ft)

| Buddlejaceae | | Malvaceae | |

BUDDLEJA CRISPA

Habit Upright, bushy. *Flowers* Small, fragrant, in dense racemes in mid- to late summer. Lilac with a white or orange throat. *Leaves* Deciduous, oval. Grey-green. *Bark* Shoots are white-woolly.
• NATIVE HABITAT On open hillsides in scrub of the Himalaya.
• CULTIVATION Thrives on chalk and lime-rich soils. In cold areas grow on a warm, south- or west-facing wall. Cut back hard in spring near to ground level or to a permanent woody framework.
• PROPAGATION By semi-ripe cuttings in summer.

HIBISCUS SINOSYRIACUS 'Lilac Queen'

Habit Vigorous, open, spreading. *Flowers* Large, with thick petals, from late summer to mid-autumn. Pale lilac, burgundy at the base. *Leaves* Deciduous, broad, lobed, finely toothed. Mid-green.
• NATIVE HABITAT Garden origin.
• CULTIVATION Prefers humus-rich soil. Flowers more freely in a warm, sunny site, such as a south-facing wall. Old plants may be cut back hard in spring.
• PROPAGATION By greenwood cuttings in late spring or by semi-ripe cuttings in summer.

HEIGHT
To 3m
(10ft)

SPREAD
2.5–3m
(8–11ft)

HEIGHT
2.5–3m
(8–10ft)

SPREAD
3m (10ft)

| Caprifoliaceae | HIMALAYAN HONEYSUCKLE |

LEYCESTERIA FORMOSA

Habit Upright, suckering. *Flowers* Small, funnel-shaped, in pendent clusters in summer and early autumn. White, enclosed in purplish-red bracts. *Fruits* Small, spherical berries. Red-purple. *Leaves* Deciduous, oval. Dark green. *Bark* Rich sea-green, bloomed when young.
• NATIVE HABITAT By streams in forests of the Himalaya.
• CULTIVATION Grow in any fertile soil, in sun or semi-shade. Sprouts freely from the base, producing young stems of much better colour. Thin out weak

and old flowered wood in spring. A beautiful specimen with a long season of interest, the Himalayan honeysuckle is ideally suited to a woodland garden or a shrub border in light, dappled shade.
• PROPAGATION By softwood cuttings in summer or by seed or division in autumn.

HEIGHT
2m (6ft)

SPREAD
2m (6ft)

Lamiaceae	MINT BUSH

PROSTANTHERA OVALIFOLIA

Habit Bushy, rounded. **Flowers** Small, cup-shaped, 2-lipped, in leafy racemes in spring and summer. Purple. **Leaves** Sweetly aromatic, evergreen, oval, thick textured. Dark green.
• NATIVE HABITAT Rocky hills of E. Australia.
• CULTIVATION Grow in a cool conservatory in fertile, freely draining soil or compost. Water potted specimens freely when in growth, otherwise moderately. Prune lightly after flowering.
• PROPAGATION By seed in spring or by semi-ripe cuttings in summer.

Min. 5°C
(41°F)

HEIGHT
2m (6ft) or
more

SPREAD
2m (6ft)

Myrtaceae	WESTERN TEA-MYRTLE

MELALEUCA NESOPHYLLA

Habit Bushy shrub or small tree.
Flowers A spherical head comprising a brush of stamens, in summer. Stamens lavender to rose-pink. **Leaves** Evergreen, small, oval, grey-green.
Bark Peeling when mature.
• NATIVE HABITAT Grasslands of W. Australia.
• CULTIVATION Dislikes chalk. Prefers low-nitrogen, well-drained soil. Water potted specimens moderately but less in low temperatures.
• PROPAGATION By seed in spring or by semi-ripe cuttings in summer.

HEIGHT
to 3m (10ft)

SPREAD
2m (6ft)

Malvaceae	

ABUTILON X SUNTENSE 'Violetta'

Habit Vigorous, upright, then arching.
Flowers Large, bowl-shaped, in late spring and early summer. Deep violet. **Leaves** Deciduous, vine-like, sharply toothed. Dark green.
• NATIVE HABITAT Garden origin.
• CULTIVATION Prefers a light soil and flowers best in a warm, sunny site such as on a south- or west-facing wall. Mature plants may have the previous season's stems cut back hard in early spring.
• PROPAGATION By softwood, greenwood, or semi-ripe cuttings in summer.

HEIGHT
3m (10ft)

SPREAD
1.5m (5ft)

Lamiaceae	ROUND-LEAVED MINT BUSH

PROSTANTHERA ROTUNDIFOLIA

Habit Bushy, dense, rounded. **Flowers** Bell-shaped, in late spring or summer. Lavender to purple-blue. **Leaves** Evergreen, aromatic, tiny, oval. Deep green.
• NATIVE HABITAT Australia and Tasmania.
• CULTIVATION Needs a warm, sunny, and sheltered site. Also good for a cool conservatory. Water freely when in growth, then moderately. Cut established plants hard back after flowering.
• PROPAGATION By seed in spring or by semi-ripe cuttings in late summer.

HEIGHT
2.5–3m
(8–10ft)

SPREAD
2.5–3m
(8–10ft)

Solanaceae	BLUE POTATO BUSH

SOLANUM 'Royal Robe'

Habit Open, loose, rounded. **Flowers** Small, saucer-shaped opening flat, in clusters in summer. Rich violet-blue with yellow centres.
Leaves Evergreen, lance-shaped, smooth. Bright green.
• NATIVE HABITAT Garden origin.
• CULTIVATION Grow in a cool conservatory in fertile, freely draining soil or compost. Water moderately in growth, then reduce in winter but do not let the plant dry out.
• PROPAGATION By semi-ripe cuttings in summer.

☀ ◊

Min. 7°C
(45°F)

HEIGHT
1.5–2m
(5–6ft)

SPREAD
2m (6ft)

Papilionaceae	

SOPHORA DAVIDII

Habit Bushy, with arching shoots and spiny branches. **Flowers** Small, pea-like, in short racemes in late spring and early summer. Purple and white. **Leaves** Deciduous, divided, with 13–19 leaflets. Grey-green.
• NATIVE HABITAT Arid and rocky valleys of China.
• CULTIVATION Tolerates very dry and chalky soils. Blooms best in a hot, sunny position. Requires no regular pruning. Usually responds to hard cutting back.
• PROPAGATION By seed in autumn.
• OTHER NAMES *S. viciifolia.*

☀ ◊
❀ ❀ ❀

HEIGHT
2–2.5m
(6–8ft)

SPREAD
2m (6ft)

Buddlejaceae	

BUDDLEJA 'Lochinch'   ♥

Habit Bushy, compact, arching. **Flowers** Small, fragrant, tubular, in long, dense, conical panicles from late summer to autumn. Lilac-blue.
Leaves Deciduous, lance-shaped. Downy grey-green when young, later smooth, white-felted beneath.
• NATIVE HABITAT Garden origin.
• CULTIVATION Thrives on chalk, and lime-rich soils. Grows in any moderately fertile soil. Cut back hard in spring. Attractive to butterflies.
• PROPAGATION By semi-ripe cuttings in summer.

☀ ◊
❀ ❀ ❀

HEIGHT
3m (10ft)

SPREAD
3m (10ft)

Solanaceae	

FABIANA IMBRICATA f. VIOLACEA   ♥

Habit Upright, bushy. **Flowers** Small, tubular, in profusion at the tips of the shoots in summer. Lilac.
Leaves Evergreen, small, heath-like. Dark green.
• NATIVE HABITAT Garden origin.
• CULTIVATION Grow in a light, moderately fertile soil. Do not grow on shallow chalk, although the plant is lime-tolerant. Flowers most profusely if given the shelter of a warm south- or west-facing wall.
• PROPAGATION By seed in spring or by greenwood cuttings in summer.

☀ ◊
❀ ❀

HEIGHT
To 2.5m
(6ft)

SPREAD
2m (6ft)

Malvaceae	

HIBISCUS SYRIACUS 'Oiseau Bleu' ♈

Habit Vigorous, upright. **Flowers** Large, mallow-like, mid- to late summer. Lilac-blue with red centres. **Leaves** Deciduous, lobed. Deep green.
• NATIVE HABITAT Garden origin.
• CULTIVATION Prefers humus-rich soils. Flowers more freely in a warm, sunny site, such as on a south-facing wall. No regular pruning needed but old plants can be cut back hard in spring.
• PROPAGATION By greenwood cuttings in late spring or by semi-ripe cuttings in summer.
• OTHER NAMES *H. syriacus* 'Blue Bird'.

HEIGHT
2.5–3m
(8–10ft)

SPREAD
2m (6ft)

Rhamnaceae	SANTA BARBARA CEANOTHUS

CEANOTHUS IMPRESSUS

Habit Bushy, dense, spreading. **Flowers** Tiny, in small, dense clusters from mid-spring to early summer. Blue. **Leaves** Evergreen, small, elliptic to almost circular, crinkled. Dark green.
• NATIVE HABITAT In scrub of S. California.
• CULTIVATION Grow in a warm, sunny, sheltered site in a light, well-drained soil. Tolerant of some lime in the soil and of coastal conditions. Cut out dead wood in spring, and trim back side-shoots after flowering.
• PROPAGATION By semi-ripe cuttings in summer.

HEIGHT
1.5m (5ft)

SPREAD
3m (10ft)

Araliaceae	

ELEUTHEROCOCCUS SIEBOLDIANUS

Habit Vigorous, scrambling, arching, and spiny.
Flowers Tiny, in clusters in early summer.
Greenish. **Fruits** Small, round berries, in clusters.
Black. **Leaves** Deciduous, divided into 5 leaflets.
Glossy bright green.
• NATIVE HABITAT Scrub and thickets of E. China.
• CULTIVATION Tolerant of poor soil and urban
pollution.
• PROPAGATION By seed in autumn, by root
cuttings in winter, or by semi-ripe cuttings in summer.
• OTHER NAMES *Acanthopanax sieboldianus.*

HEIGHT
To 3m
(10ft)

SPREAD
2.5–3m
(8–10ft)

Rutaceae	JAPAN PEPPER

ZANTHOXYLUM PIPERITUM

Habit Bushy, compact, spiny, tree-like with age.
Flowers Tiny, in spring. Greenish-yellow.
Fruits Small, round. Reddish. **Leaves** Aromatic,
deciduous, divided into many leaflets. Glossy dark
green, turning yellow in autumn.
• NATIVE HABITAT Mountain scrub in N. China,
Korea, and Japan.
• CULTIVATION Tolerates semi-shade. Grow in
any fertile soil. Cut out dead wood as seen.
• PROPAGATION By seed in autumn or by root
cuttings in late winter.

HEIGHT
2m (6ft)

SPREAD
2m (6ft)

Rutaceae	HOP TREE, WAFER ASH

PTELEA TRIFOLIATA 'Aurea'

Habit Bushy, dense, sometimes tree-like.
Flowers Tiny, very fragrant, star-shaped, in
corymbs in summer. Yellowish. **Fruits** Winged,
elm-like, in dense clusters in autumn. Green.
Leaves Deciduous, aromatic, divided into 3
leaflets. Bright yellow when young, becoming pale
green.
• NATIVE HABITAT Garden origin.
• CULTIVATION Tolerates light shade and grows
in any fertile soil.
• PROPAGATION By softwood cuttings in summer.

HEIGHT
3m (10ft)

SPREAD
3m (10ft)

Escalloniaceae	

ITEA ILICIFOLIA

Habit Bushy, with arching shoots. **Flowers** Tiny,
in long, catkin-like racemes in summer and early
autumn. Greenish. **Leaves** Evergreen, oval,
sharply toothed. Glossy dark green.
• NATIVE HABITAT On cliffs in low mountains of
W. China.
• CULTIVATION Tolerates semi-shade and most
fertile soils that are not too dry. Is best planted
against a warm, south-facing wall and protected
with a winter mulch when young.
• PROPAGATION By softwood cuttings in summer.

HEIGHT
3m (10ft)

SPREAD
3m (10ft)

Myrtaceae	LEMON BOTTLEBRUSH

CALLISTEMON PALLIDUS

Habit Bushy, arching, graceful. **Flowers** In dense, bottlebrush spikes in summer. Creamy-yellow. **Leaves** Evergreen, aromatic, long, narrow. Grey-green, pink-tinged when young.
• NATIVE HABITAT Occurs predominantly in damp situations in E. Australia.
• CULTIVATION Requires the shelter of a warm, south- or west-facing wall. Grow in fertile, moist but well-drained, preferably neutral to acid soil. Tip prune when young to encourage bushiness.
• PROPAGATION By semi-ripe cuttings in summer.

HEIGHT
3m (10ft)

SPREAD
3m (10ft)

Rosaceae	

PHYSOCARPUS OPULIFOLIUS ♥
'Dart's Gold'

Habit Compact, rounded. **Flowers** Small, shallowly cup-shaped, in clusters in late spring. White or pale pink. **Leaves** Deciduous, oval to rounded, 3-lobed. Golden-yellow. **Bark** Smooth, shredding.
• NATIVE HABITAT Garden origin.
• CULTIVATION Tolerates most fertile soils, except those on shallow chalk. Thrives on moist, slightly acid soils. Thin out crowded growth by cutting old shoots back to the base after flowering.
• PROPAGATION By softwood cuttings in summer.

HEIGHT
2.5m (8ft)

SPREAD
2.5m (8ft)

Cornaceae	

CORNUS ALBA 'Spaethii' ♥

Habit Vigorous, upright. **Flowers** Small, in small clusters in late spring and early summer. Creamy-white. **Fruits** Small, round, berry-like. White. **Leaves** Deciduous, oval to elliptic. Bright green, edged yellow. **Bark** Winter stems are bright red.
• NATIVE HABITAT Garden origin. Species occurs in forests of Siberia to N. China and Korea.
• CULTIVATION For bright winter stems, cut back almost to ground level annually in early spring.
• PROPAGATION By softwood cuttings in summer or by hardwood cuttings in autumn or winter.

HEIGHT
To 2m
(6ft)

SPREAD
2–2.5m
(6–8ft)

Umbelliferae	SHRUBBY HARE'S EAR

BUPLEURUM FRUTICOSUM

Habit Bushy, rounded, with slender, arching shoots. **Flowers** Small, in rounded heads from mid-summer to early autumn. Yellow.
Leaves Evergreen, long oval, or lance-shaped, thick. Sea green.
• NATIVE HABITAT Occurs in scrub and rocky cliffs in S. Europe.
• CULTIVATION Tolerant of coastal conditions. Grow in any not too fertile soil, in a warm and sheltered position. Cut back in spring if overgrown.
• PROPAGATION By semi-ripe cuttings in summer.

HEIGHT
2m (6ft) or
more

SPREAD
2m (6ft)

| Oleaceae | ITALIAN JASMINE, YELLOW JASMINE |

JASMINUM HUMILE

Habit Bushy, semi-climbing or mound-forming.
Flowers Small, fragrant, tubular, at the ends of
slender shoots from early spring to late autumn.
Bright yellow *Leaves* Evergreen or semi-
evergreen, divided into 5–7 leaflets. Bright green.
• NATIVE HABITAT In scrub in the dry valleys of
the Himalaya, from Afghanistan to China.
• CULTIVATION Grow in any fertile soil. In cold
areas provide the shelter of a warm south- or west-
facing wall. Thin out old shoots if necessary after
flowering, otherwise it requires little pruning. The
flowers are produced on the previous season's
wood, and on the tips of wood made in the current
season. Wall-grown plants tend to climb but will
need tying in to a strong support. This species
makes a beautiful mounded plant if grown free-
standing in the shrub border or as a specimen
where conditions permit.
• PROPAGATION By semi-ripe cuttings in
summer.

HEIGHT
2–2.5m
(6–8ft)

SPREAD
2–2.5m
(6–8ft

Solanaceae	WILLOW-LEAVED JESSAMINE

CESTRUM PARQUI

Habit Vigorous, open. **Flowers** Small, night-scented, tubular, in profuse clusters in summer. Yellow-green. **Fruits** Small berries. Brown-purple. **Leaves** Deciduous, narrowly lance-shaped. Mid-green.
• NATIVE HABITAT Poor, dry soils of Chile.
• CULTIVATION Grow in a fertile, freely draining soil, with the shelter of a warm, south- or west-facing wall. Provide a winter mulch of evergreen prunings. Will regenerate if cut by frost.
• PROPAGATION By softwood cuttings in summer.

☼ ◐
❀ ❀

HEIGHT
2–3m
(6–10ft)

SPREAD
2m (6ft)

Leguminosae	

PIPTANTHUS NEPALENSIS

Habit Open, upright. **Flowers** Pea-like, in racemes in late spring or early summer. Bright yellow. **Leaves** Deciduous or semi-evergreen, divided into 3 large leaflets. Dark blue-green.
• NATIVE HABITAT Scrub and woodland of the Himalaya.
• CULTIVATION In cold areas provide the shelter of a warm, south- or west-facing wall. Cut out old, flowered shoots in spring to relieve overcrowding.
• PROPAGATION By seed in autumn.
• OTHER NAMES *P. laburnifolius, P. forrestii.*

☼ ◐
❀ ❀

HEIGHT
2–3m
(6–10ft)

SPREAD
2m (6ft)

Leguminosae	BLADDER SENNA

COLUTEA ARBORESCENS

Habit Vigorous, open, rounded. **Flowers** Pea-like, throughout summer. Golden-yellow. **Fruits** Conspicuous, bladder-like pods in late summer and autumn. Green, brown when ripe. **Leaves** Deciduous, divided into many leaflets. Pale green.
• NATIVE HABITAT C. Europe to the Mediterranean.
• CULTIVATION Grows in any but waterlogged soil. Tolerates light shade but flowers best in sun.
• PROPAGATION By softwood cuttings in summer or by seed in autumn.

☼ ◌
❀ ❀ ❀

HEIGHT
To 3m
(10ft)

SPREAD
3m (10ft)

Dilleniaceae	

HIBBERTIA CUNEIFORMIS

Habit Bushy, upright. **Flowers** Small, with 5 spreading petals, in leafy clusters from spring to summer. Bright yellow. **Leaves** Evergreen, small, oval, serrated at tips. Dark green.
• NATIVE HABITAT W. Australia.
• CULTIVATION Grow in conservatory in a fertile, humus-rich soil or compost, with added sharp sand. Water moderately when in growth, otherwise sparingly. Maintain good ventilation.
• PROPAGATION By semi-ripe cuttings in summer.
• OTHER NAMES *Candollea cuneiformis, H. tetrandra.*

☼ ◌

Min. 5–7°C
(41–45°F)

HEIGHT
2–3m
(6–10ft)

SPREAD
1.5m (5ft)

| Paeoniaceae | TIBETAN PEONY |

PAEONIA DELAVAYI var. *LUDLOWII*

Habit Upright, open. **Flowers** Large, single, bowl-shaped, in summer. Rich golden-yellow. **Leaves** Deciduous, divided into deeply cut, pointed leaflets. Bright green.
• NATIVE HABITAT Garden origin. Species occurs in mountain gorges of S.E. Tibet.
• CULTIVATION Tolerates light shade. Grow in a fertile, neutral to alkaline soil in a sunny, sheltered position. Will re-sprout from the base if cut by frost. This is one of the loveliest of tree peonies, and is valued as much for its foliage as for its flowers.

Remove spent flower stalks after leaf fall in autumn, and in spring cut back any very old, flowered growths to the base to allow room for new growth with better foliage.
• PROPAGATION By seed in autumn (may take 3 years to germinate) or by semi-ripe cuttings in late summer.
• OTHER NAMES *P. lutea* var. *ludlowii*.

☼ ◊
❀ ❀ ❀

HEIGHT
2.5m (8ft)

SPREAD
2.5m (8ft)

Leguminosae	

COLUTEA × MEDIA

Habit Vigorous, open, rounded. **Flowers** Pea-like, in racemes throughout summer. Golden-yellow, tinted with coppery-orange.
Fruits Conspicuous, bladder-like pods, in late summer and autumn. Reddish. **Leaves** Deciduous, divided into many leaflets. Grey-green.
• NATIVE HABITAT Garden origin.
• CULTIVATION Grows in any but waterlogged soil. Tolerates light shade but flowers best in sun. Cut back hard in spring if necessary to restrict size.
• PROPAGATION By softwood cuttings in summer.

HEIGHT
To 3m
(10ft)

SPREAD
3m (10ft)

Leguminosae	

SENNA CORYMBOSA

Habit Vigorous, arching, tree-like with age.
Flowers Bowl-shaped, in large sprays in late summer. **Fruits** Oblong pod. Green, brown when ripe. **Leaves** Evergreen or semi-evergreen, divided into 4–6 oval leaflets. Bright green.
• NATIVE HABITAT In hillside thickets of S. United States, Argentina, and Uruguay.
• CULTIVATION Grow in a conservatory with good ventilation. Water freely in growth, then moderately.
• PROPAGATION By seed in spring.
• OTHER NAMES *Cassia corymbosa*.

Min. 7°C
(45°F)

HEIGHT
2–3m
(6–10ft)

SPREAD
2m (6ft)
or more

Leguminosae	SPANISH BROOM

SPARTIUM JUNCEUM

Habit Upright with slender shoots, arching with age. **Flowers** Fragrant, pea-like, from early summer to autumn. Rich golden-yellow.
Leaves Deciduous, almost leafless, with rush-like stems. Deep green.
• NATIVE HABITAT In scrub, usually on limestone, of S.W. Europe and the Mediterranean.
• CULTIVATION Grow in a warm, sunny site in any but waterlogged soil. Best on soils that are not too fertile. Trim in March, avoiding old wood.
• PROPAGATION By seed in autumn.

HEIGHT
3m (10ft)

SPREAD
3m (10ft)

Papaveraceae	TREE POPPY, BUSH POPPY

DENDROMECON RIGIDA

Habit Vigorous, upright then arching.
Flowers Large, fragrant, poppy-like, produced intermittently from spring to autumn. Golden-yellow. **Leaves** Evergreen, narrowly oval to lance-shaped. Blue-green.
• NATIVE HABITAT Dry, rocky hills of California.
• CULTIVATION Shelter against a warm, sunny wall. Protect in winter with a dry mulch.
• PROPAGATION By softwood cuttings in summer, by seed in autumn or spring, or by root cuttings in winter.

HEIGHT
3m (10ft)

SPREAD
3m (10ft)

Leguminosae	GOLDEN WONDER

SENNA DIDYMOBOTRYA

Habit Rounded or spreading. **Flowers** Large, pea-like, in dense spikes, opening from glossy brown-black bracts throughout the year. Rich yellow. **Leaves** Evergreen, with 8–18 leaflets. Yellow-green.
• NATIVE HABITAT Hillside thickets of tropical Africa.
• CULTIVATION Grow in a warm conservatory or greenhouse in freely draining soil or compost. Water freely in growth, then moderately to sparingly.
• PROPAGATION By seed in spring.
• OTHER NAMES *Cassia didymobotrya*.

Min. 13°C
(55°F)

HEIGHT
To 3m
(10ft)

SPREAD
2.5m (8ft)

Malvaceae	

ABUTILON PICTUM 'Thompsonii'

Habit Vigorous, upright, compact. **Flowers** Bell-shaped, from summer to mid-autumn. Yellow-orange, veined crimson. **Leaves** Large, 3–5 lobed. Rich green, mottled with a mosaic of yellow.
• NATIVE HABITAT Garden origin.
• CULTIVATION Grow in a conservatory in fertile, well-drained soil. Tolerates part-shade. Water freely when in growth, then moderately. Tip prune when young. Can be grown as a summer bedding plant.
• PROPAGATION By softwood, greenwood, or semi-ripe cuttings in summer.

Min. 5–7°C
(41–45°F)

HEIGHT
2.5m (8ft)

SPREAD
2m (6ft)

HYDRANGEAS

Hydrangea are deciduous shrubs and deciduous or evergreen climbers from China, Japan, the Himalaya, and both North and South America. Their flower heads vary widely but perhaps the best known are the 'mop-heads' (Hortensias), which have large, round heads of flowers, and the 'lace-caps', which have flatter heads. In some cases, depending on soil pH, the same plant may bear either blue (acid soil) or pink (neutral or alkaline soil) flowers. Each flower head usually consists of a mass of tiny, fertile flowers, surrounded by, or mixed with, much larger sterile flowers with very showy, papery, petal-like sepals. They prefer sun or semi-shade and fertile, moist, but well-drained soil. Propagate by softwood cuttings in summer.

H. PANICULATA 'Unique'

Habit Vigorous, open, upright. *Flowers* Very large, dense, conical heads in late summer and autumn. White ray flowers, turning pink or red with age. *Leaves* Deciduous, oval, toothed. Dark green.
• CULTIVATION Grow in sun or semi-shade.
• HEIGHT 3m (10ft).
• SPREAD 3m (10ft).

H. paniculata 'Unique'

☼ ◊ ❀❀❀ ♔

H. QUERCIFOLIA

Habit Bushy, mound-forming. *Flowers* In pyramidal panicles from mid-summer to mid-autumn. White, flushed purple with age. *Leaves* Deciduous, deeply-lobed. Dark green, red-purple in autumn.
• CULTIVATION Prefers a neutral to acid soil, in a frost-sheltered site.
• HEIGHT 1–1.5m (3–5ft).
• SPREAD 2m (6ft).

H. quercifolia
OAK-LEAVED HYDRANGEA

☼◑ ◊ ❀❀ ♔

H. PANICULATA 'Praecox'

Habit Vigorous, open, early flowering. *Flowers* Loose, narrowly conical heads of toothed ray flowers, in mid-summer. White. *Leaves* Deciduous, pointed, toothed. Dark green.
• CULTIVATION Grow in sun or semi-shade.
• HEIGHT 3m (10ft).
• SPREAD 3m (10ft).

H. paniculata 'Praecox'

☼ ◊ ❀❀❀ ♔

H. ARBORESCENS 'Grandiflora'

Habit Upright, open, bushy. *Flowers* Large ray flowers, in dense, rounded heads from mid-summer to early autumn. Creamy-white. *Leaves* Deciduous, broadly oval, pointed. Bright green.
• CULTIVATION Needs little pruning, but may be cut back in late winter or early spring for larger blooms.
• HEIGHT 1.5m (5ft) or more.
• SPREAD 1.5m (5ft).

H. arborescens 'Grandiflora'

☼◑ ◊ ❀❀❀ ♔

H. MACROPHYLLA 'Lanarth White'

Habit Bushy, dense, compact. *Flowers* Flat, open heads from mid- to late summer. Large, white outer flowers with tiny, bright blue or pink central flowers. *Leaves* Deciduous, oval, toothed. Glossy mid-green.
• HEIGHT 1.5m (5ft).
• SPREAD 2m (6ft).

H. macrophylla 'Lanarth White'
LACE-CAP GROUP

☼◑ ◊ ❀❀ ♔

H. PANICULATA 'Floribunda'

Habit Vigorous, open.
Flowers Large, dense, narrowly conical heads of small central flowers surrounded by very large ray flowers, in late summer. White.
Leaves Deciduous, pointed, toothed. Dark green.
• CULTIVATION Grow in sun or semi-shade in deep, fertile soils. Cut back hard in early spring for larger flower heads.
• HEIGHT 3m (10ft).
• SPREAD 3m (10ft).

H. paniculata 'Floribunda'

☼ ◊ ❀❀❀ ♛

H. HETEROMALLA, Bretschneideri Group

Habit Upright, slightly arching. **Flowers** Broad 'lace-cap' heads from mid- to late summer. Small greenish-white inner flowers and large white outer ray flowers, turning pink. **Leaves** Deciduous, narrowly oval, toothed. Dark green.
• HEIGHT 3m (10ft).
• SPREAD 3m (10ft).

H. heteromalla, **Bretschneideri Group**

☼ ◊ ❀❀❀ ♛

H. PANICULATA 'Brussels Lace'

Habit Vigorous, open.
Flowers Large, delicate, conical panicles in late summer and early autumn. White.
Leaves Deciduous, large, pointed, toothed. Dark green.
• CULTIVATION Grow in sun or semi-shade in deep, fertile soils.
• HEIGHT 3m (10ft).
• SPREAD 2m (6ft).

H. paniculata 'Brussels Lace'

☼ ◊ ❀❀❀

H. ARBORESCENS 'Annabelle'

Habit Upright, open.
Flowers Large, in dense, rounded heads, from mid-summer to early autumn. Creamy-white.
Leaves Deciduous, broadly oval, pointed Bright green.
• HEIGHT 1.5m (5ft) or more.
• SPREAD 1.5m (5ft).

H. arborescens 'Annabelle'

☼ ◊ ❀❀❀ ♛

H. INVOLUCRATA 'Hortensis'

Habit Loose, open.
Flowers Small, double, with flowers in dense clusters in late summer and autumn. Cream, pink, and green.
Leaves Deciduous, broadly heart-shaped, bristly, and finely toothed. Dark green.
• HEIGHT 1.2–1.5m (4–5ft).
• SPREAD 1.2–1.5m (4–5ft).

H. involucrata 'Hortensis'

☼ ◊ ❀❀ ♛

H. MACROPHYLLA 'Générale Vicomtesse de Vibraye'

Habit Vigorous, bushy.
Flowers Dense, rounded flower heads, from mid- to late summer. Pure, clear blue on acid soil, otherwise clear pale pink.
Leaves Deciduous, oval, toothed. Light green.
• HEIGHT 1.5m (5ft).
• SPREAD 1.5m (5ft).

H. macrophylla 'Générale Vicomtesse de Vibraye' MOP-HEAD, HORTENSIA GROUP

☼ ◊ ❀❀ ♛

H. MACROPHYLLA 'Hamburg'

Habit Vigorous, bushy.
Flowers Domed, dense heads, with large flowers from mid- to late summer. Deep rose-pink or deep blue, depending on soil.
Leaves Deciduous, oval, pointed. Deep green.
• HEIGHT 1.5–2m (5–6ft).
• SPREAD 2–2.5m (6–8ft).

H. macrophylla 'Hamburg' MOP-HEAD, HORTENSIA GROUP

☼ ◊ ❀❀

H. MACROPHYLLA 'Altona'
Habit Vigorous, bushy.
Flowers Domed, dense heads from mid- to late summer. Rich rose-pink; good blue on acid soils.
Leaves Deciduous, oval, pointed. Deep green.
• HEIGHT 1.5–2m (5–6ft).
• SPREAD 2–2.5m (6–8ft).

H. macrophylla 'Altona'
MOP-HEAD, HORTENSIA GROUP

H. ASPERA
Habit Vigorous, upright.
Flowers Flattened heads from late summer to mid-autumn. Purple central flowers, with large white ray flowers, flushed purple. *Leaves* Deciduous, lance-shaped, toothed. Dull green, bristly; grey-downy beneath.
• HEIGHT 3m (10ft).
• SPREAD 3m (10ft).

H. aspera

H. MACROPHYLLA 'Lilacina'
Habit Vigorous, bushy.
Flowers Flat, open heads from mid- to late summer. Tiny, deep lilac central flowers and larger, pink-purple outer flowers.
Leaves Deciduous, oval, toothed. Glossy mid-green.
• HEIGHT 1.5m (5ft).
• SPREAD 2m (6ft).

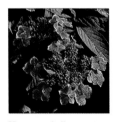

H. macrophylla 'Lilacina'
LACE-CAP GROUP

H. SERRATA
Habit Bushy, dense, with slender stems.
Flowers Flat heads, from mid- to late summer. Blue, pink, or white inner flowers; ray flowers blue on acid soil, otherwise pink. *Leaves* Deciduous, oval, toothed, pointed. Light-green.
• OTHER NAMES *H. macrophylla* subsp. *serrata*.
• HEIGHT 1.5m (5ft).
• SPREAD 1.5m (5ft).

H. serrata

H. MACROPHYLLA 'Veitchii'
Habit Vigorous, lax, bushy. *Flowers* Flat, open heads from mid- to late summer with tiny, lilac-blue central flowers and larger white then pink outer flowers.
Leaves Deciduous, oval, toothed. Glossy mid-green.
• HEIGHT 1.5m (5ft).
• SPREAD 2m (6ft).

H. macrophylla 'Veitchii'
LACE-CAP GROUP

H. MACROPHYLLA 'Mariesii Perfecta'
Habit Vigorous, bushy.
Flowers Flat heads from mid- to late summer. Tiny, blue central flowers and larger lilac-blue outer flowers. Blue on acid soils, otherwise pink.
Leaves Deciduous, oval, toothed. Light green.
• OTHER NAMES *H. macrophylla* 'Blue Wave'.
• HEIGHT 1.5–2m (5–6ft).
• SPREAD 2m (6ft).

H. macrophylla 'Mariesii Perfecta'
LACE-CAP GROUP

H. SERRATA 'Bluebird'
Habit Vigorous, bushy, stout-stemmed.
Flowers Flat, open heads from mid- to late summer. Blue, pink, or white inner flowers; ray flowers blue on acid soil, otherwise red-purple.
Leaves Deciduous, oval, toothed, pointed. Light-green, red in autumn.
• HEIGHT 1.2m (4ft).
• SPREAD 1.2m (4ft).

H. serrata 'Bluebird'

H. MACROPHYLLA 'Blue Bonnet'
Habit Vigorous, bushy.
Flowers Domed, dense heads from mid- to late summer. Rich blue or pink. True blue colour only on acid soils.
Leaves Deciduous, oval, pointed. Deep green.
• HEIGHT 1.5–2m (5–6ft).
• SPREAD 2–2.5m (6–8ft).

H. macrophylla 'Blue Bonnet'
MOP-HEAD, HORTENSIA GROUP

Rhamnaceae	

COLLETIA HYSTRIX

Habit Arching, with stout, very spiny branches.
Flowers Small, fragrant, tubular from late summer to autumn. White, pink in bud.
Leaves Deciduous, sparsely clothed with small, elliptic leaves.
• NATIVE HABITAT Rocky slopes of S. Chile.
• CULTIVATION Grow in a warm, sheltered site in well-drained, not too rich soil.
• PROPAGATION By semi-ripe cuttings in late summer.
• OTHER NAMES *C. armata.*

HEIGHT
2–2.5m
(6–8ft)

SPREAD
3m (10ft)

Caprifoliaceae	

VIBURNUM FARRERI

Habit Strongly upright, dense. **Flowers** Small, very fragrant, in rounded clusters from late autumn to early spring. White or pale pink.
Leaves Deciduous, oval. Dark green, bronze when young and also in autumn.
• NATIVE HABITAT Scrub and forests of N. China.
• CULTIVATION Grow in any deep, fertile soil that is not too dry. Thin out old shoots after flowering.
• PROPAGATION By softwood cuttings in summer or by seed in autumn (fruits rare in cultivation).
• OTHER NAMES *V. fragrans.*

HEIGHT
3m (10ft)

SPREAD
3m (10ft)

Leguminosae	POWDER PUFF TREE

CALLIANDRA HAEMATOCEPHALA (pink form)

Habit Spreading, tree-like with age.
Flowers Large, powder-puff heads consist of tiny florets carried from late autumn to spring. Pink with long pink stamens. **Leaves** Evergreen, divided, with 16–24 narrowly oval leaflets. Bright green.
• NATIVE HABITAT Dry, rocky hills of S. America.
• CULTIVATION Grow in a conservatory. Water freely in full growth, sparingly in low temperatures. Cut back by up to two-thirds after flowering.
• PROPAGATION By seed in spring.

HEIGHT
2.5m (8ft)
or more

SPREAD
3m (10ft)

Celastraceae	

EUONYMUS HAMILTONIANUS subsp. SIEBOLDIANUS 'Red Elf'

Habit Upright, sometimes tree-like. *Flowers* Tiny, inconspicuous, in early summer. Green.
Fruits 4-lobed. Deep pink, splitting to reveal red seeds in autumn. *Leaves* Deciduous, oblong, pointed. Dull green, turning rusty red in autumn.
• NATIVE HABITAT Garden origin.
• CULTIVATION Grow in any fertile soil, especially chalk. Plant two or more specimens for reliable fruiting.
• PROPAGATION By semi-ripe cuttings in summer.

HEIGHT
3m (10ft)

SPREAD
3m (10ft)

Celastraceae	

EUONYMUS EUROPAEUS 'Red Cascade' ♥

Habit Bushy, sometimes tree-like. *Flowers* Tiny, inconspicuous, in early summer. Green.
Fruits 4-lobed. Rosy-red, splitting to reveal orange seeds in autumn. *Leaves* Deciduous, narrowly oval. Mid-green, turning scarlet-red in autumn.
• NATIVE HABITAT Garden origin.
• CULTIVATION Tolerates light shade but fruiting and autumn colour are best in sun. Grow in any fertile soil, especially chalk. Plant two or more specimens for reliable fruiting.
• PROPAGATION By semi-ripe cuttings in summer.

HEIGHT
2.5–3m
(8–10ft)

SPREAD
2.5–3m
(8–10ft)

Celastraceae	

EUONYMUS LATIFOLIUS

Habit Open, upright then arching. *Flowers* Tiny, inconspicuous, in early summer. Pale green.
Fruits Large, 4-lobed. Dark red, splitting to reveal orange seeds in autumn. *Leaves* Deciduous, elliptic. Deep green, brilliant scarlet in autumn.
• NATIVE HABITAT Occurs in woodland on cliffs and in hillside scrub from S. Europe to Asia Minor.
• CULTIVATION Fruiting and autumn colour are best in sun. Grow in any fertile soil, especially chalk. Plant two or more specimens for reliable fruiting.
• PROPAGATION By semi-ripe cuttings in summer.

HEIGHT
3m (10ft)

SPREAD
3m (10ft)

Caprifoliaceae	

VIBURNUM BETULIFOLIUM

Habit Multi-stemmed, upright then arching.
Flowers Small, in compact heads in early summer.
White. *Fruits* Berries, in profusion in autumn–winter. Glossy bright red. *Leaves* Deciduous, birch-like. Glossy bright green.
• NATIVE HABITAT In scrub of W. and C. China.
• CULTIVATION Grow in any deep, fertile soil that is not too dry. Plant several specimens to ensure good fruiting. Thin out old shoots after flowering.
• PROPAGATION By softwood cuttings in summer or by seed in autumn.

HEIGHT
3m (10ft)

SPREAD
2.5–3m
(8–10ft)

Aitoniaceae (Meliaceae)	CHINESE LANTERNS, KLAPPERBOS

NYMANIA CAPENSIS

Habit Rounded, rigidly branched, tree-like with age. *Flowers* Bell-shaped, with erect petals in spring. Rose-pink. *Fruits* Papery, inflated, lantern-like, in autumn. Crimson-red. *Leaves* Evergreen, narrow, leathery, in tufts.
• NATIVE HABITAT Arid, semi-desert of S. Africa.
• CULTIVATION Grow in a fertile, freely draining soil or compost. Water carefully and moderately when in growth, otherwise sparingly.
• PROPAGATION By seed in spring or by semi-ripe cuttings in summer.

HEIGHT
To 3m
(10ft)

SPREAD
1.5–2m
(5–6ft)

Celastraceae	WINGED SPINDLE

EUONYMUS ALATUS   ♈

Habit Dense; horizontally branched shoots have corky wings. *Flowers* Inconspicuous, in summer. Pale green. *Fruits* Small, 4-lobed. Purple and red, splitting to reveal orange seeds in autumn.
Leaves Deciduous, oval to elliptic. Deep green, turning brilliant crimson in autumn.
• NATIVE HABITAT Woodland and scrub of China and Japan.
• CULTIVATION Tolerates shade, but fruiting and autumn colour are best in sun. Grow in fertile soil.
• PROPAGATION By semi-ripe cuttings in summer.

HEIGHT
To 2m (6ft)

SPREAD
3m (10ft)

Cornaceae	

CORNUS ALBA 'Kesselringii'

Habit Vigorous, upright. *Flowers* Small, in late spring–early summer. Creamy-white. *Fruits* Small, round, berry-like. White. *Leaves* Deciduous, oval to elliptic. Dark green, reddish-purple in autumn.
Bark Winter stems are dark black-purple.
• NATIVE HABITAT Garden origin.
• CULTIVATION For good winter stem colour cut back almost to ground level annually in early spring.
• PROPAGATION By softwood cuttings in summer or by hardwood cuttings in autumn or winter.

HEIGHT
To 2m (6ft)

SPREAD
2–2.5m
(6–8ft)

Verbenaceae	

CALLICARPA BODINIERI var. GIRALDII

Habit Rounded, bushy. **Flowers** Tiny, in clusters in mid-summer. Lilac. **Fruits** Small, bead-like, shining berries in clusters from early autumn. Violet. **Leaves** Deciduous, elliptic to lance-shaped, pointed. Pale green, bronze tinted when young.
• NATIVE HABITAT Woodland and scrub of C. and W. China.
• CULTIVATION Fruits more freely when several plants are grown together. Grow in any fertile soil.
• PROPAGATION By softwood cuttings in summer.

HEIGHT
2m (6ft)

SPREAD
2m (6ft)

Verbenaceae	GLORY FLOWER

CLERODENDRUM BUNGEI

Habit Upright, suckering, semi-woody.
Flowers Small, fragrant, bell-shaped, in domed clusters in late summer and early autumn. Deep pink to red-purple. **Leaves** Deciduous, malodorous, heart-shaped, coarsely serrated. Mid-green.
• NATIVE HABITAT Scrub and woodland of China.
• CULTIVATION Grow in humus-rich soil. Shelter from cold winds and late frosts. Thin out in spring.
• PROPAGATION By seed or by softwood cuttings in spring, by semi-ripe cuttings in summer, or by rooted suckers in autumn or spring.

HEIGHT
2m (6ft)

SPREAD
2m (6ft)

Rhamnaceae	

CEANOTHUS 'Autumnal Blue'

Habit Vigorous, bushy. **Flowers** Tiny, in large, loose panicles in late spring and in summer to autumn. Rich sky-blue. **Leaves** Evergreen, broadly oval. Glossy bright green.
• NATIVE HABITAT Garden origin.
• CULTIVATION Tolerant of some lime in the soil and of coastal conditions. Grow in a warm, sunny, and sheltered site, in a light, well-drained soil. Needs little pruning; side-shoots may be trimmed after flowering.
• PROPAGATION By semi-ripe cuttings in summer.

HEIGHT
3m (10ft)

SPREAD
3m (10ft)

Berberidaceae	

BERBERIS 'Barbarossa'

Habit Vigorous, arching. **Flowers** Small, in rounded panicles in late spring and early summer. Pale yellow. **Fruits** Small, globose berries in profusion from late summer. Orange-scarlet.
Leaves Semi-evergreen, narrowly oval. Dark green.
• NATIVE HABITAT Garden origin.
• CULTIVATION Tolerates light shade and any but waterlogged soils. Prefers humus-rich and fertile soil and blooms best in sun. May be cut back hard after flowering to rejuvenate.
• PROPAGATION By semi-ripe cuttings in summer.

HEIGHT
1.5–2m
(5–6ft)

SPREAD
2m (6ft)

Rutaceae	

ZANTHOXYLUM SIMULANS

Habit Bushy, spreading, spiny, tree-like with age.
Flowers Tiny, in late spring and early summer.
Greenish-yellow. **Fruits** Small, round berries, in
clusters from late summer. Orange-red.
Leaves Deciduous, aromatic, divided into 7–11
leaflets. Glossy bright green.
• NATIVE HABITAT Mountain scrub of China.
• CULTIVATION Tolerates semi-shade. Grow in
any fertile soil. Cut out dead wood as seen.
• PROPAGATION By seed in autumn or by root
cuttings in late winter.

HEIGHT
2–3m
(6–10ft)

SPREAD
2–3m
(6–10ft)

Rosaceae	

COTONEASTER SIMONSII ♥

Habit Upright. **Flowers** Small, shallowly cup-
shaped, in early summer. White. **Fruits** Small,
long-lasting berries from autumn to winter. Orange-
red. **Leaves** Semi-evergreen or deciduous, oval.
Glossy dark green.
• NATIVE HABITAT Hillside scrub of the Himalaya.
• CULTIVATION Tolerates some shade. Thrives
on most soils, including dry ones, but will not
tolerate waterlogging. Useful for hedging; clip in
late winter or early spring. Susceptible to fireblight.
• PROPAGATION By semi-ripe cuttings in summer.

HEIGHT
3m (10ft)

SPREAD
2m (6ft)

Labiatae	

COLQUHOUNIA COCCINEA ♥

Habit Upright, loose, open. **Flowers** Tubular, in
whorls in late summer and autumn. Orange-scarlet.
Leaves Evergreen or semi-evergreen, large,
aromatic, oval to heart-shaped, downy. Sage green.
• NATIVE HABITAT In scrub of the Himalaya.
• CULTIVATION Grow in well-drained soil in a
sunny site with shelter from cold winds and late
frosts. Thrives on a south- or west-facing wall. May
be cut back by frost but will regenerate from the
base. Provide a winter mulch.
• PROPAGATION By softwood cuttings in summer.

HEIGHT
To 3m
(10ft)

SPREAD
2–2.5m
(6–8ft)

Labiatae	LION'S EAR, WILD DAGGA

LEONOTIS OCYMIFOLIA

Habit Erect, sparsely branched.
Flowers Tubular, 2-lipped, in whorls in late
autumn and early winter. Bright orange-scarlet.
Leaves Semi-evergreen, lance-shaped, downy.
Blue-green.
• NATIVE HABITAT S. Africa.
• CULTIVATION Grow in a cool greenhouse or
conservatory. Water freely when in full growth,
otherwise sparingly. Cut back hard in early spring.
• PROPAGATION By greenwood cuttings in
summer or by seed in spring.

HEIGHT
1.5–2m
(5–6ft)

SPREAD
To 1.5m
(5ft)

Rosaceae	

PYRACANTHA 'Golden Charmer'

Habit Vigorous, dense, arching, spiny.
Flowers Small, shallowly cup-shaped, in clusters
in early summer. White. *Fruits* Large berries, in
early autumn. Bright orange. *Leaves* Evergreen,
narrowly oval. Glossy bright green.
• NATIVE HABITAT Garden origin.
• CULTIVATION Grow in any fertile soil. Suitable
for a north or east wall, but flowers and fruits best in
sun. Train and clip back wall-grown plants after
flowering.
• PROPAGATION By semi-ripe cuttings in summer.

HEIGHT
3m (10ft)

SPREAD
3m (10ft)

Rosaceae	

COTONEASTER STERNIANUS

Habit Arching, graceful. *Flowers* Small, in early
summer. White, pink-tinted. *Fruits* Large, almost
round berries, in profusion in early autumn.
Orange-red. *Leaves* Evergreen or semi-evergreen,
small, oval. Grey-green, white beneath.
• NATIVE HABITAT Hillside scrub of the Himalaya.
• CULTIVATION Tolerates some shade. Thrives
on most soils, including dry ones, but will not
tolerate waterlogging. Good for hedging.
• PROPAGATION By semi-ripe cuttings in summer.
• OTHER NAMES *C. franchettii* var. *sternianus.*

HEIGHT
3m (10ft)

SPREAD
3m (10ft)

Rosaceae	

PYRACANTHA 'Golden Dome'

Habit Dense, mound-forming, spiny.
Flowers Small, shallowly cup-shaped, in clusters
in early summer. White. *Fruits* Large berries, in
profusion in early autumn. Deep yellow.
Leaves Evergreen, narrowly oval. Glossy dark
green.
• NATIVE HABITAT Garden origin.
• CULTIVATION Grow in fertile soil. Suitable for a
north or east wall, but flowers and fruits best in sun.
Train and clip back wall plants after flowering.
• PROPAGATION By semi-ripe cuttings in summer.

HEIGHT
3m (10ft)

SPREAD
3m (10ft)

Rosaceae	

RUBUS BIFLORUS

Habit Upright, then arching, prickly.
Flowers Large, in late spring and early summer.
Pure white. **Fruits** Round, blackberry-like, edible.
Yellow. **Leaves** Deciduous, 5–7 lobed. Dark green,
white beneath. **Bark** Canes are chalk-white with a
waxy bloom.
• NATIVE HABITAT Scrub and woodland edge of
the Himalaya.
• CULTIVATION Grow in any fertile soil in sun or
partial shade.
• PROPAGATION By division or by layering in spring.

HEIGHT
3m (10ft)

SPREAD
3m (10ft)

Caprifoliaceae	

VIBURNUM FOETENS

Habit Open, spreading. **Flowers** Very fragrant,
opening from dense clusters of buds from mid-
winter to early spring. White, pink in bud.
Leaves Deciduous, large, aromatic, broadly oval,
smooth. Dark green.
• NATIVE HABITAT Understorey of coniferous
forest in the Himalaya of Kashmir and in Korea.
• CULTIVATION Grow in deep, fertile soil that is
not allowed to dry out during the growing season.
• PROPAGATION By softwood cuttings in summer
or by seed in autumn.

HEIGHT
1.5–2m
(5–6ft)

SPREAD
1.5–2m
(5–6ft)

Rosaceae	GHOST BRAMBLE

RUBUS THIBETANUS

Habit Arching, prickly. **Flowers** Small, with a
woolly calyx, from mid- to late summer. Pink-
purple. **Fruits** Small, blackberry-like. Black, blue-
bloomed. **Leaves** Deciduous, fern-like, divided
into 7–13 leaflets. Dark green, white beneath.
Bark Brown-purple canes covered in a waxy,
white bloom.
• NATIVE HABITAT Scrub, woodland of W. China.
• CULTIVATION Grow in any fertile soil, in sun or
partial shade.
• PROPAGATION By division or by layering in spring.

HEIGHT
2m (6ft)

SPREAD
2m (6ft)

Caprifoliaceae	LAURUSTINUS

VIBURNUM TINUS

Habit Dense, bushy. **Flowers** Small, in flat
heads, opening from buds from late autumn to early
spring. White, pink in bud. **Fruits** Oval, berry-like.
Metallic blue-black. **Leaves** Evergreen, oval.
Glossy dark green.
• NATIVE HABITAT Scrub, woodland, and coastal
garrigue around the Mediterranean and S.E. Europe.
• CULTIVATION Grow in any deep, fertile soil that
is not too dry. Provide shelter from cold winds in
inland gardens. Excellent for coastal gardens.
• PROPAGATION By semi-ripe cuttings in summer.

HEIGHT
3m (10ft)

SPREAD
3m (10ft)

Myrtaceae	GERALDTON WAXFLOWER

CHAMELAUCIUM UNCINATUM
(white form)

Habit Bushy, with wiry stems. *Flowers* Slightly fragrant, cup-shaped, in late winter or spring. White. *Leaves* Evergreen, needle-like, with hooked tips.
• NATIVE HABITAT On gravelly or sandy soils of S.W. Australia.
• CULTIVATION Grow in either a greenhouse or a conservatory in a very free-draining sandy, neutral to acid soil or compost. Water moderately when in growth, otherwise sparingly. Maintain good ventilation. To maintain a compact habit, especially when grown in a container, cut back flowered stems by up to half immediately after flowering. The shrub makes a beautiful specimen plant.
• PROPAGATION By seed in spring or by semi-ripe cuttings in summer.

☼ ◊ pH

Min. 5°C
(41°F)

HEIGHT
To 2m (6ft)

SPREAD
2m (6ft)

Leguminosae	POWDER PUFF TREE

CALLIANDRA HAEMATOCEPHALA (white form)

Habit Spreading, tree-like with age.
Flowers Large, powder-puff heads consist of tiny florets with long white stamens, carried from late autumn to spring. *Leaves* Evergreen, divided, with 16–24 narrowly oval leaflets. Bright green.
• NATIVE HABITAT Dry, rocky hills of S. America.
• CULTIVATION Grow in a conservatory or greenhouse. Water freely when in full growth, much less in low temperatures.
• PROPAGATION By seed in spring.

Min. 7°C (45°F)

HEIGHT 2.5m (8ft) or more

SPREAD 3m (10ft)

Sterculiaceae	

DOMBEYA BURGESSIAE

Habit Bushy, dense. *Flowers* Fragrant, in dense, rounded clusters in autumn and winter. White, veined pink or red. *Leaves* Evergreen, rounded, 3-lobed, downy. Mid-green.
• NATIVE HABITAT C. and S. Africa.
• CULTIVATION Grow in a conservatory or greenhouse. Shade from hot summer sun. Grow in a fertile, sandy soil or compost. Water freely in growth.
• PROPAGATION By seed in spring or by semi-ripe cuttings in summer.
• OTHER NAMES *D. mastersii.*

Min. 5°C (41°F)

HEIGHT 2m (6ft)

SPREAD 2m (6ft)

Apocynaceae	WINTERSWEET, POISON ARROW PLANT

ACOKANTHERA OBLONGIFOLIA

Habit Rounded, dense. *Flowers* Fragrant, small, in crowded clusters in late winter or spring. White or pink. *Fruits* Plum-like, highly toxic. Black. *Leaves* Evergreen, elliptic, leathery. Dark green.
• NATIVE HABITAT S. Africa.
• CULTIVATION Grow in a warm conservatory or greenhouse. Water potted specimens moderately when in growth, otherwise sparingly.
• PROPAGATION By seed in autumn or spring or by semi-ripe cuttings in summer.
• OTHER NAMES *A. spectabilis, Carissa spectabilis.*

Min.10°C (50°F)

HEIGHT 2m (6ft)

SPREAD 2m (6ft)

Thymelaeaceae	

DAPHNE BHOLUA

Habit Upright. *Flowers* Strongly fragrant, tubular with 4 spreading lobes, in terminal clusters in late winter. White and purplish-pink, opening from deep pink-purple buds. *Leaves* Evergreen or deciduous, lance-shaped, leathery. Dark green.
• NATIVE HABITAT In scrub and rhododendron forest of the Himalaya.
• CULTIVATION Grow in a warm, sheltered site in fertile soil that is not too dry.
• PROPAGATION By seed in spring or by semi-ripe cuttings in summer.

HEIGHT To 3m (10ft)

SPREAD 2m (6ft) or more

Myrtaceae	GERALDTON WAXFLOWER

CHAMELAUCIUM UNCINATUM (pink form)

Habit Bushy, with wiry stems. *Flowers* Slightly fragrant, in late winter or spring. Rose-purple to pink. *Leaves* Evergreen, needle-like, with hooked tips.
• NATIVE HABITAT Gravelly soils, S.W. Australia.
• CULTIVATION Grow under cover in a sandy, neutral to acid soil or compost. Water moderately when in growth, otherwise sparingly.
• PROPAGATION By seed in spring or by semi-ripe cuttings in summer.

☼ ◊ pH

Min. 5°C (41°F)

HEIGHT
To 2m (6ft)

SPREAD
2m (6ft)

Euphorbiaceae	POINSETTIA, CHRISTMAS STAR

EUPHORBIA PULCHERRIMA

Habit Open, sparingly branched. *Flowers* Tiny, in late autumn to spring. Greenish-red, with large, showy, bright red, pink, yellow, or white bracts. *Leaves* Evergreen, lance-shaped to oval-elliptic. Bright or dark green.
• NATIVE HABITAT W. Mexico.
• CULTIVATION Grow in the home or conservatory in a fertile, humus-rich soil or compost. Water moderately when in growth. Needs special light treatment to flower in UK.
• PROPAGATION By stem tip cuttings in spring.

☼ ◊

Min. 15°C (59°F)

HEIGHT
To 3m (10ft)

SPREAD
2.5m (8ft)

Caprifoliaceae	

VIBURNUM × BODNANTENSE 'Dawn' ♧

Habit Vigorous, strongly upright, dense. *Flowers* Small, very fragrant, tubular, in rounded clusters from late autumn to early spring. Clear pink, deep pink in bud. *Leaves* Deciduous, oval. Dark green, bronze when young and in autumn.
• NATIVE HABITAT Garden origin.
• CULTIVATION Grow in any deep, fertile soil that is not too dry. To relieve overcrowding thin out old shoots after flowering, cutting back to the base. The flowers are very resistant to frost.
• PROPAGATION By softwood cuttings in summer.

☼ ◊
❀ ❀ ❀

HEIGHT
3m (10ft)

SPREAD
3m (10ft)

Cornaceae	SIBERIAN DOGWOOD

CORNUS ALBA 'Sibirica' ♧

Habit Upright. *Flowers* Small clusters in late spring and early summer. Creamy-white. *Fruits* Small, berry-like. White. *Leaves* Deciduous, oval to elliptic. Dark green. *Bark* Young stems are bright coral-red in winter.
• NATIVE HABITAT Garden origin.
• CULTIVATION Grow in any soil. For bright winter stems cut back annually in early spring almost to ground level.
• PROPAGATION By softwood cuttings in summer or by hardwood cuttings in autumn or winter.

☼ ◊
❀ ❀ ❀

HEIGHT
To 2m (6ft)

SPREAD
2–2.5m (6–8ft)

Myrsinaceae	CORAL BERRY, SPICEBERRY

ARDISIA CRENATA

Habit Upright, open. **Flowers** Small, fragrant, star-shaped, in clusters in early summer. White. **Fruits** Round, berry-like, in profusion from autumn to winter. Bright red. **Leaves** Evergreen, elliptic to lance-shaped, crisped margins. Dark green.
• NATIVE HABITAT Forests of Japan to N. India.
• CULTIVATION Grow in the home or conservatory in moist but well-drained, humus-rich soil or compost.
• PROPAGATION By seed in spring or by semi-ripe cuttings in summer.
• OTHER NAMES *A. crenulata*.

Min. 7°C (45°F)

HEIGHT To 2m (6ft)

SPREAD 2m (6ft)

Solanaceae	

IOCHROMA CYANEA

Habit Semi-upright with slender branches. **Flowers** Tubular, in dense clusters intermittently from late autumn to the following summer. Deep blue-purple. **Leaves** Evergreen, broadly lance-shaped, pointed. Downy grey-green.
• NATIVE HABITAT Cloud forests of S. America.
• CULTIVATION Grow in the home or conservatory in fertile, well-drained soil or compost.
• PROPAGATION By greenwood or by semi-ripe cuttings in summer.
• OTHER NAMES *I. tubulosa*.

Min. 7–10°C (45–50°F)

HEIGHT To 3m (10ft)

SPREAD 1.5m (5ft)

Stachyuraceae	

STACHYURUS PRAECOX

Habit Open, arching with slender shoots. **Flowers** Tiny, bell-shaped, in pendent spikes, on bare branches in late winter and early spring. Pale yellow-green. **Leaves** Deciduous, oval to lance-shaped, pointed. Dark green. **Bark** Shoots are red-purple.
• NATIVE HABITAT Scrub, open woodland, and forest edge of Honshu, Japan.
• CULTIVATION Tolerates sun if soil is reliably moist. Prefers neutral to acid, humus-rich soil.
• PROPAGATION By softwood cuttings in summer.

HEIGHT To 2m (6ft)

SPREAD 3m (10ft)

Hamamelidaceae	

HAMAMELIS × INTERMEDIA 'Pallida'

Habit Open, spreading. **Flowers** Fragrant, spidery, with narrow petals, on bare branches, from mid- to late winter. Pale yellow.
Leaves Deciduous, broadly oval. Dark green, yellow in autumn.
• NATIVE HABITAT Garden origin.
• CULTIVATION Thrives in sun or semi-shade in fertile, well-drained, peaty soil. Provide shelter from cold winter winds. This, and other cultivars of *Hamamelis × intermedia*, are exceptionally attractive when grown in open glades in a woodland setting.

Hamamelis × intermedia 'Pallida' is the palest flowered cultivar, and is notable for its sweet, delicate fragrance. Although the flowers last well in water, and are tempting for flower arrangers, *H. × intermedia* and its cultivars regenerate slowly after cutting. Pruning is best kept to a minimum: only removing dead, diseased, and damaged growth and any badly placed or crossed branches.
• PROPAGATION By softwood cuttings in summer, by budding in late summer, or by grafting in winter.

HEIGHT
3m (10ft)

SPREAD
3m (10ft)

Berberidaceae	

MAHONIA JAPONICA

Habit Vigorous, dense, upright.
Flowers Fragrant, in long, slender, pendulous racemes from late autumn to early spring. Soft lemon-yellow. **Leaves** Evergreen, large, divided into many spiny leaflets. Glossy dark grey-green.
• NATIVE HABITAT Native range obscure but probably from China and Taiwan.
• CULTIVATION Thrives in shade or semi-shade. Grow in moist, fertile, humus-rich soil. The plant makes a beautiful specimen in a woodland garden or a shady shrub border, and is much valued for its

fragrant winter flowers that last well in water when used for flower arrangements. It is indispensable in the winter garden, as its architectural foliage and stiff, upright habit provide year-round interest. Other than the removal of dead wood, it requires little pruning. Indeed, pruning is undesirable, since the plant's beautiful form is best left to develop unchecked.
• PROPAGATION By leaf bud or semi-ripe cuttings in summer or by seed in autumn.

HEIGHT
2m (6ft) or more

SPREAD
3m (10ft)

Rutaceae	CALAMONDIN, PANAMA ORANGE

× CITROFORTUNELLA MICROCARPA

Habit Bushy, tree-like with age. *Flowers* Tiny, fragrant, waxy, intermittently through the year. White. *Fruits* Small. Orange-yellow. *Leaves* Evergreen, elliptic to broadly oval. Glossy dark green.
• NATIVE HABITAT Garden origin.
• CULTIVATION Grow in a fertile, freely draining soil or compost. Water freely when in growth, otherwise moderately.
• PROPAGATION By greenwood or semi-ripe cuttings in summer.
• OTHER NAMES × *C. mitis*, *Citrus mitis*.

Min.
5–10°C
(41–50°F)

HEIGHT
2m (6ft)

SPREAD
1.5m (5ft)

Calycanthaceae	WINTERSWEET

CHIMONANTHUS PRAECOX

Habit Bushy. *Flowers* Small, very fragrant, cup-shaped, many-petalled, waxy, on bare branches in winter. Pale yellow, with purple centres. Produced only on established plants. *Leaves* Deciduous, oval, rough. Dark green.
• NATIVE HABITAT Mountain scrub of China.
• CULTIVATION Grow in deep, fertile soil with the shelter of a warm south- or west-facing wall. Prune immediately after flowering if necessary.
• PROPAGATION By seed in late spring or by softwood cuttings in summer.

HEIGHT
2.5m (8ft)
or more

SPREAD
3m (10ft)

Oleaceae	WINTER JASMINE

JASMINUM NUDIFLORUM

Habit Arching, spreading, mound-forming. *Flowers* Small, tubular with spreading lobes, carried on leafless green shoots in winter and early spring. Bright yellow. *Leaves* Deciduous, oval. Dark green.
• NATIVE HABITAT Unknown.
• CULTIVATION. Tolerates semi-shade but flowers best in sun. Grow in any fertile soils, including dry ones. Requires support if grown on a wall. Prune to shape after flowering.
• PROPAGATION By semi-ripe cuttings in summer or by layering in autumn.

HEIGHT
To 3m
(10ft)

SPREAD
3m (10ft)

HOLLIES

Hollies (*Ilex*) are a genus of evergreen or deciduous trees and shrubs of woodland, forest, and hedgerow occurring in both temperate and tropical regions. Most hollies are tolerant of urban pollution and coastal conditions, and can be hard pruned. They are much valued for their foliage and their mainly spherical berries, which follow the insignificant flowers of spring. Many make handsome specimen plants, and the smaller types are suitable for the rock garden or pot cultivation. The taller and most vigorous forms make good wind-resistant hedging. Grow in any moderately fertile, well-drained soil, in sun or shade. Most plants are unisexual, so to achieve fruits on female plants males must also be grown. Hollies resent transplanting.

I. CILIOSPINOSA
Habit Upright.
Fruits Small, spherical berries. Red.
Leaves Small, neat, elliptic-oval, weakly spined, leathery. Dull dark green.
• CULTIVATION Grows equally well in sun or shade.
• HEIGHT 4–6m (20ft).
• SPREAD 4–6m (20ft).

I. ciliospinosa

☼ ◐ ❀❀❀

I. × KOEHNEANA
Habit Conical, shrubby, or small tree with age.
Fruits Large berries. Red. **Leaves** Large, oblong-elliptic, spiny. Glossy mid-green.
Stems Young branches are purple.
• OTHER NAMES *I. aquifolium × I. latifolia.*
• HEIGHT To 8m (25ft).
• SPREAD 5m (15ft).

I. × koehneana

☼ ◐ ❀❀❀

I. × AQUIPERNYI
Habit Upright.
Fruits Large berries. Red. **Leaves** Triangular, but rounded at the base, with long tips, and slightly wavy spines. Glossy dark green.
• OTHER NAMES *I. aquifolium × I. pernyi.*
• HEIGHT 5m (15ft).
• SPREAD 3m (10ft).

I. × aquipernyi

☼ ◐ ❀❀❀

I. CORNUTA 'Burfordii'
Habit Compact, dense, rounded. **Fruits** Large berries. Red, free-fruiting.
Leaves Rounded-oblong, with a single, terminal spine. Shiny, bright green.
• CULTIVATION May be used for hedging.
• HEIGHT To 4m (12ft).
• SPREAD 2.5m (8ft).

I. cornuta 'Burfordii'
FEMALE

☼ ◐ ❀❀❀

I. PERNYI
Habit Slow-growing, stiff. **Fruits** Small berries. Bright red.
Leaves Almost triangular, pointed, with 5 spines. Glossy dark green. **Stems** Young branches are pale green.
• CULTIVATION Makes an interesting and very beautiful specimen.
• HEIGHT To 8m (25ft).
• SPREAD 4m (12ft).

I. pernyi

☼ ◐ ❀❀❀

I. FARGESII var. *BREVIFOLIA*
Habit Dense, rounded, shrubby. **Fruits** Small berries. Red.
Leaves Smaller than the species, elliptic to elliptic-lance-shaped. Dull mid- to dark green.
Stems Shoots are green or purple.
• HEIGHT 4m (12ft).
• SPREAD 4m (12ft).

I. fargesii var. *brevifolia*

☼ ◐ ❀❀❀

I. CRENATA 'Latifolia'

Habit Vigorous, spreading to erect, may be tree-like with age. **Fruits** Small, glossy berries. Black. **Leaves** Relatively large, broadly oval. Glossy dark green. **Stems** Green.
• OTHER NAMES *I. crenata* f. *latifolia*.
• HEIGHT To 6m (20ft).
• SPREAD 3m (10ft).

I. crenata 'Latifolia'
FEMALE

☼ ◊ ❀ ❀ ❀

I. CRENATA 'Convexa'

Habit Bushy, compact, dense. **Fruits** Small berries, free-fruiting. Black. **Leaves** Small, oval-elliptic, puckered or convex between veins. Glossy dark green. **Stems** Purplish-green.
• OTHER NAMES *I. crenata* 'Bullata'.
• HEIGHT To 2.5m (8ft).
• SPREAD 1.2–1.5m (4–5ft).

I. crenata 'Convexa'
FEMALE

☼ ◊ ❀ ❀ ❀   ♈

I. CRENATA var. *PALUDOSA*

Habit Dense, low-growing, prostrate. **Fruits** Small, glossy berries. Black. **Leaves** Very small, oval, with rounded teeth. Glossy dark green.
• OTHER NAMES *I. radicans*.
• HEIGHT 15–30cm (6–12in).
• SPREAD indefinite.

I. crenata var. *paludosa*

☼ ◊ ❀ ❀ ❀

I. CRENATA 'Helleri'

Habit Low, dense, mound-forming, spreading. **Fruits** Small, glossy berries. Black. **Leaves** Very small, elliptic, with few spines. Glossy dark green. **Bark** Young stems are green.
• CULTIVATION Suitable for a rock garden.
• HEIGHT To 1.2m (4ft).
• SPREAD 1–1.2m (3–4ft).

I. crenata 'Helleri'
FEMALE

☼ ◊ ❀ ❀ ❀

I. x *MESERVEAE* 'Blue Princess'

Habit Vigorous, dense. **Fruits** Berries, usually in profusion. Red. **Leaves** Small, oval, wavy, softly spiny. Glossy greenish-blue. **Stems** Young branches are purplish-green.
• CULTIVATION Fully hardy but does not always thrive in maritime climate.
• HEIGHT 3m (10ft).
• SPREAD 1.2m (4ft).

I. x *meserveae* 'Blue Princess'
FEMALE

☼ ◊ ❀ ❀ ❀   ♈

I. VERTICILLATA

Habit Dense, suckering. **Fruits** Small berries, long-lasting on bare branches in winter. Bright red. **Leaves** Deciduous, oval to lance-shaped, saw-toothed. Bright green, yellow in autumn. **Stems** Young shoots purplish-green.
• OTHER NAMES *Prinos verticillatus*.
• HEIGHT 1–5m (3–15ft).
• SPREAD 2–5m (6–15ft).

I. verticillata

☼ ◐ pH ❀ ❀ ❀

I. CRENATA 'Variegata'

Habit Open, shy-flowering. **Leaves** Oval. Green, irregularly spotted or blotched with golden-yellow.
• CULTIVATION Good as a specimen but tends to revert to plain green.
• OTHER NAMES *I. crenata* 'Aureovariegata', *I. crenata* 'Luteovariegata'.
• HEIGHT 4m (12ft).
• SPREAD 2.5m (8ft).

I. crenata 'Variegata'

☼ ◊ ❀ ❀ ❀

I. SERRATA 'Leucocarpa'

Habit Densely branched, slow-growing. **Fruits** Tiny berries, on bare shoots. Creamy-white. **Leaves** Deciduous, small, elliptic, finely toothed. Bright green, downy when young.
• OTHER NAMES *I. serrata* f. *leucocarpa*.
• HEIGHT 4m (12ft).
• SPREAD 2.5m (8ft).

I. serrata 'Leucocarpa'

☼ ◐ pH ❀ ❀ ❀

Celastraceae	

EUONYMUS JAPONICUS 'Latifolius Albomarginatus'

Habit Bushy, dense, upright.
Flowers Insignificant, in spring. Greenish-white.
Leaves Evergreen, oval. Dark green, broadly edged with white.
• NATIVE HABITAT Garden origin.
• CULTIVATION Tolerant of urban pollution, coastal conditions, and semi-shade. Grow in any moderately fertile soil, especially chalk, and provide shelter from cold, drying winter winds.
• PROPAGATION By semi-ripe cuttings in summer.

HEIGHT
3m (10ft) or more

SPREAD
3m (10ft)

Celastraceae	

EUONYMUS FORTUNEI 'Silver Queen'

Habit Bushy, compact, upright or scrambling-climbing with aerial roots. **Flowers** Insignificant, in spring. Greenish-white. **Leaves** Evergreen, variable, oval to elliptic. Dark green, broadly edged with white, sometimes pink-tinged.
• NATIVE HABITAT Species occurs in China, Japan, and Korea. Garden origin.
• CULTIVATION Tolerates sun or shade and almost any fertile soil, including chalk. Grow as ground cover or as a self-clinging climber.
• PROPAGATION By semi-ripe cuttings in summer.

HEIGHT
2m (6ft) or more

SPREAD
1–1.5m (3–5ft)

Dracaenaceae	BELGIAN EVERGREEN

DRACAENA SANDERIANA

Habit Slow-growing, erect, sparsely branched, with slender, cane-like stems. **Leaves** Evergreen, lance-shaped. Pale to grey-green with silver-white edges.
• NATIVE HABITAT Tropical E. Africa.
• CULTIVATION Grow in the home or conservatory. Tolerates partial shade. Water moderately when in growth, otherwise sparingly, especially when temperatures are low. Rejuvenate by cutting back near to soil level in spring.
• PROPAGATION By air-layering in spring or by tip or stem cuttings in summer.

Min. 13°C (55°F)

HEIGHT
1.5–2m (5–6ft)

SPREAD
1.5m (5ft)

Araliaceae	JAPANESE FATSIA, GLOSSY-LEAVED PAPER PLANT

FATSIA JAPONICA 'Variegata'

Habit Rounded, bushy, dense. **Flowers** Tiny, in broad, upright panicles in autumn. White.
Fruits Small, round, berry-like, in clusters, ripening in spring. Black. **Leaves** Evergreen, palmate. Glossy dark green, margined creamy-white.
• NATIVE HABITAT Species occurs in coastal woodland of Japan and S. Korea. Garden origin.
• CULTIVATION Tolerates semi-shade, pollution, and maritime conditions. Grow in any fertile soil and provide shelter from winds in cold areas.
• PROPAGATION By semi-ripe cuttings in summer.

HEIGHT
3m (10ft)

SPREAD
3m (10ft)

Berberidaceae	

NANDINA DOMESTICA 'Firepower'

Habit Upright, bamboo-like. *Flowers* Small, star-shaped, in wide panicles in summer. White. *Fruits* Small, round, berry-like in autumn. Bright red. *Leaves* Evergreen or semi-evergreen, divided into 2–3 elliptic to lance-shaped leaflets. Dark green, crimson when young and in autumn.
• NATIVE HABITAT Garden origin.
• CULTIVATION Grow in fertile, moist but well-drained soil in a sunny, sheltered site. When mature cut out untidy, old stems at the base.
• PROPAGATION By semi-ripe cuttings in summer.

HEIGHT
1.5m (5ft)

SPREAD
1.5m (5ft)

Sapindaceae	

DODONAEA VISCOSA 'Purpurea'

Habit Bushy, tree-like with age. *Flowers* Insignificant. *Fruits* Small, 3-winged capsules, in clusters in late summer. Reddish. *Leaves* Evergreen, resinous, elliptic, firm-textured. Flushed coppery-purple.
• NATIVE HABITAT Species occurs in S. Africa, Australia, and Mexico. Garden origin.
• CULTIVATION Grow in a conservatory. Water freely when in growth, otherwise moderately. Cut back in late summer to shape.
• PROPAGATION By semi-ripe cuttings in summer.

Min. 5°C
(41°F)

HEIGHT
2m (6ft)

SPREAD
1.5m (5ft)

Escalloniaceae	WIRE-NETTING BUSH

COROKIA COTONEASTER

Habit Bushy, open, with interlacing shoots. *Flowers* Tiny, fragrant, star-shaped, in late spring. Yellow. *Fruits* Small, round, berry-like, in autumn. Bright red. *Leaves* Evergreen, small, spoon-shaped. Dark green.
• NATIVE HABITAT Open woodland, New Zealand.
• CULTIVATION Grow in fertile, well-drained soil. Thrives in mild coastal gardens as it has good wind tolerance. In cold areas grow in a warm, sheltered position.
• PROPAGATION By softwood cuttings in summer.

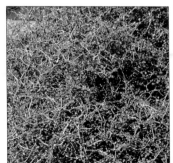

HEIGHT
To 2m (6ft)

SPREAD
2m (6ft)

Zamiaceae	

ENCEPHALARTOS FEROX

Habit Slow-growing, palm-like, developing a trunk with age. **Leaves** Evergreen, feather-shaped, 60–180cm (2–6ft) long, with many serrated and spine-tipped, leathery leaflets. Grey-green.

• NATIVE HABITAT Hot valleys and ravines of S. Africa.

• CULTIVATION Grow under glass in a freely draining, bark-based soil or compost with added leafmould and garden compost. Provide the plant with good light, but some shade, and ventilation, but take care to avoid draughts. Feed on a monthly basis with a dilute soluble fertilizer and water moderately when in growth, otherwise sparingly. *Encephalartos ferox* may take many years to form a trunk, but juvenile plants make interesting and attractive specimens for both the home or warm conservatory.

• PROPAGATION By seed in spring.

Min.
10–13°C
(50–55°F)

HEIGHT
To 1.7m
(5½ ft)

SPREAD
1.5m (5ft)

Ericaceae	GREEN MANZANITA

ARCTOSTAPHYLOS PATULA

Habit Rounded, multi-stemmed. *Flowers* Small, urn-shaped, in loose panicles from mid- to late spring. White or pale pink. *Fruits* Small, flattened-spherical. Dark brown. *Leaves* Evergreen, broadly oval, thick. Bright grey-green.
• NATIVE HABITAT Coniferous forests of the Sierra Nevada, California.
• CULTIVATION Provide shelter from cold winds and a fertile, humus-rich, acid soil.
• PROPAGATION By seed in autumn or by semi-ripe cuttings in summer.

HEIGHT
1–2m
(3–6ft)

SPREAD
To 2m (6ft)

Palmae/ Arecaceae	BAMBOO PALM, LADY PALM, GROUND RATTAN

RHAPIS EXCELSA

Habit Slender-stemmed, clump-forming with age. *Leaves* Evergreen, 20–30cm (8–12in) long, fan-shaped, divided into 20 or more narrow lobes. Glossy deep green.
• NATIVE HABITAT Warm forests of China.
• CULTIVATION Young plants make good specimens in the home or warm conservatory. Grow in a humus-rich soil or compost. Water plentifully when in growth. Mist regularly with soft water.
• PROPAGATION By seed, suckers, or division in spring.

Min. 15°C
(59°F)

HEIGHT
1.5–2m
(5–6ft) or
more

SPREAD
2m (6ft)

Moraceae	MISTLETOE FIG, MISTLETOE RUBBER PLANT

FICUS DELTOIDEA

Habit Slow-growing, bushy. *Flowers* Insignificant. *Fruits* Small, fig-like. Dull yellow to red when ripe. *Leaves* Evergreen, spatula-shaped to oval, lance-shaped in young plants. Bright green, reddish below.
• NATIVE HABITAT Sumatra to Borneo.
• CULTIVATION Grow in a warm conservatory. Tolerates semi-shade. Water moderately when in growth, otherwise sparingly.
• PROPAGATION By seed in spring or by leaf-bud, stem tip cuttings, or air-layering in summer.
• OTHER NAMES *F. diversifolia*.

Min.
15–18°C
(59–64°F)

HEIGHT
2m (6ft) or
more

SPREAD
1.5m (5ft)

Araceae	

PHILODENDRON BIPINNATIFIDUM

Habit Erect, unbranched, non-climbing habit, with aerial roots. *Flowers* Long spathes sometimes produced. Greenish-white. *Leaves* Evergreen, to 60cm (2ft) or more long, divided into 20 or more finger-like lobes. Glossy dark green.
• NATIVE HABITAT Tropical forests of S.E. Brazil.
• CULTIVATION Grow in the home or warm conservatory. Provide support. Water moderately when in growth, otherwise sparingly.
• PROPAGATION By leaf bud cuttings in summer.
• OTHER NAMES *P. selloum*.

Min.
15–18°C
(59–64°F)

HEIGHT
2m (6ft) or
more

SPREAD
2m (6ft)

Cycadaceae	JAPANESE SAGO PALM

CYCAS REVOLUTA

Habit Slow-growing, palm-like, may produce several trunks with age. *Fruits* Ovoid, in tight clusters in autumn. Yellowish. *Leaves* Evergreen, to 1.5m (5ft) long, feather-shaped, divided into many spine-tipped leaflets with rolled margins. Dark green.
• NATIVE HABITAT On open ground amongst scattered pines and on limestone cliffs of Japan.
• CULTIVATION Grow in pots in the home or a warm conservatory in open, fibrous, bark-based soil or compost. Water moderately when in growth,

otherwise sparingly. Provide good light and ventilation, but take care to avoid draughts. *C. revoluta* is very slow-growing, but the juvenile plants make interesting architectural specimens for well-lit homes and warm conservatories. Site carefully, however, to avoid brushing past and damaging the spine-tipped fronds.
• PROPAGATION By seed or suckers in spring.

☼ ◊

Min.7°C
(45°F)

HEIGHT
To 3m
(10ft)

SPREAD
3m (10ft)

Buxaceae	

BUXUS SEMPERVIRENS '**Handsworthiensis**'

Habit Vigorous, dense, upright, tree-like with age.
Flowers Tiny, without petals, in spring.
Leaves Evergreen, rounded to oblong, thick, leathery. Dark green.
• NATIVE HABITAT Species grows from S. Europe to N. Africa and S.W. Asia. Garden origin.
• CULTIVATION Tolerates semi-shade. Grow in any but waterlogged soil. An excellent hedging or screening plant; trim hedges in summer.
• PROPAGATION By semi-ripe cuttings in summer.

HEIGHT
3m (10ft)

SPREAD
3m (10ft)

Araliaceae	FERN-LEAF ARALIA

POLYSCIAS FILICIFOLIA

Habit Erect, sparsely branched.
Leaves Evergreen, 30cm (12in) long, divided into many small, serrated leaflets. Bright green.
• NATIVE HABITAT Humid tropics of E. Malaysia and W. Pacific.
• CULTIVATION Grow in the home or warm conservatory in a fertile, humus-rich soil or compost. Maintain humidity. Water plentifully when in growth, otherwise moderately.
• PROPAGATION By stem tip or leafless stem-section cuttings in summer.

Min.
15–18°C
(59–64°F)

HEIGHT
To 2m (6ft)

SPREAD
2m (6ft)

Aucubaceae	

AUCUBA JAPONICA

Habit Bushy, dense, rounded. *Flowers* Tiny, in mid-spring. Purplish. *Fruits* Small, rounded to egg-shaped berries on female plants. Bright red.
Leaves Evergreen, narrowly oval, toothed. Glossy dark green.
• NATIVE HABITAT Woodlands of Japan.
• CULTIVATION Tolerant of deep shade and any but waterlogged soils. Cut old shoots back hard in spring to restrict growth. Both male and female plants are required for good fruiting.
• PROPAGATION By semi-ripe cuttings in summer.

HEIGHT
2.5m (8ft)

SPREAD
2.5m (8ft)

Araliaceae	TREE IVY

X *FATSHEDERA LIZEI* ♀

Habit Loosely branched, mound-forming.
Flowers Small, in spherical heads in autumn. White. *Leaves* Evergreen, large, deeply lobed. Glossy dark green.
• NATIVE HABITAT Garden origin.
• CULTIVATION Tolerant of shade, coastal conditions, and urban pollution. Grow in any fertile soil. Provide shelter from winter wind in cold areas. May be trained as a climber if tied in to trellis or similar structures.
• PROPAGATION By semi-ripe cuttings in summer.

HEIGHT
1.2–2m
(4–6ft)

SPREAD
3m (10ft)

Portulacaceae	ELEPHANT BUSH

PORTULACARIA AFRA

Habit Upright, with horizontal branches.
Flowers Tiny, star-shaped, in clusters in late spring and summer. Pale pink. *Leaves* Semi-evergreen, small, oval to rounded, fleshy. Bright green.
• NATIVE HABITAT Dense thickets in hot, dry areas of S. African bush.
• CULTIVATION Grow in sandy, freely draining soil or compost. Water moderately when in growth, otherwise sparingly.
• PROPAGATION By semi-ripe cuttings in summer. Dry for 12–24 hours in a cool place before insertion.

☼ ◊

Min.
7–10°C
(45–50°F)

HEIGHT
To 3m
(10ft)

SPREAD
2m (6ft)

Palmae	DWARF MOUNTAIN PALM, PARLOUR PALM

CHAMAEDOREA ELEGANS

Habit Slender, with cane-like stems, suckering with age. *Leaves* Evergreen, feather-shaped, 60–100cm (2–3ft) long, with 12–20 leaflets. Glossy dark green.
• NATIVE HABITAT Rainforest understorey of S. Mexico and Guatemala.
• CULTIVATION Grow in the home or warm conservatory. Protect from direct sunlight. Grow in a fertile, humus-rich soil or compost. Water moderately when in growth, otherwise sparingly.
• PROPAGATION By seed in spring.
• OTHER NAMES *Neanthe bella*.

☼ ◊

Min. 18°C
(64°F)

HEIGHT
2m (6ft)

SPREAD
2m (6ft)

Agavaceae	SPANISH BAYONET, DAGGER PLANT

YUCCA ALOIFOLIA

Habit Slow-growing, upright, sparsely branched, tree-like with age. *Flowers* Large, rounded bell-shaped, pendent, in large panicles in summer to autumn. White, tinted purple. *Leaves* Evergreen, 50–75cm (20–30in) long, sword-shaped. Deep green.
• NATIVE HABITAT On sand dunes and dry hills of S.E. United States and the West Indies.
• CULTIVATION Tolerates poor soils. Water moderately when in growth, otherwise sparingly. In summer move potted plants outside.
• PROPAGATION By seed or suckers in spring.

☼ ◊

Min. 7°C
(45°F)

HEIGHT
2m (6ft) or more

SPREAD
2m (6ft)

Oleaceae	

LIGUSTRUM 'Vicaryi'

Habit Bushy, dense. *Flowers* Small, tubular, in dense racemes, in mid-summer. White.
Leaves Semi-evergreen, large, broadly oval. Golden-yellow, flushed bronze-purple in winter.
• NATIVE HABITAT Garden origin.
• CULTIVATION Thrives on any well-drained soil, including chalk. Requires little pruning, but will regenerate freely from old wood if cut back hard in mid-spring. An attractive specimen for the shrub border.
• PROPAGATION By semi-ripe cuttings in summer.

HEIGHT
3m (10ft)

SPREAD
3m(10ft)

Elaeagnaceae	

ELAEAGNUS × *EBBINGEI* 'Limelight'

Habit Vigorous, bushy, dense. *Flowers* Small, fragrant, urn-shaped, in autumn. White.
Leaves Evergreen, oval to oblong. Lustrous dark green with pale green and yellow central patch, silver beneath.
• NATIVE HABITAT Garden origin.
• CULTIVATION Given good drainage, it thrives in most fertile soils, except shallow chalk. Tolerates semi-shade. Prune out branches with all-green, mature leaves. Good for informal hedging.
• PROPAGATION By semi-ripe cuttings in summer.

HEIGHT
To 3m
(10ft)

SPREAD
3m (10ft)

Aucubaceae	

AUCUBA JAPONICA 'Crotonifolia' ♡

Habit Bushy, dense, rounded. *Flowers* Female, tiny, in mid-spring. Purplish. *Fruits* Small, rounded to egg-shaped berries. Bright red. *Leaves* Evergreen, large, oval. Glossy dark green, boldly splashed and mottled with golden-yellow.
• NATIVE HABITAT Garden origin.
• CULTIVATION Tolerates semi-shade but colours best in sun. Grows in any but waterlogged soil. Male plants are required for good fruiting by this female cultivar.
• PROPAGATION By semi-ripe cuttings in summer.

HEIGHT
2m (6ft) or
more

SPREAD
2m (6ft)

Salicaceae	

SALIX HASTATA 'Wehrhahnii'

Habit Slow-growing, spreading, with upright branches. **Flowers** Bright, male catkins on bare branches in early spring. Silver-grey.
Leaves Deciduous, oval. Bright green.
Bark Stems deep purple when young, later yellow.
• NATIVE HABITAT Garden origin. Species grows in damp places in the mountains of the Engadine, Switzerland.
• CULTIVATION Thrives in any moist soil. Needs little regular pruning, although larger catkins are

borne on young wood. Cut back older stems occasionally to stimulate the production of new wood. A beautiful specimen for the shrub border or larger rock garden. The early catkins are a valuable source of pollen for bees in spring.
• PROPAGATION By semi-ripe cuttings in summer or by hardwood cuttings in winter.

HEIGHT
1–1.5m
(3–5ft)

SPREAD
1–1.5m
(3–5ft)

Hydrangeaceae	

DEUTZIA GRACILIS

Habit Upright or spreading. *Flowers* 5 petals, in dense, upright clusters in late spring and early summer. Pure white. *Leaves* Deciduous, lance-shaped to oval, finely toothed. Bright green.
• NATIVE HABITAT Mountain scrub of Japan.
• CULTIVATION Tolerates almost any fertile, well-drained soil but grows best in humus-rich soils that do not dry out in summer. Thin out old, flowered shoots, cutting back to the base after flowering; flowers are more abundant on young wood.
• PROPAGATION By softwood cuttings in summer.

HEIGHT
To 1.5m
(5ft)

SPREAD
1–2m
(3–6ft)

Ericaceae	LABRADOR TEA

LEDUM GROENLANDICUM

Habit Erect, bushy. *Flowers* Small, in dense, rounded heads from mid-spring to early summer. White. *Leaves* Evergreen, aromatic, linear-oblong, with rolled margins, leathery. Dark green.
• NATIVE HABITAT Peat bogs and coniferous woodland of N. North America and Greenland.
• CULTIVATION Grow in woodland and bog gardens. Mulching with leafmould and dead-heading are beneficial.
• PROPAGATION By semi-ripe cuttings in summer or by seed in autumn.

HEIGHT
0.5–1.5m
(20in–5ft)

SPREAD
0.5–2m
(20in–6ft)

Rosaceae	

PRUNUS GLANDULOSA 'Alba Plena'

Habit Neat, open, with slender stems.
Flowers Large, double, in clusters along the shoots in late spring. Pure white.
Leaves Deciduous, narrowly oval. Mid-green.
• NATIVE HABITAT Garden origin. Species grows in scrub of C. and N. China and Japan.
• CULTIVATION Grow in any fertile, freely draining soil that is not too dry. Flowers best in a warm, sunny, sheltered position.
• PROPAGATION By softwood cuttings in summer.

HEIGHT
To 1.5m
(5ft)

SPREAD
1.5m (5ft)

Campanulaceae	

AZORINA VIDALII

Habit Upright sub-shrub. *Flowers* Large, bell-shaped, in racemes in spring and summer. White or pink. *Leaves* Evergreen, linear, coarsely serrated. Glossy dark green.
• NATIVE HABITAT The Azores.
• CULTIVATION Grow in a conservatory. Tolerates semi-shade. Water moderately when in full growth, otherwise sparingly. Dead-head after flowering.
• PROPAGATION By seed in spring or by softwood cuttings in spring or summer.
• OTHER NAMES *Campanula vidalii*.

Min. 5°C
(40°F)

HEIGHT
50cm (20in)

SPREAD
50cm (20in)

Rosaceae	BRIDAL WREATH

SPIRAEA × VANHOUTTEI ♟

Habit Vigorous, compact, with slender, arching shoots. **Flowers** Small, in dense clusters, all along the shoots in late spring and early summer. Pure white. **Leaves** Deciduous, diamond-shaped. Dark green.
• NATIVE HABITAT Garden origin.
• CULTIVATION Grow in any moderately fertile soil that does not dry out too much during the growing season. Prune after flowering to remove older, flowered wood.
• PROPAGATION By softwood cuttings in summer.

☼ ◊
❀ ❀ ❀

HEIGHT
1.5m (5ft)

SPREAD
1.5m (5ft)

Rosaceae	CHERRY LAUREL

PRUNUS LAUROCERASUS 'Zabeliana'

Habit Open, horizontally branching. **Flowers** Small, in slender spikes in late spring. White. **Fruits** Small, cherry-like. Red, then black. **Leaves** Evergreen, long, narrow. Glossy dark green. All parts are harmful if eaten.
• NATIVE HABITAT Garden origin.
• CULTIVATION Extremely tolerant of shade. Grows in almost any soil except waterlogged or shallow chalk soils. Cut back hard in spring if necessary to restrict growth. Good for ground cover.
• PROPAGATION By semi-ripe cuttings in summer.

☼ ◊
❀ ❀ ❀

HEIGHT
1m (3ft)

SPREAD
2.5m (8ft)

Rosaceae	

PRUNUS LAUROCERASUS 'Otto Luyken' ♟

Habit Dense, compact, upright branching. **Flowers** Small, in slender spikes, in abundance in late spring. White. **Fruits** Small, cherry-like. Red, then black. **Leaves** Evergreen, upright, long, narrow. Glossy dark green.
• NATIVE HABITAT Garden origin.
• CULTIVATION Extremely tolerant of shade. Grows in almost any soil except shallow chalk or waterlogged soils. Cut back hard in spring if necessary to restrict growth. Good for ground cover.
• PROPAGATION By semi-ripe cuttings in summer.

☼ ◊
❀ ❀ ❀

HEIGHT
75cm-1m
(30–36in)

SPREAD
2m (6ft)

Ericaceae	

GAULTHERIA × WISLEYENSIS 'Wisley Pearl'

Habit Bushy, dense, suckering. **Flowers** Small, urn-shaped, in racemes in late spring–early summer. White. **Fruits** Large, fleshy. Ox-blood red. **Leaves** Evergreen, oval. Matt dark green.
• NATIVE HABITAT Garden origin.
• CULTIVATION Thrives in shade or semi-shade. Grow in a peaty soil. Good for woodland gardens.
• PROPAGATION By suckers in spring or by semi-ripe cuttings in summer.
• OTHER NAMES × *Gaulnettya* 'Wisley Pearl'.

HEIGHT
To 1.5m
(5ft)

SPREAD
To 1.5m
(5ft)

Hydrangeaceae	

DEUTZIA × ROSEA

Habit Compact, with arching branches. **Flowers** Widely bell-shaped, with 5 petals, in broad clusters in late spring and early summer. Pale pink. **Leaves** Deciduous, oval. Dark green.
• NATIVE HABITAT Garden origin.
• CULTIVATION Tolerates almost any fertile, well-drained soil, but grows best in humus-rich soils that do not dry out in summer. Thin out old, flowered shoots, cutting back to the base after flowering; flowers are more abundant on young wood.
• PROPAGATION By softwood cuttings in summer.

HEIGHT
75cm-1m
(30–36in)

SPREAD
75cm-1m
(30–36in)

Rosaceae	

PRUNUS × CISTENA

Habit Slow-growing, upright, multi-stemmed. **Flowers** Small, from mid- to late spring. Soft pinkish-white. **Fruits** Cherry-like. Black-purple. **Leaves** Deciduous, oval to lance-shaped, pointed. Deep red-purple, red when young.
• NATIVE HABITAT Garden origin.
• CULTIVATION Grow in any but waterlogged soil. Makes an excellent hedging plant and is very hardy and wind-resistant. Trim after flowering and thin out oldest shoots to relieve overcrowding.
• PROPAGATION By softwood cuttings in summer.

HEIGHT
1.5m (5ft)

SPREAD
1.5m (5ft)

Caprifoliaceae	

VIBURNUM × JUDDII

Habit Vigorous, bushy, rounded. **Flowers** Fragrant, in large, rounded heads, in profusion from mid- to late spring. White, opening from pink buds. **Leaves** Deciduous, broadly oval to oblong. Dark green.
• NATIVE HABITAT Garden origin.
• CULTIVATION Tolerates light shade but flowers best in sun. Grow in deep, fertile soil that does not dry out during the growing season.
• PROPAGATION By softwood cuttings in early summer.

HEIGHT
1–1.5m
(3–5ft)

SPREAD
1–2m
(3–6ft)

Caprifoliaceae	

VIBURNUM CARLESII

Habit Rounded, bushy, dense. *Flowers* Very fragrant, in large, rounded heads from mid- to late spring. White, opening from pink buds.
Fruits Small, berry-like. Jet-black.
Leaves Deciduous, broadly oval. Dull dark green above, grey-downy beneath; reddish in autumn.
• NATIVE HABITAT Scrub of Korea and Japan.
• CULTIVATION Tolerates light shade. Grow in deep, fertile soil that is not too dry.
• PROPAGATION By seed in autumn or by softwood cuttings in early summer.

☼ ◊
❈ ❈ ❈

HEIGHT
To 1.5m
(5ft)

SPREAD
1.5m (5ft)

Thymelaeaceae	

DAPHNE × BURKWOODII 'Somerset'

Habit Vigorous, bushy, upright. *Flowers* Small, very fragrant, tubular with spreading lobes, in dense clusters in profusion in late spring; sometimes has repeat flowering in autumn. Tube: pink-purple; lobes: pale pink. *Leaves* Semi-evergreen, narrowly oval to lance-shaped. Pale to mid-green.
• NATIVE HABITAT Garden origin.
• CULTIVATION Grow in any fertile soil in a position sheltered from cold winter winds. One of the easiest of daphnes to grow.
• PROPAGATION By semi-ripe cuttings in summer.

☼ ◊
❈ ❈ ❈

HEIGHT
To 1.5m
(5ft)

SPREAD
To 1.5m
(5ft)

Thymelaeaceae	

DAPHNE TANGUTICA   ♥

Habit Slow-growing, densely branched.
Flowers Small, very fragrant, in dense clusters in late spring and early summer. White, flushed pink, opening from deep purple buds. *Leaves* Evergreen, oblong to lance-shaped, leathery. Glossy dark green.
• NATIVE HABITAT Mountain scrub and pine forests of the Himalaya, W. China.
• CULTIVATION Grow in fertile, humus-rich soil.
• PROPAGATION By fresh seed in autumn or by semi-ripe cuttings in summer.
• OTHER NAMES *D. retusa*.

☼ ◊
❈ ❈ ❈

HEIGHT
To 1.5m
(5ft)

SPREAD
1.5m (5ft)

Rosaceae	DWARF RUSSIAN ALMOND

PRUNUS TENELLA

Habit Bushy, with upright stems.
Flowers Shallowly cup-shaped, along the shoots from mid- to late spring. Bright pink.
Leaves Deciduous, narrowly oval. Shiny deep green above, paler beneath.
• NATIVE HABITAT Dry grassland from C. Europe to E. Siberia.
• CULTIVATION Grow in any fertile, free-draining soil that is not too dry.
• PROPAGATION By seed in autumn or by softwood cuttings in summer.

☼ ◊
❈ ❈ ❈

HEIGHT
To 1.5m
(5ft)

SPREAD
1.5m (5ft)

Grossulariaceae	

RIBES SANGUINEUM 'Brocklebankii' ♥

Habit Bushy, spreading. *Flowers* Small, tubular, in pendent clusters in spring. Pale pink.
Fruits Berries. Black, white-bloomed.
Leaves Deciduous, aromatic, 3–5 lobes. Pale yellow-green.
• NATIVE HABITAT Garden origin.
• CULTIVATION Tolerates part-day sun. Grow in any moderately fertile, well-drained soil. Cut out some older shoots after flowering and cut back overgrown specimens hard in winter or early spring.
• PROPAGATION By hardwood cuttings in winter.

HEIGHT
To 1.5m
(5ft)

SPREAD
1.5m (5ft)

Ericaceae	

MENZIESIA CILIICALYX var. *PURPUREA*

Habit Slow-growing, bushy, spreading.
Flowers Small, urn-shaped, nodding, waxy, in racemes in late spring and early summer. Purplish-pink. *Leaves* Deciduous, oval, with a short, sharp point. Bright green.
• NATIVE HABITAT Mountain scrub of Japan.
• CULTIVATION Grow in peaty soil and provide protection from cold winds and late frosts. Requires no regular pruning.
• PROPAGATION By seed in autumn or by softwood cuttings in summer.

HEIGHT
1–1.5m
(3–5ft)

SPREAD
1–1.5m
(3–5ft)

Epacridaceae	COMMON HEATH

EPACRIS IMPRESSA

Habit Erect, open, heath-like. *Flowers* Small, tubular, in spikes in late winter and spring. Pink or red. *Leaves* Evergreen, small, linear to lance-shaped. Dark green with red tips.
• NATIVE HABITAT Heathlands of S. Australia and Tasmania.
• CULTIVATION Grow in a cool conservatory in humus-rich, neutral to acid, not too fertile soil or compost. Water moderately when in growth.
• PROPAGATION By seed in spring or by semi-ripe cuttings in late summer.

Min. 5°C
(40°F)

HEIGHT
1m (3ft)

SPREAD
1m (3ft)

Polemoniaceae	MAGIC FLOWER OF THE INCAS

CANTUA BUXIFOLIA

Habit Bushy, arching. *Flowers* Large, tubular, in drooping clusters from mid- to late spring. Bright red and magenta. *Leaves* Evergreen or semi-evergreen, elliptic to lance-shaped. Grey-green.
• NATIVE HABITAT Andes of Peru, Bolivia, and N. Chile.
• CULTIVATION Grow in fertile soil or compost with the protection of a warm, sheltered, south- or west-facing wall. If necessary, prune after flowering to remove weak or overcrowded growth. In cool areas the plant should be grown in the conservatory and moved outdoors during the frost-free summer months. Water potted specimens freely when in growth, otherwise moderately.
• PROPAGATION By seed in spring or by semi-ripe cuttings in summer.
• OTHER NAMES *C. dependens.*

HEIGHT
1m (3ft) or more

SPREAD
1m (3ft)

Euphorbiaceae	CHRIST THORN, CROWN OF THORNS

EUPHORBIA MILII

Habit Slow-growing, spiny, semi-succulent.
Flowers Tiny, enclosed by 2 bracts, borne intermittently throughout the year. Yellowish; bracts bright red. *Leaves* Mainly evergreen, oval, smooth. Brilliant green.
• NATIVE HABITAT Arid areas of Madagascar.
• CULTIVATION Grow in the home or conservatory in a humus-rich soil or compost with additional grit and provide good ventilation. Water moderately when in growth, sparingly at other times.
• PROPAGATION By seed in autumn or spring.

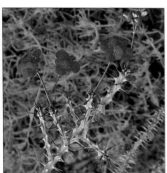

Min. 8°C
(46°F)

HEIGHT
To 1m (3ft)

SPREAD
1m (3ft)

Rosaceae	

CHAENOMELES X *SUPERBA* 'Nicoline'

Habit Vigorous, low, bushy, spreading.
Flowers Large, cup-shaped, in profusion in spring. Scarlet. *Fruits* Spherical, apple-like, aromatic. Yellow-green. *Leaves* Deciduous, oval. Glossy dark green.
• NATIVE HABITAT Garden origin.
• CULTIVATION Grow in any but waterlogged soil. If wall-grown, shorten side-shoots to 2–3 buds after flowering.
• PROPAGATION By softwood or greenwood cuttings in summer.

HEIGHT
1m (3ft)

SPREAD
1.5m (5ft)

Rosaceae	

CHAENOMELES X *SUPERBA* 'Rowallane'

Habit Low, bushy, spreading. *Flowers* Large, cup-shaped, in spring. Dark red-crimson. *Fruits* Spherical, apple-like, aromatic. Yellow-green. *Leaves* Deciduous, oval. Glossy dark green.
• NATIVE HABITAT Garden origin.
• CULTIVATION Grow in any but waterlogged soil. Tolerates shade but flowers best in sun. If wall-grown, shorten side-shoots to 2–3 buds after flowering.
• PROPAGATION By softwood or greenwood cuttings in summer.

HEIGHT
1m (3ft) or more

SPREAD
2m (6ft)

Rutaceae	SCENTED BORONIA, BROWN BORONIA

BORONIA MEGASTIGMA

Habit Slender, wiry-stemmed. *Flowers* Very fragrant, bowl-shaped, in late winter and spring. Purple-brown outside, pale yellow within.
Leaves Evergreen, divided with 3–5 soft, narrow leaflets. Dark green.
• NATIVE HABITAT Heaths of W. Australia.
• CULTIVATION Grow in a conservatory in sandy, neutral to acid soil or compost. Water moderately when in growth, otherwise sparingly.
• PROPAGATION By seed in spring or by semi-ripe cuttings in late summer.

Min.
5–7°C
(41–45°F)

HEIGHT
75cm-1m
(30–36in) or more

SPREAD
75cm (30in)

Ericaceae	

ARCTOSTAPHYLOS 'Emerald Carpet'

Habit Low, dense, mound-forming.
Flowers Small, urn-shaped, in short, dense panicles in spring. White. **Leaves** Evergreen, broadly oval, thick. Lustrous bright green.
Bark Smooth, purple-brown.
• NATIVE HABITAT Garden origin.
• CULTIVATION Provide shelter from cold winds and a fertile, humus-rich, acid soil or compost. Needs no regular pruning. Resents transplanting, so site carefully in a sunny position.
• PROPAGATION By semi-ripe cuttings in summer.

HEIGHT
To 35cm
(14in)

SPREAD
To 1.5m
(5ft)

Euphorbiaceae	MEDITERRANEAN SPURGE

EUPHORBIA CHARACIAS 🏆

Habit Upright, clump-forming, unbranched sub-shrub. **Flowers** Many bracts, in dense, rounded, terminal heads in spring and early summer. Pale yellowish-green with deep purple centres.
Leaves Evergreen, linear. Dark blue-green.
• NATIVE HABITAT Dry, rocky hills around the Mediterranean.
• CULTIVATION Grow in a warm, dry site with shelter from late frosts and cold wind.
• PROPAGATION By basal cuttings in spring or summer or by division in spring or autumn.

HEIGHT
To 1.5m
(5ft)

SPREAD
1.5m (5ft)

Salicaceae	WOOLLY WILLOW

SALIX LANATA 🏆

Habit Slow-growing, bushy, dense.
Flowers Large, erect catkins in late spring. Yellowish-green. **Leaves** Deciduous, broadly oval to rounded, downy. Silver-grey. **Bark** Young shoots are grey-woolly.
• NATIVE HABITAT On rocks and cliffs in mountains from N. Europe to E. Siberia.
• CULTIVATION Tolerates semi-shade. Provide a cool root run in moist but well-drained soil.
• PROPAGATION By semi-ripe cuttings in summer, or by hardwood cuttings in winter.

HEIGHT
60cm-1.2m
(2–4ft)

SPREAD
60cm-1.2m
(2–4ft)

Thymelaeaceae	

DAPHNE LAUREOLA subsp. PHILIPPI

Habit Compact, semi-prostrate. **Flowers** Small, fragrant, tubular with short, spreading lobes in late winter and early spring. Pale green. **Fruits** Small, berry-like. Black. **Leaves** Evergreen, oval. Glossy dark green.
• NATIVE HABITAT Pyrenees, France and Spain.
• CULTIVATION Prefers full sun but tolerates deep shade. Grow in an open position in fertile, humus-rich soil. Provide a cool root run.
• PROPAGATION By layers or by semi-ripe cuttings in summer.

HEIGHT
To 40cm
(16in)

SPREAD
40–60cm
(16–20in)

Euphorbiaceae	BALKAN SPURGE

EUPHORBIA CHARACIAS subsp. *WULFENII*

Habit Upright, clump-forming sub-shrub.
Flowers Many bracts in dense, rounded, terminal heads, in spring and early summer. Pale yellowish-green. **Leaves** Evergreen, linear, arranged in spirals along the stem. Grey-green.
• NATIVE HABITAT Dry, rocky hills and open forest in the Balkans of Turkey and S.E. Europe.
• CULTIVATION Grow in a warm, dry site in light, freely draining soil. The base of a south- or west-facing wall is ideal. Provide shelter from late frosts and cold winter winds. The unbranched stems are biennial, producing leafy growth in the first year and flowers in the second. Cut out flowered stems at the end of summer to make room for next season's flowering stems. *Euphorbia* species contain a milky sap which is toxic and irritant, so handle with care and immediately wash off any sap that comes into contact with the skin.
• PROPAGATION By basal cuttings in spring or summer or by division in spring or autumn.

HEIGHT
1m (3ft) or more

SPREAD
1.5m (5ft)

Salicaceae	CREEPING WILLOW

SALIX REPENS

Habit Bushy, prostrate or semi-upright.
Flowers Silky catkins, before the leaves, in mid- to late spring. Male catkins covered with yellow pollen when mature. Grey. *Leaves* Deciduous, small, narrowly oval. Grey-green above, silvery beneath.
• NATIVE HABITAT Heathlands and bogs, usually on acid soils, in Europe and N. Asia.
• CULTIVATION Provide a cool root run in moist but well-drained soil. Requires no regular pruning.
• PROPAGATION By semi-ripe cuttings in summer or by hardwood cuttings in winter.

☀ ◊
❀ ❀ ❀

HEIGHT
To 1.5m
(5ft), usu-
ally less

SPREAD
1.5m (5ft)

Leguminosae	WARMINSTER BROOM

CYTISUS X *PRAECOX*

Habit Compact, densely branched, arching.
Flowers Pea-like, in profusion along the shoots from mid- to late spring. Creamy-yellow.
Leaves Deciduous, tiny, divided into 3 silky leaflets. Grey-green.
• NATIVE HABITAT Garden origin.
• CULTIVATION Grow in fertile, but not over-rich, neutral to slightly acid soil. Prune after flowering, cutting back new growth by up to two-thirds.
• PROPAGATION By semi-ripe cuttings in late summer.

☀ ◊
❀ ❀ ❀

HEIGHT
75cm (30in)

SPREAD
1.5m (5ft)

Berberidaceae	OREGON GRAPE

MAHONIA AQUIFOLIUM

Habit Open, sparsely branched, suckering.
Flowers Small, in compact, dense, erect racemes in spring. Golden-yellow. *Fruits* Small, berry-like. Blue-black. *Leaves* Evergreen, divided into 5–13 spiny, oval leaflets. Glossy dark green.
• NATIVE HABITAT Coniferous woodlands of W. North America.
• CULTIVATION Grow in any fertile, moist but well-drained soil.
• PROPAGATION By fresh seed in autumn or by leaf bud or semi-ripe cuttings in summer.

☀ ◊
❀ ❀ ❀

HEIGHT
1m (3ft) or
more

SPREAD
1.5m (5ft)

Leguminosae	DWARF SIBERIAN PEA-TREE

CARAGANA ARBORESCENS 'Nana'

Habit Compact, bushy, with twisted branchlets.
Flowers Pea-like, in small clusters in late spring. Yellow. *Leaves* Deciduous, divided into 8–12 oval to elliptic, spine-tipped leaflets. Bright green.
• NATIVE HABITAT Species occurs in cold, dry regions of Siberia and Manchuria. Garden origin.
• CULTIVATION Grow in an open position in fertile, but not over-rich, soil. An attractive specimen for the rock garden.
• PROPAGATION By budding or by softwood or semi-ripe cuttings in summer.

☀ ◊
❀ ❀ ❀

HEIGHT
75cm (30in)

SPREAD
75cm (30in)

Acanthaceae	

PACHYSTACHYS LUTEA

Habit Loose, open, rounded. *Flowers* Small, tubular, tightly enclosed in bracts, in spikes in spring and summer. White; golden bracts.
Leaves Evergreen, large, narrowly oval to lance-shaped, veined. Matt dark green.
• NATIVE HABITAT Peru.
• CULTIVATION Grow in the home or conservatory in a fertile, well-drained soil or compost. Water freely when in full growth, otherwise moderately.
• PROPAGATION By greenwood cuttings in early summer.

☀ ◐ ◊

Min.
13–15°C
(55–59°F)

HEIGHT
1m (3ft)

SPREAD
1m (3ft)

Leguminosae	FURZE, GORSE, WHIN

ULEX EUROPAEUS

Habit Upright, with densely branching young growth. *Flowers* Fragrant, pea-like, throughout the year, but in profusion in spring. Bright yellow.
Fruits Hairy pod. Black. *Leaves* Leafless or almost leafless. Dark green spines and shoots give evergreen appearance.
• NATIVE HABITAT Acid, sandy soils in scrub and heathlands of W. Europe.
• CULTIVATION Grow in neutral to slightly acid soil that is not over-rich; useful on very poor soils.
• PROPAGATION By seed in autumn.

☀ ◊
❋ ❋ ❋

HEIGHT
75cm–1m
(30–36in)
or more

SPREAD
75cm–1m
(30–36in)

Leguminosae	

CYTISUS × *PRAECOX* 'Allgold'

Habit Compact, densely branched, arching.
Flowers Pea-like, in profusion along the shoots from mid- to late spring. Golden-yellow.
Leaves Deciduous, tiny, divided into 3 silky leaflets. Grey-green.
• NATIVE HABITAT Garden origin.
• CULTIVATION Grow in fertile, but not over-rich, neutral to slightly acid soil. Prune after flowering, cutting back new growth by up to two-thirds.
• PROPAGATION By semi-ripe cuttings in late summer.

☀ ◊
❋ ❋ ❋

HEIGHT
75cm-1m
(30–36in)

SPREAD
1.5m (5ft)

Berberidaceae	

BERBERIS EMPETRIFOLIA

Habit Bushy, dense, arching, semi-prostrate.
Flowers Small, globose, along the shoots in late spring. Golden-yellow. *Fruits* Globose berries in autumn. Blue-black, bloomed. *Leaves* Evergreen, small, narrowly elliptic. Grey-green.
• NATIVE HABITAT Rough, rocky areas from the coast to mountain foothills of Chile and Argentina.
• CULTIVATION Tolerates light shade and any but waterlogged soils. Prefers humus-rich, fertile soil and blooms best in sun.
• PROPAGATION By semi-ripe cuttings in summer.

HEIGHT
30–60cm
(12–24in)

SPREAD
75cm (30in)

Leguminosae	PRICKLY MOSES

ACACIA PULCHELLA

Habit Widely spreading, spiny. *Flowers* Tiny, in dense, globular heads in spring. Deep yellow.
Leaves Semi-evergreen or deciduous, divided into 2–11 pairs of tiny, narrowly oblong to oval leaflets. Rich green.
• NATIVE HABITAT W. Australia.
• CULTIVATION Grow in a conservatory in humus-rich, sandy soil or compost. Water moderately when in growth, otherwise sparingly. Maintain good ventilation.
• PROPAGATION By seed in spring.

Min. 5–7°C
(41–45°F)

HEIGHT
1m (3ft) or
more

SPREAD
1.5m (5ft)

Leguminosae	

CORONILLA VALENTINA subsp. *GLAUCA* ♀

Habit Bushy, dense, rounded. *Flowers* Fragrant, pea-like, in dense, rounded clusters from mid-spring to early summer. Bright lemon-yellow.
Leaves Evergreen, divided into 4–6, paired, broadly oval leaflets. Blue-green.
• NATIVE HABITAT Scrub and rocky places around the Mediterranean and Aegean.
• CULTIVATION Grow in a warm, sheltered position at the base of a south- or west-facing wall in light, freely draining soil.
• PROPAGATION By softwood cuttings in summer.

HEIGHT
1m (3ft)

SPREAD
1m (3ft)

Leguminosae	DYER'S GREENWEED

GENISTA TINCTORIA

Habit Erect or prostrate, compact, spreading.
Flowers Pea-like, in dense spikes, from summer to autumn. Golden-yellow. *Leaves* Deciduous, narrowly elliptic to lance-shaped. Dark green.
• NATIVE HABITAT Heathlands, meadow, and woodland from Europe to Asia Minor.
• CULTIVATION Grow in light, fertile but not too rich soil. To keep compact prune annually after flowering, taking care not to cut into older wood.
• PROPAGATION By seed in autumn or by softwood or semi-ripe cuttings in summer.

HEIGHT
60cm–1.5m
(2–5ft)

SPREAD
1m (3ft)

Leguminosae	HOLLY FLAME PEA

CHORIZEMA ILICIFOLIUM

Habit Upright to sprawling. **Flowers** Pea-like, in loose racemes in spring and summer. Standard petal orange-yellow; keel rosy-mauve.
Leaves Evergreen, spiny-toothed, holly-like. Dark green.
• NATIVE HABITAT By the coast and on riverbanks in gravelly soils of W. Australia.
• CULTIVATION Grow in a conservatory in fertile, neutral to acid soil or compost, with additional sharp sand. Water moderately in growth, then sparingly.
• PROPAGATION By seed in spring.

☼ ◊ pH

Min. 7°C
(45°F)

HEIGHT
50cm–1m
(20–36in)

SPREAD
75cm (30in)

Gesneriaceae	CLOG PLANT

NEMATANTHUS GREGARIUS

Habit Climbing or sprawling. **Flowers** Inflated, tubular, 1–3 in loose clusters, from spring to autumn. Bright orange and yellow. **Leaves** Evergreen, elliptic to oval, fleshy. Dark green.
• NATIVE HABITAT Eastern S. America.
• CULTIVATION Grow in the home or conservatory in a humus-rich soil or compost. Water moderately in full growth; allow to almost dry out in between.
• PROPAGATION By softwood or greenwood cuttings in summer.
• OTHER NAMES N. radicans, Hypocyrta radicans.

☼ ◑

Min.
13–15°C
(55–59°F)

HEIGHT
To 80cm
(32in)

SPREAD
80cm (32in)

Hydrangeaceae	

DEUTZIA MONBEIGII

Habit Arching, with slender branches.
Flowers Small, star-shaped, in profuse clusters from early to mid-summer. Glistening white.
Leaves Deciduous, small, oval to lance-shaped. Dark green.
• NATIVE HABITAT In scrub at high altitudes of Yunnan, China.
• CULTIVATION Tolerates partial shade and almost any fertile, well-drained soil, but grows best in humus-rich soils that do not dry out in summer.
• PROPAGATION By softwood cuttings in summer.

☼ ◊
❀ ❀ ❀

HEIGHT
1–1.5m
(3–5ft)

SPREAD
1.5m (5ft)

Scrophulariaceae	

HEBE BRACHYSIPHON 'White Gem'

Habit Low-growing, dense, rounded.
Flowers Small, 4-lobed, in tight racemes in early summer. White. **Leaves** Evergreen, small, oval to lance-shaped, smooth. Bright green.
• NATIVE HABITAT Garden origin.
• CULTIVATION Thrives in seaside gardens. Grow in any fertile, freely draining soil, with shelter from cold winter winds. Growth may be restricted and leggy plants tidied by cutting back in spring. Useful for contrasts of form and texture in the shrub border.
• PROPAGATION By semi-ripe cuttings in summer.

☼ ◊
❀ ❀ ❀

HEIGHT
75cm–1m
(30–36in)

SPREAD
1m (3ft)

Rosaceae	

RHODOTYPOS SCANDENS

Habit Upright or slightly arching. **Flowers** Large, shallowly cup-shaped, in profusion in late spring and early summer. White. **Fruits** Small, pea-shaped, shining. Black. **Leaves** Deciduous, oval, sharply toothed, veined. Mid-green.
• NATIVE HABITAT China and Japan.
• CULTIVATION Tolerates semi-shade and most soils. After flowering cut back oldest shoots to base.
• PROPAGATION By seed in autumn or by softwood cuttings in summer.
• OTHER NAMES *R. kerrioides*.

HEIGHT
To 1.5m
(5ft)

SPREAD
1.5m (5ft)

Compositae	

OLEARIA PHLOGOPAPPA var. SUBREPANDA

Habit Compact, upright. **Flowers** Daisy-like, in dense panicles along the shoots, from mid-spring to early summer. White. **Leaves** Evergreen, aromatic, narrowly oval, toothed. Dull grey-green, white and downy beneath.
• NATIVE HABITAT Tasmania and S. Australia.
• CULTIVATION Grow in any fertile, well-drained soil, including chalk. Tolerant of salt-laden winds but when grown inland will need some protection from cold, dry wind.
• PROPAGATION By softwood cuttings in summer.

HEIGHT
To 1.5m
(5ft)

SPREAD
1.5m (5ft)

Lythraceae	ELFIN HERB, FALSE HEATHER

CUPHEA HYSSOPIFOLIA

Habit Dense, rounded. **Flowers** Small, 6-petalled, in summer and autumn. Rose-purple, lilac, or white. **Leaves** Evergreen, narrowly lance-shaped. Dark green.
• NATIVE HABITAT Mexico and Guatemala.
• CULTIVATION Grow in a conservatory in a moderately fertile soil or compost. Water freely when in growth, otherwise moderately. Cut back flowered stems after flowering.
• PROPAGATION By seed in spring or by greenwood cuttings in spring or summer.

HEIGHT
To 60cm
(24in)

SPREAD
60cm (24in)

Labiatae	AUSTRALIAN ROSEMARY

WESTRINGIA FRUTICOSA ♥

Habit Compact, rounded. **Flowers** Delicate, irregularly 5-lobed, in loose clusters in spring and summer. White to palest blue. **Leaves** Evergreen, in whorls of 4. Dark green, white-felted beneath.
• NATIVE HABITAT New South Wales.
• CULTIVATION Grow in a conservatory or greenhouse in a humus-rich, neutral to acid soil or compost. Water moderately when in growth.
• PROPAGATION By seed in spring or by semi-ripe cuttings in late summer.
• OTHER NAMES *W. rosmariniformis.*

Min. 5–7°C
(41–45°F)

HEIGHT
1.2m (4ft)

SPREAD
1.2m (4ft)

Hydrangeaceae	

PHILADELPHUS 'Manteau d'Hermine' ♥

Habit Bushy, compact. **Flowers** Large, fragrant, double, in clusters from early to mid-summer. Creamy-white. **Leaves** Deciduous, small, broadly oval. Pale to mid-green.
• NATIVE HABITAT Garden origin.
• CULTIVATION Tolerant of a range of soils, including shallow chalk, and of part-shade, although flowers better in sun. Cut back some older shoots to new young growth after flowering, leaving young shoots to flower in the following year.
• PROPAGATION By softwood cuttings in summer.

HEIGHT
75cm–1m
(30–36in)

SPREAD
1.5m (5ft)

Rubiaceae	

GARDENIA AUGUSTA 'Fortuniana'

Habit Slow-growing, rounded. **Flowers** Large, fragrant, double, from summer to winter. White, becoming creamy with age. **Leaves** Evergreen, large, oval, leathery. Glossy dark green.
• NATIVE HABITAT Garden origin.
• CULTIVATION Grow in a conservatory or greenhouse in a humus-rich, non-soil medium. Avoid direct sun. Needs humid atmosphere.
• PROPAGATION By greenwood cuttings in spring or by semi-ripe cuttings in summer.
• OTHER NAMES *G. jasminoides* 'Fortuniana'.

Min. 15°C
(59°F)

HEIGHT
To 1.5m
(5ft)

SPREAD
1.5m (5ft)

Rosaceae	

POTENTILLA FRUTICOSA 'Abbotswood' ♥

Habit Bushy, spreading. **Flowers** Large, single, in profusion throughout summer to autumn. Pure white. **Leaves** Deciduous, divided into 5 narrowly oval leaflets. Dark blue-green.
• NATIVE HABITAT Garden origin.
• CULTIVATION Tolerates light shade. Grow in any moderately fertile but not too rich soil. In early spring cut out crowded growth at the base, tipping back strong growth by one-third.
• PROPAGATION By softwood or greenwood cuttings in summer.

HEIGHT
60cm (24in)

SPREAD
90cm (36in)

Rosaceae	

POTENTILLA FRUTICOSA var. MANDSHURICA 'Manchu'

Habit Dense, mound-forming. *Flowers* Appear from late spring to early autumn. Pure white. *Leaves* Deciduous, divided into 5 narrowly oval leaflets. Silvery-grey. *Bark* Young shoots red-pink.
• NATIVE HABITAT Garden origin.
• CULTIVATION Tolerates light shade. Grow in any moderately fertile but not too rich soil. Cut out crowded growth at the base in early spring.
• PROPAGATION By softwood or greenwood cuttings in summer.

☼ ◊
❀❀❀

HEIGHT
45cm (18in)
or more

SPREAD
45cm (18in)

Cistaceae	

HALIMIUM UMBELLATUM

Habit Upright or spreading, twisted branches. *Flowers* Small, in clusters in early summer. White with yellow centres, reddish in bud. *Leaves* Evergreen, narrowly lance-shaped. Glossy dark green, white-felted beneath.
• NATIVE HABITAT Scrub and pinewoods around the Mediterranean. ·
• CULTIVATION Grow in a warm, sheltered position in light, freely draining soil. Good for seaside gardens and suitable for the rock garden.
• PROPAGATION By semi-ripe cuttings in summer.

 ☼ ◊
❀❀

HEIGHT
40cm (16in)

SPREAD
40cm (16in)

Convolvulaceae	SILVER BUSH

CONVOLVULUS CNEORUM ♥

Habit Bushy, dense, rounded. *Flowers* Funnel-shaped, in profusion from late spring to late summer. Shining white, opening from pink buds. *Leaves* Evergreen, narrowly lance-shaped to linear, glistening, silky. Silvery-green.
• NATIVE HABITAT On limestone around the Mediterranean coast.
• CULTIVATION Grow in a warm, sheltered position in gritty and not too rich soil.
• PROPAGATION By softwood cuttings in early summer.

☼ ◊
❀❀

HEIGHT
50–75cm
(20–30in)

SPREAD
50–75cm
(20–30in)

Rosaceae	

POTENTILLA FRUTICOSA 'Farrer's White'

Habit Bushy, erect, rounded. *Flowers* Large, single, in profusion throughout summer to autumn. Pure white. *Leaves* Deciduous, divided into 5 narrowly oval leaflets. Grey-green.
• NATIVE HABITAT Garden origin.
• CULTIVATION Tolerates light shade. Grow in any moderately fertile but not too rich soil. In early spring cut out crowded growth at the base, tipping back strong growth by about one-third.
• PROPAGATION By softwood or greenwood cuttings in summer.

☼ ◊
❀❀❀

HEIGHT
60–90cm
(24–36in)

SPREAD
60–90cm
(24–36in)

Cistaceae	

× *HALIMIOCISTUS SAHUCII*

Habit Bushy, dense, mound-forming.
Flowers Single, in abundance in late spring and early summer. Pure white. **Leaves** Evergreen, linear to narrowly lance-shaped. Dark green, downy beneath.
• NATIVE HABITAT Scrub and open woodland, usually on limestone, of S. France.
• CULTIVATION Grow in a warm, sheltered site, in light, gritty, freely draining soil. A top dressing of grit affords protection from winter wet.
• PROPAGATION By semi-ripe cuttings in summer.

HEIGHT
50cm (20in)
or more

SPREAD
50cm (20in)

Cistaceae	MONTPELIER ROCK ROSE

CISTUS MONSPELIENSIS

Habit Bushy, compact, erect. **Flowers** Single, in small clusters from early to mid-summer. Pure white. **Leaves** Evergreen, linear to oblong, sticky, slightly wrinkled. Dark green.
• NATIVE HABITAT In scrub on dry hills from S. Europe to N. Africa and the Canary Islands.
• CULTIVATION Tolerates drought. Grow in a warm, sheltered position in light, freely draining soil. Good for seaside gardens and dry, sunny banks.
• PROPAGATION By seed in autumn or by softwood or greenwood cuttings in summer.

HEIGHT
To 1.5m
(5ft)

SPREAD
1.5m (5ft)

Cistaceae	ROCK ROSE

CISTUS SALVIIFOLIUS

Habit Bushy, dense. **Flowers** Single, solitary, or in small clusters in early summer. Pure white, with a central yellow blotch. **Leaves** Evergreen, oval to oblong, slightly wrinkled. Grey-green, paler beneath.
• NATIVE HABITAT On dry limestone hills of the Mediterranean and S. Europe.
• CULTIVATION Grow in a warm, sheltered position in light, freely draining soil.
• PROPAGATION By seed in autumn or by softwood or greenwood cuttings in summer.

HEIGHT
50cm (20in)

SPREAD
50cm (20in)
or more

Cistaceae	ROCK ROSE

CISTUS × *HYBRIDUS*

Habit Bushy, dense, spreading. **Flowers** Single, in late spring to early summer. Pure white, with a central yellow blotch; crimson-tinged in bud.
Leaves Evergreen, aromatic, oval, wrinkled. Dark green.
• NATIVE HABITAT S. Europe and N.W. Africa.
• CULTIVATION Grow in a warm position, in light, freely draining soil. Shelter from cold, dry winds.
• PROPAGATION By softwood or greenwood cuttings in summer.
• OTHER NAMES *C.* × *corbariensis.*

HEIGHT
To 1m (3ft)

SPREAD
1m (3ft)

| Cistaceae | ROCK ROSE |

CISTUS × CYPRIUS

Habit Vigorous, bushy. **Flowers** Large, single, opening in succession for several weeks, each bloom lasting only a day. Pure white, with a red-carmine blotch at each petal base.
Leaves Evergreen, aromatic, oblong to lance-shaped, sticky, wavy-edged. Glossy dark green above, grey-downy beneath.
• NATIVE HABITAT In scrub on dry granite hills and in open coniferous forests of S. Europe and N. Africa.
• CULTIVATION Grow in a warm, sunny position in light, freely draining but not too rich soil. Provide shelter from cold, dry, winter winds and late frosts. As with other *Cistus*, it dislikes the combination of cold and wet in winter and also resents transplanting and pruning. Young plants may be carefully tipped back in early spring to encourage a bushy habit. Cut out dead wood in spring. Excellent for seaside gardens, dry, sunny banks, and terrace wall planting.
• PROPAGATION By softwood or greenwood cuttings in summer.

HEIGHT
To 1.5m
(5t)

SPREAD
1.5–2m
(5–6ft)

Cistaceae	ROCK ROSE

CISTUS × AGUILARII 'Maculatus'

Habit Vigorous, bushy. **Flowers** Large, single, from early to mid-summer. Pure white, with a crimson blotch at each petal base.
Leaves Evergreen, aromatic, lance-shaped, sticky, wavy-edged. Rich bright green.
• NATIVE HABITAT Garden origin.
• CULTIVATION Grow in a warm, sunny position in light, freely draining but not too rich soil. Provide shelter from cold, dry winds and late frosts.
• PROPAGATION By softwood or greenwood cuttings in summer.

HEIGHT
To 1.5m
(5ft)

SPREAD
1.5–2m
(5–6ft)

Cistaceae	GUM CISTUS

CISTUS LADANIFER

Habit Open, upright. **Flowers** Large, single, from early to mid-summer. Pure white, with a chocolate-red blotch at each petal base.
Leaves Evergreen, aromatic, narrowly lance-shaped, sticky. Dark green.
• NATIVE HABITAT S. Europe and N. Africa.
• CULTIVATION Grow in a warm, sunny position in light, freely draining but not too rich soil. Shelter from cold, dry winter winds and late frosts.
• PROPAGATION By seed in autumn or by softwood or greenwood cuttings in summer.

HEIGHT
To 1.5m
(5ft)

SPREAD
1.5–2m
(5–6ft)

Apocynaceae	MADAGASCAR PERIWINKLE, ROSE PERIWINKLE

CATHARANTHUS ROSEUS

Habit Upright, fleshy, spreading with age.
Flowers Large, periwinkle-like, from spring to autumn. White to rose-pink. **Leaves** Evergreen, oblong to spoon-shaped, smooth. Dark green.
• NATIVE HABITAT Madagascar.
• CULTIVATION Water potted specimens moderately when in growth, otherwise sparingly. Popular for summer bedding.
• PROPAGATION By seed in spring or by greenwood or semi-ripe cuttings in summer.
• OTHER NAMES *Vinca rosea.*

Min 5–7°C
(41–45°F)

HEIGHT
To 60cm
(24in)

SPREAD
60cm (24in)

Rosaceae	

RHAPHIOLEPIS UMBELLATA

Habit Slow-growing, bushy, rounded.
Flowers Small, fragrant, in terminal clusters in early summer. White. **Fruits** Small, pear-shaped, berry-like. Blue-black. **Leaves** Evergreen, broadly oval, leathery. Glossy dark green.
• NATIVE HABITAT Coastal scrub of Japan.
• CULTIVATION Grow in fertile, well-drained soil, against a warm south- or west-facing wall in cool areas. Shelter from cold, dry winds.
• PROPAGATION By semi-ripe cuttings in late summer.

HEIGHT
1.5m (5ft)

SPREAD
1.5m (5ft)
or more

Myrtaceae	

LEPTOSPERMUM RUPESTRE

Habit Semi-prostrate, widely arching.
Flowers Small, open cup-shaped, carried along the length of shoots in early summer. White.
Leaves Evergreen, aromatic, narrowly oval-elliptic. Glossy dark green, bronze-purple in winter.
• NATIVE HABITAT Coastal to mountain habitats of Tasmania.
• CULTIVATION Grow in a humus-rich, neutral to acid soil. Provide the shelter of a warm wall in cold areas. In cold areas mulch with a deep, dry mix of

bracken litter or similar material in winter.
Trim lightly after flowering to maintain bushiness, as plants will not regenerate from older wood.
Much valued for their glossy, aromatic foliage and the generous profusion of flowers, *Leptospermum* species are useful in mild, coastal gardens as specimens or as informal, low hedging.
• PROPAGATION By semi-ripe cuttings in summer.
• OTHER NAMES *L. humifusum.*

HEIGHT
50cm–1m
(20–36in)

SPREAD
1.5m (5ft)

Agavaceae	OUR LORD'S CANDLE

YUCCA WHIPPLEI

Habit Stemless, forming a dense, rounded, basal clump. *Flowers* Fragrant, bell-shaped, in long, dense panicles in late spring and early summer. Greenish-white. *Leaves* Evergreen, long, narrow, lance-shaped, stiff. Blue-green.
• NATIVE HABITAT Dry scrub and chaparral of California.
• CULTIVATION Grow in well-drained soil. Needs a hot, dry, sunny position to bloom well.
• PROPAGATION By root cuttings in winter.
• OTHER NAMES *Hesperaloë whipplei.*

HEIGHT
1.5m (5ft)

SPREAD
1m (3ft)

Caprifoliaceae	

WEIGELA FLORIDA 'Variegata'

Habit Bushy, compact, dense. *Flowers* Showy, funnel-shaped, in profusion in late spring and early summer. Rose-pink. *Leaves* Deciduous, oval to oblong, pointed. Mid-green, broadly edged with creamy-white.
• NATIVE HABITAT Garden origin.
• CULTIVATION Tolerant of urban pollution and of most soils. Prefers a fertile, humus-rich soil and a warm, sunny site. Prune out some of the oldest branches annually after flowering.
• PROPAGATION By softwood cuttings in summer.

HEIGHT
To 1.5m
(5ft)

SPREAD
1.5m (5ft)

Ericaceae	HIGHBUSH BLUEBERRY, SWAMP BLUEBERRY

VACCINIUM CORYMBOSUM

Habit Upright, dense, slightly arching. *Flowers* Small, urn-shaped, in clusters in late spring and early summer. White or pinkish. *Fruits* Globose, edible, and sweet. Blue-black, bloomed. *Leaves* Deciduous, oval to lance-shaped. Bright green, red in autumn.
• NATIVE HABITAT E. North America.
• CULTIVATION Tolerates shade. Grow in moist but well-drained, peaty or sandy acid soils.
• PROPAGATION By seed in autumn or by semi-ripe cuttings in summer.

HEIGHT
1.5m (5ft)

SPREAD
1–2m
(3–6ft)

Agavaceae	

YUCCA FLACCIDA 'Ivory'

Habit Short-stemmed, forming a dense, basal clump. **Flowers** Fragrant, bell-shaped, in long, dense panicles from mid- to late summer. Ivory-white. **Leaves** Evergreen, long, narrow, lance-shaped, reflexed above the middle. Dark green.
• NATIVE HABITAT Garden origin.
• CULTIVATION Needs a hot, dry, sunny position to bloom well. Grows well in seaside gardens and on sandy soils.
• PROPAGATION By root cuttings in winter.
• OTHER NAMES *Y. filifera* 'Ivory'.

HEIGHT
1.2–1.5m
(4–5ft)

SPREAD
75cm–1m
(30–36in)

Compositae	KEROSCENE WEED

OZOTHAMNUS LEDIFOLIUS

Habit Dense, rounded. **Flowers** Small, daisy-like, in dense heads in early summer. White. **Leaves** Evergreen, aromatic, broadly linear with recurved margins. Dark green above, sticky and yellow beneath.
• NATIVE HABITAT Mountains of Tasmania.
• CULTIVATION Grow in any moderately fertile, freely draining soil. In cold areas provide a warm, sheltered site such as a south- or west-facing wall.
• PROPAGATION By semi-ripe cuttings in summer.
• OTHER NAMES *Helichrysum ledifolium*.

HEIGHT
1m (3ft)

SPREAD
1m (3ft)

Proteaecae	

LOMATIA SILAIFOLIA

Habit Bushy. **Flowers** Small, fragrant, with 4 narrow, twisted petals, in clustered spikes from mid- to late summer. Creamy-white.
Leaves Evergreen, finely divided leaflets. Dark green.
• NATIVE HABITAT Coastal thickets, E. Australia.
• CULTIVATION Thrives in light shade. Grow in moist but well-drained, neutral to acid soil, with shelter from cold, dry winds.
• PROPAGATION By softwood or semi-ripe cuttings in summer.

HEIGHT
75–90cm
(30–36in)

SPREAD
1m (3ft)

Caprifoliaceae	DOCKMACKIE, MAPLE LEAF VIBURNUM

VIBURNUM ACERIFOLIUM

Habit Rounded. **Flowers** Small, in large heads in early summer. Creamy-white. **Fruits** Ovoid, berry-like. Red then shining black. **Leaves** Deciduous, 3-lobed, coarsely toothed. Bright green, turning crimson in autumn.
• NATIVE HABITAT Deciduous woodland of E. North America.
• CULTIVATION Grow in deep, fertile, not too dry soil, in sun or semi-shade.
• PROPAGATION By seed in autumn or by softwood cuttings in early summer.

HEIGHT
To 1.5m
(5ft)

SPREAD
1.5m (5ft)

Compositae	

CASSINIA LEPTOPHYLLA subsp. VAUVILLIERSII var. ALBIDA

Habit Dense, upright. **Flowers** Small, daisy-like, in dense heads from mid- to late summer. White. **Leaves** Evergreen, tiny, narrowly oval, leathery. Dark green, with white down beneath. **Bark** Shoots sticky, with white down.
• NATIVE HABITAT New Zealand.
• CULTIVATION Grow in any moderately fertile, freely draining soil. Provide a warm, sunny site with shelter from cold, dry winds.
• PROPAGATION By softwood cuttings in summer.

HEIGHT
To 1.5m
(5ft)

SPREAD
1.5m (5ft)

Polygonaceae	WILD BUCKWHEAT

ERIOGONUM ARBORESCENS

Habit Rounded, sparingly branched. **Flowers** Tiny, in broad, leafy umbels from spring to autumn. White or pink. **Leaves** Evergreen, linear to oblong, with recurved edges, smooth. Dark green above, white-woolly beneath.
• NATIVE HABITAT Coastal areas of California.
• CULTIVATION Grow in a conservatory. Prefers very well-drained soil or compost of low fertility. Provide good ventilation. Water moderately when in growth, otherwise sparingly.
• PROPAGATION By seed in spring or autumn.

Min. 5°C
(41°F)

HEIGHT
To 1.5m
(5ft)

SPREAD
1.5m (5ft)

Scrophulariaceae	

HEBE RECURVA

Habit Low-growing, open, spreading. **Flowers** Small, 4-lobed, in small spikes from mid- to late summer. White. **Leaves** Evergreen, curved, narrowly lance-shaped, smooth. Blue-grey.
• NATIVE HABITAT Rocky areas of South Island, New Zealand.
• CULTIVATION Thrives in seaside gardens. Grow in any fertile, freely draining soil with shelter from cold winter winds. Growth may be restricted or leggy plants tidied by cutting back in spring.
• PROPAGATION By semi-ripe cuttings in summer.

HEIGHT
75cm–1m
(30–36in)

SPREAD
1m (3ft)

Scrophulariaceae	

HEBE ALBICANS

Habit Low-growing, dense, mound-forming.
Flowers Small, 4-lobed, in short, dense spikes
from early to mid-summer. White.
Leaves Evergreen, oval to oblong, fleshy, smooth.
Blue-grey.
• NATIVE HABITAT Rocky areas in the mountains
of South Island, New Zealand.
• CULTIVATION Thrives in seaside gardens. Grow
in any fertile, freely draining soil with shelter from
cold winter winds.
• PROPAGATION By semi-ripe cuttings in summer.

☼ ◊
❄❄

HEIGHT
To 60cm
(24in)

SPREAD
60cm (24in)

Hydrangeaceae	

DEUTZIA × HYBRIDA 'Mont Rose'

Habit Bushy, dense, upright. **Flowers** Small,
star-shaped, in profuse clusters in early summer.
Pink or pinkish-purple, with yellow anthers.
Leaves Deciduous, oval to lance-shaped, sharply
toothed. Mid-green.
• NATIVE HABITAT Garden origin.
• CULTIVATION Tolerates almost any fertile, well-
drained soil but grows best in humus-rich soils that
do not dry out in summer. Thin out old, flowered
shoots, cutting back to the base after flowering.
• PROPAGATION By softwood cuttings in summer.

☼ ◊
❄❄❄

HEIGHT
1–1.5m
(3–5ft)

SPREAD
1.5m (5ft)

Rosaceae	

POTENTILLA FRUTICOSA 'Daydawn'

Habit Bushy, slightly arching. **Flowers** Large,
from early summer to mid-autumn. Creamy-yellow,
flushed orange-pink. **Leaves** Deciduous, divided
into 5–7 narrowly oval leaflets. Mid-green.
• NATIVE HABITAT Garden origin.
• CULTIVATION Tolerates light shade and any
moderately fertile but not too rich soil. Prune in
early spring, cutting out weak growth at the base
and tipping back strong growth by about one-third.
• PROPAGATION By softwood or greenwood
cuttings in summer.

☼ ◊
❄❄❄

HEIGHT
To 1m (3ft)

SPREAD
1m (3ft)

Proteaceae	KING PROTEA

PROTEA CYNAROÏDES

Habit Bushy, rounded. **Flowers** Many small,
slender florets, waterlily-shaped, with silky-haired,
petal-like bracts in spring to summer. Pink to red.
Leaves Evergreen, oval, smooth. Mid- to dark green.
• NATIVE HABITAT Cape province, S. Africa.
• CULTIVATION Grow in a conservatory or
greenhouse in neutral to acid soil or compost low in
phosphates and nitrates. Water moderately when in
growth, otherwise sparingly.
• PROPAGATION By seed in spring or by semi-ripe
cuttings in summer.

☼ ◊ pH

Min. 5–7°C
(41–45°F)

HEIGHT
To 1.5m
(5ft)

SPREAD
1.5m (5ft)

Caprifoliaceae	GOUCHER ABELIA

ABELIA 'Edward Goucher'

Habit Compact, arching. *Flowers* Funnel-shaped, in profuse clusters from mid-summer to autumn. Lilac-pink. *Leaves* Deciduous or semi-evergreen, oval. Lustrous bright green, bronze when young.
• NATIVE HABITAT Garden origin.
• CULTIVATION Grow in a warm, sunny situation in any fertile soil. Provide shelter from cold winds. In cold areas, grow against a south- or west-facing wall.
• PROPAGATION By softwood cuttings in summer.

HEIGHT
To 1.5m
(5ft)

SPREAD
1.5m (5ft)

Caprifoliaceae	

ABELIA SCHUMANNII

Habit Arching, with slender branches. *Flowers* Funnel-shaped, from mid-summer to mid-autumn. Rose-purple and white. *Leaves* Deciduous or semi-evergreen, pointed. Mid-green, bronze when young.
• NATIVE HABITAT Dry valleys and riversides of C. China.
• CULTIVATION Grow in a sunny situation in any fertile soil. Shelter from cold winds. In cold areas grow against a south- or west-facing wall.
• PROPAGATION By softwood cuttings in summer.

HEIGHT
To 1.5m
(5ft)

SPREAD
1.5m (5ft)

Ericaceae	SALAL, SHALLON

GAULTHERIA SHALLON

Habit Vigorous, bushy, suckering. *Flowers* Small, urn-shaped, in pendulous racemes in late spring and early summer. Pink. *Fruits* Rounded, in dense clusters. Dark purple. *Leaves* Evergreen, broadly oval, sharply pointed, leathery. Dark green.
• NATIVE HABITAT Coastal scrub and coniferous woodland of W. North America.
• CULTIVATION Thrives in shade or semi-shade in moist, peaty soil. Excellent ground cover.
• PROPAGATION By seed in autumn, by semi-ripe cuttings in summer or by division in spring or autumn.

HEIGHT
60cm–1m
(2–3ft)

SPREAD
1–1.5m
(3–5ft) or
more

Labiatae	

PHLOMIS ITALICA

Habit Upright sub-shrub. *Flowers* 2-lipped: upper lip hooded; lower lip lobed, in whorls at the ends of shoots in mid-summer. Pale lilac-pink. *Leaves* Evergreen, oblong to lance-shaped, very woolly. Grey-green.
• NATIVE HABITAT Dry, rocky areas of the Balearic Islands.
• CULTIVATION Grow in a sunny, sheltered position in light, gritty, not too rich soil.
• PROPAGATION By seed in autumn or by softwood cuttings in summer.

HEIGHT
30–45cm
(12–18in)

SPREAD
30cm (12in)

Myoporaceae	

MYOPORUM PARVIFOLIUM

Habit Spreading to semi-prostrate.
Flowers Honey-scented, small, in clusters in summer. Purple spotted, white or pink.
Fruits Tiny, berry-like. Purple. **Leaves** Evergreen, small, linear, somewhat fleshy. Mid-green.
• NATIVE HABITAT S. Australia.
• CULTIVATION Grow in a conservatory in sandy, not too rich soil or compost. Water moderately when in growth; keep almost dry in winter.
• PROPAGATION By seed when ripe or in spring, or by semi-ripe cuttings in late summer.

☼ ◊

Min. 2–5°C
(36–41°F)

HEIGHT
To 50cm
(20in)

SPREAD
75cm (30in)

Cistaceae	ROCK ROSE

CISTUS × SKANBERGII ♥

Habit Bushy, compact. **Flowers** Single, in small clusters from early to mid-summer. Pure clear pink.
Leaves Evergreen, oblong to lance-shaped, wavy-edged. Grey-green, white-downy beneath.
• NATIVE HABITAT In scrub on dry hills in Greece and Lampedusa, Sicily.
• CULTIVATION Tolerates drought. Grow in a warm, sheltered position in light, freely draining soil. Good for dry, sunny banks.
• PROPAGATION By softwood or greenwood cuttings in summer.

☼ ◊
❀ ❀

HEIGHT
To 1m (3ft)

SPREAD
1m (3ft)

Leguminosae	

INDIGOFERA DIELSIANA

Habit Upright, open. **Flowers** Small, in erect racemes along the length of new growth, from early summer to early autumn. Pale pink.
Leaves Deciduous, finely divided into 7–11 oval, downy leaflets. Dark green.
• NATIVE HABITAT Dry scrub in Yunnan, China.
• CULTIVATION Tolerates any but waterlogged soil. In cold areas provide the shelter of a warm, south- or west-facing wall.
• PROPAGATION By softwood cuttings in summer or by seed in autumn.

☼ ◊
❀ ❀

HEIGHT
1m–1.5m
(3–5ft)

SPREAD
1.5m (5ft)

Thymelaeaceae	RICE FLOWER

PIMELEA FERRUGINEA

Habit Dense, rounded, with upright branches.
Flowers Small, tubular, in dense, almost spherical heads in spring or early summer. Rich pink.
Leaves Evergreen, tiny, oval to oblong, recurved. Deep green, downy beneath.
• NATIVE HABITAT W. Australia.
• CULTIVATION Grow in a conservatory in well-drained neutral to acid soil or compost. Water moderately when in growth. Needs good ventilation.
• PROPAGATION By seed in spring or by semi-ripe cuttings in late summer.

☼ ◊ pH

Min. 7°C
(45°F)

HEIGHT
75cm (30in)
or more

SPREAD
75–80cm
(30–32in)
or more

Hydrangeaceae	

DEUTZIA × *ELEGANTISSIMA* 'Rosealind'

Habit Bushy, dense, rounded. *Flowers* Small, 5-petalled, in profuse clusters from late spring to early summer. Deep carmine-pink. *Leaves* Deciduous, small, oval to oblong-oval. Dark green.
• NATIVE HABITAT Garden origin.
• CULTIVATION Tolerates almost any fertile, well-drained soil but grows best in humus-rich soils that do not dry out in summer. Thin out old, flowered shoots, cutting back to the base after flowering; flowers are more abundant on young wood.
• PROPAGATION By softwood cuttings in summer.

HEIGHT
To 1.5m
(5ft)

SPREAD
1.5m (5ft)

Caprifoliaceae	

WEIGELA FLORIDA 'Foliis Purpureis'

Habit Bushy, compact, dense. *Flowers* Showy, funnel-shaped, in profusion in late spring and early summer. Deep pink, pale pink within.
Leaves Deciduous, oval to oblong, pointed. Dull purple or purplish-green.
• NATIVE HABITAT Garden origin.
• CULTIVATION Tolerant of pollution and of most soils. Prefers a fertile, humus-rich soil and a warm, sunny site. Prune out some old branches at ground level annually after flowering to maintain vigour.
• PROPAGATION By softwood cuttings in summer.

HEIGHT
75cm–1m
(30–36in)

SPREAD
1–1.5m
(3–5ft)

Rosaceae	

SPIRAEA JAPONICA 'Little Princess'

Habit Slow-growing, compact, mound-forming.
Flowers Tiny, in small, dense heads, in profusion from mid- to late summer. Rose-pink.
Leaves Deciduous, small, oval to lance-shaped, coarsely toothed. Dark green, red-tinted in autumn.
• NATIVE HABITAT Garden origin.
• CULTIVATION Grow in any moderately fertile soil that does not dry out too much during the growing season. Cut young stems back and remove very old shoots at the base in spring.
• PROPAGATION By softwood cuttings in summer.

HEIGHT
50cm–1m
(20–36in)

SPREAD
50cm–1m
(20–36in)

Rosaceae	

SPIRAEA JAPONICA 'Goldflame'

Habit Compact, upright, slightly arching.
Flowers Tiny, in flattened, dense heads from mid- to late summer. Deep rose-red. *Leaves* Deciduous, small, oval to lance-shaped, coarsely toothed. Orange-red when young, then bright yellow, and finally pale green.
• NATIVE HABITAT Garden origin.
• CULTIVATION Grow in any moderately fertile soil that does not dry out too much during the growing season.
• PROPAGATION By softwood cuttings in summer.

HEIGHT
75cm–1m
(30–36in)

SPREAD
75cm–1m
(30–36in)

Rhamnaceae	

CEANOTHUS × PALLIDUS 'Perle Rose'

Habit Bushy, rounded. **Flowers** Tiny, in dense racemes, from mid-summer to early autumn. Bright carmine-pink. **Leaves** Deciduous, broadly oval. Mid-green.
• NATIVE HABITAT Garden origin.
• CULTIVATION Tolerant of some lime in the soil and of coastal conditions. Grow in a warm, sunny, sheltered site in a light, well-drained soil. Cut back in spring to a basal framework or to within 8–10cm (3–4in) of previous year's growth.
• PROPAGATION By semi-ripe cuttings in summer.

HEIGHT
To 1.5m
(5ft)

SPREAD
1.5m (5ft)

Acanthaceae	KING'S CROWN, BRAZILIAN PLUME

JUSTICIA CARNEA

Habit Upright, sparingly branched.
Flowers Tubular, with conspicuous bracts, in dense spikes in summer to autumn. Bright pink to rose-purple. **Leaves** Evergreen, oval, pointed, velvety. Mid-green.
• NATIVE HABITAT Northern S. America.
• CULTIVATION Grow in a fertile, humus-rich soil or compost. Water freely only when in full growth.
• PROPAGATION By softwood or greenwood cuttings in spring or early summer.
• OTHER NAMES *Jacobinia carnea, J. pohliana.*

Min.
10–15°C
(50–59°F)

HEIGHT
To 1.5m
(5ft)

SPREAD
75cm (30in)

Scrophulariaceae	

HEBE 'Great Orme' ♥

Habit Open, rounded. **Flowers** Small, 4-lobed, in slender spikes from mid-summer to mid-autumn. Clear, deep pink, fading to white.
Leaves Evergreen, long, lance-shaped. Glossy dark green. **Bark** Shoots deep purple.
• NATIVE HABITAT Garden origin.
• CULTIVATION Thrives in seaside gardens. Grow in any fertile, freely draining soil, with shelter from cold winter winds. Growth may be restricted or leggy plants tidied by cutting back in spring.
• PROPAGATION By semi-ripe cuttings in summer.

HEIGHT
To 1.5m
(5ft)

SPREAD
1.5m (5ft)

Scrophulariaceae	

PENSTEMON ISOPHYLLUS ♥

Habit Loose, open, with upright, slender stems.
Flowers Large, tubular, in long sprays from mid- to late summer. Deep pink, with white and red markings at the throat. **Leaves** Deciduous, spear-shaped. Glossy mid-green.
• NATIVE HABITAT Mexico.
• CULTIVATION Grow in a warm, dry, sunny position in well-drained but not too rich soil.
• PROPAGATION By seed in autumn or spring, or by softwood or semi-ripe cuttings of non-flowering shoots in mid-summer.

HEIGHT
70cm (28in)

SPREAD
70cm (28in)

Rubiaceae	EGYPTIAN STAR, STAR-CLUSTER

PENTAS LANCEOLATA

Habit Loosely rounded, with upright or spreading stems. **Flowers** Tiny, star-shaped, in flattened clusters in summer to autumn. Pink, lilac, red, or white. **Leaves** Evergreen, oval to lance-shaped, hairy. Bright green.
• NATIVE HABITAT Tropical Arabia to E. Africa.
• CULTIVATION Grow in a warm conservatory in fertile soil or compost. Water freely when in growth.
• PROPAGATION By seed in spring or by softwood cuttings in summer.
• OTHER NAMES *P. carnea.*

Min.
10–15°C
(50–59°F)

HEIGHT
1m (3ft) or more

SPREAD
1m (3ft)

Cistaceae	

CISTUS INCANUS subsp. CRETICUS

Habit Bushy, rounded. **Flowers** Single, from early to mid-summer. Pink or rose-purple.
Leaves Evergreen, oval, wavy-edged. Grey-green.
• NATIVE HABITAT Hillside scrub and open woodland around the Mediterranean.
• CULTIVATION Grow in a warm, sunny position in light, freely draining but not too rich soil. Provide shelter from cold, dry winter winds and late frosts.
• PROPAGATION By seed in autumn or by softwood or greenwood cuttings in summer.
• OTHER NAMES *C. creticus.*

HEIGHT
To 1m (3ft)

SPREAD
1.5–2m
(5–6ft)

Rosaceae	

SPIRAEA JAPONICA 'Anthony Waterer' ⚥

Habit Compact, upright. **Flowers** Tiny, in dense heads, from mid- to late summer. Deep crimson-pink. **Leaves** Deciduous, small, oval to lance-shaped, coarsely toothed. Red when young, then dark green, sometimes variegated cream and pink.
• NATIVE HABITAT Garden origin.
• CULTIVATION Grow in any moderately fertile soil that does not dry out too much during the growing season. Cut young stems back and remove very old shoots at the base in spring.
• PROPAGATION By softwood cuttings in summer.

HEIGHT
1m (3ft) or more

SPREAD
1m (3ft)

Ericaceae	

KALMIA ANGUSTIFOLIA f. RUBRA ⚥

Habit Bushy, mound-forming. **Flowers** Saucer-shaped, in dense clusters in early summer. Dark rosy-red. **Leaves** Evergreen, oblong to elliptic. Glossy dark green. The whole plant is poisonous.
• NATIVE HABITAT Acid bogs and heaths of E. United States.
• CULTIVATION Tolerates semi-shade. Grow in moist, humus-rich, peaty or sandy acid soil.
• PROPAGATION By seed in autumn or by softwood cuttings in summer.
• OTHER NAMES *K. angustifolia* 'Rubra'.

HEIGHT
50cm–1m
(20–36in)

SPREAD
1.5m (5ft)

FUCHSIAS

Fuchsia is a genus of deciduous or evergreen shrubs and trees, originating mainly in the mountain forests of Central and South America. The shrubby species, depending on growth habit, may be trained as bush, pyramid or standard specimens; the lax or trailing species are ideal for hanging baskets. They flower from summer to autumn. Almost all fuchsias, including standards, except *F. magellanica* and *F.* 'Riccartonii', will be cut back to the ground by frost. Pot-grown fuchsias should be moved indoors to overwinter. Grow hardy, outdoor species in a fertile, moist but well-drained soil in a partially shady site, and shelter from cold winds. Cut back dead top growth to ground level in spring. Propagate by softwood cuttings in any season.

F. 'Harry Gray'
Habit Lax, open, very free-flowering, self-branching.
Flowers Double. Tube pale rose-pink; sepals white, tipped green, flushed pale pink; petals white to pale pink.
Leaves Mid-green with red stems.
• CULTIVATION Good for hanging baskets.
• HEIGHT 2m (6ft).
• SPREAD indefinite.

F. 'Harry Gray'
BASKET TYPE

☀ ◌ ❀

F. 'Annabel'
Habit Upright, very free-flowering.
Flowers Large, double. Tube is long, striped pink; sepals are white, pink-tinged; petals are creamy-white.
Leaves Pale green.
• CULTIVATION Makes an excellent standard.
• HEIGHT 75cm (30in).
• SPREAD 75cm (30in).

F. 'Annabel'

☀ ◌ ❀   ♛

F. 'Ann Howard Tripp'
Habit Vigorous, upright, self-branching, very free-flowering.
Flowers Single or semi-double. Tube is white; sepals are white, tipped pale green; petals are white, veined pale pink. Flowers are held clear of foliage. *Leaves* Pale green.
• HEIGHT 75cm (30in).
• SPREAD 75cm (30in).

F. 'Ann Howard Tripp'

☀ ◌ ❀

F. 'Other Fellow'
Habit Bushy, upright, self-branching.
Flowers Small, single. Tube and sepals are waxy-white; petals are rich coral-pink.
Leaves Mid-green.
• HEIGHT 1.5m (5ft).
• SPREAD 75cm (30in).

F. 'Other Fellow'

☀ ◌ ❀

F. 'White Spider'
Habit Vigorous, bushy, horizontally branching, free-flowering.
Flowers Large, single. Very pale pink, with long, narrow, twisted, green-tipped sepals.
Leaves Mid-green.
• CULTIVATION Excellent for hanging baskets, or trained as a weeping standard.
• HEIGHT 2m (6ft).
• SPREAD Indefinite.

F. 'White Spider'
BASKET TYPE

☀ ◌ ❀

F. 'Pink Galore'
Habit Trailing.
Flowers Large, double. Pale pink. *Leaves* Glossy dark green.
• CULTIVATION Excellent for large hanging baskets, as a weeping standard, and for training against a trellis. Also suitable for bedding in semi-shade.
• HEIGHT 1.5m (5ft).
• SPREAD indefinite.

F. 'Pink Galore'
BASKET TYPE

☀ ◌ ❀

F. 'Leonora'
Habit Vigorous, bushy, upright, self-branching.
Flowers Single. Clear pink, sepals tipped green.
Leaves Mid-green.
• CULTIVATION Good for training as a standard.
• HEIGHT 1.5m (5ft).
• SPREAD 1m (3ft).

F. 'Leonora'

F. 'Jack Acland'
Habit Bushy, upright.
Flowers Large, semi-double. Tube and sepals are bright pink; petals are deep rose-pink, fading to pale pink with age.
Leaves Mid-green.
• CULTIVATION Makes a good standard and is useful for hanging baskets.
• HEIGHT 1.5m (5ft).
• SPREAD 1m (3ft).

F. 'Jack Acland'
BASKET TYPE

F. 'Jack Shahan'
Habit Vigorous, trailing, free-flowering.
Flowers Large. Pale to deep pink. **Leaves** Mid-green.
• CULTIVATION Excellent for hanging baskets, as a weeping standard, or for training against a trellis.
• HEIGHT 2m (6ft).
• SPREAD Indefinite.

F. 'Jack Shahan'
BASKET TYPE

F. ARBORESCENS
Habit Upright, shrubby, or tree-like with age.
Flowers Tiny, in upright heads, throughout the year. Pale pink-purple.
Fruits Berries, almost globose. Black, blue-bloomed.
Leaves Evergreen, laurel-like. Mid- to dark green.
• HEIGHT 3–8m (10–25ft).
• SPREAD 2.5m (8ft).

F. arborescens
Lilac fuchsia, Tree fuchsia

Min. 5°C (41°F)

F. 'Swingtime'
Habit Vigorous, open, self-branching.
Flowers Large, double. Tube and sepals are red; petals are creamy-white, veined pink.
Leaves Dark green.
• CULTIVATION Good as a standard and as an espalier. Suitable for bedding and hanging baskets.
• HEIGHT 1m (3ft).
• SPREAD 1m (3ft).

F. 'Swingtime'
BASKET TYPE

F. 'Lady Thumb'
Habit Vigorous, bushy, compact, upright.
Flowers Small, semi-double. Tube and sepals are reddish-pink; petals are white, veined pink.
Leaves Narrowly oval. Mid-green.
• CULTIVATION May be trained as a miniature standard. Suitable for the shrub or mixed border.
• HEIGHT 50cm (20in).
• SPREAD 50cm (20in).

F. 'Lady Thumb'

F. 'White Ann'
Habit Upright.
Flowers Double. Tube and sepals are red; petals are white, veined cerise.
Leaves Mid-green.
• CULTIVATION Good for training as a standard.
• HEIGHT 1m (3ft).
• SPREAD 75cm (30in).

F. 'White Ann'

F. 'Nellie Nuttall'
Habit Vigorous, bushy, upright. **Flowers** Single. Tube and sepals are rose-red; petals are white, with red veins. Blooms are carried well above the foliage. **Leaves** Light green.
• CULTIVATION Good for summer bedding and for training as a standard.
• HEIGHT 1m (3ft).
• SPREAD 75cm (30in).

F. 'Nellie Nuttall'

F. 'Golden Dawn'
Habit Upright.
Flowers Single. Tube and sepals are light salmon-pink; petals are orange, tinted fuchsia pink. *Leaves* Pale green.
• CULTIVATION Good for training as a standard. Pinch early to ensure bushiness.
• HEIGHT 1.5m (5ft).
• SPREAD 75cm (30in).

F. 'Golden Dawn'

☀ ◊ ❄

F. 'Peppermint Stick'
Habit Bushy, upright.
Flowers Large, double. Tube and sepals are carmine-red; petals are rich purple, splashed pink. *Leaves* Mid-green.
• CULTIVATION Good for training as a standard.
• HEIGHT 1.5m (5ft).
• SPREAD 1m (3ft).

F. 'Peppermint Stick'

☀ ◊ ❄

F. 'Kwintet'
Habit Vigorous, upright.
Flowers Single, slender. Tube and sepals are deep rose-pink; petals are red-pink. *Leaves* Mid-green.
• HEIGHT 1.5m (5ft).
• SPREAD 1m (3ft).

F. 'Kwintet'

☀ ◊ ❄

F. 'Autumnale'
Habit Loose, open, late-flowering.
Flowers Single. Tube and sepals are scarlet-pink; petals are reddish-purple.
Leaves Variegated red, gold, and bronze.
• CULTIVATION Suitable for hanging baskets and for training as a weeping standard.
• HEIGHT 2m (6ft).
• SPREAD 50cm (20in).

F. 'Autumnale'
BASKET TYPE

☀ ◊ ❄

F. 'Rufus'
Habit Vigorous, bushy, upright, free-flowering.
Flowers Small, single, bright red. *Leaves* Mid-green.
• CULTIVATION Excellent for bedding. Suitable for training as a standard. Will tolerate to –10°C (14°F) if given good drainage and shelter from cold, dry winds .
• HEIGHT 1.5m (5ft).
• SPREAD 75cm (30in).

F. 'Rufus'

☀ ◊ ❄❄

F. 'Riccartonii'
Habit Stiff, upright, very free-flowering.
Flowers Small, single. Tube, short, red; sepals, long, narrow, recurved, red; petals are purple.
Leaves Mid-green, tinted bronze.
• OTHER NAMES
F. magellanica 'Riccartonii'.
• HEIGHT 2m (6ft).
• SPREAD 1.5m (5ft).

F. 'Riccartonii'

☀ ◊ ❄❄❄   ♈

F. 'Red Spider'
Habit Vigorous, trailing.
Flowers Long. Tube, slender, red; sepals, narrow, spreading, rose-pink, veined crimson; petals are a slightly darker red. *Leaves* Mid-green.
• CULTIVATION Excellent for large hanging baskets and good for training against trellis.
• HEIGHT 1.5m (5ft).
• SPREAD Indefinite.

F. 'Red Spider'
BASKET TYPE

☀ ◊ ❄

F. 'Dollar Princess'
Habit Vigorous, bushy, upright, early-flowering.
Flowers Small, double. Tube and sepals are cerise-red; petals are rich purple. *Leaves* Mid-green.
• CULTIVATION Easily cultivated. Excellent as a bush, pyramid or standard. Must have good drainage and wind protection.
• HEIGHT 1m (3ft).
• SPREAD 75cm (30in).

F. 'Dollar Princess'

☀ ◊ ❄❄   ♈

F. 'Royal Velvet'

Habit Vigorous, upright.
Flowers Large, double. Tube and sepals are red; petals are deep purple, splashed deep pink.
Leaves Mid-green.
• CULTIVATION Makes an excellent standard.
• HEIGHT 1.5m (5ft).
• SPREAD 75cm (30in).

F. 'Royal Velvet'

F. 'Gruss aus dem Bodethal'

Habit Bushy, upright, late-flowering.
Flowers Small, single or semi-double. Crimson, opening almost black, becoming larger and paler with age.
Leaves Mid-green.
• CULTIVATION Good for bedding or for a cool conservatory.
• HEIGHT 1m (3ft).
• SPREAD 75cm (30in).

F. 'Gruss aus dem Bodethal'

F. 'Genii'

Habit Upright.
Flowers Small, single. Tube and sepals are cerise red; petals are reddish purple.
Leaves Golden-green.
• CULTIVATION Makes a good standard.
• HEIGHT 1.5m (5ft).
• SPREAD 75cm (30in).

F. 'Genii'

F. 'Tom Thumb'

Habit Bushy, upright, very free-flowering.
Flowers Small, single. Tube and sepals are red; petals are violet.
Leaves Bright green.
• CULTIVATION May be trained as a miniature standard. Suitable for the shrub or mixed border. Must have good drainage and wind protection.
• HEIGHT 50cm (20in).
• SPREAD 50cm (20in).

F. 'Tom Thumb'

F. MAGELLANICA

Habit Upright, very free-flowering.
Flowers Small, slender. Tube and sepals are deep crimson; petals are violet.
Leaves Oval to elliptic. Bright green.
• CULTIVATION Grow in moist but well-drained soil. Shelter from cold, dry winds. Re-sprouts at base if cut by frost.
• HEIGHT 3m (10ft).
• SPREAD 2m (6ft).

F. magellanica
Lady's eardrops

F. 'Mrs Popple'

Habit Vigorous, bushy, upright, free-flowering.
Flowers Large, single. Very long stamens and style. Tube and sepals are scarlet; petals are violet; stamens and style are crimson.
Leaves Mid-green.
• CULTIVATION Excellent for hedging in sheltered areas. Thrives in sun. Needs good drainage and wind protection.
• HEIGHT 1.5m (5ft).
• SPREAD 75cm (30in).

F. 'Mrs Popple'

F. 'Marinka'

Habit Vigorous, bushy, trailing. *Flowers* Single. Tube and sepals are red; petals are darker red, folded at margins. *Leaves* Dark green with crimson midribs.
• CULTIVATION Excellent for large hanging baskets and good for training against trellis. Foliage may be discoloured by cold winds.
• HEIGHT 2m (6ft).
• SPREAD Indefinite.

F. 'Marinka'
BASKET TYPE

☀◐ ◊ ❄   ♔

F. 'Checkerboard'

Habit Vigorous, dense, upright. *Flowers* Single. Tube is red; sepals are red, turning white with age; petals are dark red. *Leaves* Mid-green.
• CULTIVATION Good for summer bedding.
• HEIGHT To 1.2m (4ft).
• SPREAD 75cm (30in).

F. 'Checkerboard'

☀◐ ◊ ❄   ♔

F. 'Golden Marinka'

Habit Trailing. *Flowers* Single. Tube and sepals are rich red; petals are slightly darker red. *Leaves* Variegated golden-yellow, red veins.
• CULTIVATION Good for hanging baskets and as a weeping standard. Leaf colour is best in good light but may be discoloured by wind.
• HEIGHT 2m (6ft).
• SPREAD Indefinite.

F. 'Golden Marinka'
BASKET TYPE

☀ ◊ ❄   ♔

F. BOLIVIANA var. ALBA

Habit Upright, with arching branches, tree-like with age. *Flowers* Long, very slender, in clusters at branch tips. Tube and sepals are white; petals are scarlet. *Leaves* Large. Bright grey-green with reddish midribs.
• HEIGHT 3m (10ft).
• SPREAD 1m (3ft).

F. boliviana var. *alba*

☀ ◊   Min. 5°C (41°F) ♔

F. 'Celia Smedley'

Habit Very vigorous, upright. *Flowers* Large, single or semi-double. Tube is greenish-white; sepals are pale pinkish-white; petals are currant-red. *Leaves* Large. Mid-green.
• CULTIVATION Best when trained as a standard. Makes an excellent bush for tubs.
• HEIGHT 1.5m (5ft).
• SPREAD 1m (3ft).

F. 'Celia Smedley'

☀ ◊ ❄   ♔

F. 'Lye's Unique'

Habit Vigorous, bushy, upright. *Flowers* Small, single. Tube, long, waxy-white; sepals and petals are orange-red. *Leaves* Mid-green.
• CULTIVATION Excellent for training as a large pyramid.
• HEIGHT 1.5m (5ft).
• SPREAD 1m (3ft).

F. 'Lye's Unique'

☀ ◊ ❄

F. 'Mary Poppins'
Habit Bushy, upright.
Flowers Single, slender.
Tube and sepals are
apricot-pink; petals are
vermilion. **Leaves** Mid-
green.
• HEIGHT 1.5m (5ft).
• SPREAD 75cm (30in).

F. 'Mary Poppins'

☼ ◊ ❄

F. 'Cascade'
Habit Trailing,
pendulous, very free-
flowering.
Flowers Single. Tube
and sepals are white,
tinged red; petals are
deep carmine.
Leaves Mid-green.
• CULTIVATION
Excellent for hanging
baskets.
• HEIGHT 2m (6ft).
• SPREAD Indefinite.

F. 'Cascade'
BASKET TYPE

☼ ◊ ❄

F. 'Garden News'
Habit Vigorous, upright.
Flowers Large, double.
Tube and sepals are pale
pink; petals are magenta-
rose. **Leaves** Mid-green.
• HEIGHT 1.5m (5ft).
• SPREAD 1m (3ft).

F. 'Garden News'

☼ ◊ ❄❄❄   ♔

F. 'Lena'
Habit Loose, open.
Flowers Double. Tube
and sepals are pale pink;
petals are pink-flushed,
purple. **Leaves** Mid-
green.
• CULTIVATION Makes
a good standard.
• HEIGHT 1m (3ft).
• SPREAD 1m (3ft).

F. 'Lena'

☼ ◊ ❄❄   ♔

F. × BACILLARIS
Habit Upright, or
spreading. **Flowers** Tiny.
Pale pink to crimson.
Fruits Small, rounded
berries. Glossy black.
Leaves Deciduous,
lance-shaped to oval,
finely serrated. Mid- to
dark green.
• CULTIVATION Good
for hanging baskets.
• HEIGHT 75cm (30in).
• SPREAD 75cm (30in).

F. × bacillaris

☼ ◊ ❄❄

F. 'Joy Patmore'
Habit Vigorous, upright.
Flowers Single. Tube is
white; sepals are white,
tipped green; petals are
cerise with white bases.
Leaves Mid-green.
• CULTIVATION Makes
a good standard.
• HEIGHT 1.5m (5ft).
• SPREAD 1m (3ft).

F. 'Thalia'
Habit Vigorous, upright,
very free-flowering.
Flowers Single, slender,
with long, narrow tube,
small sepals, and small
petals in dense clusters at
the ends of branches.
Sepals are red; petals are
orange-red.
Leaves Velvety. Veined
olive-green, ribbed dark
magenta.
• HEIGHT 1m (3ft).
• SPREAD 1m (3ft).

F. 'Thalia'

☼ ◊ Min. 5°C (41°F) ♔

F. 'Joy Patmore'

☼ ◊ ❄   ♔

F. 'La Campanella'

Habit Trailing, self-branching, very free-flowering.
Flowers Small, semi-double. Tube is white, flushed pink; sepals are white; petals are cerise-purple, fading to lavender. *Leaves* Mid-green.
• CULTIVATION Excellent for hanging baskets and suitable for training against a trellis. Pinch back hard for bushy plants.
• HEIGHT 1.5m (5ft).
• SPREAD Indefinite.

F. 'La Campanella'
BASKET TYPE

☼ ◊ ❋   ♈

F. 'Rose of Castile'

Habit Vigorous, bushy, upright. *Flowers* Small, single. Tube is white; sepals are white, tipped green; petals are pink, flushed purple.
Leaves Mid-green.
• CULTIVATION Makes a good standard. If given good drainage and wind shelter, it will withstand –10°C (14°F).
• HEIGHT 1.5m (5ft).
• SPREAD 1m (3ft).

F. 'Rose of Castile'

☼ ◊ ❋❋   ♈

F. 'Estelle Marie'

Habit Bushy, upright, self-branching.
Flowers Single. Tube is greenish-white; sepals are white; petals are blue-violet, ageing to violet.
Leaves Dark green.
• CULTIVATION Excellent for summer bedding.
• HEIGHT 1m (3ft).
• SPREAD 50cm (20in).

F. 'Estelle Marie'

☼ ◔ ◊ ❋

F. PROCUMBENS

Habit Prostrate, very free-flowering.
Flowers Tiny, erect, petalless. Tube is yellow; sepals are purple; pollen is bright blue.
Fruits Large, long-persistent berries. Red.
Leaves Almost circular, heart-shaped at base.
• CULTIVATION Blooms best on sandy soil.
• HEIGHT 10cm (4in).
• SPREAD Indefinite.

F. procumbens

☼ ◐ ◊ ❋❋

F. FULGENS

Habit Upright, tuberous-rooted.
Flowers Long-tubed, in short clusters. Orange.
Fruits Large, oval berries. Deep purple.
Leaves Large, oval to heart-shaped, finely toothed. Sage green.
• CULTIVATION Prone to vine weevil and whitefly.
• HEIGHT To 3m (10ft).
• SPREAD 1m (3ft).

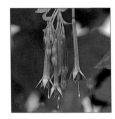

F. fulgens

☼ ◊ Min. 5°C (41°F) ♈

F. 'Coralle'

Habit Vigorous, upright.
Flowers Small, with long, narrow tubes and small sepals and petals, carried in dense clusters at the ends of branches in summer. Salmon-orange.
Leaves Velvety. Deep blue-green.
• CULTIVATION Useful as summer bedding and excellent as a specimen plant in the conservatory.
• HEIGHT 1m (3ft).
• SPREAD 1m (3ft).

F. 'Coralle'

☼ ◊ Min. 7°C (45°F) ♈

Acanthaceae	

CROSSANDRA NILOTICA

Habit Upright to spreading. *Flowers* Small, tubular with spreading petals, in short spikes in summer. Apricot to pale brick-red.
Leaves Evergreen, oval, pointed. Glossy rich green.
• NATIVE HABITAT Scrub of tropical Africa.
• CULTIVATION Grow in a warm conservatory in a fertile, humus-rich soil or compost. Water freely in full growth, then moderately. Cut back flowered stems by half in late winter. Shade in summer.
• PROPAGATION By seed in spring or by greenwood cuttings in late spring or summer.

Min. 15°C
(59°F)

HEIGHT
To 50cm
(20in) or
more

SPREAD
50–75cm
(20–30in)

Escalloniaceae	

ESCALLONIA RUBRA 'Woodside'

Habit Bushy, compact, dense, spreading.
Flowers Small, tubular, in short racemes in summer and autumn. Crimson. *Leaves* Evergreen, oval to lance-shaped. Glossy dark green.
• NATIVE HABITAT Garden origin.
• CULTIVATION Tolerant of lime-rich and dry soils. Thrives in mild areas and in seaside gardens. Provide shelter from wind in inland gardens. Prune in early spring if necessary.
• PROPAGATION By softwood or semi-ripe cuttings in summer.

HEIGHT
50cm (20in)
or more

SPREAD
1.5m (5ft)

Leguminosae	BALLOON PEA, DUCK PLANT

SUTHERLANDIA FRUTESCENS

Habit Upright, open. *Flowers* Large, pea-like, in racemes in late spring and summer. Terracotta-red.
Fruits Large, inflated papery pods. Green, then flushed red. *Leaves* Evergreen, divided into 13–21 narrow leaflets. Silvery grey-green.
• NATIVE HABITAT Dry hills of S. Africa.
• CULTIVATION Grow in light soil, with the shelter of a warm, south- or west-facing wall. Protect with a dry mulch, such as bracken litter, in winter. Will re-sprout from the base if cut back by frost.
• PROPAGATION By seed in spring.

HEIGHT
1.5m (5ft)

SPREAD
1.5m (5ft)

Rubiaceae	FLAME OF THE WOODS, JUNGLE FLAME

IXORA COCCINEA

Habit Bushy, rounded. *Flowers* Small, tubular, in dense heads in summer. Red, pink, orange, or yellow. *Leaves* Evergreen, elliptic to oblong-oval. Glossy dark green.
• NATIVE HABITAT Tropical forests of India and Sri Lanka.
• CULTIVATION Grow in a warm conservatory or well-lit site in the home in a fertile, loamless compost. Water freely when in growth, otherwise moderately.
• PROPAGATION By seed in spring or by semi-ripe cuttings in summer.

Min.
13–16°C
(55–61°F)

HEIGHT
1m (3ft) or
more

SPREAD
1m (3ft)

Rosaceae	

POTENTILLA FRUTICOSA 'Red Ace'

Habit Bushy, compact, dense, mound-forming.
Flowers Large, single, in profusion from late
spring to mid-autumn. Vermilion, with pale creamy-
yellow reverse.
Leaves Deciduous, divided into 5 narrowly oval
leaflets. Bright green.
• NATIVE HABITAT Garden origin.
• CULTIVATION Grow in any moderately fertile
but not too rich soil. Will grow well in sun, although
the bright flower colour will then fade to a washed-
out red. Preserve good colour in this cultivar, and

others with orange, red, or pink flowers, by
growing in semi-shade. Cut out weak and crowded
growth at the base in spring. If necessary, trim
back strong shoots in early spring by about one-
third to maintain compactness or restrict spread.
• PROPAGATION By softwood or greenwood
cuttings in summer.

HEIGHT
1m (3ft)

SPREAD
1m (3ft)

Scrophulariaceae	

PHYGELIUS AEQUALIS

Habit Upright sub-shrub. *Flowers* Tubular, in one-sided panicles from mid-summer to early autumn. Dusky orange-pink with yellow throats. *Leaves* Evergreen or semi-evergreen, oval. Dark green.
• NATIVE HABITAT S. Africa.
• CULTIVATION Grow in light but not too dry soil, in a sheltered position. Grow against a south- or west-facing wall in cool areas.
• PROPAGATION By seed in spring or by softwood cuttings in summer.

HEIGHT
1–1.2m
(3–4ft)

SPREAD
1–1.2m
(3–4ft)

Labiatae	MEXICAN RED SAGE

SALVIA FULGENS

Habit Upright sub-shrub. *Flowers* Tubular, 2-lipped, in whorls in late summer. Brilliant scarlet. *Leaves* Evergreen or semi-evergreen, oval to heart-shaped, hairy. Mid-green above, white downy beneath.
• NATIVE HABITAT Oak woods and coniferous mountain woodland of Mexico.
• CULTIVATION Grow in light, freely draining, fertile soil in a warm, sunny, sheltered site.
• PROPAGATION By seed in spring or by softwood cuttings in mid-summer.

HEIGHT
To 1m (3ft)
or more

SPREAD
1m (3ft)

Labiatae	

SALVIA MICROPHYLLA var. *NEUREPIA*

Habit Upright, well-branched. *Flowers* Tubular, 2-lipped, in racemes in late summer and autumn. Bright rosy-red. *Leaves* Evergreen, triangular to oval. Pale green.
• NATIVE HABITAT Mountain scrub, oak woods, and coniferous woodland of Mexico.
• CULTIVATION Grow in light, freely draining fertile soil in a warm, sunny, sheltered site. Protect from cold and wet in winter.
• PROPAGATION By softwood cuttings in mid-summer.

HEIGHT
To 1.2m
(4ft)

SPREAD
1m (3ft)

Proteaceae	

GREVILLEA 'Robyn Gordon'

Habit Rounded, then spreading with age. *Flowers* Tubular, with protruding, recurved styles, in dense racemes at intervals from early spring to late summer. Crimson. *Leaves* Evergreen, narrow, fern-like, leathery. Dark green.
• NATIVE HABITAT Garden origin.
• CULTIVATION Grow in a conservatory in a neutral to acid soil or compost. Water moderately in growth, then sparingly. Provide good ventilation. Prune to shape after flowering if necessary.
• PROPAGATION By semi-ripe cuttings in summer.

Min.
5–10°C
(41–50°F)

HEIGHT
1m (3ft)

SPREAD
1m (3ft)

Acanthaceae	SHRIMP PLANT

Aceraceae	

JUSTICIA BRANDEGEEANA ♉

Habit Bushy, rounded. *Flowers* Small, appearing mainly in summer. White, with overlapping shrimp-pink bracts. *Leaves* Evergreen, oval to elliptic, soft. Mid-green.
- NATIVE HABITAT Mexico.
- CULTIVATION Grow in the home or a warm conservatory in a fertile, humus-rich soil or compost. Water freely only when in full growth.
- PROPAGATION By softwood or greenwood cuttings in spring or early summer.
- OTHER NAMES *Beloperone guttata, Drejerella guttata.*

ACER PALMATUM 'Chitoseyama' ♉

Habit Arching, mound-forming
Flowers Tiny, in drooping clusters, in spring. Red-purple. *Fruits* Sycamore-like. *Leaves* Deciduous, deeply divided. Greenish-bronze, turning brilliant red from late summer to autumn.
- NATIVE HABITAT Garden origin.
- CULTIVATION Grow in a moist but well-drained, neutral to acid soil. Provide shelter from cold wind.
- PROPAGATION By softwood cuttings in spring, by budding in summer, or by grafting in late winter or early spring.

☀ ◊

Min.
7–10°C
(45–50°F)

HEIGHT
75cm–1m
(30–36in)

SPREAD
50cm (20in)

☀ ◊
❄ ❄ ❄

HEIGHT
1–1.5m
(3–5ft)

SPREAD
1.5m (5ft)

Aceraceae	

ACER PALMATUM var. *DISSECTUM*
Dissectum Atropurpureum Group

Habit Bushy, mound-forming. *Flowers* Tiny, in drooping clusters in spring. Red-purple.
Fruits Sycamore-like, with red or green wings.
Leaves Deciduous, deeply divided. Rich bronze-red or purple, turning brilliant red, orange, or yellow in autumn.
- NATIVE HABITAT Garden origin. Species grows in hill and mountainside thickets of China, Japan, and Korea.
- CULTIVATION Tolerates light shade. Colours

best in sun, but should be given a position with some shade from the hottest midday sun in summer. Grow in a well-drained, neutral to acid soil that remains reliably moist during the growing season. Provide shelter from cold winds, to avoid leaf scorch. Suitable for small courtyard gardens and may be trained as a bonsai specimen.
- PROPAGATION By softwood cuttings in spring, by budding in summer, or by grafting in late winter or early spring.

☀ ◊
❄ ❄ ❄

HEIGHT
1–1.5m
(3–5ft)

SPREAD
1.5m (5ft)

Scrophulariaceae	

HEBE HULKEANA 'Lilac Hint'

Habit Upright, open-branched. **Flowers** Small, 4-lobed, in large panicles, in profusion in late spring and early summer. Pale lilac-blue. **Leaves** Evergreen, oval, toothed. Glossy pale green.
• NATIVE HABITAT Garden origin.
• CULTIVATION Thrives in seaside gardens. Grow in any fertile, freely draining soil and shelter from cold winter winds. Needs little pruning but benefits from trimming back after flowering.
• PROPAGATION By semi-ripe cuttings in summer.

HEIGHT
60cm (24in)
or more

SPREAD
60cm (24in)

Leguminosae	

DESMODIUM ELEGANS

Habit Upright sub-shrub. **Flowers** Small, pea-like, in large panicles from late summer to mid-autumn. Pale lilac. **Leaves** Deciduous, divided into 3 large, rounded-oval leaflets. Mid-green.
• NATIVE HABITAT In scrubland of the Himalaya.
• CULTIVATION Grow in light soil. In cold areas provide the shelter of a warm, south- or west-facing wall. Protect with a dry mulch in winter.
• PROPAGATION By softwood cuttings in summer or by seed in autumn.
• OTHER NAMES D. tiliifolium.

HEIGHT
90cm–1.5m
(3–5ft) or
more

SPREAD
1.5m (5ft)

Scrophulariaceae	

HEBE 'E. A. Bowles'

Habit Bushy, rounded. **Flowers** Small, 4-lobed, in slender spikes from mid-summer to late autumn. Soft lilac. **Leaves** Evergreen, narrowly oval. Glossy pale green.
• NATIVE HABITAT Garden origin.
• CULTIVATION Thrives in seaside gardens. Grow in any fertile, freely draining soil, with shelter from cold winter winds. Seldom needs much pruning but leggy specimens may be cut back in spring.
• PROPAGATION By semi-ripe cuttings in summer.

HEIGHT
75cm (30in)
or more

SPREAD
1m (3ft)

Verbenaceae	

LANTANA MONTEVIDENSIS

Habit Trailing or mat-forming. **Flowers** Tiny, in dense heads throughout the year, mainly in summer. Rose-purple with a yellow eye. **Leaves** Evergreen, oval-oblong to lance-shaped, serrated. Mid-green.
• NATIVE HABITAT S. America.
• CULTIVATION Grow in a well-lit position in the home or in a conservatory in a freely draining, fertile soil or compost. Water freely when in growth, otherwise moderately. Tip back shoots when young to promote bushiness. Susceptible to red spider mite and whitefly when grown under glass. Valued for its long flowering period and makes an attractive specimen for a warm conservatory or well-lit place in the home. It also makes good, free-flowering ground cover in warm, frost-free climates.
• PROPAGATION By seed in spring or by semi-ripe cuttings in summer.
• OTHER NAMES *L. delicatissima, L. sellowiana.*

☀ ◊

Min.
7–10°C
(45–50°F)

HEIGHT
50cm (20in)
or more

SPREAD
1.2m (4ft)

Boraginaceae	CHERRY-PIE, HELIOTROPE

HELIOTROPIUM ARBORESCENS

Habit Bushy. **Flowers** Small, very fragrant, in dense, flat clusters from late spring to winter. Purple to lavender. **Leaves** Evergreen, elliptic-oblong to oval, finely wrinkled. Dark green.
• NATIVE HABITAT Dry, open sites in Peru.
• CULTIVATION Grow in a conservatory in fertile, well-drained soil or compost. Water freely in growth, then moderately. Can be used for summer bedding.
• PROPAGATION By seed in spring, or by greenwood or semi-ripe cuttings in late summer.
• OTHER NAMES *H. peruvianum.*

☀ ◊

Min. 5°C
(41°F)

HEIGHT
1m (3ft) or
more

SPREAD
75cm–2m
(2½–6ft)

Polygalaceae	

POLYGALA × DALMAISIANA   ♥

Habit Upright, much-branched. **Flowers** Pea-like, in short racemes from late spring to autumn. White-veined, rich purple. **Leaves** Evergreen, small, elliptic-oblong or oval. Greyish-green.
• NATIVE HABITAT S. Africa.
• CULTIVATION Grow in a conservatory in a fertile, humus-rich soil or compost with added sharp sand. Water freely in growth, then moderately.
• PROPAGATION By seed in spring or by semi-ripe cuttings in summer.
• OTHER NAMES *P. myrtifolia* 'Grandiflora'.

☀ ◊

Min. 5°C
(41°F)

HEIGHT
1m (3ft) or
more

SPREAD
1.5m (5ft)

Solanaceae	

BRUNFELSIA PAUCIFLORA 'Macrantha'

Habit Spreading, much-branched.
Flowers Large, saucer-shaped, from winter to summer. Rich blue-purple, ageing to white.
Leaves Evergreen, oblong to lance-shaped, leathery. Deep green.
• NATIVE HABITAT Garden origin.
• CULTIVATION Grow in the home or conservatory in a fertile, humus-rich soil, with good light but not direct sun. Water moderately when in growth, otherwise sparingly.
• PROPAGATION By semi-ripe cuttings in summer.

Min.
7–10°C
(45–50°F)

HEIGHT
1.5m (5ft)

SPREAD
1.5m (5ft)

Labiatae	FRENCH LAVENDER

LAVANDULA STOECHAS ♥

Habit Bushy, dense. *Flowers* Tiny, strongly fragrant, in dense spikes in late spring and summer. Deep purple, topped by rose-purple bracts.
Leaves Evergreen, aromatic, linear to oblong-lance-shaped, woolly. Silver-grey.
• NATIVE HABITAT In scrub and open coniferous woodland on dry hills around the Mediterranean.
• CULTIVATION Grow in any freely draining, fertile soil in a warm, sunny site.
• PROPAGATION By seed in spring or by semi-ripe cuttings in summer.

HEIGHT
30cm–1m
(1–3ft)

SPREAD
30cm–1m
(1–3ft)

Scrophulariaceae	

HEBE 'Autumn Glory'

Habit Open, mound-forming. *Flowers* Small, 4-lobed, in dense racemes from mid-summer to early winter. Deep blue-purple. *Leaves* Evergreen, broadly oval. Glossy deep green, tinted purple.
Bark Shoots glossy and dark red-purple.
• NATIVE HABITAT Garden origin.
• CULTIVATION Grow in any fertile, freely draining soil, with shelter from cold winter winds. Thrives in seaside gardens and is tolerant of urban pollution. Cut back leggy specimens in spring.
• PROPAGATION By semi-ripe cuttings in summer.

HEIGHT
60cm (24in)

SPREAD
75cm (30in)

Labiatae	HIDCOTE LAVENDER

LAVANDULA ANGUSTIFOLIA 'Hidcote' ♥

Habit Bushy, dense. *Flowers* Tiny, fragrant, in dense, slender-stemmed spikes from mid- to late summer. Deep purple. *Leaves* Evergreen, aromatic, narrowly lance-shaped. Silver-grey.
• NATIVE HABITAT Garden origin.
• CULTIVATION Grow in any freely draining, fertile soil in a warm, sunny site. Excellent for low hedging. Trim in spring to maintain compactness. Pick flowers for drying before fully open.
• PROPAGATION By semi-ripe cuttings in summer.

HEIGHT
To 30cm
(1ft)

SPREAD
60–80cm
(24–32in)

Labiatae	HYSSOP

HYSSOPUS OFFICINALIS

Habit Bushy, compact, erect, many-stemmed.
Flowers Small, tubular, 2-lipped, in slender spikes
from mid-summer to early autumn. Blue-violet.
Leaves Semi-evergreen or deciduous, aromatic,
narrowly oval. Deep green.
• NATIVE HABITAT Dry slopes, S. and E. Europe.
• CULTIVATION Grow in freely draining, fertile
soil in a warm, sunny site. Excellent for low hedging;
trim lightly in spring. Leaves used in cooking.
• PROPAGATION By seed in autumn or by
softwood cuttings in summer.

HEIGHT
To 60cm
(24in)

SPREAD
60cm (24in)

Scrophulariaceae	

HEBE 'Amy'

Habit Bushy, compact. *Flowers* Small, 4-lobed,
in racemes from early summer to mid-autumn.
Deep blue-purple. *Leaves* Evergreen, broadly oval
to elliptic. Purple-tinted, then glossy deep green.
• NATIVE HABITAT Garden origin.
• CULTIVATION Thrives in seaside gardens and
tolerates urban pollution. Grow in any fertile, freely
draining soil, with shelter from cold winter winds.
Leggy specimens may be cut back in spring.
• PROPAGATION By semi-ripe cuttings in summer.
• OTHER NAMES *H.* 'Purple Queen'.

HEIGHT
75cm (30in)

SPREAD
75cm (30in)

Rhamnaceae	CREEPING BLUE BLOSSOM

CEANOTHUS THYRSIFLORUS var. *REPENS* ♀

Habit Vigorous, dense, mound-forming.
Flowers Tiny, in dense, rounded racemes in late
spring and early summer. Blue. *Leaves* Evergreen,
broadly elliptic. Glossy dark green.
• NATIVE HABITAT Coastal scrub of N. California.
• CULTIVATION Tolerant of semi-shade on light
soils and of coastal conditions. Grow in a warm,
sunny, sheltered site, in a light, well-drained soil.
Cut out dead wood in spring and trim back side-
shoots after flowering.
• PROPAGATION By semi-ripe cuttings in summer.

HEIGHT
To 1m (3ft)

SPREAD
2.5m (8ft)

Rhamnaceae	

CEANOTHUS X *DELILEANUS* 'Gloire de Versailles'

Habit Vigorous, bushy. **Flowers** Tiny, in large racemes from mid-summer to early autumn. Pale blue. **Leaves** Deciduous, broadly oval. Mid-green.
• NATIVE HABITAT Garden origin.
• CULTIVATION Grow in a warm, sheltered site, in a light and well-drained soil. Tolerant of some lime in the soil and of coastal conditions. Cut back in spring to a basal framework or to within 8–10cm (3–4in) of the previous year's growth.
• PROPAGATION By semi-ripe cuttings in summer.

☀ ◊
❀❀

HEIGHT
To 1.5m
(5ft)

SPREAD
1.5m (5ft)

Verbenaceae	

CARYOPTERIS X *CLANDONENSIS* 'Arthur Simmonds'

Habit Bushy, rounded sub-shrub. **Flowers** Tiny, in dense, many-flowered clusters from late summer to autumn. Bright blue-purple.
Leaves Deciduous, narrowly oval, irregularly toothed. Grey-green.
• NATIVE HABITAT Garden origin.
• CULTIVATION Grow in light, fertile soil in a warm, sheltered position. Tolerant of chalky soils.
• PROPAGATION By greenwood or semi-ripe cuttings in summer.

☀ ◊
❀❀

HEIGHT
75cm (30in)

SPREAD
75cm (30in)

Compositae	BLUE DAISY, BLUE MARGUERITE

FELICIA AMELLOIDES 'Santa Anita'

Habit Bushy, spreading sub-shrub.
Flowers Large, daisy-like heads, on long stalks from late spring to autumn. Blue with bright yellow centres. **Leaves** Evergreen, round to oval. Bright green.
• NATIVE HABITAT Species found in dry, rocky areas of South Africa.
• CULTIVATION Grow in light soil in a sheltered site. Protect in cold weather. Dead-head regularly.
• PROPAGATION By greenwood cuttings in summer or early autumn.

☀ ◊
❀

HEIGHT
To 30cm
(12in)

SPREAD
60cm (24in)

Labiatae	

PEROVSKIA ATRIPLICIFOLIA 'Blue Spire'

Habit Upright sub-shrub. **Flowers** Tiny, tubular, 2-lipped, in long, narrow panicles from late summer to mid-autumn. Violet-blue. **Leaves** Deciduous, aromatic, deeply cut. Grey-green. **Bark** Shoots white.
• NATIVE HABITAT Garden origin.
• CULTIVATION Grow in a warm, sunny position. Tolerates any freely draining soil. Cut back hard almost to the base in spring as new growth begins.
• PROPAGATION By softwood cuttings in late spring.

☀ ◊
❀❀❀

HEIGHT
To 1.5m
(5ft)

SPREAD
1.5m (5ft)

Caprifoliaceae	

SYMPHORICARPOS ORBICULATUS 'Foliis Variegatis'

Habit Bushy, suckering. *Flowers* Occasionally bears flowers in summer to autumn. White or pink. *Leaves* Deciduous, oval. Green with yellow margins.
• NATIVE HABITAT Garden origin.
• CULTIVATION Tolerant of urban pollution, coastal conditions, and dry soil.
• PROPAGATION By softwood cuttings in summer or by rooted suckers in autumn.
• OTHER NAMES *S. o.* 'Variegatus', *S. o.* 'Aureovariegatus'.

HEIGHT
To 1.5m
(5ft)

SPREAD
1.5m (5ft)

Caprifoliaceae	

WEIGELA MIDDENDORFFIANA

Habit Bushy, arching. *Flowers* Large, funnel-shaped. Soft sulphur-yellow, spotted orange at the throat. *Leaves* Deciduous, oblong to narrowly oval, pointed, serrated. Bright green.
• NATIVE HABITAT Mountain thickets of Japan and N. China.
• CULTIVATION Prefers a fertile, humus-rich soil and a warm, sunny site. Tolerant of urban pollution and of most soils. Prune out some of the oldest branches at ground level annually after flowering.
• PROPAGATION By softwood cuttings in summer.

HEIGHT
To 1.5m
(5ft)

SPREAD
1.5m (5ft)

Acanthaceae	

JUSTICIA BRANDEGEEANA 'Chartreuse'

Habit Bushy, arching. *Flowers* Small, tubular, in arching spikes mainly in summer. White, enclosed in overlapping pale yellow-green bracts. *Leaves* Evergreen, oval to elliptic, soft. Mid-green.
• NATIVE HABITAT Garden origin.
• CULTIVATION Grow in a well-lit area of the home or in a conservatory in a fertile, humus-rich soil or compost. Water freely when in full growth, then moderately. Cut back leggy plants in spring.
• PROPAGATION By softwood or greenwood cuttings in spring or early summer.

Min.
7–10°C
(45–50°F)

HEIGHT
75cm–1m
(30–36in)

SPREAD
50–75cm
(20–30in)

Compositae	

SANTOLINA PINNATA subsp. *NEAPOLITANA* 'Sulphurea'

Habit Bushy, rounded. *Flowers* Minute, in dense, button-like heads on slender stems in mid-summer. Pale primrose-yellow. *Leaves* Evergreen, aromatic, deeply cut, feathery. Grey-green.
• NATIVE HABITAT Species occurs on dry, rocky, coastal hills of S. Italy. Garden origin.
• CULTIVATION Grow in any well-drained, not too fertile soil, in a warm, sunny site. Dead-head and reduce long stems in autumn.
• PROPAGATION By semi-ripe cuttings in summer.

HEIGHT
60–75cm
(24–30in)

SPREAD
60–75cm
(24–30in)

Rosaceae	

POTENTILLA FRUTICOSA 'Vilmoriniana'

Habit Vigorous, bushy, with upright branches.
Flowers Large, single, in profusion from late spring to autumn. Pale yellow or creamy-white.
Leaves Deciduous, divided into 5 narrowly oval leaflets. Silvery-grey.
• NATIVE HABITAT Garden origin.
• CULTIVATION Tolerates light shade, although flowers best in sun. Grow in any moderately fertile, but not too rich soil; very fertile soils promote leafy growth with few flowers. Prune in early spring, cutting out weak and crowded growth at the base,

and tipping back strong growth by about one-third. Old, congested specimens may be rejuvenated over 2–3 seasons by cutting a proportion of the plant back hard in early spring. This cultivar, and other shrubby potentillas, are invaluable in shrub and mixed borders.
• PROPAGATION By softwood or greenwood cuttings in summer.

HEIGHT
To 1.5m
(5ft)

SPREAD
1m (3ft)

Leguminosae	TREE LUPIN

LUPINUS ARBOREUS

Habit Fast-growing, sprawling, usually short-lived.
Flowers Fragrant, appearing in short spikes from
early to late summer. Shades of soft, clear yellow.
Leaves Semi-evergreen, divided into 6–9 leaflets,
often silky-hairy. Pale green.
• NATIVE HABITAT Dunes and coastal scrub of
California.
• CULTIVATION Tolerant of coastal conditions.
Grow in any light, freely draining, not too rich soil,
in a warm, sunny site with shelter from cold winds.
• PROPAGATION By fresh seed in autumn.

HEIGHT
To 1.5m
(5ft)

SPREAD
1.5–2m
(5–6ft)

Scrophulariaceae	

PHYGELIUS AEQUALIS 'Yellow Trumpet'

Habit Upright sub-shrub. *Flowers* Tubular, in
one-sided panicles from mid-summer to early
autumn. Pale creamy-yellow. *Leaves* Evergreen or
semi-evergreen, oval. Dark green.
• NATIVE HABITAT Garden origin.
• CULTIVATION Grow in light but not too dry soil,
in a sheltered position, and against a south- or west-
facing wall in cool areas. Prune back to a permanent
woody framework in spring. May be cut back by
frost but will regenerate from the base.
• PROPAGATION By softwood cuttings in summer.

HEIGHT
1–1.2m
(3–4ft)

SPREAD
1–1.2m
(3–4ft)

Rosaceae	

POTENTILLA FRUTICOSA 'Elizabeth'

Habit Vigorous, bushy, mound-forming.
Flowers Large, single, in profusion from late
spring to mid-autumn. Rich bright yellow.
Leaves Deciduous, divided into 5 narrowly oval
leaflets. Soft green.
• NATIVE HABITAT Garden origin.
• CULTIVATION Grow in any moderately fertile,
but not too rich soil. In early spring cut out crowded
growth; tip back strong growth by about one-third.
• PROPAGATION By softwood or greenwood
cuttings in summer.

HEIGHT
1m (3ft)

SPREAD
1.2m (4ft)

Proteaceae	

GREVILLEA JUNIPERINA f. *SULPHUREA*

Habit Bushy, rounded. *Flowers* Tubular, with
protruding, recurved styles, in dense racemes at
intervals from early spring to late summer. Pale
yellow. *Leaves* Evergreen, needle-like, recurved.
Dark green above, silky-haired beneath.
• NATIVE HABITAT New South Wales, Australia.
• CULTIVATION Grow in a cool conservatory in
areas prone to hard frosts in neutral to acid, freely
draining soil in a warm, sunny, sheltered site. Prune
after flowering if necessary.
• PROPAGATION By semi-ripe cuttings in summer.

HEIGHT
1m (3ft) or
more

SPREAD
1m (3ft) or
more

Rosaceae	

POTENTILLA FRUTICOSA 'Friedrichsenii'

Habit Vigorous, bushy, upright. ***Flowers*** Large, single, in profusion from late spring to mid-autumn. Bright yellow. ***Leaves*** Deciduous, divided into 5 narrowly oval leaflets. Grey-green.
• NATIVE HABITAT Garden origin.
• CULTIVATION Grow in any moderately fertile but not too rich soil. Prune in early spring, cutting out weak and crowded growth at the base. Tip back strong growth by about one-third.
• PROPAGATION By softwood or greenwood cuttings in summer.

HEIGHT
To 1.5m
(5ft)

SPREAD
1.2m (4ft)

Cistaceae	

HALIMIUM OCIYMOÏDES 'Susan' ♀

Habit Compact, spreading. ***Flowers*** Small, single or semi-double, in small, few-flowered panicles along the branches in summer. Bright yellow with central, deep purple-red markings.
Leaves Evergreen, narrowly oval. Grey-green.
• NATIVE HABITAT Species occurs in heathland and pinewoods on sandy soils of the Mediterranean.
• CULTIVATION Grow in a warm, sheltered position in light, freely draining soil. Good for seaside gardens and suitable for the rock garden.
• PROPAGATION By semi-ripe cuttings in summer.

HEIGHT
60cm (24in)

SPREAD
60cm (24in)

Cistaceae	

HALIMIUM LASIANTHUM
subsp. *FORMOSUM*

Habit Bushy, spreading, with upright branches. ***Flowers*** Small, single, in early summer. Golden-yellow with central deep red blotches.
Leaves Evergreen, narrowly oval. Grey-green.
• NATIVE HABITAT Scrub and open woodland of S. Portugal and S. Spain.
• CULTIVATION Grow in a warm, sheltered position, in light, freely draining soil. Good for seaside gardens.
• PROPAGATION By semi-ripe cuttings in summer.

HEIGHT
75cm–1m
(30–36in)

SPREAD
75cm–1m
(30–36in)

Labiatae	JERUSALEM SAGE

PHLOMIS FRUTICOSA ♀

Habit Spreading, with upright shoots.
Flowers 2-lipped, upper lip hooded, lower lip lobed, in whorls along the shoots from early to mid-summer. Golden-yellow. ***Leaves*** Evergreen, aromatic, oval to lance-shaped. Grey-green.
• NATIVE HABITAT Dry, rocky hillsides, usually on limestone, around the Mediterranean.
• CULTIVATION Grow in a sheltered position in light, freely draining, not too rich soil.
• PROPAGATION By seed in autumn or by softwood cuttings in summer.

HEIGHT
1–1.5m
(3–5ft)

SPREAD
1–1.5m
(3–5ft)

Berberidaceae	

BERBERIS THUNBERGII 'Aurea'

Habit Low-growing, compact, spiny.
Flowers Globose to cup-shaped, in mid-spring.
Red-tinged, pale yellow. *Fruits* Small, elliptic
berries. Red. *Leaves* Deciduous, oval. Yellow
when young, later pale green.
• NATIVE HABITAT Species occurs in woodland in
Japan. Garden origin.
• CULTIVATION Grows in any but waterlogged soils.
Leaves may scorch in sun. Tolerates semi-shade.
• PROPAGATION By softwood or semi-ripe
cuttings in summer.

☼ ◊
❀ ❀ ❀

HEIGHT
50cm (20in)

SPREAD
50cm (20in)

Leguminosae	BLACK BROOM

CYTISUS NIGRICANS

Habit Compact, upright. *Flowers* Pea-like, in long,
slender, silky spires, in profusion in mid- to late
summer. Yellow. *Leaves* Deciduous, tiny, divided
into 3 leaflets. Dark green.
• NATIVE HABITAT Woodland edge on dry soils of
C. and S.E. Europe to C. Russia.
• CULTIVATION Grow in fertile, but not over-rich,
neutral to slightly acid soil. Prune in spring, cutting
back to new growth. Resents transplanting.
• PROPAGATION By semi-ripe cuttings in late
summer.

☼ ◊
❀ ❀ ❀

HEIGHT
1–1.5m
(3–5ft)

SPREAD
75cm (30in)

Leguminosae	SPANISH GORSE

GENISTA HISPANICA

Habit Bushy, compact, mound-forming, spiny.
Flowers Pea-like, in dense clusters in late spring
and early summer. Golden-yellow.
Leaves Deciduous, tiny, oval-oblong. Dark green.
• NATIVE HABITAT On dry, rocky hillsides in
scrub of S. France and N. Spain.
• CULTIVATION Grow in light, fertile, but not too
rich soil. Prune annually after flowering to keep
compact, taking care not to cut into older wood.
• PROPAGATION By seed in autumn or by
softwood or semi-ripe cuttings in summer.

☼ ◊
❀ ❀

HEIGHT
50–75cm
(20–30in)

SPREAD
1.5m (5ft)

Compositae	

BRACHYGLOTTIS Dunedin Hybrids ♀
Group

Habit Bushy, mound-forming. *Flowers* Daisy-
like heads, in clusters, on white-felted shoots from
early to mid-summer. Bright yellow.
Leaves Evergreen, oval. Silver-grey when young,
later dark green and white-felted beneath.
• NATIVE HABITAT Garden origin.
• CULTIVATION Thrives in coastal conditions.
Grow in any well-drained soil in a sheltered site.
• PROPAGATION Semi-ripe cuttings in summer.
• OTHER NAMES *Senecio* 'Sunshine'.

☼ ◊
❀ ❀

HEIGHT
To 1m (3ft)
or more

SPREAD
1.5m (5ft)

Guttiferae	AARON'S BEARD, ROSE OF SHARON

HYPERICUM CALYCINUM

Habit Suckering, with upright stems.
Flowers Large, from mid-summer to mid-autumn. Bright yellow. **Leaves** Evergreen or semi-evergreen, oblong to narrowly oval. Dark green.
• NATIVE HABITAT S.E. Bulgaria and N. Turkey.
• CULTIVATION Tolerates drought, shade, and any but waterlogged soil. Cut back to ground every other year in spring. Excellent ground cover but can be invasive.
• PROPAGATION By seed or by division in autumn or by softwood cuttings in summer.

HEIGHT
20–60cm
(8–24in)

SPREAD
1.5m (5ft)
or more

Guttiferae	

HYPERICUM 'Hidcote'

Habit Bushy, with semi-arching stems.
Flowers Large, cupped, in abundant clusters from mid-summer to early autumn. Rich golden-yellow. **Leaves** Evergreen or semi-evergreen, triangular lance-shaped. Dark green.
• NATIVE HABITAT Garden origin.
• CULTIVATION Tolerates semi-shade but flowers best in sun. Grow in any well-drained soil. Cut out dead wood in spring. May be cut by hard frost but re-sprouts from base. Can be hard pruned to shape.
• PROPAGATION By semi-ripe cuttings in summer.

HEIGHT
To 1.5m
(5ft)

SPREAD
To 2.5m
(8ft)

HYPERICUM × *INODORUM* 'Elstead'

Habit Bushy, upright. **Flowers** Small, star-shaped, in abundant clusters from mid-summer to early autumn. Yellow. **Fruits** Oval, fleshy capsule. Orange-red. **Leaves** Semi-evergreen or deciduous, oblong-lance-shaped to broadly oval; aromatic when crushed. Dark green.
• NATIVE HABITAT Garden origin.
• CULTIVATION Tolerates semi-shade but flowers best in sun. Grow in any well-drained soil. Cut out dead wood in spring.
• PROPAGATION By semi-ripe cuttings in summer.

HEIGHT
1m (3ft)

SPREAD
1m (3ft)

Guttiferae	

HYPERICUM KOUYTCHENSE

Habit Bushy, arching. **Flowers** Small, star-shaped, in abundance from mid-summer to early autumn. Yellow. **Fruits** Oval, fleshy capsule. Bronze-red. **Leaves** Semi-evergreen or deciduous, elliptic to oval or lance-shaped. Dark green.
• NATIVE HABITAT In open scrub of China.
• CULTIVATION Tolerates semi-shade but flowers best in sun. Grow in any moderately fertile, well-drained soil. Cut out dead wood in spring.
• PROPAGATION By seed in autumn or by semi-ripe cuttings in summer.

HEIGHT
1m (3ft) or
more

SPREAD
1.5m (5ft)

SHRUBS SMALL/Summer

Linaceae	YELLOW FLAX

REINWARDTIA INDICA

Habit Upright sub-shrub. ***Flowers*** Large, flax-like, in short, dense racemes, mainly in summer but sporadically throughout the year. Yellow.
Leaves Evergreen, elliptic. Grey-green.
• NATIVE HABITAT N. India and China.
• CULTIVATION Grow in a well-lit area of the home or in a conservatory in fertile, freely draining soil or compost. Water freely in growth, then moderately.
• PROPAGATION By softwood cuttings in late spring.
• OTHER NAMES *R. trigyna*.

Min.
7–10°C
(45–50°F)

HEIGHT
60–90cm
(24–36in)

SPREAD
60–90cm
(24–36in)

Compositae	

EURYOPS PECTINATUS

Habit Vigorous, upright. ***Flowers*** Delicate, daisy-like heads in late spring and early summer. Clear yellow. ***Leaves*** Evergreen, deeply cut, downy. Grey-green.
• NATIVE HABITAT Mountains of S. Africa.
• CULTIVATION Grow in a conservatory in neutral to slightly acid, light, gritty, freely draining soil. In almost frost-free areas grow outside but provide the shelter of a south- or west-facing wall and a dry mulch in winter.
• PROPAGATION By softwood cuttings in summer.

Min 5–7°C
(41–45°F)

HEIGHT
1m (3ft) or
more

SPREAD
75cm (30in)

Compositae	

BRACHYGLOTTIS MONROI

Habit Bushy, compact, dense. ***Flowers*** Small, daisy-like, in clusters in mid-summer. Yellow.
Leaves Evergreen, small, oblong to oval, with wavy edges. Dark green, white-felted beneath.
• NATIVE HABITAT Sub-alpine scrub of New Zealand.
• CULTIVATION Grow in any well-drained soil in a sheltered site. Prune in spring for best foliage effects, otherwise trim after flowering.
• PROPAGATION By semi-ripe cuttings in summer.
• OTHER NAMES *Senecio monroi*.

HEIGHT
To 1m (3ft)

SPREAD
1m (3ft)

Compositae	

GRINDELIA CHILOENSIS

Habit Bushy sub-shrub with upright stems.
Flowers Large, daisy-like, in summer; covered in sticky, white gum when in bud. Clear yellow.
Leaves Evergreen, lance-shaped, serrated, sticky. Dark green.
• NATIVE HABITAT Patagonia.
• CULTIVATION Tolerant of poor, dry soils. Grow in gritty, well drained, not too rich soil in a warm, sheltered site.
• PROPAGATION By semi-ripe cuttings in summer.
• OTHER NAMES *G. speciosa*.

HEIGHT
1m (3ft)

SPREAD
75cm (30in)

Leguminosae	

CYTISUS SCOPARIUS f. ANDREANUS ♀

Habit Densely branched, arching. **Flowers** Pea-like, in profusion along slender shoots, in late spring and early summer. Bright yellow, marked brown-crimson. **Leaves** Deciduous, divided into 3 leaflets. Dark green.
• NATIVE HABITAT Normandy, France.
• CULTIVATION Grow in fertile, but not over-rich, neutral to slightly acid soil. After flowering, cut back flowered stems by about half. Do not cut old wood.
• PROPAGATION By semi-ripe cuttings in late summer.

HEIGHT
75cm (30in)

SPREAD
1.5m (5ft)

Malvaceae	

ABUTILON 'Kentish Belle' ♀

Habit Vigorous, arching. **Flowers** Large, pendent, bell-shaped, in summer and autumn. Orange-yellow and red. **Leaves** Semi-evergreen, deeply lobed. Dark green, purple veined.
• NATIVE HABITAT Garden origin.
• CULTIVATION Prefers a light soil and requires a warm, sunny site, such as a south- or west-facing wall. Provide a dry winter mulch in cool areas. Cut back previous year's growth hard in early spring.
• PROPAGATION By softwood, greenwood, or semi-ripe cuttings in summer.

HEIGHT
To 1.5m
(5ft)

SPREAD
1m (3ft)

Paeoniaceae	

PAEONIA × LEMOINEI 'Souvenir de Maxime Cornu'

Habit Upright. **Flowers** Very large, fragrant, bowl-shaped, double, in summer. Yellow, with ruffled reddish-orange petal margins. **Leaves** Deciduous, divided into pointed leaflets. Bright green.
• NATIVE HABITAT Garden origin.
• CULTIVATION Tolerates chalk and light shade. Grow in fertile, neutral to alkaline soil, in a sunny, sheltered position protected from early sun.
• PROPAGATION By semi-ripe cuttings in late summer or by grafting in winter.

HEIGHT
To 1.5m
(5ft)

SPREAD
1.5m (5ft)

Paeoniaceae	

PAEONIA 'Mme Louis Henri'

Habit Upright. **Flowers** Very large, bowl-shaped, loosely semi-double, in summer. Russet red. **Leaves** Deciduous, divided into deeply cut, pointed leaflets. Bright green.
• NATIVE HABITAT Garden origin.
• CULTIVATION Tolerates chalk and light shade. Grow in fertile, neutral to alkaline soil, in a sunny, sheltered position but protect from early sun. Will re-sprout from the base if cut by frost.
• PROPAGATION By semi-ripe cuttings in late summer or by grafting in winter.

HEIGHT
To 1.5m
(5ft)

SPREAD
1.5m (5ft)

Scrophulariaceae	BUSH MONKEY FLOWER

MIMULUS AURANTIACUS

Habit Domed, or sprawling. *Flowers* Tubular, from late spring to autumn. Orange, yellow, or red-purple. *Leaves* Evergreen, lance-shaped. Rich green.
• NATIVE HABITAT Dry, rocky foothills of coastal mountains of S. Oregon and N. California.
• CULTIVATION Prefers a light, dry soil and requires a warm, sunny site.
• PROPAGATION By semi-ripe cuttings in late summer.
• OTHER NAMES *M. glutinosus, Diplacus glutinosus.*

☀ ◊
❄

HEIGHT
To 1.2m
(4ft)

SPREAD
1.2m (4ft)

Scrophulariaceae	

ISOPLEXIS CANARIENSIS

Habit Rounded, with upright stems.
Flowers Large, foxglove-like, in dense, upright spikes in summer. Orange-yellow to yellow-brown.
Leaves Evergreen, lance-shaped to narrowly oval, toothed. Mid-green.
• NATIVE HABITAT Canary Islands.
• CULTIVATION Grow in a conservatory in light, dry soil. In almost frost-free areas grow outside but provide the shelter of a south- or west-facing wall.
• PROPAGATION By semi-ripe cuttings in summer.
• OTHER NAMES *Digitalis canariensis.*

☀ ◊

Min 7°C
(45°F)

HEIGHT
1.2m (4ft)

SPREAD
75cm (30in)
or more

Rosaceae	

POTENTILLA FRUTICOSA 'Sunset'

Habit Bushy, arching with age. *Flowers* Large, single, in profusion from early summer to mid-autumn. Deep orange. *Leaves* Deciduous, divided into 5 narrowly oval leaflets. Mid-green.
• NATIVE HABITAT Garden origin.
• CULTIVATION Grow in any moderately fertile but not too rich soil. Flowers fade in sun. In early spring cut out crowded growth at the base, tipping back strong growth by about one-third.
• PROPAGATION By softwood or greenwood cuttings in summer.

☀ ◊
❄ ❄ ❄

HEIGHT
1m (3ft)

SPREAD
1m (3ft)

Solanaceae	

JUANULLOA MEXICANA

Habit Upright, sparingly branched.
Flowers Tubular, waxy, with urn-shaped, ribbed calyxes, in nodding clusters in summer. Orange.
Leaves Evergreen, oblong, leathery. Dark green.
• NATIVE HABITAT Peru, Colombia, and C. America.
• CULTIVATION Grow in a warm conservatory in a fertile soil or compost. Water moderately in growth, then sparingly. Pinch out shoots of young plants.
• PROPAGATION By semi-ripe cuttings in summer.
• OTHER NAMES *J. aurantiaca.*

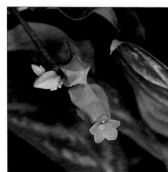

☀ ◊

Min.
13–15°C
(55–59°F)

HEIGHT
1m (3ft) or
more

SPREAD
1m (3ft)

Verbenaceae	

LANTANA 'Spreading Sunset'

Habit Rounded to spreading. *Flowers* Tiny, tubular, in rounded heads from spring to autumn. Golden-yellow to soft pink. *Leaves* Evergreen, oval, pointed, finely wrinkled. Dark green.
• NATIVE HABITAT Garden origin.
• CULTIVATION Grow in a conservatory in a fertile soil or compost. Water freely when in growth, otherwise moderately. Tip prune when young to promote bushiness. Also useful for summer bedding; plant out in early summer.
• PROPAGATION By semi-ripe cuttings in summer.

☼ ◊

Min.
10–13°C
(50–55°F)

HEIGHT
60cm (20in)

SPREAD
1.2m (4ft)

Lythraceae	CIGAR FLOWER

CUPHEA IGNEA ♥

Habit Spreading, bushy. *Flowers* Small, tubular, from spring to autumn. Dark orange-red, each with a dark band and white ring at the mouth.
Leaves Evergreen, lance-shaped. Dark green.
• NATIVE HABITAT Mexico and Jamaica.
• CULTIVATION Grow in a moderately fertile soil or compost. Water freely when in growth, otherwise moderately. Feed weekly in spring and summer. For summer bedding or a cool conservatory.
• PROPAGATION By seed in spring or by greenwood cuttings in spring or summer.

☼ ◊

Min. 2°C
(36°F)

HEIGHT
To 60cm
(24in)

SPREAD
60cm (24in)

Lythraceae	

CUPHEA CYANAEA

Habit Rounded sub-shrub. *Flowers* Small, tubular, in summer. Orange-red, yellow, and violet-blue. *Leaves* Evergreen, narrowly oval, sticky-haired. Dark green.
• NATIVE HABITAT Dry areas of Mexico.
• CULTIVATION Grow in a moderately fertile soil or compost. Water freely when in growth, otherwise moderately. Feed weekly in spring and summer. Suitable for summer bedding or a cool conservatory.
• PROPAGATION By seed in spring or by greenwood cuttings in spring or summer.

☼ ◊

Min. 2°C
(36°F)

HEIGHT
To 60cm
(24in)

SPREAD
60cm (24in)

Acanthaceae	

JUSTICIA SPICIGERA

Habit Bushy, much-branched. *Flowers* Small, tubular, in terminal spikes, mainly in summer. Orange or red. *Leaves* Evergreen, large, lance-shaped to oval, soft. Mid-green.
• NATIVE HABITAT Mexico and Colombia.
• CULTIVATION Grow in a conservatory in a fertile, humus-rich soil or compost. Water freely when in full growth, otherwise moderately.
• PROPAGATION By softwood or greenwood cuttings in spring or early summer.
• OTHER NAMES *Jacobinia spicigera*.

☼ ◊

Min.
10°C (50°F)

HEIGHT
To 1.5m
(5ft)

SPREAD
1m (3ft)

Meliaceae	

TURRAEA OBTUSIFOLIA

Habit Bushy, rounded, arching. *Flowers* Star-shaped, fragrant, from autumn to spring. White. *Fruits* Small, flattened-globose, segmented. Orange-yellow. *Leaves* Evergreen, oval to lance-shaped. Dark green.
• NATIVE HABITAT S. Africa.
• CULTIVATION Grow in a warm conservatory in fertile soil or compost. Water freely when in growth, otherwise moderately.
• PROPAGATION By seed in spring or by semi-ripe cuttings in summer.

Min. 13°C
(55°F)

HEIGHT
To 1.5m
(5ft)

SPREAD
1m (3ft)

Berberidaceae	

BERBERIS 'Rubrostilla'

Habit Vigorous, arching. *Flowers* Small, globose to cup-shaped, in racemes in early summer. Pale yellow. *Fruits* Large, ovoid berries, in profusion from late summer. Coral-red. *Leaves* Deciduous, oval. Grey-green, turning brilliant red in autumn.
• NATIVE HABITAT Garden origin.
• CULTIVATION Tolerates light shade, and any but waterlogged soils. Prefers humus-rich, fertile soil, and blooms best in sun. May be cut back hard after flowering to rejuvenate.
• PROPAGATION By semi-ripe cuttings in summer.

HEIGHT
To 1.5m
(5ft)

SPREAD
1.5m (5ft)

Leguminosae	FAIRY DUSTER, MESQUITILLA

CALLIANDRA ERIOPHYLLA

Habit Dense, stiff, spreading. *Flowers* Small, powder-puff heads consist of tiny florets with long stamens, carried from late spring to autumn. White. *Leaves* Evergreen, divided, with 12–20 narrowly elliptic leaflets. Bright green.
• NATIVE HABITAT California and New Mexico.
• CULTIVATION Grow in a conservatory. Shade from the hottest summer sun. Will tolerate partial shade. Water freely when in full growth and sparingly in low temperatures.
• PROPAGATION By seed in spring.

Min. 10°C
(50°F)

HEIGHT
To 1m (3ft)

SPREAD
1m (3ft)

Rosaceae	

COTONEASTER HORIZONTALIS

Habit Spreading, with herringbone branching pattern. *Flowers* Small, from late spring to summer. Pinkish-white. *Fruits* Small, globose, berry-like, from autumn to winter. Bright red. *Leaves* Deciduous, broadly elliptic. Glossy dark green, turning red in autumn.
• NATIVE HABITAT Rocky areas of W. China.
• CULTIVATION Grow in any but waterlogged soils. Tolerates semi-shade but fruits best in sun.
• PROPAGATION By seed in autumn or by softwood cuttings in summer.

HEIGHT
50cm (20in)
or more

SPREAD
1.5m (5ft)

Ericaceae	

VACCINIUM ANGUSTIFOLIUM var. LAEVIFOLIUM

Habit Bushy, suckering. *Flowers* Small, cylindrical or bell-shaped, in late spring and early summer. White or pinkish. *Fruits* Globose. Edible. Blue-black, bloomed. *Leaves* Deciduous, oblong to lance-shaped. Glossy green, then red in autumn.
• NATIVE HABITAT N.E. North America.
• CULTIVATION Tolerates shade. Grow in well-drained but moist, peaty or sandy, acid soils.
• PROPAGATION By seed in autumn or by semi-ripe cuttings in summer.

HEIGHT
50–60cm
(20–24in)

SPREAD
80cm (32in)
or more

Rubiaceae	

BOUVARDIA TERNIFOLIA

Habit Bushy, upright. *Flowers* Tubular, in clusters from summer to early winter. Bright scarlet. *Leaves* Mainly evergreen, oval to lance-shaped, in whorls of 3, smooth. Mid-green.
• NATIVE HABITAT Mountains of the Trans-Pecos, Texas, New Mexico, and Mexico.
• CULTIVATION Grow in a conservatory in a fertile, freely draining soil or compost. Water freely when in full growth, otherwise moderately.
• PROPAGATION By softwood cuttings in spring or by greenwood or semi-ripe cuttings in summer.

Min.
7–10°C
(45–50°F)

HEIGHT
To 1m (3ft)

SPREAD
75cm (30in)

Caprifoliaceae	

VIBURNUM OPULUS 'Compactum'

Habit Dense, compact. *Flowers* Showy, flattened 'lace-cap' heads in early summer. White. *Fruits* Glossy berries, in clusters in autumn. Red. *Leaves* Deciduous, 3–5 lobes. Dark green, turning red in autumn.
• NATIVE HABITAT Species grows in hedgerows and woods from Europe to Siberia. Garden origin.
• CULTIVATION Tolerates semi-shade. Grow in any deep, fertile, not too dry soil. Some older shoots may be cut out after flowering if overcrowded.
• PROPAGATION By softwood cuttings in summer.

HEIGHT
To 1.5m
(5ft)

SPREAD
1.5m (5ft)

Ericaceae	HIGHBUSH BLUEBERRY

VACCINIUM CORYMBOSUM 'Pioneer'

Habit Upright, dense, slightly arching. *Flowers* Small, urn-shaped, in clusters in late spring and early summer. White or pinkish. *Fruits* Globose, edible, and sweet. Blue-black, bloomed. *Leaves* Deciduous, oval to lance-shaped. Dark green, turning red in autumn.
• NATIVE HABITAT Garden origin.
• CULTIVATION Tolerates shade. Grow in open, well-drained but moist, peaty or sandy, acid soils. Apply general fertilizer in spring for good cropping.
• PROPAGATION By semi-ripe cuttings in summer.

HEIGHT
To 1.5m
(5ft)

SPREAD
1–2m
(3–6ft)

Ericaceae	RED BILBERRY, RED HUCKLEBERRY

VACCINIUM PARVIFOLIUM

Habit Upright, dense. **Flowers** Small, globose, in late spring and early summer. White or pinkish. **Fruits** Egg-shaped, translucent, edible but acidic. Coral-red. **Leaves** Deciduous, small, variable in shape. Dark green, turning red in autumn.
• NATIVE HABITAT Dry and damp woodlands in the mountain foothills of W. North America.
• CULTIVATION Tolerates shade. Grow in open, well-drained but moist, peaty or sandy, acid soil.
• PROPAGATION By seed in autumn or by semi-ripe cuttings in summer.

HEIGHT To 1.5m (5ft)

SPREAD 1.5m (5ft)

Labiatae	

ELSHOLTZIA STAUNTONII

Habit Rounded, open sub-shrub. **Flowers** Small, 2-lipped, hooded, in slender spires during late summer and autumn. Deep pink-purple. **Leaves** Deciduous, aromatic, oval to elliptic, sharply toothed. Dark green, red in autumn.
• NATIVE HABITAT N. China.
• CULTIVATION Grow in any fertile soil. Top growth may be cut back by frost but will re-sprout from the base. The best foliage and flowers are produced by cutting back hard in spring.
• PROPAGATION By softwood cuttings in summer.

HEIGHT 1–1.5m (3–5ft) or more

SPREAD 1.5m (5ft)

Plumbaginaceae	CHINESE PLUMBAGO

CERATOSTIGMA WILLMOTTIANUM

Habit Low-growing, open. **Flowers** Small, tubular, with spreading lobes, from late summer to autumn. Bright, rich blue. **Leaves** Deciduous, lance-shaped to oval, pointed, bristly. Mid-green, turning red in autumn.
• NATIVE HABITAT Dry slopes in river valleys from W. China to Tibet.
• CULTIVATION Tolerant of dry soils. Grow in any fertile soil. May die back to the base in winter but will re-sprout in spring.
• PROPAGATION By softwood cuttings in summer.

HEIGHT To 1m (3ft)

SPREAD 1m (3ft)

Coriariaceae	

CORIARIA TERMINALIS var. XANTHOCARPA

Habit Arching, suckering. **Flowers** Small, in long racemes in late spring. Greenish. **Fruits** Translucent, berry-like, enclosed by the fleshy petals. Yellow. **Leaves** Deciduous, frond-like, with oval leaflets. Mid-green, red in autumn.
• NATIVE HABITAT Sikkim and Nepal.
• CULTIVATION Grow in any deep, moderately fertile soil.
• PROPAGATION By seed in autumn or by softwood cuttings in summer.

HEIGHT 60cm–1.5m (2–5ft)

SPREAD 1m (3ft) or more

Rutaceae	

SKIMMIA JAPONICA 'Fructo-alba'

Habit Bushy, dense, low-growing.
Flowers Female only, fragrant, small, from mid-to late spring. Creamy-white. *Fruits* Globose berries persisting into winter. White. *Leaves* Evergreen, aromatic, lance-shaped or elliptic. Dark green.
• NATIVE HABITAT Garden origin. Species grows in forests of Japan.
• CULTIVATION Tolerant of urban pollution and coastal conditions. Grow in moist, fertile, neutral to slightly acid soil. Needs male plant to fruit.
• PROPAGATION By semi-ripe cuttings in summer.

HEIGHT
75cm (30in)

SPREAD
75cm (30in)

Ericaceae	

GAULTHERIA MUCRONATA 'Wintertime' ♀

Habit Bushy, suckering. *Flowers* Small, urn-shaped, in late spring and early summer. White. *Fruits* Large, globose, and long-persistent. White. *Leaves* Evergreen, oblong-elliptic. Glossy dark green.
• NATIVE HABITAT Garden origin.
• CULTIVATION Grow in a moist, acid soil in semi-shade. Grow with a male clone for reliable fruiting.
• PROPAGATION By semi-ripe cuttings in summer or by division in autumn or spring.
• OTHER NAMES *Pernettya mucronata* 'Wintertime'.

HEIGHT
1m (3ft)

SPREAD
1.2m (4ft)

Caprifoliaceae	SHRUBBY HONEYSUCKLE

LONICERA × *PURPUSII*

Habit Bushy, dense. *Flowers* Small, very fragrant, short-tubed with spreading lobes, in winter and early spring. Creamy-white with yellow anthers. *Leaves* Semi-evergreen, oval. Dark green above, paler beneath.
• NATIVE HABITAT Garden origin.
• CULTIVATION Tolerates semi-shade but flowers best in sun. Grow in any fertile soil. Prune after flowering only to remove dead wood or restrict size.
• PROPAGATION By semi-ripe cuttings in summer or by hardwood cuttings in autumn.

HEIGHT
To 1.5m
(5ft)

SPREAD
1.5m (5ft)

Buxaceae	

SARCOCOCCA HOOKERIANA var. *HUMILIS*

Habit Low, clump-forming, suckering.
Flowers Tiny, fragrant, in late winter. White with pink anthers. *Fruits* Small, round, berry-like. Black. *Leaves* Evergreen, elliptic. Glossy dark green.
• NATIVE HABITAT Mountain scrub of China.
• CULTIVATION Tolerates dry or chalky soils, and sun where soils are reliably moist. Prefers a humus-rich and fertile soil. Useful for cutting in winter.
• PROPAGATION By seed in autumn or by semi-ripe cuttings in summer.

HEIGHT
60cm (24in)

SPREAD
75cm (30in)
or more

Thymelaeaceae	

DAPHNE ODORA 'Aureomarginata'

Habit Bushy, with upright branches.
Flowers Small, very fragrant, tubular, with spreading lobes, in dense clusters from mid-winter to early spring. Deep pink-purple and white.
Leaves Evergreen, narrowly oval. Glossy dark green, edged with creamy-yellow.
• NATIVE HABITAT Species occurs on low mountainsides of China. Garden origin.
• CULTIVATION Grow in any fertile, not too dry soil, in a position sheltered from cold wind.
• PROPAGATION By semi-ripe cuttings in summer.

☼ ◊
❀ ❀

HEIGHT
To 1.5m
(5ft)

SPREAD
To 1.5m
(5ft)

Buxaceae	

SARCOCOCCA HOOKERIANA var. DIGYNA ♀

Habit Dense, clump-forming, suckering.
Flowers Tiny, fragrant, in late winter. White with pink anthers. **Fruits** Small, spherical, berry-like. Black. **Leaves** Evergreen, narrowly elliptic. Glossy bright green.
• NATIVE HABITAT Mountain scrub of W. China.
• CULTIVATION Tolerates dry or chalky soils and sun where soils are reliably moist. Prefers shade or semi-shade and a humus-rich, fertile soil.
• PROPAGATION By seed in autumn or by semi-ripe cuttings in summer.

☼ ◊
❀ ❀

HEIGHT
To 1m (3ft)

SPREAD
1m (3ft)

Thymelaeaceae	MEZEREON, FEBRUARY DAPHNE

DAPHNE MEZEREUM

Habit Upright. **Flowers** Small, fragrant, tubular, with spreading lobes, along bare stems in late winter and early spring. Deep pink or purple.
Fruits Globose, fleshy, poisonous berries. Bright scarlet. **Leaves** Deciduous, narrowly oval. Dull grey-green.
• NATIVE HABITAT Scrub and woodland from Europe to Asia Minor and Siberia.
• CULTIVATION Grow in any fertile soil in full sun.
• PROPAGATION By fresh seed in early summer or by semi-ripe cuttings in summer.

☼ ◊
❀ ❀ ❀

HEIGHT
To 1.5m
(5ft)

SPREAD
1.5m (5ft)

Ericaceae

GAULTHERIA MUCRONATA 'Mulberry Wine'

Habit Bushy, suckering. *Flowers* Female, small, urn-shaped, in late spring and early summer. White. *Fruits* Large, globose, persistent. Magenta to purple. *Leaves* Evergreen, oblong-elliptic. Glossy dark green.
• NATIVE HABITAT Garden origin.
• CULTIVATION Grow in moist, acid soil. Grow with a male clone for reliable fruiting.
• PROPAGATION By semi-ripe cuttings in summer.
• OTHER NAMES *Pernettya mucronata* 'Mulberry Wine'.

HEIGHT
1.2m (4ft)

SPREAD
1.2m (4ft)

Rutaceae

CORREA PULCHELLA

Habit Bushy, slender-stemmed. *Flowers* Small, pendent, tubular, from summer to winter and sometimes at other seasons. Rose-red. *Leaves* Evergreen, oval, smooth. Light green.
• NATIVE HABITAT S. Australia.
• CULTIVATION Grow in a cool conservatory in a fertile, neutral to acid soil or compost. In mild areas grow outside in a warm, sheltered site. Water moderately when in growth, otherwise sparingly.
• PROPAGATION By seed in spring or by semi-ripe cuttings in summer.

HEIGHT
1–1.5m
(3–5ft)

SPREAD
1m (3ft)

Rutaceae

SKIMMIA JAPONICA 'Rubella'

Habit Bushy, dense, upright. *Flowers* Male. Dense clusters of dark red buds during autumn to winter, open to fragrant heads in spring. Creamy-white. *Leaves* Evergreen, aromatic, oval to elliptic. Dark green, with red rim.
• NATIVE HABITAT Garden origin.
• CULTIVATION Tolerant of urban pollution and coastal conditions. Grow in a moist, fertile, neutral to slightly acid soil, and in shade or semi-shade. Leaves may become yellow in sun and in poor soils.
• PROPAGATION By semi-ripe cuttings in summer.

HEIGHT
75cm (30in)

SPREAD
75cm (30in)

Rutaceae

SKIMMIA JAPONICA subsp. REEVESIANA 'Robert Fortune'

Habit Bushy, upright. *Flowers* Hermaphrodite, small, fragrant, in clusters in spring. Creamy-white. *Fruits* Ovoid berries. Deep crimson. *Leaves* Evergreen, aromatic, lance-shaped or elliptic. Dark green.
• NATIVE HABITAT Garden origin.
• CULTIVATION Tolerant of urban pollution and coastal conditions. Grow in a moist, fertile, neutral to slightly acid soil in shade or semi-shade.
• PROPAGATION By semi-ripe cuttings in summer.

HEIGHT
1m (3ft)

SPREAD
1m (3ft)

Rutaceae	

SKIMMIA JAPONICA

Habit Bushy, dense. *Flowers* Small, fragrant, in clusters from mid- to late spring. Creamy-white. *Fruits* Globose berries on female plants, persisting into winter. Bright red. *Leaves* Evergreen, aromatic, oval to elliptic. Mid- to dark green.
• NATIVE HABITAT In forests of China and Japan.
• CULTIVATION Grow in moist, fertile, neutral to slightly acid soils in shade or semi-shade. Both male and female plants are required to ensure fruit.
• PROPAGATION By seed in spring or by semi-ripe cuttings in summer.

HEIGHT
To 1.5m
(5ft)

SPREAD
1.5m (5ft)

Caprifoliaceae	

VIBURNUM DAVIDII

Habit Dense, mound-forming. *Flowers* Small, in open heads, in late spring. White. *Fruits* Egg-shaped, berry-like, on female plants. Metallic turquoise-blue. *Leaves* Evergreen, narrowly oval, with 3 deep veins. Glossy dark green.
• NATIVE HABITAT Mountain woodlands of China.
• CULTIVATION Grow in any deep, fertile soil that is not too dry. Male and female plants should be grown together to ensure fruit.
• PROPAGATION By semi-ripe cuttings in summer.

HEIGHT
1m (3ft) or
more

SPREAD
1.5m (5ft)

Grossulariaceae	

RIBES LAURIFOLIUM

Habit Semi-prostrate, spreading. *Flowers* Small, tubular, in pendent clusters in spring; larger on male plants. *Fruits* Small, currant-like, edible, on female plants where plants of both sexes are grown together. Black.
Leaves Evergreen, narrowly elliptic, leathery. Dark green.
• NATIVE HABITAT Mountain rocks of China.
• CULTIVATION Tolerates semi-shade. Grow in any moderately fertile, well-drained soil.
• PROPAGATION By semi-ripe cuttings in summer.

HEIGHT
To 1m (3ft)

SPREAD
1.5m (5ft)

Euphorbiaceae	SNOW BUSH

BREYNIA NIVOSA

Habit Well-branched, with slender, zigzag stems. *Flowers* Tiny, insignificant, without petals. Greenish. *Leaves* Evergreen, oval. Green with white marbling.
• NATIVE HABITAT Pacific Islands.
• CULTIVATION Grow in a warm conservatory in a fertile soil or compost. Water freely in growth, then moderately. Shade from high summer sun.
• PROPAGATION By greenwood or semi-ripe cuttings in summer.
• OTHER NAMES *B. disticha, Phyllanthus nivosus.*

Min. 13°C
(55°F)

HEIGHT
To 1.2m
(4ft)

SPREAD
1.2m (4ft)

Rubiaceae	

COPROSMA × *KIRKII* 'Kirkii Variegata'

Habit Densely branched, prostrate, semi-erect with age. *Flowers* Insignificant. *Fruits* Small, berry-like, translucent, on female plants. White. *Leaves* Evergreen, linear-oblong to lance-shaped. Pale green, edged with white.
• NATIVE HABITAT Garden origin.
• CULTIVATION Grow in cool conservatory in areas with hard frosts. Grow in a fertile soil or compost. Water freely in growth, then moderately. Needs male and female plants to fruit.
• PROPAGATION By semi-ripe cuttings in late summer.

HEIGHT
50cm (20in)

SPREAD
1.2m (4ft)

Apocynaceae	

VINCA MAJOR 'Variegata' ♥

Habit Vigorous, prostrate, arching, spreading. *Flowers* Large, tubular, with 5 spreading lobes, from late spring to early autumn. Bright blue. *Leaves* Evergreen, broadly oval to lance-shaped. Bright green, broadly edged with creamy-white.
• NATIVE HABITAT Garden origin.
• CULTIVATION Grow in any moist but well-drained soil. Tolerates deep shade but flowers best with part-day sun.
• PROPAGATION By semi-ripe cuttings in summer, by division from autumn to spring, or by layering.

HEIGHT
30cm (12in)

SPREAD
1.5m (5ft)

Pandanaceae	

PANDANUS VEITCHII ♥

Habit Upright, arching. *Leaves* Evergreen, long, narrow, slightly drooping. Light green with spiny, white to cream margins.
• NATIVE HABITAT Uncertain; probably from Polynesia.
• CULTIVATION Grow in a warm conservatory in a fertile soil or compost. Water freely when in growth, otherwise sparingly. Tolerates semi-shade.
• PROPAGATION By seed or by suckers in spring, or by cuttings of lateral shoots in summer.
• OTHER NAMES *P. tectorius* 'Veitchii'.

Min.
13–16°C
(55–61°F)

HEIGHT
To 1m (3ft)

SPREAD
1m (3ft)

Compositae	

ARTEMISIA ARBORESCENS

Habit Upright, rounded. *Flowers* Small, daisy-like, in large, rounded panicles in summer and early autumn. Yellow-brown. *Leaves* Evergreen, finely divided. Silvery-white.
• NATIVE HABITAT Dry, rocky hills, usually on limestone, around the Mediterranean.
• CULTIVATION Tolerant of poor, dry soils. Grow in a warm, sunny, and sheltered position.
• PROPAGATION By softwood or semi-ripe cuttings in summer.
• OTHER NAMES *A. arborea*, *A. argentea* of gardens.

HEIGHT
1m (3ft)

SPREAD
50–75cm
(20–30in)

Compositae	LIQUORICE PLANT

HELICHRYSUM PETIOLARE ♼

Habit Mound-forming, with trailing shoots.
Flowers Small, in loose heads in summer. Creamy-yellow. **Leaves** Evergreen, almost round to broadly oval, densely felted. Silver-grey.
• NATIVE HABITAT Transkei, S. Africa.
• CULTIVATION Grow in any well-drained, not too rich soil. Usually grown annually from cuttings as ground cover or edging. Suitable for hanging baskets.
• PROPAGATION By semi-ripe cuttings in summer.
• OTHER NAMES *H. petiolatum.*

HEIGHT
50cm–1m
(20–36in)

SPREAD
1.5m (5ft)

Labiatae	

BALLOTA ACETABULOSA

Habit Dense, mound-forming, with upright stems.
Flowers Small, 2-lipped, in whorls in late spring and early summer. Pink. **Leaves** Evergreen, broadly heart-shaped, densely woolly. Grey-green.
• NATIVE HABITAT Dry areas, usually on alkaline soils, of Greece and around the E. Mediterranean.
• CULTIVATION Grow in a hot, dry site. Tolerant of poor, dry soil. Protect with a dry mulch in winter.
• PROPAGATION By semi-ripe cuttings in summer.

HEIGHT
To 60cm
(24in)

SPREAD
75cm (30in)

Compositae	

CALOCEPHALUS BROWNII

Habit Rounded, intricately branched.
Flowers Tiny, insignificant, in small, slender clusters in summer. Silver in bud, yellowish on emergence. **Leaves** Evergreen, tiny, scale-like.
• NATIVE HABITAT Rocky coastal areas, Australia.
• CULTIVATION Grow in sandy, not too rich soil. Water potted plants moderately when in growth, otherwise sparingly. Grown for its 'foliage' effect.
• PROPAGATION By semi-ripe cuttings in late summer.

Min.
7–10°C
(45–50°F)

HEIGHT
40cm (16in)

SPREAD
To 75cm
(30in)

Apocynaceae	

VINCA MINOR

Habit Vigorous, prostrate, mat-forming.
Flowers Small, tubular, with 5 spreading lobes, from mid-spring to early summer. Bright blue.
Leaves Evergreen, lance-shaped. Glossy dark green.
• NATIVE HABITAT Scrub and woodland from Europe to S. Russia and N. Caucasus.
• CULTIVATION Flowers best with part-day sun. Grow in any soil that is not too dry.
• PROPAGATION By semi-ripe cuttings in summer, by division from autumn to spring, or by layering.

HEIGHT
10–20cm
(4–8in)

SPREAD
1.5m (5ft)

Palmae	

CHAMAEROPS HUMILIS

Habit Slow-growing, upright then arching, suckering with age. **Leaves** Evergreen, fan-shaped, to 60–90cm (2–3ft) across, with narrow lobes. Green to grey-green.
• NATIVE HABITAT W. Portugal to Morocco.
• CULTIVATION Grow in a cool conservatory or in a warm, sheltered site in mild areas. Grow in fertile soil or compost. Water moderately when in growth, otherwise sparingly. Tolerant of semi-shade.
• PROPAGATION By seed in spring or by suckers in late spring.

☀ ◊
❄

HEIGHT
1.5m (5ft)
or more

SPREAD
1.5m (5ft)

Ericaceae	

VACCINIUM GLAUCOALBUM

Habit Dense, suckering. **Flowers** Small, cylindrical, in clusters in late spring and early summer. White, tinged pink. **Fruits** Small, globose, berry-like, persisting into winter. Blue-black, white-bloomed. **Leaves** Evergreen, oval-oblong, leathery. Dark green, blue-white below.
• NATIVE HABITAT The Himalaya and S. Tibet.
• CULTIVATION Grow in open, moist but well-drained, acid, peaty soil.
• PROPAGATION By seed in autumn or by semi-ripe cuttings in summer.

☀ ◊ pH
❄ ❄

HEIGHT
50cm–1m
(20–36in)

SPREAD
1m (3ft)

Leguminosae	HUMBLE PLANT, SENSITIVE PLANT

MIMOSA PUDICA

Habit Short-lived, prostrate or semi-erect, thorny. **Flowers** Tiny, fluffy, in summer to autumn. Pale pink. **Leaves** Evergreen, finely divided, fern-like, folding when touched. Bright green.
• NATIVE HABITAT Tropical C. America.
• CULTIVATION Grow in a warm conservatory or in bright, indirect light in the home in fertile, humus-rich soil or compost. Provide support. Feed weekly with liquid fertilizer and water freely when in growth. Water moderately at other times.
• PROPAGATION By seed in spring.

☀ ◊

Min.
13–16°C
(55–61°F)

HEIGHT
30–80cm
(12–32in)

SPREAD
30–80cm
(12–32in)

Compositae	SOUTHERNWOOD

ARTEMISIA ABROTANUM

Habit Bushy, rounded, upright. *Flowers* Tiny, daisy-like, in small clusters in summer. Yellowish. *Leaves* Aromatic, deciduous or semi-evergreen, finely divided into slender lobes. Grey-green.
• NATIVE HABITAT Origin uncertain but naturalised in dry, sandy, and rocky areas of E. to S.C. Europe.
• CULTIVATION Tolerant of poor, dry soils but prefers moderately fertile, freely drained soil.
• PROPAGATION By heeled or semi-ripe cuttings in summer.

HEIGHT
To 1m (3ft)

SPREAD
1m (3ft)

Theaceae	

EURYA EMARGINATA

Habit Slow-growing, densely branched, rounded. *Flowers* Inconspicuous, in late spring. Pale yellow-green. *Fruits* Tiny, globose, glossy berries. Purple-black. *Leaves* Evergreen, small, oval, toothed, leathery. Deep green, tinted red in winter.
• NATIVE HABITAT Coasts of S. Japan.
• CULTIVATION Tolerates semi-shade. Grow in any fertile, freely draining soil, with shelter from cold winds. In cold areas grow in a conservatory.
• PROPAGATION By seed in autumn or spring or by semi-ripe cuttings in summer.

HEIGHT
To 1.5m (5ft)

SPREAD
1.5m (5ft)

Scrophulariaceae	

HEBE CUPRESSOÏDES

Habit Dense, rounded, upright. *Flowers* Tiny, in broad clusters from early to mid-summer. Pale lilac-blue. *Leaves* Evergreen, aromatic, cypress-like. Grey-green.
• NATIVE HABITAT Mountain valleys of New Zealand, South Island.
• CULTIVATION Thrives in seaside gardens. Grow in any fertile, freely draining soil. Shelter from cold winter winds. Growth may be restricted, or leggy plants tidied, by cutting back in spring.
• PROPAGATION By semi-ripe cuttings in summer.

HEIGHT
To 1.5m (5ft)

SPREAD
1.5m (5ft) or more

Buxaceae	

BUXUS MICROPHYLLA 'Green Pillow'

Habit Compact, dense, dome-forming. *Flowers* Insignificant, without petals, in spring. *Leaves* Evergreen, small, oval. Dark green.
• NATIVE HABITAT Garden origin.
• CULTIVATION Tolerates any but waterlogged soil, and sun or semi-shade. Best given some shade from the hottest sun in summer, and shelter from cold winds to avoid leaf scorch. Clip over to shape in spring but otherwise needs little pruning.
• PROPAGATION By semi-ripe cuttings in late summer.

HEIGHT
30–50cm (12–20in)

SPREAD
30–50cm (12–20in)

Liliaceae/ Ruscaceae	

RUSCUS HYPOGLOSSUM

Habit Arching, clump-forming. **Flowers** Tiny, on the surface of the 'leaves' in spring. Yellow. **Fruits** Large, cherry-like berries, on female plants. Bright red. **Leaves** True leaves are evergreen, tiny, scale-like. The apparent, large, oval, pointed 'leaves' are actually flattened stems. Glossy green.
• NATIVE HABITAT Woodland of S. Europe.
• CULTIVATION Tolerant of any but waterlogged soil, and especially useful as ground cover in dry shade. Grow plants of both sexes to ensure berries.
• PROPAGATION By division in spring.

HEIGHT
To 40cm
(16in)

SPREAD
75cm (30in)
or more

Palmae	DWARF PALMETTO

SABAL MINOR

Habit Suckering, with stems mainly underground. **Flowers** Small, in erect sprays. Cream. **Fruits** Small, almost globose, glossy berries. Black. **Leaves** Large, fan-shaped, with 20–30 narrow lobes. Grey-green.
• NATIVE HABITAT S.E to S. United States.
• CULTIVATION Grow in a conservatory in fertile, humus-rich, freely draining soil or compost. Young plants may be grown in a well-lit site in the home. Water freely in growth, otherwise moderately.
• PROPAGATION By seed in spring.

Min. 5°C
(41°F)

HEIGHT
1m (3ft) or
more

SPREAD
75cm (30in)

Caprifoliaceae	

LONICERA PILEATA

Habit Dense, low, spreading with horizontal branches. **Flowers** Tiny, short-tubed, in late spring. Creamy-white. **Fruits** Small, translucent, globose berries. Amethyst-violet.
Leaves Evergreen or semi-deciduous, narrowly oval-oblong. Glossy dark green.
• NATIVE HABITAT Low mountain scrub and by streamsides of Hubei and Sichuan in China.
• CULTIVATION Tolerant of semi-shade. Grow in any fertile, well-drained soil. Good ground cover.
• PROPAGATION By semi-ripe cuttings in summer.

HEIGHT
75cm (30in)
or more

SPREAD
2.5m (8ft)

Buxaceae	BOX, EDGING BOX

BUXUS SEMPERVIRENS 'Suffruticosa'

Habit Compact, very dense.
Flowers Insignificant, without petals, in late spring or early summer. **Leaves** Evergreen, small, oval. Glossy bright green.
• NATIVE HABITAT Garden origin.
• CULTIVATION Tolerates any but waterlogged soil and thrives in sun or semi-shade. May be clipped back to about 15cm (6in) in spring. Used as edging and for formal knot gardens.
• PROPAGATION By semi-ripe cuttings in late summer.

HEIGHT
To 1m (3ft)

SPREAD
30–50cm
(12–20in)

Labiatae	

SALVIA OFFICINALIS 'Icterina'

Habit Bushy, low, spreading. *Flowers* Small, tubular, 2-lipped, in small spikes, appearing occasionally in summer. Purplish.
Leaves Evergreen or semi-evergreen, aromatic, oblong to elliptic. Grey-green, variegated with pale green and yellow.
• NATIVE HABITAT Garden origin.
• CULTIVATION Tolerant of dry soils. Grow in any well-drained, not too rich soil in a sheltered site.
• PROPAGATION By softwood cuttings in mid-summer.

HEIGHT
50cm (20in)

SPREAD
To 1.2m
(4ft)

Acanthaceae	

SANCHEZIA SPECIOSA

Habit Upright, soft-stemmed. *Flowers* Large, tubular, in summer. Yellow, with conspicuous red bracts. *Leaves* Evergreen, oval-elliptic to lance-shaped. Glossy mid-green with yellow or white veins.
• NATIVE HABITAT Tropical forests, Ecuador, Peru.
• CULTIVATION Grow in a warm conservatory or a well-lit position in the home. Tolerates partial shade. Water freely in growth, then moderately.
• PROPAGATION By greenwood cuttings in spring or summer.
• OTHER NAMES *S. nobilis* of gardens.

Min.
13–15°C
(55–59°F)

HEIGHT
1.5m (5ft)

SPREAD
1m (3ft)

Rutaceae	

RUTA GRAVEOLENS 'Jackman's Blue'

Habit Bushy, compact sub-shrub. *Flowers* Small, in clusters in summer. Mustard-yellow.
Leaves Evergreen, aromatic, divided into lance-shaped to narrowly oblong leaflets. Bright blue-green.
• NATIVE HABITAT Garden origin.
• CULTIVATION Tolerant of light shade and of poor, dry soils, but prefers a warm site in any well drained soil. Cut back to old wood in spring. Contact with the skin can cause blistering.
• PROPAGATION By semi-ripe cuttings in summer.

HEIGHT
20–50cm
(8–20in)

SPREAD
20–50cm
(8–20in)

Celastraceae	

EUONYMUS FORTUNEI 'Emerald 'n' Gold'

Habit Bushy, compact, upright or scrambling.
Flowers Insignificant, in spring. Greenish-white.
Leaves Evergreen, oval to elliptic. Bright green, broadly edged with bright yellow; pink-tinged in winter.
• NATIVE HABITAT Garden origin. Species occurs in scrub and woodland of China, Japan, and Korea.
• CULTIVATION Tolerates sun or shade and almost any fertile soil, including chalk. Good ground cover.
• PROPAGATION By semi-ripe cuttings in summer.

HEIGHT
50cm (20in)
or more

SPREAD
1m (3ft)

Ericaceae	

LEUCOTHOË FONTANESIANA 'Rainbow'

Habit Arching, clump-forming. *Flowers* Small, urn-shaped, in short, drooping racemes in spring. White. *Leaves* Evergreen, lance-shaped, pointed, toothed, leathery. Dark green with cream, yellow, and pink variegations.
• NATIVE HABITAT Species occurs in moist mountain woods of S.E. United States. Garden origin.
• CULTIVATION Grow in shade or semi-shade in moist, peaty soils. Makes excellent ground cover for the peat terrace or woodland garden.
• PROPAGATION By semi-ripe cuttings in summer.

HEIGHT
To 1.5m
(5ft)

SPREAD
1.5m (5ft)

Euphorbiaceae	CROTON

CODIAEUM VARIEGATUM

Habit Erect, sparingly branched.
Leaves Evergreen, leathery, very variable in shape, glossy. Variegated red, pink, orange, and yellow.
• NATIVE HABITAT S. India, Sri Lanka, Malaya.
• CULTIVATION Grow in the home or a warm conservatory in a humus-rich, neutral to slightly acid soil or compost. Water freely when in full growth, otherwise moderately.
• PROPAGATION By greenwood cuttings from firm stem tips in spring or summer.
• OTHER NAMES *Croton pictum.*

Min.
10–13°C
(50–55°F)

HEIGHT
1m (3ft) or
more

SPREAD
1m (3ft) or
more

Caprifoliaceae	

LONICERA NITIDA 'Baggesen's Gold' ♥

Habit Dense, with long, arching shoots.
Flowers Insignificant, in mid-spring. Yellowish-green. *Fruits* Small, translucent, globose berries. Purple. Produced only occasionally.
Leaves Evergreen, tiny, oval. Bright yellow.
• NATIVE HABITAT Garden origin.
• CULTIVATION Tolerant of urban pollution. Grow in any fertile, well-drained soil. Good for formal and informal hedging and sometimes used for topiary.
• PROPAGATION By semi-ripe cuttings in summer.

HEIGHT
To 1.5m
(5ft)

SPREAD
1.5m (5ft)

Pittosporaceae	

PITTOSPORUM TENUIFOLIUM 'Tom Thumb' ♥

Habit Dense, rounded. *Flowers* Small, cup-shaped, in summer. Purplish. *Leaves* Evergreen, oblong-elliptic, with waved margins. Pale green when young, becoming bronzed red-purple.
• NATIVE HABITAT Garden origin. Species occurs in lowland and coastal forests of New Zealand.
• CULTIVATION Thrives in mild areas, especially on the coast. In cold areas site against a south-facing wall. Shelter from cold winds.
• PROPAGATION By semi-ripe cuttings in summer.

HEIGHT
75cm–1m
(30–36in)
or more

SPREAD
50–75cm
(20–30in)

HEATHERS

The heaths (*Erica* and *Daboecia* species) and heathers (*Calluna vulgaris* and its cultivars) form a diverse group of fine-leaved, evergreen shrubs that vary in habit from low, ground-hugging types, to the tree heaths, such as *Erica arborea* which grows to 6m (20ft) or more. They occur mainly in cool temperate zones, in exposed and inhospitable conditions, often on poor soils, and in areas of high rainfall. The tender South African species of *Erica* occur in similar conditions.

With rich colours, ranging from pure paper-white to deepest carmine and crimson, heaths and heathers offer colour throughout the year. Seasonal interest is enhanced by those with coloured foliage. Those with soft, silver-grey foliage and golden-leaved forms often have russet and burnt orange tints in winter and provide beautiful textural contrasts. The main seasons of interest are given for each plant.

Prostrate forms make excellent ground cover. Heathers make good companion plants for dwarf conifers and other members of the Ericaceae, especially those with dark, glossy leaves such as *Gaultheria*, *Pieris*, and *Leucothoë*.

Grow in an open site in full sun, in a humus-rich, sandy or peaty, acid soil. Some *Erica* species and cultivars are tolerant of alkaline soils. Many tolerate light shade, but all bloom best in sun. Clear all perennial weeds before planting: weed control is extremely difficult once plants have formed close cover. Mulch to conserve moisture and control weeds. Plants take 2–3 years to achieve full cover. Shear over annually after flowering to maintain dense growth.

Propagate species by seed in spring, by softwood cuttings in spring, or by division or layering in summer. All cultivars must be vegetatively propagated.

CALLUNA VULGARIS 'Kinlochruel'
Habit Compact, dense, slightly spreading, very free-flowering.
Flowers Large, double, white, in dense spikes.
Leaves Linear, scale-like, fleshy. Bright green.
• SEASON Summer–autumn.
• HEIGHT 30cm (12in).
• SPREAD 35cm (14in).

C. vulgaris 'Kinlochruel'

DABOECIA CANTABRICA 'Snowdrift'
Habit Straggling.
Flowers Large, urn-shaped, in slender spikes. White. *Leaves* Lance-shaped to oval. Bright green above, silver-grey beneath.
• SEASON Spring–autumn.
• HEIGHT 45cm (18in).
• SPREAD 60cm (24in).

D. cantabrica 'Snowdrift'

CALLUNA VULGARIS 'Spring Cream'
Habit Vigorous, dense.
Flowers Small, urn- to bell-shaped, single, in long spikes. White.
Leaves Linear, scale-like. Bright green, tipped creamy-white in spring.
• SEASON Summer–autumn.
• HEIGHT 45–50cm (18–20in).
• SPREAD 45–50cm (18–20in).

C. vulgaris 'Spring Cream'

ERICA x *VEITCHII* 'Exeter'
Habit Bushy, shrub-like tree heath.
Flowers Fragrant, tubular to bell-shaped, in dense clusters, and in profusion. White. *Leaves* Needle-like. Bright green.
• CULTIVATION Tolerates some lime.
• SEASON Mid-winter–spring.
• HEIGHT To 2m (6ft).
• SPREAD 2m (6ft).

E. x *veitchii* 'Exeter'

ERICA CINEREA
'Hookstone White'
Habit Straggling,
spreading. *Flowers* Urn-
shaped, in long racemes,
in profusion. White.
Leaves Needle-like, in
whorls of 3. Bright green.
• SEASON Early
summer–early autumn.
• CULTIVATION Prefers
a warm, dry position.
• HEIGHT 35cm (14in).
• SPREAD 50cm (20in).

E. cinerea 'Hookstone
White'

ERICA VAGANS
'Lyonesse'
Habit Vigorous, bushy.
Flowers Rounded, bell-
shaped, in long, tapering
spikes. White, with brown
anthers. *Leaves* Long,
needle-like, in whorls of
4–5. Dark green.
• SEASON Mid-summer–
late autumn.
• HEIGHT 45cm (18in).
• SPREAD 45cm (18in).

E. vagans 'Lyonesse'

ERICA MACKAYANA
'Dr Ronald Gray'
Habit Compact.
Flowers Small, urn-
shaped, in rounded
clusters. White.
Leaves Small, lance-
shaped, in whorls of 4.
Dark green.
• SEASON Mid-summer–
early autumn.
• HEIGHT 15cm (6in).
• SPREAD 15cm (6in).

E. mackayana
'Dr Ronald Gray'

ERICA ARBOREA var.
ALPINA
Habit Dense, upright.
Flowers Fragrant,
globular, in compact
racemes. White.
Leaves Needle-like, in
whorls of 3–4. Bright
green.
• CULTIVATION
Tolerates lime.
• SEASON Late winter–
late spring.
• HEIGHT To 2m (6ft).
• SPREAD 2m (6ft).

E. arborea var. *alpina*

ERICA MACKAYANA
'Shining Light'
Habit Dense, spreading.
Flowers Small, urn-
shaped, in rounded
clusters. Pure white.
Leaves Small, lance-
shaped, in whorls of 4.
Dark green.
• SEASON Mid-summer–
early autumn.
• HEIGHT 15cm (6in).
• SPREAD 15cm (6in).

E. mackayana
'Shining Light'

ERICA CANICULATA
Habit Erect, densely
branched. *Flowers* Cup-
shaped, in spring (winter
if under glass). Pearl-
white, pink-flushed, with
brown-black anthers.
Leaves Needle-like, in
whorls of 3. Dark green.
• CULTIVATION Needs
a warm, sheltered site.
• SEASON Winter or
spring.
• HEIGHT To 3m (10ft).
• SPREAD 1m (3ft).

E. caniculata

ERICA TETRALIX
'Alba Mollis'
Habit Vigorous, with
upright branches, free-
flowering. *Flowers* Large,
globular, in dense,
rounded clusters. White.
Leaves Lance-shaped to
linear, in whorls of 4.
silver-grey, then green.
• SEASON Early
summer–late autumn.
• HEIGHT 22cm (9in).
• SPREAD 22cm (9in).

E. tetralix 'Alba Mollis'

ERICA x *DARLEYENSIS*
'White Perfection'
Habit Vigorous, dense,
bushy. *Flowers* Bell-
shaped, in profuse
racemes. White.
Leaves Long, needle-
like, in whorls of 4.
Bright green.
• CULTIVATION
Tolerates some lime.
• SEASON Mid-winter–
spring.
• HEIGHT 60cm (24in).
• SPREAD 60cm (24in).

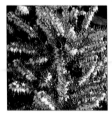

E. x *darleyensis* 'White
Perfection'

ERICA X DARLEYENSIS 'White Glow'
Habit Vigorous, dense, bushy. *Flowers* Bell-shaped, in profuse racemes. White. *Leaves* Long, needle-like, in whorls of 4. Dark green.
• CULTIVATION Tolerates some lime.
• SEASON Mid-winter–spring.
• HEIGHT 60cm (24in).
• SPREAD 60cm (24in).

E. x *darleyensis* 'White Glow'

☀ ◐ pH ✾✾✾

ERICA CILIARIS 'David McClintock'
Habit Low, spreading. *Flowers* Large, urn-shaped, in long racemes. White with deep pink tips. *Leaves* Oval to lance-shaped, in whorls of 3–4. Pale grey-green.
• CULTIVATION Prefers warm, moist conditions.
• SEASON Summer–autumn.
• HEIGHT 35cm (14in).
• SPREAD 30cm (12in).

E. ciliaris 'David McClintock'

☀ ◐ pH ✾✾✾ 🏆

ERICA X VEITCHII 'Pink Joy'
Habit Bushy, shrub-like tree heath. *Flowers* Fragrant, tubular to bell-shaped, in dense clusters. Clear white, opening from pink buds. *Leaves* Needle-like. Bright green, golden in spring.
• SEASON Mid-winter–spring.
• HEIGHT To 2m (6ft).
• SPREAD 2m (6ft).

E. x *veitchii* 'Pink Joy'

☀ ◐ ✾✾

CALLUNA VULGARIS 'My Dream'
Habit Vigorous, compact, upright. *Flowers* Large, double, in long, tapering spikes. White. *Leaves* Linear, scale-like, fleshy. Dark green.
• SEASON Summer–autumn.
• HEIGHT 50cm (20in).
• SPREAD 50cm (20in).

C. vulgaris 'My Dream'

☀ ◐ pH ✾✾✾

ERICA CILIARIS 'White Wings'
Habit Bushy, compact. *Flowers* Large, urn-shaped, in long racemes. White. *Leaves* Small, oval to lance-shaped, in whorls of 3 or 4. Dark grey-green.
• CULTIVATION Prefers warm, moist conditions.
• SEASON Summer–early autumn.
• HEIGHT 30cm (12in).
• SPREAD 30cm (12in).

E. ciliaris 'White Wings'

☀ ◐ pH ✾✾✾

ERICA CARNEA 'Springwood White'
Habit Vigorous, trailing. *Flowers* Large, long, urn-shaped. White, with brown anthers. *Leaves* Needle-like, in whorls. Rich dark green.
• CULTIVATION Tolerant of lime and some shade.
• SEASON Late winter–spring.
• HEIGHT 15cm (6in).
• SPREAD 45cm (18in).

E. carnea 'Springwood White'

☀ ◐ ✾✾✾ 🏆

CALLUNA VULGARIS
'Anthony Davis'
Habit Dense, compact, free-flowering.
Flowers Small, urn- to bell-shaped, single, in upright spikes. White.
Leaves Linear, scale-like, fleshy. Silver-grey.
• SEASON Summer–autumn.
• HEIGHT 38–45cm (15–18in).
• SPREAD 38–45cm (15–18in).

C. vulgaris 'Anthony Davis'

☼ ◊ pH ✿✿✿   ♔

CALLUNA VULGARIS
'Elsie Purnell'
Habit Vigorous, spreading.
Flowers Double. Pale silvery pink, deeper pink in bud. *Leaves* Linear, scale-like, fleshy. Greyish-green.
• SEASON Summer–autumn.
• HEIGHT 60–80cm (24–32in).
• SPREAD 60–80cm (24–32in).

C. vulgaris 'Elsie Purnell'

☼ ◊ pH ✿✿✿   ♔

CALLUNA VULGARIS
'J. H. Hamilton'
Habit Compact, dense, spreading.
Flowers Large, double, in short, dense spikes in profusion. Salmon-pink.
Leaves Linear, scale-like, fleshy. Dark green.
• SEASON Summer–autumn.
• HEIGHT 20cm (8in).
• SPREAD 40cm (16in).

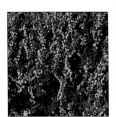

C. vulgaris 'J. H. Hamilton'

☼ ◊ pH ✿✿✿   ♔

CALLUNA VULGARIS
'County Wicklow'
Habit Compact, dense, very free-flowering.
Flowers Double, in dense spikes, from summer to autumn. Shell-pink.
Leaves Linear, scale-like, fleshy. Dark green.
• OTHER NAMES
Calluna vulgaris 'Camla'.
• SEASON Summer–autumn.
• HEIGHT 30cm (12in).
• SPREAD 35cm (14in).

C. vulgaris 'County Wicklow'

☼ ◊ pH ✿✿✿   ♔

CALLUNA VULGARIS
'Silver Queen'
Habit Dense, spreading.
Flowers Small, urn- to bell-shaped, single. Deep mauve-pink.
Leaves Linear, scale-like. Soft silver-grey.
• SEASON Summer–autumn.
• HEIGHT 40–60cm (16–24in).
• SPREAD 55cm (22in).

C. vulgaris 'Silver Queen'

☼ ◊ pH ✿✿✿   ♔

ERICA X
DARLEYENSIS **'Ghost Hills'**
Habit Vigorous, dense, bushy. *Flowers* Bell-shaped, in profuse racemes. Pink, with darker pink tips.
Leaves Long, needle-like, in whorls of 4. Dark green, cream-tipped in spring.
• SEASON Mid-winter–spring.
• CULTIVATION Tolerates some lime.
• HEIGHT 60cm (24in).
• SPREAD 60cm (24in).

E. x *darleyensis* 'Ghost Hills'

☼ ◊ pH ✿✿✿   ♔

ERICA x DARLEYENSIS 'Archie Graham'
Habit Vigorous, dense.
Flowers Bell-shaped, in racemes. Mauve-pink.
Leaves Long, needle-like, in whorls of 4. Dark green.
• SEASON Early winter–late spring.
• CULTIVATION Tolerates lime.
• HEIGHT 50cm (20in).
• SPREAD 50cm (20in).

E. x *darleyensis* 'Archie Graham'

☼ ◊ ❀❀❀

ERICA x WATSONII 'Dawn'
Habit Compact, spreading.
Flowers Rounded, bell-shaped, in large clusters. Deep mauve-pink.
Leaves Needle-like. Mid-green, with orange-yellow tips in spring.
• SEASON Mid–late summer.
• HEIGHT 30cm (12in).
• SPREAD 38cm (15in).

E. x *watsonii* 'Dawn'

☼ ◊ pH ❀❀❀ ♔

ERICA x DARLEYENSIS 'Darley Dale'
Habit Vigorous, dense, bushy. **Flowers** Bell-shaped, in profuse racemes. Pale mauve.
Leaves Long, needle-like, in whorls of 4. Dark green.
• CULTIVATION Tolerates some lime.
• SEASON Mid-winter–spring.
• HEIGHT 60cm (24in).
• SPREAD 60cm (24in).

E. x *darleyensis* 'Darley Dale'

☼ ◊ pH ❀❀❀

ERICA x WILLIAMSII 'P. D. Williams'
Habit Compact, bushy, spreading.
Flowers Small, urn-shaped, in dense, leafy, rounded clusters. Deep mauve-pink.
Leaves Small, needle-like, in whorls of 4. Dark green, with golden tips.
• SEASON Mid–late summer.
• HEIGHT 15cm (6in).
• SPREAD 15cm (6in).

E. x *williamsii* 'P. D. Williams'

☼ ◗ pH ❀❀❀ ♔

ERICA MACKAYANA 'Plena'
Habit Compact.
Flowers Small, urn-shaped, double, in rounded clusters. Deep-pink, fading to white in the centres.
Leaves Small, lance-shaped, in whorls of 4. Dark green.
• SEASON Mid-summer–early autumn.
• HEIGHT 15cm (6in).
• SPREAD 15cm (6in).

E. mackayana 'Plena'

☼ ◗ pH ❀❀❀

DABOECIA CANTABRICA 'Bicolor'
Habit Straggling.
Flowers Urn-shaped, in slender spikes. White, purple, and white/purple striped. **Leaves** Lance-shaped to oval. Dark green above, silver-grey beneath.
• SEASON Spring–autumn.
• HEIGHT 45cm (18in).
• SPREAD 60cm (24in).

D. cantabrica 'Bicolor'

☼ ◊ pH ❀❀ ♔

DABOECIA x SCOTICA 'William Buchanan'
Habit Vigorous, compact.
Flowers Large, bell- to urn-shaped, in slender spikes. Deep purple.
Leaves Lance-shaped to oval. Dark green above, silver-grey beneath.
• SEASON Late spring–mid-autumn.
• HEIGHT 45cm (18in).
• SPREAD 60cm (24in).

D. x *scotica* 'William Buchanan'

☼ ◊ pH ❀❀ ♔

ERICA VAGANS 'Birch Glow'
Habit Vigorous, bushy.
Flowers Rounded, bell-shaped. Rose-pink.
Leaves Long, needle-like, in whorls of 4–5. Bright green.
• CULTIVATION Tolerates some lime.
• SEASON Mid-summer–late autumn.
• HEIGHT 45cm (18in).
• SPREAD 45cm (18in).

E. vagans 'Birch Glow'

☼ ◊ pH ❀❀❀ ♔

ERICA TETRALIX
'Pink Star'
Habit Low-growing, spreading. *Flowers* Bell-shaped, in dense, rounded, star-like heads, on erect stems. Pink. *Leaves* Lance-shaped to linear, in whorls of 4. Grey-green.
• SEASON Summer–early autumn.
• HEIGHT 22cm (9in).
• SPREAD 22cm (9in).

E. tetralix 'Pink Star'

☀ ◊ pH ✤✤✤   ♈

ERICA CILIARIS
'Corfe Castle'
Habit Compact. *Flowers* Large, urn-shaped, in long racemes. Salmon-pink. *Leaves* Oval-to lance-shaped, in whorls of 3–4. Dark green, bronze in winter.
• SEASON Summer–early autumn.
• HEIGHT 30cm (12in).
• SPREAD 30cm (12in).

E. ciliaris 'Corfe Castle'

☀ ◊ pH ✤✤✤   ♈

ERICA CINEREA
'C. D. Eason'
Habit Dense, bushy, compact. *Flowers* Urn-shaped. Bright rosy-red. *Leaves* Needle-like, in whorls of 3. Dull deep green.
• CULTIVATION Prefers a warm, dry position.
• SEASON Early summer–early autumn.
• HEIGHT 20cm (8in).
• SPREAD 20cm (8in).

E. cinerea 'C. D. Eason'

☀ ◊ pH ✤✤✤   ♈

ERICA CINEREA
'Romiley'
Habit Dense, bushy, compact. *Flowers* Urn-shaped. Bright ruby-red. *Leaves* Needle-like, in whorls of 3. Dark grey-green.
• SEASON Early–late summer.
• CULTIVATION Prefers a warm, dry position.
• HEIGHT 15cm (6in).
• SPREAD 15cm (6in).

E. cinerea 'Romiley'

☀ ◊ pH ✤✤✤

ERICA CINEREA
'Glencairn'
Habit Dense, neat, spreading. *Flowers* Urn-shaped. Magenta. *Leaves* Needle-like, in whorls of 3. Green, tipped pink and red, especially in spring.
• SEASON Early summer–early autumn.
• CULTIVATION Prefers a warm, dry position.
• HEIGHT 20cm (8in).
• SPREAD 55cm (22in).

E. cinerea 'Glencairn'

☀ ◊ pH ✤✤✤

ERICA TETRALIX
'Con Underwood'
Habit Vigorous, hummock-forming. *Flowers* Large, globular, in dense, rounded clusters. Dark red-crimson. *Leaves* Lance-shaped to linear, in whorls of 4. Grey-green.
• SEASON Summer–early autumn.
• HEIGHT 22cm (9in).
• SPREAD 22cm (9in).

E. tetralix 'Con Underwood'

☀ ◊ pH ✤✤✤   ♈

ERICA CINEREA 'Eden Valley'

Habit Dense, neat, spreading. **Flowers** Urn-shaped. White, tipped with lavender-mauve. **Leaves** Needle-like, in whorls of 3. Glossy deep green.
• CULTIVATION Prefers a warm, dry position.
• SEASON Early summer–early autumn.
• HEIGHT 20cm (8in).
• SPREAD 55cm (22in).

E. cinerea 'Eden Valley'

☼ ◊ pH ❀ ❀ ❀　　♛

ERICA ERIGENA 'Brightness'

Habit Low-growing, dense. **Flowers** Fragrant, bell-shaped. Mauve-pink. **Leaves** Needle-like. Sea-green, tinted bronze-purple in winter.
• SEASON Early winter–late spring.
• HEIGHT 45–50cm (18–20in).
• SPREAD 45–50cm (18–20in).

E. erigena 'Brightness'

☼ ◊ pH ❀ ❀

ERICA CARNEA 'C. J. Backhouse'

Habit Compact, dense. **Flowers** Small, tubular to bell-shaped. Pale pink. **Leaves** Needle-like, in whorls of 4. Dark green.
• SEASON Mid-winter–late spring.
• CULTIVATION Lime-tolerant.
• HEIGHT 15–23cm (6–9in).
• SPREAD 15–23cm (6–9in).

E. carnea 'C. J. Backhouse'

☼ ◊ ❀ ❀ ❀

CALLUNA VULGARIS 'Peter Sparkes'

Habit Loose, graceful. **Flowers** Large, double, in long spikes. Deep pink, fading with maturity. Good for cutting and drying. **Leaves** Linear, scale-like, fleshy. Dark grey-green.
• SEASON Summer–late autumn.
• HEIGHT 50cm (20in).
• SPREAD 55cm (22in).

C. vulgaris 'Peter Sparkes'

☼ ◊ pH ❀ ❀ ❀

CALLUNA VULGARIS 'Silver Knight'

Habit Dense, upright. **Flowers** Large, urn- to bell-shaped, single, in dense spikes. Mauve-pink. **Leaves** Linear, scale-like. Soft silver-grey.
• SEASON Summer–autumn.
• HEIGHT 30cm (12in).
• SPREAD 30cm (12in).

C. vulgaris 'Silver Knight'

☼ ◊ pH ❀ ❀ ❀

ERICA CINEREA 'Hookstone Lavender'

Habit Straggling, spreading. **Flowers** Urn-shaped, in long racemes, in profusion. Pale lavender. **Leaves** Needle-like, in whorls of 3. Bright green.
• SEASON Early summer–early autumn.
• HEIGHT 38cm (15in).
• SPREAD 50cm (20in).

E. cinerea 'Hookstone Lavender'

☼ ◊ pH ❀ ❀ ❀

CALLUNA VULGARIS 'Tib'

Habit Compact, dense, rounded, very free-flowering. **Flowers** Small, tightly double. Deep rosy-pink. **Leaves** Linear, scale-like. Dark green.
• SEASON Mid-summer–autumn.
• HEIGHT 30–60cm (12–24in).
• SPREAD 40–60cm (16–24in).

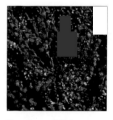

C. vulgaris 'Tib'

☼ ◊ pH ❀ ❀ ❀　　♛

ERICA CARNEA
'December Red'
Habit Vigorous,
spreading.
Flowers Small, tubular
to bell-shaped, in robust
spikes. Deep rose-red.
Leaves Needle-like, in
whorls of 4. Rich dark
green.
• SEASON Mid-winter.
• CULTIVATION
Tolerant of lime and
some shade.
• HEIGHT 20cm (8in).
• SPREAD 45cm (18in).

E. carnea 'December
Red'

ERICA CINEREA
'Purple Beauty'
Habit Dense, bushy.
Flowers Urn-shaped, in
long racemes. Dark rose-
purple. *Leaves* Needle-
like, in whorls of 3. Dark
green.
• SEASON Early
summer–early autumn.
• HEIGHT 25–30cm
(10–12in).
• SPREAD 25–30cm
(10–12in).

E. cinerea 'Purple
Beauty'

☼ ◊ ᴾᴴ ✿ ✿ ✿

ERICA CARNEA
'Vivellii'
Habit Dense, compact.
Flowers Small, tubular
to bell-shaped. Deep
purple-pink, with darker
tips. *Leaves* Needle-
like, in whorls. Rich dark
green, bronze in winter.
• SEASON Late winter–
spring.
• CULTIVATION
Tolerant of lime.
• HEIGHT 15cm (6in).
• SPREAD 30cm (12in).

E. carnea 'Vivellii'

☼ ◊ ✿ ✿ ✿   ♈

CALLUNA VULGARIS
'Darkness'
Habit Dense, compact.
Flowers Small, urn- to
bell-shaped, single, in
short, dense spikes, in
profusion. Deep carmine.
Leaves Linear, scale-
like, fleshy. Bright green.
• SEASON Summer–
autumn.
• HEIGHT 30–40cm
(12–16in).
• SPREAD 35cm (14in).

C. vulgaris 'Darkness'

☼ ◊ ᴾᴴ ✿ ✿ ✿   ♈

CALLUNA VULGARIS
'Firefly'
Habit Vigorous, dense.
Flowers Small, urn- to
bell-shaped, single. Deep
lilac. *Leaves* Linear,
scale-like. Red-brown,
turning bright orange in
winter.
• SEASON Late summer–
early autumn.
• HEIGHT 45–50cm
(18–20in).
• SPREAD 45–50cm
(18–20in).

C. vulgaris 'Firefly'

☼ ◊ ᴾᴴ ✿ ✿ ✿   ♈

ERICA × STUARTII
'Irish Lemon'
Habit Dense, compact.
Flowers Large, bell-shaped, in rounded umbels. Pale mauve.
Leaves Small, narrowly lance-shaped, in whorls of 4. Dark green, tipped lemon-yellow in spring.
• OTHER NAMES
E. × *praegeri.*
• SEASON Late spring–summer.
• HEIGHT 15cm (6in).
• SPREAD 30cm (12in).

E. × *stuartii* 'Irish Lemon'

☼ ◑ pH ❄❄❄ ⚱

CALLUNA VULGARIS
'Foxii Nana'
Habit Very compact, dense, mound-forming.
Flowers Small, urn- to bell-shaped, single. Mauve-pink.
Leaves Moss-like. Bright green.
• SEASON Summer–autumn.
• HEIGHT 10–15cm (4–6in).
• SPREAD 10–15cm (4–6in).

C. vulgaris 'Foxii Nana'

☼ ◌ pH ❄❄❄

ERICA CARNEA
'Westwood Yellow'
Habit Dense, compact.
Flowers Small, tubular to bell-shaped. Deep pink. *Leaves* Needle-like, in whorls of 4. Golden-yellow.
• SEASON Mid-winter–spring.
• HEIGHT 15–23cm (6–9in).
• SPREAD 15–23cm (6–9in).

E. carnea 'Westwood Yellow'

☼ ◌ ❄❄❄ ⚱

ERICA CARNEA
'Foxhollow'
Habit Vigorous, spreading. *Flowers* Few, small, tubular to bell-shaped. Pale pink.
Leaves Needle-like, in whorls of 4. Golden yellow in summer, tipped orange in spring.
• SEASON Early winter–late spring.
• HEIGHT 30cm (12in).
• SPREAD 45cm (18in) or more.

E. carnea 'Foxhollow'

☼ ◌ ❄❄❄ ⚱

ERICA ERIGENA
'Golden Lady'
Habit Compact, shy-flowering.
Flowers Fragrant, bell-shaped. White.
Leaves Needle-like. Golden-yellow.
• CULTIVATION Tolerates some lime.
• SEASON Early winter–late spring.
• HEIGHT 30cm (12in).
• SPREAD 30cm (12in).

E. erigena 'Golden Lady'

☼ ◌ pH ❄❄ ⚱

ERICA VAGANS
'Valerie Proudley'
Habit Vigorous, bushy, shy-flowering.
Flowers Rounded, bell-shaped. White.
Leaves Long, needle-like, in whorls of 4–5. Golden.
• CULTIVATION Tolerates some lime.
• SEASON Late summer–autumn.
• HEIGHT 45cm (18in).
• SPREAD 45cm (18in).

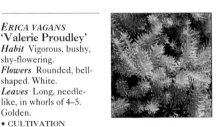

E. vagans 'Valerie Proudley'

☼ ◌ pH ❄❄❄ ⚱

ERICA CARNEA 'Ann Sparkes'
Habit Slow-growing, spreading.
Flowers Small, tubular to bell-shaped. Rose-pink. *Leaves* Needle-like, in whorls of 4. Golden, bronze in winter.
• SEASON Early winter–late spring.
• HEIGHT 15cm (6in).
• SPREAD 15cm (6in) or more.

E. carnea 'Ann Sparkes'

☼ ◌ ❄❄❄

CALLUNA VULGARIS
'Golden Feather'
Habit Vigorous, dense.
Flowers Small, urn- to
bell-shaped, single.
Mauve-pink.
Leaves Feathery. Golden-
yellow and bright green,
tipped with red young
growth; orange in winter.
• SEASON Summer–
autumn.
• HEIGHT 38–50cm
(15–20in).
• SPREAD 60cm (24in).

C. vulgaris 'Golden
Feather'

☼ ◊ pH ✽✽✽

CALLUNA VULGARIS
'Robert Chapman'
Habit Dense, spreading.
Flowers Small, urn- to
bell-shaped, single. Soft
purple. *Leaves* Linear,
scale-like. Mid-green,
overlaid golden-yellow;
orange and red in winter.
• SEASON Summer–
autumn.
• HEIGHT 25cm–60cm
(10–24in).
• SPREAD 35–60cm
(14–24in).

C. vulgaris 'Robert
Chapman'

☼ ◊ pH ✽✽✽   ♈

CALLUNA VULGARIS
'Gold Haze'
Habit Vigorous, dense.
Flowers Small, urn- to
bell-shaped, single.
White. *Leaves* Linear,
scale-like. Bright golden-
yellow.
• SEASON Summer–
autumn.
• HEIGHT 45–60cm
(18–24in).
• SPREAD 25–45cm
(10–18in).

C. vulgaris 'Gold
Haze'

☼ ◊ pH ✽✽✽   ♈

CALLUNA VULGARIS
'Beoley Gold'
Habit Vigorous, dense.
Flowers Small, urn- to
bell-shaped, single, in
short spikes. White.
Leaves Linear, scale-
like, fleshy. Light green,
flushed gold and cream.
• SEASON Summer–
autumn.
• HEIGHT 50cm (20in).
• SPREAD 60cm (24in).

C. vulgaris 'Beoley
Gold'

☼ ◊ pH ✽✽✽   ♈

ERICA CINEREA
'Windlebrooke'
Habit Vigorous, dense,
bushy. *Flowers* Urn-
shaped. Mauve.
Leaves Needle-like, in
whorls of 3. Golden,
tinted bright orange and
red in winter.
• SEASON Early
summer–early autumn.
• CULTIVATION Prefers
a warm, dry position.
• HEIGHT 15cm (6in).
• SPREAD 15cm (6in).

E. cinerea
'Windlebrooke'

☼ ◊ pH ✽✽✽

CALLUNA VULGARIS
'Multicolor'
Habit Compact, dense.
Flowers Small, urn- to
bell-shaped, single. Soft
mauve-pink.
Leaves Linear, scale-like.
Bright green, red-tipped
in summer; tinted yellow
and orange in winter.
• SEASON Summer–
autumn.
• HEIGHT 10–20cm
(4–8in).
• SPREAD 10–20cm
(4–8in).

C. vulgaris 'Multicolor'

☼ ◊ pH ✽✽✽

ERICA CINEREA
'Rock Pool'
Habit Dense, bushy,
compact. *Flowers* Urn-
shaped. Mauve.
Leaves Needle-like, in
whorls of 3. Golden,
tinted orange and red in
winter.
• SEASON Early
summer–early autumn.
• CULTIVATION Prefers
a warm, dry position.
• HEIGHT 15cm (6in).
• SPREAD 15cm (6in).

E. cinerea 'Rock Pool'

☼ ◊ pH ✽✽✽

CALLUNA VULGARIS
'Boskoop'
Habit Dense, compact.
Flowers Small, urn- to
bell-shaped, single. Soft
lilac-pink.
Leaves Linear, scale-
like, fleshy. Rich golden-
yellow, turning deep
orange-red in winter.
• SEASON
Summer–autumn.
• HEIGHT 30cm (12in).
• SPREAD 30cm (12in).

C. vulgaris 'Boskoop'

☼ ◊ pH ✽✽✽

Apocynaceae	HERALD'S TRUMPET, NEPAL TRUMPET FLOWER

BEAUMONTIA GRANDIFLORA

Habit Woody-stemmed, twining. *Flowers* Large, fragrant, funnel- to bell-shaped, from late spring to summer. White. *Leaves* Evergreen, broadly oblong-oval. Glossy green, rusty-downy beneath.
• NATIVE HABITAT Scrub, forest, and rocky areas of the E. Himalaya.
• CULTIVATION Grow in a conservatory in fertile soil or compost. Water freely when in full growth, otherwise sparingly. Prune after flowering.
• PROPAGATION By seed or by heeled semi-ripe cuttings in summer.

☀ ◊

Min.
7–10°C
(45–50°F)

HEIGHT
15m (50ft)
or more

Leguminosae	

CLIANTHUS PUNICEUS 'Albus'   ♥

Habit Woody-stemmed, scrambling.
Flowers Large, claw-like, in drooping clusters in spring and early summer. Creamy-white.
Leaves Evergreen or semi-evergreen, divided into many, narrowly oblong leaflets. Mid-green.
• NATIVE HABITAT New Zealand.
• CULTIVATION Provide a warm, sheltered site such as a south- or west-facing wall. Tip back shoots in spring. In cold areas grow in a cool conservatory.
• PROPAGATION By seed in spring or by stem cuttings in late summer.

☀ ◊

HEIGHT
To 5m
(15ft)

Asclepiadaceae	MADAGASCAR JASMINE, WAX FLOWER

STEPHANOTIS FLORIBUNDA   ♥

Habit Woody-stemmed, twining. *Flowers* Small, fragrant, funnel-shaped, waxy, in clusters from spring to autumn. White. *Leaves* Evergreen, oval to oblong-elliptic, leathery. Glossy deep green.
• NATIVE HABITAT Madagascar.
• CULTIVATION Grow in the home or conservatory in a fertile, humus-rich soil or compost. Water moderately when in full growth, less in winter. Cut back long shoots and crowded growth in spring.
• PROPAGATION By seed in spring or by semi-ripe cuttings in summer.

◑ ◊

Min.
13–16°C
(55–61°F)

HEIGHT
To 5m
(15ft)

Apocynaceae	

MANDEVILLA SPLENDENS

Habit Woody-stemmed, twining. *Flowers* Large, funnel-shaped, in late spring or early summer. Rose-pink with yellow centres. *Leaves* Evergreen, broadly elliptic, pointed. Lustrous dark green.
• NATIVE HABITAT Mountain forests of S.E. Brazil.
• CULTIVATION Grow in a conservatory in fertile soil or compost. Water freely when in growth, otherwise sparingly. Thin out and spur back congested growth in early spring.
• PROPAGATION By seed in spring or by semi-ripe cuttings in summer.

◑ ◊

Min.
7–10°C
(45–50°F)

HEIGHT
3–6m
(10–20ft)

Bignoniaceae

DISTICTIS BUCCINATORIA

Habit Vigorous, woody-stemmed, tendril climber.
Flowers Large, tubular to funnel-shaped, in clusters from early spring to summer. Rose-crimson, with orange-yellow tube. *Leaves* Evergreen, oval to lance-shaped, pointed, smooth. Mid-green.
• NATIVE HABITAT Mexico.
• CULTIVATION Grow in a fertile, humus-rich soil or compost. Water freely when plant is in full growth, otherwise sparingly. Maintain good ventilation under glass. Cut back hard at planting time and prune in spring to thin out any congested growth. Tie the shoots in to a support as growth progresses. The Mexican blood flower makes an unusual and beautiful specimen for the conservatory.
• PROPAGATION By softwood cuttings in early summer or by semi-ripe cuttings in late summer.
• OTHER NAMES *Phaedranthus buccinatorius*.

Min. 5°C
(41°F)

HEIGHT
5m (15ft) or
more

Leguminosae	GLORY PEA, LOBSTER CLAW, PARROT'S BILL

CLIANTHUS PUNICEUS ♀

Habit Woody-stemmed, scrambling.
Flowers Large, claw-like, in drooping clusters in spring and early summer. Brilliant red.
Leaves Evergreen or semi-evergreen, divided into many narrowly oblong leaflets. Mid-green.
• NATIVE HABITAT New Zealand.
• CULTIVATION Provide a warm, sheltered site such as a south- or west-facing wall. Tip back in spring. In cold areas grow in a cool conservatory.
• PROPAGATION By seed in spring or by stem cuttings in late summer.

☼ ◊ ❀

HEIGHT
To 5m
(15ft)

Passifloraceae	RED GRANADILLA, RED PASSION FLOWER

PASSIFLORA COCCINEA

Habit Vigorous, woody-stemmed, tendril climber.
Flowers Large, complex, very showy, from spring to autumn. Deep scarlet, with red, pink, and white corona of filaments. **Leaves** Evergreen, rounded-oblong. Mid-green, downy beneath.
• NATIVE HABITAT Venezuela, Peru, and Brazil.
• CULTIVATION Grow in a conservatory in sandy, humus-rich soil or compost. Water freely in growth, then moderately. Thin congested growth in spring.
• PROPAGATION By seed in spring or by semi-ripe cuttings in summer.

☼ ◊

Min.15°C
(59°F)

HEIGHT
3–4m
(10–12ft)

Leguminosae	DUSKY CORAL PEA

KENNEDIA RUBICUNDA

Habit Fast-growing, woody-stemmed, twining.
Flowers Pea-like, in small trusses in spring and summer. Rich coral-red. **Leaves** Evergreen, divided into 3 oval leaflets. Dull green.
• NATIVE HABITAT E. Australia.
• CULTIVATION Grow in a conservatory in a sandy, moderately fertile soil or compost. Water moderately and regularly when in full growth, otherwise sparingly.
• PROPAGATION By seed in spring or by semi-ripe cuttings in summer.

☼ ◊

Min. 5–7°C
(41–45°F)

HEIGHT
To 3m
(10ft)

Tropaeolaceae	

TROPAEOLUM TRICOLORUM ♀

Habit Herbaceous, tuberous-rooted, with twining leaf stalks. **Flowers** Small, spurred, from early spring to summer. Orange-yellow, with orange-red, black-tipped calyces. **Leaves** Deciduous, 5–7 lobes. Rich green.
• NATIVE HABITAT Chile and Bolivia.
• CULTIVATION Grows best in a cool conservatory in sandy, humus-rich, neutral to slightly acid soil or compost. Store tubers dry in winter.
• PROPAGATION By seed, tubers, or basal stem cuttings in spring.

☼ ◊

Min. 5°C
(41°F)

HEIGHT
1m (3ft)

Ericaceae	

AGAPETES SERPENS ♼

Habit Arching, scandent. **Flowers** Small, goblet-shaped, pendent, carried beneath slender shoots in spring. Rich rose-red with darker veins.
Leaves Evergreen, small, lance-shaped. Lustrous dark green.
• NATIVE HABITAT Mountain forest, E. Himalaya.
• CULTIVATION Grow in a cool conservatory. In mild areas grow against a sheltered, shady wall in a humus-rich, moisture-retentive but well-drained soil.
• PROPAGATION By seed in spring or by semi-ripe cuttings in summer.

☀ ◌ pH

Min. 5°C
(41°F)

HEIGHT
2–3m
(6–10ft)

Rubiaceae	BRAZILIAN FIRECRACKER

MANETTIA LUTEORUBRA

Habit Fast-growing, twining. **Flowers** Small, funnel-shaped, in spring and summer. Red with yellow tips. **Leaves** Evergreen, lance-shaped or oblong. Glossy dark green.
• NATIVE HABITAT Forests of South America.
• CULTIVATION Grow in a fertile, humus-rich soil or compost. Water freely when in growth, less in autumn and winter.
• PROPAGATION By softwood cuttings in spring or by semi-ripe cuttings in summer.
• OTHER NAMES *M. inflata.*

☀ ◌

Min. 5°C
(41°F)

HEIGHT
2m (6ft)

Gesneriaceae	

MITRARIA COCCINEA

Habit Woody-stemmed, scrambling or climbing.
Flowers Small, tubular, carried in leaf axils during late spring and summer. Bright orange-red.
Leaves Evergreen, small, toothed, leathery. Glossy green.
• NATIVE HABITAT Chile and Argentina.
• CULTIVATION Grow in a sheltered and shaded site, in a humus-rich, acid soil. If grown as a climber, tie in shoots to support as growth proceeds.
• PROPAGATION By seed in spring or by stem cuttings in summer.

☀ ◐ pH
❄

HEIGHT
To 2m (6ft)

Lardizabalaceae	CHOCOLATE VINE

AKEBIA QUINATA

Habit Vigorous, woody-stemmed, twining.
Flowers Small, vanilla-scented, in racemes in late spring. Chocolate-maroon. **Fruits** Sausage-shaped. Purplish. **Leaves** Deciduous or semi-evergreen, divided into 5 oblong-oval leaflets. Deep green, blue-green beneath.
• NATIVE HABITAT Japan, China, and Korea.
• CULTIVATION Tolerates a north- or east-facing wall. Grow in any fertile soil.
• PROPAGATION By seed in autumn or spring, by semi-ripe cuttings in summer or by layering in winter.

☀ ◌
❄❄

HEIGHT
10m (30ft)
or more

Lardizabalaceae	

HOLBOELLIA CORIACEA

Habit Fast-growing, twining. **Flowers** Fragrant, in spring. Male: small. White-mauve. Female: larger. Greenish-white, flushed purple. **Fruits** Sausage-shaped, 4–6cm (1.5–2.5in) long. Purple.
Leaves Evergreen, with 3 oval to lance-shaped, leathery leaflets. Dark green.
• NATIVE HABITAT C. China.
• CULTIVATION Tolerates semi-shade but needs sun for flowers and fruit. Grow in any fertile soil in a warm, sheltered site.
• PROPAGATION By stem cuttings in late summer.

☀ ◊
❀❀❀

HEIGHT
To 7m
(22ft)

Bignoniaceae	ARGENTINE TRUMPET VINE, LOVE-CHARM

CLYTOSTOMA CALLISTEGIOÏDES

Habit Vigorous, woody-stemmed, tendril climber.
Flowers Funnel- to bell-shaped, in small clusters from spring to summer. Lilac, veined purple.
Leaves Evergreen, each with 2 oval, shining leaflets and a tendril. Green.
• NATIVE HABITAT Lowland forests of Brazil and Argentina.
• CULTIVATION Grow in a warm conservatory in fertile, sandy, humus-rich soil or compost. Water freely when in growth, otherwise moderately.
• PROPAGATION By semi-ripe cuttings in summer.

☀ ◊

Min.
10–13°C
(50–55°F)

HEIGHT
To 5m
(15ft)

Lardizabalaceae	

STAUNTONIA HEXAPHYLLA

Habit Woody-stemmed, twining. **Flowers** Small, fragrant, cup-shaped, in racemes in spring. Pale violet. Male and female on separate plants. **Fruits** Egg-shaped, edible. Purple. **Leaves** Evergreen, with 3–7 oval, leathery leaflets. Dark green.
• NATIVE HABITAT Japan, Korea, and Taiwan.
• CULTIVATION Tolerates semi-shade but needs sun for fruits. Grow in any fertile soil, in a warm, sheltered site.
• PROPAGATION By seed in spring or by stem cuttings in spring or summer.

☀ ◊
❀❀

HEIGHT
To 10m
(30ft) or
more

Leguminosae	WESTERN AUSTRALIA CORAL PEA

HARDENBERGIA COMPTONIANA ♥

Habit Woody-stemmed, twining. **Flowers** Small, pea-like, in profuse, slender racemes in spring. Deep purple-blue. **Leaves** Evergreen, divided into 3–5 lance-shaped, pointed leaflets. Mid-green.
• NATIVE HABITAT Dry eucalypt forest and coastal scrub of W. Australia.
• CULTIVATION Grow in a cool conservatory in neutral to slightly acid, humus-rich soil that does not dry out during the growing season.
• PROPAGATION By pre-soaked seed or tip cuttings in spring or by stem cuttings in late summer.

☀ ◊

Min. 5°C
(41°F)

HEIGHT
To 2.5m
(8ft)

Verbenaceae	PURPLE WREATH, SANDPAPER VINE

PETREA VOLUBILIS

Habit Vigorous, woody-stemmed, twining.
Flowers Small, tubular with spreading lobes, in spikes from late winter to late summer. Indigo and lilac-blue. *Leaves* Evergreen, elliptic, rough-textured. Deep green above, paler beneath.
• NATIVE HABITAT Lowland forests of C. America.
• CULTIVATION Grow in a warm conservatory in fertile, neutral to acid soil or compost. Water regularly and moderately when in growth, otherwise sparingly.
• PROPAGATION By semi-ripe cuttings in summer.

☀ ◊

Min.
13–15°C
(55–59°F)

HEIGHT
To 6m
(20ft) or
more

Pittosporaceae	AUSTRALIAN BLUEBELL, BLUEBELL CREEPER

SOLLYA HETEROPHYLLA ♟

Habit Woody-based, twining. *Flowers* Small, bell-shaped, in clusters from spring to autumn. Sky-blue. *Leaves* Evergreen, lance-shaped to oval. Mid-green.
• NATIVE HABITAT Coastal plains and mountains of W. Australia.
• CULTIVATION Grow in a fertile, humus-rich soil or compost against a warm, sheltered wall. Water moderately when in growth, otherwise sparingly.
• PROPAGATION By seed in spring or by softwood or greenwood cuttings in summer.

☀ ◊

Min. 5°C
(45°F)

HEIGHT
To 3m
(10ft)

Leguminosae	EMERALD CREEPER, JADE VINE

STRONGYLODON MACROBOTRYS

Habit Vigorous, woody-stemmed, twining.
Flowers Claw-like, waxy, in long pendent racemes in winter and spring. Luminescent blue-green.
Leaves Evergreen, divided into 3 oblong-oval leaflets. Dark green, bronzed pink when young.
• NATIVE HABITAT Philippines.
• CULTIVATION Grow in a warm conservatory in fertile, humus-rich, preferably neutral to acid soil or compost. Water freely in full growth, then moderately.
• PROPAGATION By seed or stem cuttings in summer or by air-layering in spring.

☀ ◊

Min. 18°C
(64°F)

HEIGHT
To 20m
(70ft)

Cannabiaceae	GOLDEN HOP, BINE, EUROPEAN HOP

HUMULUS LUPULUS 'Aureus' ♟

Habit Herbaceous, twining. *Flowers* Small, female, in rounded spikes, carried in pendent clusters in autumn. Greenish-yellow, with papery bracts.
Fruits Papery, cone-like (hops). *Leaves* Deciduous, with 3–5 lobes. Lime-green to yellow.
• NATIVE HABITAT Garden origin.
• CULTIVATION Tolerates shade and any well-drained soil but colours best in sun. Provide support of a pergola or trellis.
• PROPAGATION By tip cuttings or division in spring.

☀ ◊
❄ ❄ ❄

HEIGHT
To 6m
(20ft)

Solanaceae	

SOLANDRA MAXIMA

Habit Vigorous, woody-stemmed, scrambling.
Flowers Large, night-scented, broadly trumpet-shaped, in spring to summer. Pale yellow with purple veins, then golden. **Leaves** Evergreen, elliptic. Glossy mid-green.
• NATIVE HABITAT By water in tropical forests of Mexico, C. America, Venezuela.
• CULTIVATION Grow in a warm conservatory. Water freely in growth, then sparingly. Induce flowers by temporarily reducing water after first flush of growth.
• PROPAGATION By semi-ripe cuttings in summer.

☼ ◊

Min.
10–13°C
(50–55°F)

HEIGHT
7–10m
(23–30ft)

Acanthaceae	

THUNBERGIA MYSORENSIS ♥

Habit Woody-stemmed, twining. **Flowers** Large, tubular, with recurved lobes, in long, pendent racemes from spring to autumn. Yellow, with red-brown lobes. **Leaves** Evergreen, narrowly elliptic, toothed, smooth. Mid-green.
• NATIVE HABITAT Hillsides of Nilgiri, India.
• CULTIVATION Grow in a warm conservatory in fertile, humus-rich soil or compost. Water freely in growth; keep just moist in winter. Shade in summer.
• PROPAGATION By seed in spring or by softwood or semi-ripe cuttings in summer.

☼ ◊

Min. 15°C
(59°F)

HEIGHT
To 6m
(20ft)

Oleaceae	PRIMROSE JASMINE

JASMINUM MESNYI ♥

Habit Woody-stemmed, scrambling.
Flowers Large, semi-double, in spring. Pale yellow. **Leaves** Evergreen or semi-evergreen, divided into 3 lance-shaped leaflets. Glossy dark green.
• NATIVE HABITAT W. China.
• CULTIVATION Grow in any fertile soil, including dry soil. Suitable for a warm south- or south-west wall in mild areas or otherwise in a conservatory.
• PROPAGATION By heeled semi-ripe cuttings in late summer.

☼ ◊
❄

HEIGHT
To 3m
(10ft)

Nyctaginaceae	

BOUGAINVILLEA GLABRA 'Snow White'

Habit Woody-stemmed, scrambling.
Flowers Tiny, with conspicuous, papery bracts, in clusters throughout the year, mainly in summer. Bracts are white, with green veins. *Leaves* Evergreen or semi-evergreen, round-oval. Glossy bright green.
• NATIVE HABITAT Garden origin.
• CULTIVATION Grown in a conservatory. Water moderately when in growth but keep almost dry when dormant.
• PROPAGATION By semi-ripe cuttings in summer or by hardwood cuttings in winter.

☼ ◊

Min.
7–10°C
(45–50°F)

HEIGHT
To 5m
(15ft)

Apocynaceae	

TRACHELOSPERMUM JASMINOÏDES ♔

Habit Woody-stemmed, twining.
Flowers Very fragrant, with 5 twisted petal lobes, in clusters in summer. White. *Fruits* Pods, to 15cm (6in) long, in pairs. *Leaves* Evergreen, oval to lance-shaped. Dark green.
• NATIVE HABITAT China and Taiwan.
• CULTIVATION Grow in any moderately fertile soil. Provide the shelter of a warm, south-facing wall.
• PROPAGATION By seed in spring, by layering in summer, or by semi-ripe cuttings in late summer.

☼ ◊
❁ ❁

HEIGHT
To 9m
(28ft)

Solanaceae	

SOLANUM JASMINOÏDES 'Album' ♔

Habit Woody-stemmed, scrambling.
Flowers Star-shaped, in broad clusters in summer to autumn. Milk-white with lemon-yellow stamens.
Leaves Semi-evergreen or deciduous, oval to lance-shaped. Dark green.
• NATIVE HABITAT Garden origin.
• CULTIVATION Grow in any fertile soil. Provide support and the shelter of a warm, south- or south-west-facing wall. Thin out and spur back shoots in spring.
• PROPAGATION By semi-ripe cuttings in summer.

☼ ◊
❁

HEIGHT
To 6m
(20ft)

Leguminosae	

WISTERIA SINENSIS 'Alba' ♔

Habit Vigorous, woody-stemmed, twining anti-clockwise. *Flowers* Small, strongly fragrant, pea-like, in slender, drooping racemes, 20–30cm (8–12in) long, in early summer. White. *Leaves* Deciduous, divided into 7–13 elliptic-oblong leaflets. Bright green.
• NATIVE HABITAT Garden origin.
• CULTIVATION Grow in any moderately fertile soil in a sheltered south- or west-facing site. Prune in summer and in late winter.
• PROPAGATION By bench grafting in winter or by layering in summer.

☼ ◊
❁ ❁ ❁

HEIGHT
To 30m
(100ft)

Leguminosae	

WISTERIA FLORIBUNDA 'Alba'

Habit Vigorous, woody-stemmed, twining anti-clockwise. **Flowers** Small, fragrant, pea-like, in slender, drooping racemes, to 60cm (24in) long in early summer. White, sometimes ageing to pale mauve. **Leaves** Deciduous, divided into 11–19 oval leaflets. Bright green.
• NATIVE HABITAT Garden origin.
• CULTIVATION Grows in any fertile soil but prefers deep loam. Prune in summer and in late winter.
• PROPAGATION By bench grafting in winter or by layering in summer.

HEIGHT
To 9m
(28ft)

Asclepiadaceae	CRUEL PLANT

ARAUJIA SERICIFERA

Habit Woody-stemmed, twining.
Flowers Fragrant, tubular with spreading lobes, from late summer to autumn. White.
Leaves Evergreen, oval-oblong. Pale green.
• NATIVE HABITAT S. America.
• CULTIVATION In mild areas grow in fertile soil against a south- or west-facing wall. In colder areas grow in a cool conservatory.
• PROPAGATION By seed in spring or by stem cuttings in late summer or early autumn.
• OTHER NAMES *A. sericofera.*

HEIGHT
To 7m
(23ft)

Hydrangeaceae	CLIMBING HYDRANGEA

HYDRANGEA ANOMALA subsp. *PETIOLARIS*

Habit Woody-stemmed, with aerial roots.
Flowers Large, 'lace-cap' heads, in summer on mature plants. Creamy-white inner and ray florets.
Leaves Deciduous, oval, pointed, coarsely toothed. Mid-green.
• NATIVE HABITAT Japan, Korea, and Taiwan.
• CULTIVATION Grow in any moist, fertile soil, including chalk. Excellent climber for a north wall.
• PROPAGATION By softwood cuttings in summer.
• OTHER NAMES *H. petiolaris.*

HEIGHT
18–25m
(60–80ft)

Hydrangeaceae	

PILEOSTEGIA VIBURNOÏDES ♥

Habit Slow-growing, woody-stemmed, with aerial roots. **Flowers** Tiny, with prominent stamens, in dense panicles from late summer to autumn. Creamy-white. **Leaves** Evergreen, narrowly oblong to lance-shaped, leathery. Glossy dark green.
• NATIVE HABITAT India, China, and Taiwan.
• CULTIVATION Grow in any fertile soil. Tolerates shade and is useful for north walls.
• PROPAGATION By seed in autumn or by tip cuttings in spring or early summer.
• OTHER NAMES *Schizophragma viburnoïdes.*

HEIGHT
6–10m
(20–30ft)

Hydrangeaceae	

SCHIZOPHRAGMA INTEGRIFOLIUM ♥

Habit Woody-stemmed, with aerial roots. **Flowers** Large, flat heads with tiny inner florets, and outer narrowly oval, petal-like sepals. Creamy-white. **Leaves** Deciduous, oval or heart-shaped. Bright green.
• NATIVE HABITAT Rocky cliffs of China.
• CULTIVATION Shade tolerant, but flowers best in sun and with its roots in the shade. Grow in any fertile soil.
• PROPAGATION By seed in spring or by greenwood or semi-ripe cuttings in summer.

HEIGHT
To 12m
(40ft)

Verbenaceae	BAG FLOWER, BLEEDING HEART VINE

CLERODENDRUM THOMSONIAE

Habit Vigorous, woody-stemmed, scrambling. **Flowers** Tubular, partly enclosed in a calyx, in large clusters in summer. Rich crimson, with pure white calyx. **Leaves** Evergreen, oval. Rich green.
• NATIVE HABITAT Tropical West Africa.
• CULTIVATION Grow in a warm conservatory in fertile, humus-rich soil or compost. Water freely when in growth, reducing to almost dry in winter.
• PROPAGATION By seed in spring, by softwood cuttings in late spring, or by semi-ripe cuttings in late summer.

Min. 16°C
(61°F)

HEIGHT
3m (10ft) or
more

Asclepiadaceae	

DREGEA SINENSIS

Habit Woody-stemmed, twining. **Flowers** Small, fragrant, star-shaped, in broad, rounded clusters in summer. White or cream, with red dots and streaks. **Fruits** Slender pods, 5–7cm (2–3in) long. **Leaves** Evergreen, heart-shaped. Mid-green.
• NATIVE HABITAT China.
• CULTIVATION Grow in any well-drained soil in a warm, sheltered site. Provide support.
• PROPAGATION By seed in spring or by stem cuttings in summer or autumn.
• OTHER NAMES *Wattakaka sinensis.*

HEIGHT
To 3m
(10ft)

Bignoniaceae	BOWER PLANT

PANDOREA JASMINOÏDES

Habit Woody-stemmed, twining. **Flowers** Funnel-shaped, in clusters from late winter to summer. White with pink-flushed throat. **Leaves** Evergreen, oval to lance-shaped, 5–9 leaflets. Glossy pale green.
• NATIVE HABITAT N.E. Australia.
• CULTIVATION Grow in a cool conservatory in fertile, humus-rich soil or compost. Water freely in growth, reducing in winter. Needs good ventilation.
• PROPAGATION by seed in spring or by stem cuttings or layering in summer.
• OTHER NAMES *Bignonia jasminoïdes*.

☼ ◊

Min. 5°C
(41°F)

HEIGHT
To 5m
(15ft)

Oleaceae	

JASMINUM OFFICINALE f. AFFINE

Habit Woody-stemmed, twining. **Flowers** Small, fragrant, tubular with spreading lobes, in clusters in summer to autumn. White; pink exterior and buds. **Leaves** Semi-evergreen or deciduous, divided into 5–9 elliptic leaflets. Dark green.
• NATIVE HABITAT Forests and scrub, from Asia Minor to the Himalaya and China.
• CULTIVATION Tolerates shade of a north wall but flowers best in sun. Grow in any moderately fertile soil.
• PROPAGATION By semi-ripe cuttings in summer.

☼ ◊

HEIGHT
To 12m
(40ft)

Asclepiadaceae	

HOYA AUSTRALIS

Habit Woody-stemmed, twining, with aerial roots, epiphytic. **Flowers** Star-shaped, fragrant, waxy, in dense trusses in summer. White with maroon markings. **Leaves** Evergreen, oval to rounded, fleshy. Rich green.
• NATIVE HABITAT Coastal forests of Australia.
• CULTIVATION Grow in a warm conservatory in fibrous, humus-rich soil or compost with added charcoal. Water freely when in growth, otherwise moderately. Provide some shade and support.
• PROPAGATION By semi-ripe cuttings in summer.

☼ ◊

Min. 15°C
(59°F)

HEIGHT
To 5m
(15ft)

Asclepiadaceae	WAX PLANT

HOYA CARNOSA

Habit Woody-stemmed, twining, with aerial roots.
Flowers Star-shaped, fragrant, waxy, in dense trusses in summer to autumn. White, fading to pink, with red centres. ***Leaves*** Evergreen, ovate. Dark green.
• NATIVE HABITAT India, Burma, and S. China.
• CULTIVATION Grow in a fibrous, humus-rich soil or compost with added charcoal. Feed every fortnight and water freely when in growth, then moderately, keeping just moist in winter. Provide support and shade.
• PROPAGATION By semi-ripe cuttings in summer.

Min. 5°C
(41°F)

HEIGHT
To 5m
(15ft)

Leguminosae	SWEET PEA

LATHYRUS ODORATUS 'Selana'

Habit Vigorous, annual, tendril climber.
Flowers Large, sweetly scented, from summer to early autumn. White, flushed pink. ***Leaves*** Pairs of oval leaflets. Mid-green.
• NATIVE HABITAT Garden origin.
• CULTIVATION Grow in any fertile, humus-rich soil. Provide support with canes or trellis and attach until established. Excellent as cut flowers.
• PROPAGATION By seed in autumn or spring. Overwinter autumn-sown plants in a cold frame or greenhouse.

HEIGHT
2m (6ft)

Actinidiaceae	

ACTINIDIA KOLOMIKTA

Habit Woody-stemmed, twining. ***Flowers*** Small, fragrant, cup-shaped, in summer. White. Male and female on separate plants. ***Leaves*** Deciduous, long and narrowly oval. Mid-green, splashed or banded with creamy-white and pink.
• NATIVE HABITAT Coniferous forests of E. Asia.
• CULTIVATION Tolerates semi-shade and any moderately fertile soil.
• PROPAGATION By seed in spring or autumn, by semi-ripe cuttings in summer, or by layering in winter.

HEIGHT
To 6m
(20ft)

Leguminosae	SWEET PEA

LATHYRUS ODORATUS 'Xenia Field'

Habit Vigorous, annual, tendril climber.
Flowers Large, sweetly scented, from summer to early autumn. Deep pink and cream.
Leaves Pairs of oval leaflets. Mid-green.
• NATIVE HABITAT Garden origin.
• CULTIVATION Grow in any fertile, humus-rich soil. Provide support with canes or trellis and attach until established. Excellent for cut flowers.
• PROPAGATION By seed in autumn or spring. Overwinter autumn-sown plants in a cold frame or greenhouse.

☼ ◊
❋ ❋ ❋

HEIGHT
2m (6ft)

Polygonaceae	CORAL VINE

ANTIGONON LEPTOPUS

Habit Vigorous, woody-stemmed, scandent.
Flowers Small, in dense trusses, mainly summer but to early autumn if conditions are favourable. Coral-pink, sometimes white. *Leaves* Evergreen, diamond-heart-shaped, crinkly. Pale green.
• NATIVE HABITAT Tropical forests of Mexico.
• CULTIVATION Grow in warm conservatory in a sandy, humus-rich soil or compost that is not too nitrogen-rich. Water freely in growth, then sparingly.
• PROPAGATION By seed in spring or by softwood cuttings in summer.

☼ ◊

Min. 15°C
(59°F)

HEIGHT
6m (20ft) or more

Apocynaceae	

MANDEVILLA × *AMOENA* 'Alice du Pont' ♛

Habit Woody-stemmed, twining. *Flowers* Large, funnel-shaped, in clusters in summer. Bright, glowing rose-pink. *Leaves* Evergreen, oval with deeply impressed veins. Dark green.
• NATIVE HABITAT Garden origin.
• CULTIVATION Grow in a conservatory in fertile, fibrous, humus-rich soil or compost. Water freely when in growth but keep almost dry in winter. Provide shade and support.
• PROPAGATION By semi-ripe cuttings in summer.

☼ ◊

Min.
7–10°C
(45–50°F)

HEIGHT
To 4m
(12ft)

Scrophulariaceae	CREEPING GLOXINIA

LOPHOSPERMUM ERUBESCENS

Habit Perennial, soft-stemmed, scandent.
Flowers Tubular, with spreading lobes, in summer and autumn. Soft rose-pink. **Leaves** Evergreen, triangular, toothed, softly hairy. Greyish-green.
• NATIVE HABITAT Mexico.
• CULTIVATION Grow in a cool conservatory in any fertile soil. Often grown outdoors as an annual.
• PROPAGATION By seed in spring or by soft tip cuttings in late summer.
• OTHER NAMES *Asarina erubescens, Maurandia erubescens.*

☼ ◊

Min. 5°C
(41°F)

HEIGHT
To 3m
(10ft)

Leguminosae	EVERLASTING PEA

LATHYRUS GRANDIFLORUS

Habit Herbaceous, tendril climber with ridged stems. **Flowers** Pea-like, in neat racemes in summer. Pink-purple and red. **Leaves** Deciduous, divided into 1–3 pairs of oval leaflets. Light green.
• NATIVE HABITAT Mountain scrub of S. Italy, S. Balkans, and N.W. Africa.
• CULTIVATION Tolerant of dry soils. Grow in any moderately fertile soil. Cut down in autumn. Useful for scrambling through hedges or other supports.
• PROPAGATION By seed in autumn or by division in spring.

☼ ◊
❄ ❄ ❄

HEIGHT
To 2m (6ft)

Caprifoliaceae	HONEYSUCKLE

LONICERA × HECKROTTII

Habit Woody-stemmed, twining. **Flowers** Large, fragrant, slender-tubular, in abundant clusters in summer. Bright pink with orange-yellow throat.
Leaves Deciduous, oblong-oval. Dark green.
• NATIVE HABITAT Garden origin.
• CULTIVATION Will tolerate sun, preferably with roots in shade. Grow in any fertile, well-drained soil. Provide support.
• PROPAGATION By semi-ripe cuttings in summer or by hardwood cuttings in late autumn.

☼ ◊
❄ ❄

HEIGHT
To 5m
(15ft)

Convolvulaceae	

IPOMOEA HORSFALLIAE ♔

Habit Vigorous, woody-stemmed, twining.
Flowers Funnel-shaped, vivid, in stalked clusters from summer to winter. Deep rose-pink.
Leaves Evergreen, with 5–7 radiating, elliptic to narrowly lance-shaped lobes. Mid-green.
• NATIVE HABITAT Tropical forests of Mexico.
• CULTIVATION Grow in a conservatory in fertile soil or compost. Water freely in growth, then moderately. Cut back congested growth in spring.
• PROPAGATION By seed in spring or by softwood or semi-ripe cuttings in summer.

☼ ◊

Min.
7–10°C
(45–50°F)

HEIGHT
2–3m
(6–10ft)

Caprifoliaceae	CORAL HONEYSUCKLE, TRUMPET HONEYSUCKLE

LONICERA SEMPERVIRENS ♀

Habit Woody-stemmed, twining. **Flowers** Large, narrowly trumpet-shaped, in abundant whorls at the ends of shoot tips in summer. Bright salmon-red, yellow inside. **Leaves** Evergreen, oval. Rich green, bluish beneath. Upper leaves perfoliate.
• NATIVE HABITAT E. and S. United States.
• CULTIVATION Will tolerate sun, preferably with roots in shade. Grow in fertile, well-drained soil. Provide protection of a south- or west-facing wall.
• PROPAGATION By semi-ripe cuttings in summer or by hardwood cuttings in late autumn.

HEIGHT
To 4m
(12ft)

Nyctaginaceae	

BOUGAINVILLEA 'Miss Manila'

Habit Woody-stemmed, scrambling. **Flowers** Tiny, surrounded by conspicuous, papery bracts, in clusters in summer. Red-pink bracts. **Leaves** Evergreen or semi-evergreen, oval, pointed, smooth. Mid-green.
• NATIVE HABITAT Garden origin.
• CULTIVATION Grow in a conservatory in fertile soil or compost. Water moderately when in growth; keep almost dry from late autumn to early spring. Provide support. Prune lateral growths in spring.
• PROPAGATION By semi-ripe cuttings in summer or by hardwood cuttings in winter.

Min.
7–10°C
(45–50°F)

HEIGHT
To 5m
(15ft)

Nyctaginaceae	

BOUGAINVILLEA 'Dania'

Habit Woody-stemmed, scrambling. **Flowers** Tiny, surrounded by conspicuous, papery bracts, in clusters in summer. Deep pink bracts. **Leaves** Evergreen or semi-evergreen, oval, pointed, smooth. Mid-green.
• NATIVE HABITAT Garden origin.
• CULTIVATION Grow in a conservatory in fertile soil or compost. Water moderately when in growth. Keep almost dry from late autumn to early spring. Provide support. Prune lateral growths in spring.
• PROPAGATION By semi-ripe cuttings in summer or by hardwood cuttings in winter.

Min.
7–10°C
(45–50°F)

HEIGHT
To 5m
(15ft)

Liliaceae	CHILEAN BELL FLOWER, COPIHUE

LAPAGERIA ROSEA ♀

Habit Woody-stemmed, twining. **Flowers** Large, bell-shaped, pendent, waxy, from summer to late autumn. Creamy-pink to crimson.
Leaves Evergreen, oblong, leathery. Dark green.
• NATIVE HABITAT Andes of Chile and Argentina.
• CULTIVATION Grow in a humus-rich, neutral to acid soil or compost. Water moderately in growth, but keep almost dry from late autumn to spring. Provide support and shade.
• PROPAGATION By seed in spring or by layering in spring or autumn.

HEIGHT
To 5m
(15ft)

Convolvulaceae	SPANISH FLAG

IPOMOEA LOBATA

Habit Vigorous, woody-stemmed, twining.
Usually grown as an annual. **Flowers** Small,
tubular, one-sided racemes. Short-lived but profuse
from summer to winter. Scarlet, turning yellow,
then white. **Leaves** Deciduous or semi-evergreen,
entire or 3-lobed, with toothed margins. Mid-green.
• NATIVE HABITAT Mexico.
• CULTIVATION Grow in any fertile soil in a sunny
and sheltered site. Water freely when in growth.
• PROPAGATION By seed in spring.
• OTHER NAMES *Mina lobata*.

HEIGHT
To 5m
(15ft)

Convolvulaceae	CYPRESS VINE, INDIAN PINK

IPOMOEA QUAMOCLIT

Habit Twining annual. **Flowers** Slender, tubular,
from summer to autumn. Orange or scarlet.
Leaves Oval, divided into many thread-like
segments. Bright green.
• NATIVE HABITAT Forests of tropical S. America.
• CULTIVATION Grow in a warm, sunny, sheltered
site, in a sandy, freely draining soil. Water freely in
dry periods.
• PROPAGATION By seed in spring.
• OTHER NAMES *Quamoclit pennata*.

HEIGHT
2–4m
(6–12ft)

Leguminosae	SWEET PEA

LATHYRUS ODORATUS 'Red Ensign'

Habit Vigorous, annual, tendril climber.
Flowers Large, sweetly scented, from summer to
early autumn. Rich scarlet. **Leaves** Pairs of oval
leaflets. Mid-green.
• NATIVE HABITAT Garden origin.
• CULTIVATION Grow in any fertile, humus-rich
soil. Provide support of canes or trellis, and attach
to support until established. Excellent for cutting.
• PROPAGATION By seed in autumn or spring.
Overwinter autumn-sown plants in a cold frame or
greenhouse.

HEIGHT
2m (6ft)

Caprifoliaceae	

LONICERA × BROWNII 'Dropmore Scarlet'

Habit Woody-stemmed, twining. **Flowers** Small,
narrowly trumpet-shaped, in abundant whorls
throughout summer. Scarlet with orange throats.
Leaves Deciduous or semi-evergreen, oval. Blue-
green. Upper leaves perfoliate.
• NATIVE HABITAT Garden origin.
• CULTIVATION Will tolerate sun, preferably with
roots in shade. Grow in fertile, well-drained soil.
Provide protection of a south- or west-facing wall.
• PROPAGATION By semi-ripe cuttings in summer
or by hardwood cuttings in late autumn.

HEIGHT
To 4m
(12ft)

Tropaeolaceae	FLAME NASTURTIUM, SCOTTISH FLAME FLOWER

TROPAEOLUM SPECIOSUM

Habit Herbaceous, twining, rhizomatous.
Flowers Large, spurred, in summer. Rich scarlet.
Fruits Small, fleshy, rounded. Bright blue with deep red calyces. *Leaves* Divided into 5–7 lobes. Bright green.
• NATIVE HABITAT Cool, humid, mountain forests of Chile.
• CULTIVATION Prefers a fertile, humus-rich, neutral to acid soil or compost. Provide shade at the roots. This climber is excellent for growing through yew hedging or other dark-leaved evergreens, which provide a beautiful contrast to its brilliantly coloured flowers. It is also useful for growing against a north-facing wall, provided it has support. It may be difficult to establish. Grows best in cool, moist areas.
• PROPAGATION By seed in autumn or by division in spring.

HEIGHT
To 3m
(10ft)

Liliaceae	

GLORIOSA SUPERBA 'Rothschildiana'

Habit Tuberous-rooted, perennial, tendril climber. All parts are toxic. **Flowers** Large, lily-like, with 6 strongly reflexed, wavy-edged petals in summer. Red with yellow margins. **Leaves** Deciduous, oval to lance-shaped. Glossy bright green.
• NATIVE HABITAT Garden origin.
• CULTIVATION Grow in a cool conservatory in fertile, humus-rich soil, with additional sharp sand. Water freely when in growth. Provide support. Store tubers in dry, frost-free conditions in winter.
• PROPAGATION By division in spring.

Min. 8°C
(46°F)

HEIGHT
2.5m (8ft)

Combretaceae	RANGOON CREEPER

QUISQUALIS INDICA

Habit Vigorous, scandent. **Flowers** Small, fragrant, tubular with spreading lobes, from late spring to late summer. White, turning red. **Leaves** Semi-evergreen, elliptic to oblong. Bright green.
• NATIVE HABITAT S. Africa and Indo-Malaysia.
• CULTIVATION Grow in a warm conservatory in humus-rich, moist but well-drained soil or compost that is not too rich in nitrogen. Water freely in growth; keep almost dry in winter. Provide shade.
• PROPAGATION By seed in spring or by semi-ripe cuttings in summer.

Min. 10°C
(50°F)

HEIGHT
3–5m
(10–15ft)

Schisandraceae	

SCHISANDRA RUBRIFLORA

Habit Woody-stemmed, twining. **Flowers** Small, fragrant, in spring or early summer. Crimson. **Fruits** Long, pendent clusters of berries on female plants. Scarlet. **Leaves** Deciduous, lance-shaped, leathery, toothed. Mid-green.
• NATIVE HABITAT The Himalaya.
• CULTIVATION Grow in any fertile, humus-rich, neutral to acid soil. Male and female plants are required for fruiting. Provide support and some shade.
• PROPAGATION By greenwood or semi-ripe cuttings in summer.

HEIGHT
To 6m
(20ft)

Flacourtiaceae	CORAL PLANT

BERBERIDOPSIS CORALLINA

Habit Woody-stemmed, scrambling or twining.
Flowers Small, globular, in pendent clusters in
summer and early autumn. Deep red.
Leaves Evergreen, oval to heart-shaped, leathery,
edged with small spines. Bright green.
• NATIVE HABITAT Damp woodlands of Chile.
• CULTIVATION Grows best in acid or neutral soil.
Shelter from cold winds. Tie in to support as
growth proceeds. Mulch at the roots in winter; will
re-sprout from the base if frost-damaged.
• PROPAGATION By semi-ripe cuttings in summer.

☼ ◊
❀❀

HEIGHT
4.5m (14ft)

Scrophulariaceae	

RHODOCHITON ATROSANGUINEUM ♛

Habit Slender-stemmed, leaf-stalk climber.
Flowers Pendent, tubular, with bell-shape calyces,
from late spring to late autumn. Black-purple, with
reddish calyces. *Leaves* Evergreen, almost heart-
shaped, distinctly toothed. Mid-green.
• NATIVE HABITAT Dry, sandy areas of Mexico.
• CULTIVATION Needs protection unless grown
outdoors as an annual. Grow in fertile, humus-rich
soil. Water freely in growth; keep nearly dry in winter.
• PROPAGATION By seed when fresh or in spring.
• OTHER NAMES *R. volubilis*.

☼ ◊
Min. 5°C
(41°F)

HEIGHT
To 3m
(10ft)

Vitaceae	

PARTHENOCISSUS HENRYANA ♛

Habit Woody-stemmed, tendril climber, with
adhesive pads. *Flowers* Tiny, insignificant.
Fruits Small, berry-like, in clusters in autumn.
Bright blue. *Leaves* Deciduous, with 3–5 toothed,
oval leaflets. Velvety deep green or bronze, with
white-pink veins.
• NATIVE HABITAT Damp woodlands of China.
• CULTIVATION Grow in fertile, well-drained,
moist soil. Colours best with a north or east aspect.
• PROPAGATION By softwood or greenwood
cuttings in summer or by hardwood cuttings in spring.

☼ ◐ ◊
❀❀❀

HEIGHT
To 10m
(30ft)

Aristolochiaceae	CALICO FLOWER

ARISTOLOCHIA LITTORALIS ♛

Habit Vigorous, woody-stemmed, twining.
Flowers Large, heart-shaped, to 12cm (5in) wide,
in summer. Maroon with white marbling.
Leaves Evergreen, heart- to kidney-shaped,
smooth. Mid-green above, blue-green beneath.
• NATIVE HABITAT S. America.
• CULTIVATION Grow in a conservatory. Water
freely in growth, then sparingly. Cut back in spring.
• PROPAGATION By seed in spring or by semi-ripe
cuttings in summer.
• OTHER NAMES *A. elegans*.

☼ ◊
Min. 13°C
(55°F)

HEIGHT
To 7m
(23ft)

Gesneriaceae	

ASTERANTHERA OVATA

Habit Woody-stemmed, scrambling, aerial root climber. *Flowers* Tubular, 5–6cm (2–2.5in) long, in pairs in the leaf axils in summer. Bright red with white throat. *Leaves* Evergreen, small, oblong, toothed. Mid- to dark green.
• NATIVE HABITAT Chile.
• CULTIVATION Grow in a moist, leafy, neutral to acid soil, in a sheltered, shady site. Good in woodland when grown up trees or as ground cover.
• PROPAGATION By tip cuttings in summer or by stem cuttings in late summer or early autumn.

HEIGHT
To 4m
(12ft)

Leguminosae	PERENNIAL PEA

LATHYRUS LATIFOLIUS ♔

Habit Herbaceous, tendril climber with winged stems. *Flowers* Pea-like, in small, dense racemes in summer and early autumn. Pink-purple. *Leaves* Deciduous, with a pair of branched tendrils and linear to oval leaflets. Mid-green.
• NATIVE HABITAT Scrub and waste ground of S. and C. Europe.
• CULTIVATION Tolerant of dry soils. Grow in any moderately fertile soil. Provide support.
• PROPAGATION By seed in autumn or by division in spring.

HEIGHT
2m (6ft) or more

Nyctaginaceae	

BOUGAINVILLEA GLABRA 'Variegata'

Habit Woody-stemmed, scrambling. *Flowers* Tiny, with conspicuous, papery bracts, in clusters throughout the year, mainly in summer. Bright purple bracts. *Leaves* Evergreen or semi-evergreen, round-oval. Dark green edged with creamy-white.
• NATIVE HABITAT Garden origin.
• CULTIVATION Grow in a conservatory. Water moderately in growth. Keep almost dry when dormant.
• PROPAGATION By semi-ripe cuttings in summer or by hardwood cuttings in winter.

Min.
7–10°C
(45–50°F)

HEIGHT
To 5m
(15ft)

Nyctaginaceae	PAPER FLOWER

BOUGAINVILLEA GLABRA ♔

Habit Woody-stemmed, scrambling. *Flowers* Tiny, with conspicuous, papery bracts, in clusters, mainly in summer. Cyclamen-purple bracts. *Leaves* Evergreen or semi-evergreen, round-oval. Dark green.
• NATIVE HABITAT Coastal areas and dry mountain valleys of Brazil.
• CULTIVATION Grow in a conservatory. Water moderately in growth. Keep almost dry when dormant.
• PROPAGATION By semi-ripe cuttings in summer or by hardwood cuttings in winter.

Min.
7–10°C
(45–50°F)

HEIGHT
To 5m
(15ft)

Convolvulaceae	

IPOMOEA HEDERACEA

Habit Twining annual. *Flowers* Funnel-shaped, from summer to early autumn. Blue, sometimes purplish. *Leaves* Heart-shaped or 3-lobed. Bright green.
• NATIVE HABITAT Tropical America.
• CULTIVATION Grow in a warm, sheltered site, in a sandy, but humus-rich, freely draining soil. Provide support with canes, wire, or trellis.
• PROPAGATION By pre-soaked seed in spring at 18°C (65°F). Sowing too early or at too low temperatures are common causes of failure.

HEIGHT
3–4m
(10–12ft)

Leguminosae	SWEET PEA

LATHYRUS ODORATUS 'Lady Diana'

Habit Moderately vigorous, annual, tendril climber. *Flowers* Large, sweetly scented, from summer to early autumn. Pale violet-blue. *Leaves* Pairs of oval leaflets. Mid-green.
• NATIVE HABITAT Garden origin.
• CULTIVATION Grow in any fertile, humus-rich soil. Provide support with canes or trellis and attach to support until established. Excellent for cutting.
• PROPAGATION By seed in autumn or spring. Overwinter autumn-sown plants in a cold frame or greenhouse.

HEIGHT
2m (6ft)

Cobaeaceae	CUP-AND-SAUCER VINE

COBAEA SCANDENS ♔

Habit Woody-stemmed, tendril climber.
Flowers Large, fragrant, bell-shaped, carried from late summer to first frosts. Opening yellow-green, ageing to purple. *Leaves* Evergreen, divided into 4–6 leaflets. Mid- to bright green.
• NATIVE HABITAT Mountains of Mexico.
• CULTIVATION May be grown outdoors as an annual. Grow in not too rich soil. Water potted plants freely in growth, then sparingly. Provide support.
• PROPAGATION By seed in spring or by softwood stem cuttings in summer.

Min. 4°C
(39°F)

HEIGHT
4–5m
(12–15ft)

Campanulaceae	

CODONOPSIS CONVOLVULACEA ♔

Habit Twining, herbaceous perennial.
Flowers Delicate, widely bell- to saucer-shaped, in summer. Soft blue-violet. *Leaves* Lance-shaped to oval. Bright green.
• NATIVE HABITAT Scrub and rocky slopes of the Himalaya.
• CULTIVATION Prefers dappled shade. Grow in light, fertile, moisture-retentive but freely drained soil. Provide support, or grow through other shrubs.
• PROPAGATION By seed in autumn or spring.

HEIGHT
To 2m (6ft)

Solanaceae	PARADISE FLOWER, POTATO VINE	

SOLANUM WENDLANDII

Habit Robust, scrambling, with prickly stems.
Flowers Widely funnel-shaped, in slender-stemmed
sprays in late summer and autumn. Lavender-blue.
Leaves Mainly evergreen, variable, lobed or
pinnate, with oblong to oval leaflets. Bright green.
• NATIVE HABITAT Costa Rica.
• CULTIVATION Grow in a warm conservatory in
fertile soil or compost. Water freely when in growth,
otherwise sparingly.
• PROPAGATION By seed in spring or by semi-ripe
cuttings in summer.

☼ ◊

Min. 10°C
(50°F)

HEIGHT
3–6m
(10–20ft)

Solanaceae		

SOLANUM CRISPUM 'Glasnevin' ♥

Habit Vigorous, woody-stemmed, scrambling.
Flowers Small, potato-like, in large clusters in
summer. Deep blue-purple with yellow anthers.
Leaves Evergreen or semi-evergreen, oval to
lance-shaped. Bright green.
• NATIVE HABITAT Garden origin.
• CULTIVATION Tolerant of semi-shade and of
any fertile soil, including chalk. Cut back weak and
badly placed growth in spring. Tie in to support as
growth proceeds. Needs a sheltered position.
• PROPAGATION By semi-ripe cuttings in summer.

☼ ◊
❄ ❄

HEIGHT
To 6m
(20ft)

Passifloraceae		

PASSIFLORA × *CAPONII* 'John Innes'

Habit Vigorous, woody-stemmed, tendril climber.
Flowers Large, bowl-shaped, nodding, in summer
to autumn. White, flushed claret-purple, with white
corona of filaments banded with purple.
Leaves Evergreen, 3-lobed. Bright green.
• NATIVE HABITAT Garden origin.
• CULTIVATION Grow in a conservatory in a
sandy, humus-rich soil or compost. Water freely
when in growth, otherwise moderately.
• PROPAGATION By seed in spring or by semi-ripe
cuttings in summer.

☼ ◊

Min.
7–10°C
(45–50°F)

HEIGHT
8m (25ft)

Passifloraceae	GIANT GRANADILLA	

PASSIFLORA QUADRANGULARIS ♥

Habit Vigorous, woody-stemmed, tendril climber.
Flowers Large, in summer. White, pink, red, or
pale violet, with a corona of wavy filaments, banded
white and deep purple. *Leaves* Evergreen, oval to
lance-shaped. Bright green.
• NATIVE HABITAT Tropical America.
• CULTIVATION Grow in a conservatory in a
sandy, humus-rich soil or compost. Water freely
when in growth, otherwise moderately.
• PROPAGATION By seed in spring or by semi-ripe
cuttings in summer.

☼ ◊

Min. 10°C
(50°F)

HEIGHT
5–8m
(15–25ft)

| Passifloraceae | BLUE PASSION FLOWER, COMMON PASSION FLOWER |

PASSIFLORA CAERULEA

Habit Vigorous, woody-stemmed, tendril climber. **Flowers** Large, in summer to autumn. White, sometimes flushed pink, with blue or purple banded filaments. **Fruits** Large, egg-shaped. Orange. **Leaves** Evergreen or semi-evergreen, 5–7 lobes. Dark green.
• NATIVE HABITAT S. Brazil.
• CULTIVATION Grow in any moderately fertile soil and provide the shelter of a warm, south- or west-facing wall. In general, passion flowers bloom best in soils that are not too rich in nitrogen, as this promotes vigorous leaf growth at the expense of flowering. Provide support. Thin out and spur back crowded growth in spring. In regions at the limits of hardiness the plant performs best if sheltered from cold, dry winds, with top growth and base of plant given the additional protection of hessian or other covering in the coldest months. Fruits only produced after hot summers.
• PROPAGATION By seed in spring or by semi-ripe cuttings in summer.

HEIGHT
10m (30ft)

Leguminosae	

WISTERIA × FORMOSA

Habit Vigorous, woody-stemmed, twining anti-clockwise. **Flowers** Small, fragrant, pea-like, in racemes to 25cm (10in) long, in early summer. Mauve and pale lilac. **Leaves** Deciduous, divided into 9–15 narrowly oval leaflets. Bright green.
• NATIVE HABITAT Garden origin.
• CULTIVATION Grow in any fertile soil in a warm, sheltered position. Cut back leafy shoots in mid- to late summer; in late winter, cut back long shoots to 2–3 buds.
• PROPAGATION By layering in summer.

HEIGHT
To 25m
(80ft) or
more

Leguminosae	CHINESE WISTERIA

WISTERIA SINENSIS ♈

Habit Vigorous, woody-stemmed, twining anti-clockwise. **Flowers** Small, fragrant, pea-like, in racemes 20–30cm (8–12in) long, in early summer. Lilac or pale violet. **Leaves** Deciduous, divided into 11 oval leaflets. Bright green.
• NATIVE HABITAT China.
• CULTIVATION Grow in any fertile soil in a warm, sheltered position. Cut back leafy shoots in mid- to late summer; in late winter, cut back long shoots to 2–3 buds.
• PROPAGATION By layering in summer.

HEIGHT
To 30m
(100ft) or
more

Leguminosae	LORD ANSON'S BLUE PEA

LATHYRUS NERVOSUS

Habit Herbaceous, tendril climber. **Flowers** Fragrant, pea-like, in long-stalked racemes, in summer. Blue-purple. **Leaves** Divided into a pair of oval to oblong leaflets. Blue-green.
• NATIVE HABITAT In scrub of S. Chile.
• CULTIVATION Tolerates full sun where soils are moist throughout the growing season. Grow in a fertile, moisture-retentive, humus-rich soil. Provide support of pea sticks or trellis.
• PROPAGATION By seed in autumn or by division in spring.

HEIGHT
1m (3ft)

Convolvulaceae	

IPOMOEA TRICOLOR 'Heavenly Blue' ♈

Habit Fast-growing, twining annual.
Flowers Large, funnel-shaped, silky, from summer to early autumn. Sky-blue.
Leaves Heart-shaped. Mid- to bright green.
• NATIVE HABITAT Garden origin.
• CULTIVATION Grow in a warm, sheltered site in a sandy, humus-rich soil. Provide support. May need protection.
• PROPAGATION By pre-soaked seed in spring. Sowing too early or in too low temperatures are common causes of failure.

HEIGHT
3m (10ft)

CLEMATIS

Clematis comprise a genus of evergreen or deciduous, mainly twining climbers, and herbaceous perennials (not included here).

They are unsurpassed for their profusion of flowers, usually carried over long periods, with species in bloom in almost every month of the year. Many are vigorous, and will cover large areas of wall or disguise unsightly buildings. Large-flowering types are usually less vigorous. Site the plants with their roots in the shade and allow their heads to get the sun, or grow them in shade, in rich, well-drained soil. Propagate cultivars by softwood or semi-ripe cuttings or by layering in early summer, and species by seed in autumn.

Clematis are divided into three groups according to flowering time, habit, and pruning requirements. Leaf descriptions are given below, but those plants that have leaves differing from their type are specified on the entry.

EARLY-FLOWERING SPECIES, *macropetala*, *alpina*, and *montana* types and cultivars

Flowers are carried on the previous season's ripened shoots. Prune after flowering to allow new growth to be produced and ripened to bloom the following year. Cut back lateral shoots to 1 or 2 buds from the framework branches. If overgrown, these types will tolerate drastic cutting back. *Macropetala* and *alpina* types have pale to mid-green leaves divided into 3–5 lance-shaped to broadly oval, serrated leaflets. The *montana* types are similar but leaves range from mid- to purplish-green in colour.

EARLY, LARGE-FLOWERED CULTIVARS, such as *C.* 'Nellie Moser', and *C.* 'The President'

The early, large-flowered cultivars flower on the previous season's ripened shoots and on new shoots produced in the current season, blooming from early to late summer.

Prune in late winter before new growth starts. Remove dead or damaged stems and cut back all other shoots to where strong leaf-axil buds are clearly visible. These buds will produce the first flush of flowers. Their leaves are pale to mid-green and simple, or divided into 3 leaflets.

LATE, LARGE-FLOWERED CULTIVARS, LATE-FLOWERING SPECIES, AND LATE SMALL-FLOWERED CULTIVARS, such as *C.* 'Duchess of Albany, and *C.* 'Etoile Violette'

Flowers are borne on the current season's growth in summer and autumn. Prune in late winter before growth begins. Cut back all the previous season's stems to a pair of strong leaf-axil buds, 15–30cm (6–12in) above ground level. Leaves on large-flowered cultivars are similar to the early, large-flowered cultivars described above. Late, large-flowered species and small-flowered cultivars have pale to dark green or grey-green leaves, divided into 3 or 3–5 leaflets.

C. MONTANA

Habit Very vigorous, floriferous.
Flowers Single, 5–7cm (2–3in) across, in late spring. White, with yellow anthers.
Leaves Divided into 3 long, oval to lance-shaped, lobed, coarsely serrated leaflets. Mid-green.
• CULTIVATION Tolerates sun and shade. Excellent for clothing fences, walls, and buildings, and for growing up trees.
• HEIGHT 7–12m (22–40ft).
• SPREAD 2–3m (6–10ft).

C. montana
EARLY-FLOWERING

☼ ◐ ◊ ✿✿✿

C. 'Henryi'

Habit Vigorous, floriferous.
Flowers Single, 12–18cm (5–7in) across, with pointed petals. White with chocolate anthers.
• HEIGHT 3m (10ft).
• SPREAD 1m (3ft).

C. 'Henryi'
EARLY LARGE-FLOWERING

☼ ◊ ✿✿✿   ♔

C. ARMANDII

Habit Vigorous.
Flowers Single, scented, flattish, 5cm (2in) across, in early spring. White.
Leaves Evergreen, with 3 long leaflets. Glossy dark green.
• CULTIVATION Best against a sheltered, south- or south-west-facing wall.
• HEIGHT 3–5m (10–15ft).
• SPREAD 2–3m (6–10ft).

C. armandii
EARLY-FLOWERING

☼ ◊ ✿✿

C. 'Mrs George Jackman'

Habit Moderately vigorous. **Flowers** Semi-double, 10cm (4in) across, in early summer, and again in early autumn when flowers are single. Creamy-white with light brown anthers,
• HEIGHT 2–3m (6–10ft).
• SPREAD 1m (3ft).

C. 'Mrs George Jackman'
EARLY LARGE-FLOWERING

☼ ◊ ✿✿   ♔

C. FLAMMULA

Habit Vigorous, dense.
Flowers Single, almond-scented, flattish, 2.5cm (1in) across, in abundance in summer and early autumn. Creamy-white.
Leaves Deciduous or semi-evergreen, with 3–5 narrowly lance-shaped leaflets. Dull green to grey.
• HEIGHT 3–5m (10–15ft).
• SPREAD 2m (6ft) or more.

C. flammula
LATE-FLOWERING

☼ ◊ ✿✿

C. FLORIDA 'Sieboldii'

Habit Weak-growing, with wiry stems.
Flowers Single, 8cm (3in) across, in mid- to late summer. Creamy-white with a domed boss of purple stamens.
Leaves Deciduous, or semi-evergreen, divided, with oval to lance-shaped leaflets. Glossy dark green.
• CULTIVATION Needs a warm, sunny, and sheltered site.
• OTHER NAMES C. florida 'Bicolor'.
• HEIGHT 2–3m (6–10ft).
• SPREAD 1m (3ft).

C. florida 'Sieboldii'
LATE SMALL-FLOWERING

☼ ◊ ✿✿✿

C. 'Huldine'

Habit Very vigorous, usually floriferous.
Flowers Single, from mid-summer to early autumn. Pearly-white with mauve reverse and cream anthers.
• CULTIVATION Good for archways and pergolas. Best grown in full sun.
• HEIGHT 3–4m (10–12ft) or more.
• SPREAD 2m (6ft).

C. 'Huldine'
LATE SMALL-FLOWERING

☼ ◊ ❀❀❀

C. MACROPETALA 'Markham's Pink'

Habit Floriferous.
Flowers Semi-double, 8cm (3in) long, in late spring-early summer. Strawberry-pink.
Leaves Divided, with oval to lance-shaped, serrated leaflets. Mid-green.
• HEIGHT 3.5m (11ft).
• SPREAD 1.5m (5ft).

C. macropetala 'Markham's Pink'
EARLY-FLOWERING

☼ ◊ ❀❀❀   ♒

C. 'Nelly Moser'

Habit Vigorous, very floriferous.
Flowers Single, 12–18cm (5–7in) across. Rose-mauve, with red-purple anthers, each petal with a central carmine stripe.
• CULTIVATION Excellent for east-, west- or north-facing walls. Flower colour fades in sun.
• HEIGHT 3.5m (11ft).
• SPREAD 1m (3ft).

C. 'Nelly Moser'
EARLY LARGE-FLOWERING

☼ ◊ ❀❀❀   ♒

C. MONTANA var. RUBENS

Habit Very vigorous, floriferous.
Flowers Single, 5cm (2in) across, in late spring. Pale pink, yellow anthers.
Leaves Divided into 3 long, oval to lance-shaped, coarsely serrated leaflets. Bronze-tinted.
• HEIGHT 7–12m (22–40ft).
• SPREAD 2–3m (6–10ft).

C. montana var. *rubens*
EARLY-FLOWERING

☼ ◊ ❀❀❀   ♒

C. MONTANA 'Tetrarose'

Habit Vigorous, floriferous.
Flowers Single, 7–10cm (3–4in) across, thick-textured, in late spring. Deep satin pink.
Leaves Divided into long, oval to lance-shaped, coarsely serrated leaflets. Bronze-flushed.
• HEIGHT 7–8m (22–25ft).
• SPREAD 2–3m (6–10ft).

C. montana 'Tetrarose'
EARLY-FLOWERING

☼ ◊ ❀❀❀   ♒

C. 'Hagley Hybrid'

Habit Vigorous, very floriferous.
Flowers Single, 8–10cm (3–4in) across, with boat-shaped petals, in summer-early autumn. Rose-mauve petals, and red anthers.
• CULTIVATION Best planted out of direct sun.
• HEIGHT 2.5m (8ft).
• SPREAD 1m (3ft).

C. 'Hagley Hybrid'
LATE LARGE-FLOWERING

☼ ◊ ❀❀❀

C. 'Lincoln Star'

Habit Moderately vigorous. **Flowers** Single, 10–12cm (4–5in) across, in early summer, and again in autumn. Bright raspberry-pink petals, and red anthers; late flowers are paler in colour.
• HEIGHT 2–3m (6–10ft).
• SPREAD 1m (3ft).

C. 'Lincoln Star'
EARLY LARGE-FLOWERING

☼ ◊ ❀❀❀

C. 'Duchess of Albany'

Habit Vigorous, very floriferous.
Flowers Small, single, upright, tulip-like, 6cm (2½in) long, in summer and early autumn. Soft pink with brown anthers and a deeper pink stripe inside each petal.
• HEIGHT 2.5m (8ft).
• SPREAD 1m (3ft).

C. 'Duchess of Albany'
LATE SMALL-FLOWERING

C. VITICELLA 'Purpurea Plena Elegans'

Habit Vigorous.
Flowers Very double, to 6cm (2½in) across, with tight rosettes of petals. Rose-purple, sometimes with green outer petals.
Leaves Divided, with broadly oval leaflets. Mid-green.
• HEIGHT 3–4m (10–12ft).
• SPREAD 1.5m (5ft).

C. viticella 'Purpurea Plena Elegans'
LATE SMALL-FLOWERING

C. 'Proteus'

Habit Moderately vigorous.
Flowers Double, 10–12cm (4–5in) across, in early summer, with a second flush of single flowers in late summer. Deep mauve-pink, flushed coral-pink at the centres.
• CULTIVATION Performs best in semi-shade. Although fully hardy, if top growth is killed in severe winters, only single flowers will be produced.
• HEIGHT 2.5–3m (8–10ft).
• SPREAD 1m (3ft).

C. 'Proteus'
EARLY LARGE-FLOWERING

C. 'Abundance'

Habit Vigorous.
Flowers Single, flattish, 2cm (1in) across, in summer and early autumn. Rose-pink with delicately veined petals and yellow anthers.
Leaves Divided, with long, lance-shaped to broadly oval leaflets. Bright green.
• HEIGHT 2–3m (6–10ft).
• SPREAD 1m (3ft).

C. 'Abundance'
LATE SMALL-FLOWERING

C. 'Ville de Lyon'

Habit Very vigorous.
Flowers Single, 10–13cm (4–5in) across, rounded petals. Bright carmine red, darker at the edges, and yellow anthers.
• CULTIVATION Thrives in sun or semi-shade.
• HEIGHT 3–4m (10–12ft) or more.
• SPREAD 1m (3ft).

C. 'Ville de Lyon'
LATE LARGE-FLOWERING

C. 'Mme Julia Correvon'

Habit Very vigorous, floriferous.
Flowers Single, flattish, to 5–7cm (2–3in) across, with twisted petals, from mid-summer to early autumn. Wine-red, with creamy stamens.
Leaves Divided, with lobed, veined leaflets. Mid-green.
• HEIGHT 2.5–3.5m (8–11ft).
• SPREAD 1m (3ft).

C. 'Mme Julia Correvon'
LATE SMALL-FLOWERING

C. 'Gravetye Beauty'
Habit Vigorous, shrubby, floriferous.
Flowers Small, single, tulip-like, with slender petals, later opening to 8cm (3in) across. Deep cherry-red.
• CULTIVATION Thrives in semi-shade or sun.
• HEIGHT 2.5m (8ft).
• SPREAD 1m (3ft).

C. 'Gravetye Beauty'
LATE SMALL-FLOWERING

☀ ◊ ❀❀❀

C. 'Ernest Markham'
Habit Vigorous.
Flowers Single, 10cm (4in) across, with blunt-tipped petals. Vivid magenta, with chocolate anthers.
• CULTIVATION Thrives in full sun.
• HEIGHT 3–4m (10–12ft).
• SPREAD 1m (3ft).

C. 'Ernest Markham'
LATE LARGE-FLOWERING

☀◑ ◊ ❀❀❀   ♛

C. 'Countess of Lovelace'
Habit Weak habit.
Flowers Double, 10cm (4in) across, with pointed petals, in early summer, and single flowers in late summer. Bluish-lilac, with cream anthers.
• CULTIVATION If top growth is killed in severe winters only single flowers will be produced.
• HEIGHT 2.5m (8ft).
• SPREAD 1m (3ft).

C. 'Countess of Lovelace'
EARLY LARGE-FLOWERING

◑ ◊ ❀❀❀

C. 'Ascotiensis'
Habit Vigorous, very floriferous.
Flowers Single, 9–12cm (3½–5in) across, with pointed petals. Bright violet-blue with brownish-green anthers.
• HEIGHT 3–4m (10–12ft).
• SPREAD 1m (3ft).

C. 'Ascotiensis'
LATE LARGE-FLOWERING

☀ ◊ ❀❀❀   ♛

C. 'Star of India'
Habit Vigorous, very floriferous.
Flowers Single, 8–10cm (3–4in) across. Deep red-purple, fading to purple-blue. Each broad petal has a central, deep carmine stripe, with light brown anthers.
• HEIGHT 3m (10ft).
• SPREAD 1m (3ft).

C. 'Star of India'
LATE LARGE-FLOWERING

☀ ◊ ❀❀❀   ♛

C. 'The President'
Habit Vigorous, floriferous.
Flowers Single, slightly cupped, to 18cm (7in) across, from early summer to early autumn. Rich purple, silvery beneath, with red anthers.
• HEIGHT 2–3m (6–10ft).
• SPREAD 1m (3ft).

C. 'The President'
EARLY LARGE-FLOWERING

☀ ◊ ❀❀❀   ♛

C. 'Richard Pennell'
Habit Moderately vigorous. *Flowers* Single, 12–15cm (5–6in) across, in late spring to mid-summer. Rich purple-blue, with golden-yellow anthers.
• HEIGHT 2–3m (6–10ft).
• SPREAD 1m (3ft).

C. 'Richard Pennell'
EARLY LARGE-FLOWERING

☀ ◊ ❀❀❀   ♛

C. 'Elsa Spath'
Habit Moderately vigorous. *Flowers* Single, 15–20cm (6–8in) across, with overlapping petals, carried throughout summer. Rich lavender-blue, each with a darker central stripe, and plum-purple stamens.
• HEIGHT 2–3m (6–10ft).
• SPREAD 1m (3ft).

C. 'Elsa Spath'
EARLY LARGE-FLOWERING

☀ ◊ ❀❀❀

C. 'H. F. Young'
Habit Compact.
Flowers Single, 10cm (4in) across, in early summer, and sometimes again in autumn. Blue, violet tinted, with cream anthers.
• CULTIVATION Ideal for containers and courtyard or patio gardens.
• HEIGHT 2.5m (8ft).
• SPREAD 1m (3ft).

C. 'H. F. Young'
EARLY LARGE-FLOWERING

☀ ◊ ✿✿✿ ♀

C. 'Beauty of Worcester'
Habit Less vigorous than others of its group.
Flowers Double, 10cm (4in) across, in early summer, and single flowers in late summer. Rich deep violet-blue, with cream anthers.
• CULTIVATION Single flowers only produced if top growth is killed.
• HEIGHT 2.5–3m (8–10ft).
• SPREAD 1m (3ft).

C. 'Beauty of Worcester'
EARLY LARGE-FLOWERING

☀ ◊ ✿✿✿

C. 'Etoile Violette'
Habit Very vigorous, floriferous.
Flowers Single, flattish, to 4–6cm (1½–2½in) across, from mid- to late summer. Rich, deep violet-purple. *Leaves* Divided, with long, lance-shaped to broadly oval leaflets. Green.
• HEIGHT 3–4m (10–12ft).
• SPREAD 1.5m (5ft).

C. 'Etoile Violette'
LATE SMALL-FLOWERING

☀ ◊ ✿✿✿ ♀

C. 'Jackmanii'
Habit Vigorous, very floriferous.
Flowers Single, 8–10cm (3–4in) or more across, velvety, from mid- to late summer. Rich deep purple, fading to violet, with light brown anthers.
• CULTIVATION Thrives in sun or shade.
• HEIGHT 3–4m (10–12ft).
• SPREAD 1m (3ft).

C. 'Jackmanii'
LATE LARGE-FLOWERING

☀ ◊ ✿✿✿ ♀

C. 'Lasurstern'
Habit Vigorous.
Flowers Single, 15–20cm (6–8in) across, with overlapping, wavy-edged petals. Deep lavender-blue, with cream anthers.
• HEIGHT 2–3m (6–10ft).
• SPREAD 1m (3ft).

C. 'Lasurstern'
EARLY LARGE-FLOWERING

☀ ◊ ✿✿✿ ♀

C. 'William Kennett'
Habit Vigorous, floriferous.
Flowers Single, 10–12cm (4–5in) across or more, in summer. Lavender blue with a central, darker stripe which fades with maturity.
• HEIGHT 2–3m (6–10ft).
• SPREAD 1m (3ft).

C. 'William Kennett'
EARLY LARGE-FLOWERING

☀ ◊ ✿✿✿

C. 'Vyvyan Pennell'
Habit Vigorous.
Flowers Double, to 15cm (6in) or more across, in summer. Deep violet-blue, flushed purple and carmine at the centre; a second flush of single, lavender-blue flowers in autumn.
• CULTIVATION Single flowers only produced if top growth is killed off.
• HEIGHT To 3.5m (11ft).
• SPREAD 1m (3ft).

C. 'Vyvyan Pennell'
EARLY LARGE-FLOWERING

C. ALPINA 'Frances Rivis'
Habit Vigorous.
Flowers Single, lantern-shaped, 7cm (3in) long, with slightly twisted petals. Mid-blue.
Leaves Divided, with 9 oval to lance-shaped, toothed leaflets. Light green.
• OTHER NAMES
C. a. 'Blue Giant'.
• HEIGHT 2–3m (6–10ft).
• SPREAD 1.5m (5ft).

C. alpina 'Frances Rivis'
EARLY-FLOWERING

C. 'Perle d'Azur'
Habit Vigorous, floriferous.
Flowers Single, 10–15cm (4–6in) across, recurved at the tips, in summer. Azure petals, with creamy-green anthers.
• CULTIVATION Thrives in sun or semi-shade.
• HEIGHT 3–4m (10–12ft).
• SPREAD 1m (3ft).

C. 'Perle d'Azur'
LATE LARGE-FLOWERING

C. MACROPETALA
Habit Open, floriferous.
Flowers Semi-double, 5cm (2in) long, in late spring and summer. Mauve-blue, paler towards the centre.
Leaves Divided, with oval to lance-shaped, lobed, serrated leaflets. Fresh green.
• HEIGHT To 3m (10ft).
• SPREAD 1.5m (5ft).

C. macropetala
EARLY-FLOWERING

C. REHDERIANA
Habit Very vigorous.
Flowers Single, fragrant, tubular, 1–2cm (½–¾in) long, in loose, upright clusters in late summer and early autumn. Pale yellow. **Leaves** Divided, with 7–9 coarsely textured, toothed leaflets. Light green.
• HEIGHT 6–7m (20–22ft).
• SPREAD 2–3m (6–10ft).

C. rehderiana
LATE-FLOWERING

C. CIRRHOSA
Habit Vigorous.
Flowers Bell-shaped, 3cm (3¼in) across, in late winter and early spring. Cream, sometimes spotted red inside.
Leaves Evergreen, simple or 3-lobed. Glossy dark green, sometimes flushed purple in winter.
• HEIGHT 3–4m (10–12ft) or more.
• SPREAD 2–3m (6–10ft).

C. cirrhosa
EARLY-FLOWERING

C. TANGUTICA
Habit Vigorous, dense.
Flowers Single, lantern-shaped, to 5cm (2in) long, silky, fleshy petals, in summer and early autumn. Golden-yellow.
Leaves Divided, with oval to lance-shaped, lobed leaflets. Green.
• CULTIVATION Good for walls, trees, and sunny banks.
• HEIGHT 5–6m (15–20ft).
• SPREAD 2–3m (6–10ft).

C. tangutica
LATE-FLOWERING

C. 'Bill Mackenzie'
Habit Very vigorous.
Flowers Single, lantern-shaped, nodding, 7cm (3in) across, with silky, fleshy petals, recurved at the tips, in late summer. Yellow. **Leaves** Divided, smooth leaflets. Green.
• HEIGHT 7m (22ft).
• SPREAD 3–4m (10–12ft).

C. 'Bill Mackenzie'
LATE SMALL-FLOWERING

Plumbaginaceae	CAPE LEADWORT

PLUMBAGO AURICULATA ♀

Habit Vigorous, woody-stemmed, scrambling.
Flowers Small, tubular with spreading lobes, in panicles from summer to early winter. Sky-blue.
Leaves Evergreen, oblong to spatula-shaped. Green.
• NATIVE HABITAT S. Africa.
• CULTIVATION Grow in a conservatory in a highly fertile humus-rich soil or compost. Feed and water freely when in growth but sparingly in winter. Provide protection and support.
• PROPAGATION By semi-ripe cuttings in summer.
• OTHER NAMES *P. capensis.*

☼ ◊

Min. 5–7°C
(41–45°F)

HEIGHT
3–6m
(10–20ft)

Asclepiadaceae	

TWEEDIA CAERULEA ♀

Habit Herbaceous, twining stems. *Flowers* Small, fleshy, in clusters in summer to early autumn. Sky-blue, maturing purple. Stems white-hairy.
Leaves Oblong to heart-shaped. Soft green.
• NATIVE HABITAT S. Brazil and Uruguay.
• CULTIVATION Grow in a conservatory or outdoors as an annual, in any moderately fertile soil. Pinch out shoots when young to promote branching.
• PROPAGATION By seed in spring.
• OTHER NAMES *Oxypetalum caeruleum.*

☼ ◊

Min 5°C
(41°F)

HEIGHT
To 1m (3ft)
or more

Caprifoliaceae	HONEYSUCKLE

LONICERA x AMERICANA ♀

Habit Woody-stemmed, twining-scrambling, free-flowering. *Flowers* Large, very fragrant, trumpet-shaped, in abundant whorls at the ends of shoot tips in summer. Soft flesh pink, flushed red-purple, yellow inside. *Leaves* Deciduous, oval. Rich green.
• NATIVE HABITAT S. and E. Europe.
• CULTIVATION Will tolerate sun, preferably with roots in shade. Grow in any fertile, well-drained soil. Provide support.
• PROPAGATION By semi-ripe cuttings in summer or by hardwood cuttings in late autumn.

☼ ◊
❀ ❀ ❀

HEIGHT
To 7m
(23ft)

Caprifoliaceae	JAPANESE HONEYSUCKLE

LONICERA JAPONICA 'Halliana' ♀

Habit Woody-stemmed, twining stems softly hairy. *Flowers* Delicate, very fragrant, slender-tubular, from summer to autumn. White, ageing to pale yellow. *Leaves* Evergreen or semi-evergreen, oblong-oval, sometimes lobed. Bright green.
• NATIVE HABITAT Garden origin. Species occurs in woodland of China, Japan, and Korea.
• CULTIVATION Prefers roots in shade. Grow in any fertile, well-drained soil. Provide support.
• PROPAGATION By semi-ripe cuttings in summer or by hardwood cuttings in late autumn.

☼ ◊
❀ ❀ ❀

HEIGHT
To 10m
(30ft)

Caprifoliaceae	COMMON HONEY-SUCKLE, WOODBINE

LONICERA PERICLYMENUM
'Graham Thomas'
Habit Woody-stemmed, twining, free-flowering.
Flowers Large, very fragrant, trumpet-shaped, in abundant whorls, in summer. White, ageing to yellow.
Leaves Deciduous, oval to oblong. Rich green.
• NATIVE HABITAT Natural variant of English honeysuckle.
• CULTIVATION Thrives in full sun, but prefers shade at the roots. Grow in fertile, humus-rich soil.
• PROPAGATION By semi-ripe cuttings in summer or by hardwood cuttings in late autumn.

HEIGHT
To 4m
(12ft)

Tropaeolaceae	CANARY CREEPER

TROPAEOLUM PEREGRINUM
Habit Herbaceous, leaf stalk climber.
Flowers Small, 2 upper petals large, fringed, in profusion from summer to first frost. Bright yellow.
Leaves With 5 deeply cut lobes. Pale grey-green.
• NATIVE HABITAT Mountain forests of Peru and Ecuador.
• CULTIVATION Treat as an annual in cool areas. Grow in any not too fertile soil, in a warm, sheltered position. Provide support with pea sticks or canes.
• PROPAGATION By seed in spring.
• OTHER NAMES *T. canariense.*

HEIGHT
To 2m (6ft)

Cucurbitaceae	

THLADIANTHA DUBIA
Habit Fast-growing, tendril climber.
Flowers Conspicuous, bell-shaped, in summer. Bright yellow. *Leaves* Deciduous or evergreen, oval to heart-shaped. Mid-green, hairy beneath.
• NATIVE HABITAT Scrub, thickets, and woods of Korea and N.E. China.
• CULTIVATION Grow in a fertile, well-drained soil in a warm, sunny, sheltered site. Provide support.
• PROPAGATION By seed or division in early spring.

HEIGHT
3m (10ft)

Apocynaceae

ALLAMANDA CATHARTICA 'Hendersonii'

Habit Vigorous, woody-stemmed, scrambling.
Flowers Large, trumpet-shaped, waxy, and thick-textured, from summer to autumn. Rich bright yellow, bronze tinted, with white spots at the throat. **Leaves** Evergreen, lance-shaped, leathery, in whorls. Glossy mid-green.
• NATIVE HABITAT Species occurs in forest in mountain valleys of tropical S. America.
• CULTIVATION Grow in a conservatory in fertile, humus-rich, neutral to acid soil or compost, with additional sharp sand. Ensure partial shade in high summer to avoid foliage scorch. Water freely when in growth, otherwise sparingly. Keep almost dry in winter. Tie in to supports. Cut back the previous season's growth to 1–2 nodes in spring.
• PROPAGATION By softwood cuttings in spring or summer.

Min.
13–15°C
(55–59°F)

HEIGHT
To 5m
(15ft)

Malpighiaceae	GOLDEN VINE

STIGMAPHYLLON CILIATUM

Habit Fast-growing, woody-stemmed, twining.
Flowers Small, clawed, with 5 unequal, ruffled
petals, in clusters in spring to summer. Bright yellow.
Leaves Evergreen, heart-shaped, fringed. Pale green.
• NATIVE HABITAT Belize to Uruguay.
• CULTIVATION Grow in a conservatory in well-
drained, fertile soil or compost. Grow in good light
but ensure shade from hot sun. Water freely when
in growth, less in low temperatures. Shoots may be
thinned in spring. Provide protection.
• PROPAGATION By semi-ripe cuttings in summer.

☀ ◐ ◊

Min.
10–13°C
(50–55°F)

HEIGHT
5m (15ft) or
more

Bignoniaceae	ANIKAB

MACFADYENA UNGUIS-CATI

Habit Fast-growing, woody-stemmed, tendril
climber. **Flowers** Large, to 10cm (4in), tubular, in
late spring or early summer. Yellow, striped orange
at the throat. **Leaves** Evergreen, divided into 2
narrowly oval leaflets, with a claw-like tendril. Green.
• NATIVE HABITAT Mexico to Argentina.
• CULTIVATION Grow in a cool conservatory in
fertile soil or compost. Water freely when in growth.
Provide support.
• PROPAGATION By semi-ripe cuttings in summer.
• OTHER NAMES *Doxantha unguis-cati.*

☀ ◊

Min. 5°C
(41°F)

HEIGHT
8–10m
(25–30ft)

Acanthaceae	BLACK-EYED SUSAN

THUNBERGIA ALATA

Habit Fast-growing, twining perennial.
Flowers Small, short-tubed, with rounded, flattened
lobes, from early summer to early autumn. Creamy
yellow-orange, with very dark brown centres. Colours
vary from light to dark shades. **Leaves** Toothed,
oval-elliptic to heart-shaped. Mid-green.
• NATIVE HABITAT Tropical Africa.
• CULTIVATION Usually grown as an annual but
makes an attractive climber for a cool conservatory.
Grow in any moderately fertile soil. Provide support.
• PROPAGATION By seed in spring.

☀ ◊
❄

HEIGHT
3m (10ft)

Liliaceae	

LITTONIA MODESTA

Habit Tuberous-rooted, perennial, tendril
climber. **Flowers** Bell-shaped, pendent, in
summer. Golden-orange. **Leaves** Deciduous,
linear to oval-lance-shaped. Rich emerald green.
• NATIVE HABITAT S. Africa.
• CULTIVATION Grow in a conservatory in fertile,
humus-rich soil, with additional sharp sand. Feed
fortnightly, and water freely when in growth.
Provide support. Store tubers in dry, frost-free
conditions in winter.
• PROPAGATION By seed or division in spring.

☀ ◊

Min. 8°C
(46°F)

HEIGHT
2.5m (8ft)

Liliaceae	CHINESE-LANTERN LILY, CHRISTMAS BELLS

SANDERSONIA AURANTIACA

Habit Tuberous-rooted, slender-stemmed, perennial, tendril climber. **Flowers** Lantern-shaped, pendent, on long stalks in summer. Soft orange. **Leaves** Deciduous, few, lance-shaped. Bright green.
• NATIVE HABITAT Open, scrubby grasslands of S. Africa.
• CULTIVATION Grow in a conservatory in fertile, humus-rich soil with additional sharp sand. Feed fortnightly. Water freely when in growth.
• PROPAGATION By seed or division in spring.

☼ ◊
Min. 8°C (46°F)

HEIGHT 60cm (24in)

Tropaeolaceae	

TROPAEOLUM TUBEROSUM var. LINEAMACULATUM 'Ken Aslet' ♖

Habit Tuberous, herbaceous climber. **Flowers** Long-stalked, spurred, tubular, from mid-summer to autumn. Yellow, with orange-red sepals. **Leaves** 3–5 lobes, with long stalks. Grey-green.
• NATIVE HABITAT Garden origin.
• CULTIVATION Grow in a warm, sunny, sheltered position, in light, well-drained soil. Provide support. Lift and store tubers over winter.
• PROPAGATION By basal stem cuttings or by separation of tubers in spring.

☼ ◊
❄

HEIGHT To 2.5m (8ft)

Liliaceae	

BOMAREA CALDASII ♖

Habit Herbaceous, tuberous-rooted, twining. **Flowers** Tubular to funnel-shaped, in rounded clusters of 5–40, in summer. Orange-red, spotted crimson within. **Leaves** Oblong to lance-shaped, smooth. Mid-green.
• NATIVE HABITAT Northern S. America.
• CULTIVATION Grow in sandy, fertile soil. Water freely in growth. Cut old flowering stems to ground when leaves turn yellow. Protect from frost.
• PROPAGATION By seed or division in early spring.
• OTHER NAMES B. kalbreyeri of gardens.

☼ ◊
❄

HEIGHT 3–4m (10–12ft)

Bignoniaceae	CROSS VINE, TRUMPET FLOWER

BIGNONIA CAPREOLATA

Habit Vigorous, leaf tendril climber. **Flowers** Funnel-shaped, in clusters in the leaf axils, in summer. Reddish-orange. **Fruits** Pods, in autumn. **Leaves** Evergreen or semi-evergreen, divided into 2 narrowly oblong leaflets. Dark green.
• NATIVE HABITAT S.E. United States.
• CULTIVATION Grow in fertile soil in a warm, sunny, sheltered site. Spring prune if necessary.
• PROPAGATION By stem cuttings in summer or autumn or by layering in winter.
• OTHER NAMES Doxantha capreolata.

☼ ◊
❄ ❄

HEIGHT 10m (30ft) or more

Bignoniaceae	

ECCREMOCARPUS SCABER ♀

Habit Sub-shrubby, tendril climber.
Flowers Tubular, in racemes throughout summer.
Orange-red. **Fruits** Inflated pods to 3.5cm (1½in).
Leaves Divided into toothed, heart-shaped
leaflets. Mid-green.
• NATIVE HABITAT High Andes of Chile.
• CULTIVATION Usually grown as an annual.
Grow in a warm, sunny, sheltered position in fertile,
freely draining soil.
• PROPAGATION By seed in spring.

Compositae	MEXICAN FLAME VINE

PSEUDOGYNOXYS CHENOPODIOIDES

Habit Woody-stemmed, twining. **Flowers** Daisy-
like, in clusters, mainly in summer. Orange-yellow,
ageing to orange-red. **Leaves** Evergreen, narrowly
oval, toothed. Light green.
• NATIVE HABITAT Colombia.
• CULTIVATION Grow in a conservatory in fertile,
freely draining soil or compost. Water moderately
when in growth, otherwise sparingly.
• PROPAGATION By semi-ripe cuttings in summer.
• OTHER NAMES *Senecio confusus*.

☼ ◊

Min.
7–10°C
(45–50°F)

HEIGHT
To 3m
(10ft)

☼ ◊
❄

HEIGHT
2–3m
(6–10ft)

Caprifoliaceae	

LONICERA × *TELLMANNIANA* ♀

Habit Woody-stemmed, twining. **Flowers** Large,
slender-tubular, rich coppery-orange, flushed red in
bud, in abundant clusters in late spring and
summer. **Leaves** Deciduous, oval to oblong, deep
green above, white beneath.
• NATIVE HABITAT Garden origin.
• CULTIVATION Tolerates sun, but blooms well in
shade or semi-shade. Grow in any fertile, well-
drained soil. Provide a sheltered position.
• PROPAGATION By semi-ripe cuttings in summer
or by hardwood cuttings in late autumn.

☼ ◊
❄ ❄

HEIGHT
To 5m
(15ft)

Acanthaceae	

THUNBERGIA GREGORII

Habit Woody-stemmed, twining.
Flowers Tubular, with spreading lobes, in summer. Rich glowing orange. *Leaves* Triangular to oval, toothed, with winged stalks. Bright green.
• NATIVE HABITAT Tropical Africa.
• CULTIVATION Usually grown as an annual. Grow in any moderately fertile soil, in a warm, sunny, sheltered position. Provide support. If grown under glass, water freely when in growth and keep almost dry in winter.
• PROPAGATION By seed in spring.

Min. 10°C
(50°F)
HEIGHT
To 3m
(10ft)

Compositae	

MUTISIA DECURRENS

Habit Shrubby, tendril climber. *Flowers* Large, daisy-like, in summer. Rich orange-red.
Leaves Evergreen, narrowly oblong. Grey-green.
• NATIVE HABITAT Forests in the foothills of the Andes of Chile and Argentina.
• CULTIVATION Grow in any fertile, well-drained soil in a warm, sunny, sheltered site, with roots in shade. Thin crowded growth in spring. May prove difficult to establish.
• PROPAGATION By seed in spring, by stem cuttings in summer, or by layering in autumn.

HEIGHT
To 3m
(10ft)

Polygonaceae	MILE-A-MINUTE PLANT, RUSSIAN VINE

FALLOPIA BALDSCHUANICA

Habit Vigorous, woody-stemmed, twining, extremely rampant. *Flowers* Tiny, in drooping clusters in summer and autumn. White, tinted pink.
Leaves Deciduous, oval. Mid-green.
• NATIVE HABITAT Iran and Uzbekistan.
• CULTIVATION Tolerates dry soils and semi-shade, although blooms best in sun. Grow in any soil that is not too rich in nitrogen as this will promote leafy growth at the expense of flowering.
• PROPAGATION Semi-ripe cuttings in summer.
• OTHER NAMES *Polygonum baldschuanicum.*

HEIGHT
12m (40ft)

Bignoniaceae	

CAMPSIS × *TAGLIABUANA* 'Madame Galen' ♈

Habit Woody-stemmed, aerial root climber.
Flowers Trumpet-shaped, in pendent clusters from late summer to autumn. Dark apricot-pink.
Leaves Deciduous, divided into 7 or more narrowly oval, toothed leaflets. Dark green.
• NATIVE HABITAT Garden origin.
• CULTIVATION Grow in a warm, sunny, sheltered site, in fertile soil. Thin in late winter to early spring.
• PROPAGATION By semi-ripe cuttings in summer or by layering in winter.

☼ ◊
❄❄
HEIGHT
To 10m
(30ft)

Passifloraceae	RED PASSION FLOWER

PASSIFLORA MANICATA

Habit Vigorous, woody-stemmed, tendril climber.
Flowers Large, with narrow petals, in summer to autumn. Rich scarlet, with white filaments banded purple. **Leaves** Evergreen, 3-lobed. Bright green.
• NATIVE HABITAT S. America.
• CULTIVATION Grow in a conservatory in a sandy, humus-rich soil or compost. Water freely in growth, then moderately. Provide support with wires or trellis. Thin out congested growth in spring.
• PROPAGATION By seed in spring or by semi-ripe cuttings in summer.

☼ ◊
Min.7°C
(45°F)

HEIGHT
3–5m
(10–15ft)

Vitaceae	MINIATURE JAPANESE IVY

PARTHENOCISSUS TRICUSPIDATA 'Lowii'

Habit Vigorous, woody-stemmed, tendril climber with adhesive pads at tendril tips. **Flowers** Tiny, inconspicuous. Yellow-green. **Leaves** Deciduous, deeply cut, with 3–7 crinkled lobes. Dark green, turning crimson in autumn.
• NATIVE HABITAT Garden origin.
• CULTIVATION Grow in any fertile, humus-rich soil in sun or semi-shade.
• PROPAGATION By softwood or greenwood cuttings in summer, or by hardwood cuttings in early spring.

☼ ◊
❄❄❄
HEIGHT
To 20m
(70ft)

Vitaceae	VIRGINIA CREEPER

PARTHENOCISSUS QUINQUEFOLIA ♈

Habit Vigorous, woody-stemmed, tendril climber with adhesive pads. **Flowers** Tiny. Yellow-green. **Leaves** Deciduous, with 5 oval, toothed leaflets. Dark green, turning brilliant crimson in autumn.
• NATIVE HABITAT E. United States.
• CULTIVATION Grow in any fertile soil. Excellent for north- or east-facing walls.
• PROPAGATION By softwood or greenwood cuttings in summer or by hardwood cuttings in early spring.
• OTHER NAMES *Vitis quinquefolia*.

☼ ◊
❄❄❄
HEIGHT
To 15m
(50ft) or
more

Vitaceae	BOSTON IVY, JAPANESE IVY

PARTHENOCISSUS TRICUSPIDATA

Habit Vigorous, woody-stemmed, tendril climber with adhesive pads at tendril tips. *Flowers* Tiny, inconspicuous. Yellow-green. *Fruits* Small, berry-like. Dull deep blue, bloomed.
Leaves Deciduous, variable, sometimes broadly oval or divided into 3 rounded-triangular, pointed lobes. Green, turning brilliant crimson and scarlet in autumn.
• NATIVE HABITAT Damp forests of China and Japan.
• CULTIVATION Grow in any fertile, humus-rich soil, in shade or semi-shade. Excellent for covering large areas of a north- or east-facing wall, and for disguising unsightly buildings. Prune annually in autumn to confine shoots to allotted space and to direct away from eaves and gutters. May need initial support until adhesive pads develop.
• PROPAGATION By softwood or greenwood cuttings in summer or by hardwood cuttings in early spring.
• OTHER NAMES *Ampelopsis tricuspidata.*

HEIGHT
To 20m
(70ft)

| Vitaceae | CRIMSON GLORY VINE |

VITIS COIGNETIAE

Habit Vigorous, woody-stemmed, tendril climber.
Flowers Tiny, insignificant. Pale green.
Fruits Tiny grapes. Black. *Leaves* Deciduous,
with 3–5 rounded, toothed lobes. Dark green,
brown-hairy beneath. Rich crimson in autumn.
• NATIVE HABITAT Japan, Korea, and Sakhalin.
• CULTIVATION Grow in well-drained, neutral to
alkaline soil. Autumn colour is best on soils that are
not too fertile.
• PROPAGATION By hardwood cuttings in late
autumn.

HEIGHT
25m (80ft)
or more

| Vitaceae | TEINTURIER GRAPE |

VITIS VINIFERA 'Purpurea'

Habit Woody-stemmed, tendril climber.
Flowers Tiny, in summer. Pale green.
Fruits Small grapes. Green or black.
Leaves Deciduous, 3–5 lobes, white-downy,
turning claret red, then deep purple with age.
• NATIVE HABITAT Garden origin.
• CULTIVATION Grow in well-drained, neutral to
alkaline soil. Autumn colour is best on soils that are
not too fertile.
• PROPAGATION By hardwood cuttings in late
autumn.

HEIGHT
To 7m
(22ft)

| Vitaceae | |

CAYRATIA THOMSONII

Habit Slender, woody-stemmed, tendril climber.
Flowers Tiny, inconspicuous. *Fruits* Small,
globose, berry-like, in autumn. Black.
Leaves Deciduous, divided into 5 oval leaflets.
Glossy dark green, then maroon-purple in autumn.
• NATIVE HABITAT Forests in W. and C. China.
• CULTIVATION Grow in any fertile, humus-rich
soil. Excellent for north-facing walls.
• PROPAGATION By softwood or greenwood
cuttings in summer.
• OTHER NAMES *Parthenocissus thomsonii.*

HEIGHT
To 10m
(30ft)

| Vitaceae | JAPANESE IVY |

PARTHENOCISSUS TRICUSPIDATA 'Veitchii'

Habit Vigorous, woody-stemmed, tendril climber
with adhesive pads. *Flowers* Tiny. Yellow-green.
Fruits Small, berry-like. Dull deep blue, bloomed.
Leaves Deciduous, oval, or with 3 lobes. Purple
when young, turning rich red-purple in autumn.
• NATIVE HABITAT Garden origin.
• CULTIVATION Grow in any fertile, humus-rich
soil in sun or semi-shade.
• PROPAGATION By softwood cuttings in summer
or by hardwood cuttings in early spring.

HEIGHT
To 20m
(70ft)

Vitaceae	

AMPELOPSIS GLANDULOSA var. *BREVIPEDUNCULATA*

Habit Vigorous, woody-stemmed, twining, tendril climber. *Flowers* Inconspicuous; late summer. *Fruits* Small berries. Bright blue. *Leaves* Deciduous, heart-shaped or 3–5 lobes, smooth. Dark green.
• NATIVE HABITAT China, Japan, and Korea.
• CULTIVATION Tolerates partial shade but needs full sun to fruit well. Grow in any fertile soil.
• PROPAGATION By greenwood or semi-ripe cuttings in mid-summer.

HEIGHT
5m (15ft) or
more

Tropaeoleaceae	

TROPAEOLUM TUBEROSUM

Habit Tuberous, herbaceous climber.
Flowers Long-stalked, spurred, tubular, in late autumn. Rich yellow, with orange-red sepals.
Leaves 3–5 lobes, long-stalked. Grey-green.
• NATIVE HABITAT Peru, Bolivia, and Ecuador.
• CULTIVATION Grow in a warm, sunny, sheltered position in light, well-drained soil. Provide support. In cool areas lift and store tubers over winter.
• PROPAGATION By basal stem cuttings or by separation of small tubers in spring.

HEIGHT
To 2.5m
(8ft)

Pittosporaceae	

BILLARDIERA LONGIFLORA

Habit Woody-stemmed, twining. *Flowers* Small, bell-shaped, in summer. Greenish-yellow, sometimes tinged purple. *Fruits* Rounded oblong, fleshy berries. Blue-purple. *Leaves* Evergreen, narrowly elliptic to lance-shaped. Mid-green.
• NATIVE HABITAT Tasmania.
• CULTIVATION Grow in any well-drained soil and shelter from cold winds. In cool areas grow in a conservatory. Provide support.
• PROPAGATION By seed in spring or by stem cuttings in summer or autumn.

HEIGHT
To 2m (6ft)

Bignoniaceae	FLAME FLOWER

PYROSTEGIA VENUSTA

Habit Fast-growing, woody-stemmed, tendril climber. *Flowers* Tubular, in dense clusters from autumn to spring. Glowing golden-orange.
Leaves Evergreen, large, oval to oblong-lance-shaped, leathery. Dark green.
• NATIVE HABITAT Forests of S. America.
• CULTIVATION Grow in a conservatory in fertile, humus-rich soil or compost with added sharp sand. Water moderately in full growth; sparingly in winter.
• PROPAGATION By semi-ripe cuttings in summer.
• OTHER NAMES *Pyrostegia ignea*.

Min.
13–15°C
(55–59°F)

HEIGHT
10m (30ft)
or more

Oleaceae	

JASMINUM POLYANTHUM

Habit Vigorous, woody-stemmed, twining.
Flowers Small, very fragrant, tubular with 5
spreading lobes, in clusters from spring to autumn,
depending on temperature. White, flushed pink
outside. *Leaves* Evergreen, or semi-evergreen,
divided into 5–7 elliptic leaflets. Dark green.
• NATIVE HABITAT Yunnan, China.
• CULTIVATION Tolerates semi-shade but flowers
best in sun. Grow in a warm, sheltered site, in any
moderately fertile soil. Needs protection in cool areas.
• PROPAGATION By semi-ripe cuttings in summer.

☼ ◌
❋

HEIGHT
3m (10ft) or
more

Ericaceae	

AGAPETES MACRANTHA

Habit Loose, arching, scandent. *Flowers* Small,
goblet-shaped, pendent, in clusters in winter.
White or pinkish-white, patterned with dark red.
Leaves Evergreen, lance-shaped to elliptic. Dark
green.
• NATIVE HABITAT N.E. India.
• CULTIVATION Grow in a conservatory in coarse,
open, humus-rich, acid soil or compost. Water freely
when in growth, otherwise moderately.
• PROPAGATION By seed in spring or by semi-ripe
cuttings in summer.

☼ ◌ pH

Min. 10°C
(50°F)

HEIGHT
1–2m
(3–6ft)

Campanulaceae	CANARY ISLAND BELLFLOWER

CANARINA CANARIENSIS

Habit Herbaceous, tuberous, scrambling.
Flowers Bell-shaped, pendent, waxy, from late
autumn to spring. Golden-orange, with maroon
veins. *Leaves* Triangular, serrated. Mid-green.
• NATIVE HABITAT The Canary Islands.
• CULTIVATION Grow in a conservatory in fertile
soil or compost. Water moderately from early
autumn to spring. Keep dry and remove dead stems
when dormant.
• PROPAGATION By seed in autumn or spring or
by basal cuttings in spring.

☼ ◌

Min. 7°C
(45°F)

HEIGHT
2–3m
(6–10ft)

Liliaceae	

ASPARAGUS SCANDENS

Habit Scrambling, with lax stems. *Flowers* Tiny, nodding, in clusters of 2–3 in summer. White.
Fruits Small, globose berries. Red.
Leaves Evergreen, short, curved, flattened, leaf-like stems, in whorls of 2–3. Light green.
• NATIVE HABITAT S. Africa.
• CULTIVATION Grow in the home or conservatory in any fertile soil, in bright light or semi-shade but not in direct sun. Water freely when in growth, otherwise moderately.
• PROPAGATION By seed or division in spring.

☀ ◊

Min. 10°C
(50°F)

HEIGHT
1m (3ft) or
more

Araceae	

EPIPREMNUM AUREUM 'Marble Queen'

Habit Fast-growing, woody-stemmed, aerial root climber. *Leaves* Evergreen, oval. Rich green, streaked and marbled white, with white leaf stalks.
• NATIVE HABITAT Garden origin.
• CULTIVATION Grow in the home or conservatory in a humus-rich, moisture-retentive soil or compost. Water regularly when in growth, less in cold weather. Provide support.
• PROPAGATION By leaf-bud or stem cuttings in late spring or by layering in summer.
• OTHER NAMES *Scindapsus aureus* 'Marble Queen'.

☀ ◊

Min.
15–18°C
(59–64°F)

HEIGHT
3–10m
(10–30ft)

Compositae	VARIEGATED NATAL IVY, VARIEGATED WAX VINE

SENECIO MACROGLOSSUS 'Variegatus' ♀

Habit Woody-stemmed, twining.
Flowers Conspicuous, daisy-like, on long stems, mainly in winter. Pale creamy-yellow.
Leaves Evergreen, triangular, fleshy. Dark green, broadly margined with white and cream.
• NATIVE HABITAT S.E. Africa, Zimbabwe, and Mozambique.
• CULTIVATION Grow in a conservatory in fertile, freely draining soil or compost. Feed regularly and water moderately when in growth.
• PROPAGATION By semi-ripe cuttings in summer.

☀ ◊

Min.
7–10°C
(45–50°F)

HEIGHT
3m (10ft)

Araceae	

SCINDAPSUS PICTUS 'Argyraeus'

Habit Slow-growing, woody-stemmed, aerial root climber. *Leaves* Evergreen, heart-shaped,. Rich silvery-green, marked with silver-white spots.
• NATIVE HABITAT Garden origin.
• CULTIVATION Grow in the home or conservatory in semi-shade or in bright light out of direct sun, in a humus-rich, moisture-retentive soil or compost. Water regularly in growth, less in cold weather.
• PROPAGATION By leaf-bud or stem cuttings in late spring or by layering in summer.
• OTHER NAMES *Epipremnum pictum* 'Argyraeus'.

☀ ◊

Min.
15–18°C
(59–64°F)

HEIGHT
2–3m
(6–10ft) or
more

Araceae	

SYNGONIUM PODOPHYLLUM
'Trileaf Wonder'

Habit Woody-stemmed, aerial root climber.
Flowers Insignificant. **Leaves** Evergreen. Young
leaves arrowhead-shaped; mature leaves divided
into 3 leaflets. Grey-green with silvery-white veins.
• NATIVE HABITAT Garden origin.
• CULTIVATION Grow in the home or conservatory
in a humus-rich, freely draining soil or compost.
Water moderately in growth, less in cold weather.
• PROPAGATION By leaf-bud or stem-tip cuttings
in summer.

☀ ◊

Min. 18°C
(64°F)

HEIGHT
2m (6ft) or
more

Vitaceae	IVY OF URUGUAY, MINIATURE GRAPE IVY

CISSUS STRIATA

Habit Fast-growing, woody-stemmed, tendril
climber. **Leaves** Evergreen, divided into 3–5 oval,
serrated leaflets. Lustrous rich green.
• NATIVE HABITAT Chile and S. Brazil.
• CULTIVATION Grow in the home or conservatory,
or outdoors in warm areas, in fertile soil or compost
with added organic matter and sharp sand. Water
regularly when in growth, less in low temperatures.
• PROPAGATION By semi-ripe cuttings in summer.
• OTHER NAMES *Ampelopsis sempervirens, Vitis
striata*.

☀ ◊
❄

HEIGHT
10m (30ft)
or more

Dioscoreaceae	

DIOSCOREA DISCOLOR

Habit Woody-stemmed, twining, with tuberous
roots. **Leaves** Evergreen, 12–15cm (5–6in) long,
heart-shaped. Deep olive green, marbled with
silver, pale green and brown; red beneath.
• NATIVE HABITAT Tropical S. America.
• CULTIVATION Grow in a conservatory in semi-
shade or sun, in a humus-rich, freely draining soil or
compost. Water moderately when in growth, less in
cold weather. Provide support.
• PROPAGATION By division or by sections of
tuber in spring or autumn.

☀ ◊

Min. 5°C
(41°F)

HEIGHT
2–3m
(6–10ft)

Araceae	

SYNGONIUM PODOPHYLLUM   ♈

Habit Woody-stemmed, aerial root climber.
Leaves Evergreen, juvenile leaves arrowhead-
shaped; mature leaves to 30cm (12in) long, divided
into 7–9 glossy, rich green leaflets, with paler veins.
• NATIVE HABITAT Mexico to Brazil and Bolivia.
• CULTIVATION Grow in the home or conservatory.
Water moderately when in growth, less in cold
weather. Provide support.
• PROPAGATION By leaf-bud or stem-tip cuttings
in summer.
• OTHER NAMES *Nephthytis triphylla* of gardens.

☀ ◊

Min.
16–18°C
(61–64°F)

HEIGHT
2m (6ft) or
more

Araceae	BLACK-GOLD PHILODENDRON

PHILODENDRON MELANOCHRYSUM

Habit Robust, slow-growing, woody-based, aerial root climber. **Leaves** Evergreen, to 75cm (30in) long, heart-shaped. Lustrous deep olive green with a coppery sheen, and pale veins.
• NATIVE HABITAT Colombia.
• CULTIVATION Grow in the home or conservatory in semi-shade in humus-rich, freely draining soil or compost. Water moderately in growth, sparingly in cold weather.
• PROPAGATION By leaf-bud or stem-tip cuttings in summer.

☼ ◊

Min.
15–18°C
(59–64°F)

HEIGHT
3m (10ft) or
more

Compositae	VELVET PLANT

GYNURA AURANTIACA

Habit Woody-based, soft-stemmed, semi-scrambling, or shrubby. **Flowers** Daisy-like, in clusters in winter. Orange-yellow.
Leaves Evergreen, oval to elliptic. Dark green with fine, velvety, purple-violet hairs.
• NATIVE HABITAT Java.
• CULTIVATION Grow in a conservatory in any fertile, well-drained soil or compost. Water moderately, and sparingly in cool conditions.
• PROPAGATION By softwood or semi-ripe cuttings in spring or summer.

☼ ◊

Min. 16°C
(61°F)

HEIGHT
2–3m
(6–10ft)
often less

Vitaceae	CHESTNUT VINE, LIZARD PLANT

TETRASTIGMA VOINIERIANUM ♥

Habit Vigorous, woody-stemmed, tendril climber. **Leaves** Evergreen, with 3–5 oval to diamond-shaped leaflets. Lustrous dark green, rust-coloured and hairy when young.
• NATIVE HABITAT Tropical forests of S.E. Asia.
• CULTIVATION Grow in the home or conservatory in fertile, humus-rich soil or compost. Grow in shade. Water freely when in growth, less in low temperatures.
• PROPAGATION By layering in spring or by semi-ripe cuttings in summer.
• OTHER NAMES *Cissus voinieriana.*

☼ ◊

Min.
15–18°C
(59–64°F)

HEIGHT
10m (30ft)
or more

Vitaceae	KANGAROO VINE

CISSUS ANTARCTICA ♥

Habit Fairly vigorous, woody-stemmed, tendril climber. **Leaves** Evergreen, oval, pointed, coarsely serrated. Lustrous rich green.
• NATIVE HABITAT Rainforests of Australasia.
• CULTIVATION Grow in a cool conservatory in fertile soil or compost with added organic matter and sharp sand. Feed and water regularly when in growth, less in low temperatures. Provide good ventilation. Tie in to support. Thin out crowded growth in spring. Direct sun will scorch the foliage.
• PROPAGATION By semi-ripe cuttings in summer.

☼ ◊

Min. 5°C
(44°F)

HEIGHT
To 5m
(15ft)

Araceae	SWISS-CHEESE PLANT

MONSTERA DELICIOSA 🏆

Habit Robust, woody-stemmed, root climber.
Flowers Large spathes on mature plants. Creamy.
Fruits Tight clusters of aromatic, edible berries.
White. *Leaves* Evergreen, large-lobed, with
oblong holes when mature, leathery. Rich green.
• NATIVE HABITAT Tropical forests of S. America.
• CULTIVATION Grow in in a humus-rich, freely
draining soil or compost. Water moderately in growth,
sparingly in cold weather. Protect from draughts.
• PROPAGATION By leaf-bud or stem-tip cuttings
in spring.

☼ ◊

Min.
15–18°C
(59–64°F)

HEIGHT
To 6m
(20ft)

Araceae	HEART LEAF PHILODENDRON

PHILODENDRON SCANDENS 🏆

Habit Fairly fast-growing, woody-based, root
climber. *Leaves* Evergreen, heart-shaped,
10–15cm (4–6in) long when young, to 30cm (12in)
long on mature plants. Glossy rich green.
• NATIVE HABITAT Moist, tropical forests of
Mexico, West Indies, and S.E. Brazil.
• CULTIVATION Use a coarse, open, humus-rich
soil or compost. Water moderately in growth,
sparingly in cold weather. Provide shade in summer.
• PROPAGATION By leaf-bud or stem-tip cuttings
in summer.

☼ ◊

Min.
15–18°C
(59–64°F)

HEIGHT
4m (12ft)

Vitaceae	VENEZUELA TREEBINE

CISSUS RHOMBIFOLIA 🏆

Habit Fairly vigorous, woody-stemmed, tendril
climber. *Leaves* Evergreen, divided into 3
diamond-shaped to oval, sharply toothed leaflets.
Lustrous rich green.
• NATIVE HABITAT Tropical forests of S. America.
• CULTIVATION Grow in a fertile soil or compost
with added organic matter and sharp sand. Feed
and water regularly when in growth; water less in
low temperatures. Provide good ventilation. Tie in
to support. Thin out crowded growth in spring.
• PROPAGATION By semi-ripe cuttings in summer.

☼ ◊

Min. 7°C
(45°F)

HEIGHT
3m (10ft) or
more

Solanaceae	ORANGE BROWALLIA, MARMALADE BUSH

STREPTOSOLEN JAMESONII 🏆

Habit Slender, loosely scrambling.
Flowers Trumpet-shaped, in clusters in spring to
summer. Tube: yellow; lobes: deep orange.
Leaves Evergreen or semi-evergreen, oval,
corrugated. Dark green.
• NATIVE HABITAT Colombia and Peru.
• CULTIVATION Grow in a fertile, humus-rich soil
or compost. Water freely when in growth, less at
other times. Feed when in growth.
• PROPAGATION By softwood or semi-ripe
cuttings in summer.

☼ ◊

Min. 7°C
(45°F)

HEIGHT
2–3m
(6–10ft)

IVIES

Ivies (*Hedera*) are evergreen, woody-stemmed, trailing perennials and self-clinging climbers. Most occur in woodland and hedgerow, often in densely shaded conditions, in Europe, Asia, and N. Africa.

Ivies are ideal for covering walls and fences, especially the golden or creamy variegated forms, as these need more light, or those which assume bronze or purple tints in winter. Non-variegated types make ideal ground cover plants for shaded sites. Ivies take about a year to establish, and are not all fully hardy; those with variegated leaves may sustain frost and wind damage in severe winters. Less hardy varieties may be grown in a conservatory. Ivies prefer alkaline soil. Propagate by softwood cuttings or rooted layers in summer.

H. HELIX 'Erecta'
Habit Slow-growing, non-climbing, stiffly upright. *Leaves* 3-lobed, arrow-shaped. Dark green, with paler veins.
• CULTIVATION Suitable for the rock garden.
• HEIGHT 1m (3ft).
• SPREAD 1.2m (4ft).

H. helix 'Erecta'

☀ ◊ ❄❄❄   ♔

H. COLCHICA 'Dentata'
Habit Very vigorous, self-clinging or trailing. *Leaves* Large, irregularly oval, unlobed, drooping. Glossy light green.
• CULTIVATION Excellent for north-facing walls. Tolerates acid soils.
• HEIGHT 10m (30ft).
• SPREAD 5m (15ft).

H. colchica 'Dentata'

☀ ◊ ❄❄❄   ♔

H. HELIX 'Pedata'
Habit Moderately vigorous.
Leaves 5 very slender lobes, resembling a bird's foot. Metallic grey-green, veins grey-white.
• CULTIVATION Not suitable for ground cover.
• OTHER NAMES
H. helix 'Caenwoodiana'.
• HEIGHT 4m (12ft).
• SPREAD 3m (10ft).

H. helix 'Pedata'

☀ ◊ ❄❄❄   ♔

H. HELIX 'Green Ripple'
Habit Bushy, weakly climbing. *Leaves* Small, with 5 deeply cut, and slightly jagged lobes. Mid-green, with prominent light green veins.
• CULTIVATION Good for ground cover or for growing against a low wall.
• HEIGHT 1.2m (4ft).
• SPREAD 1.2m (4ft).

H. helix 'Green Ripple'

☀ ◊ ❄❄

H. HELIX 'Telecurl'
Habit Slender, open. *Leaves* 5 neat and distinct lobes, elegantly twisted. Glossy light green.
• HEIGHT 1m (3ft).
• SPREAD 1m (3ft).

H. helix 'Telecurl'

☀ ◊ ❄❄❄

H. HIBERNICA 'Deltoidea'
Habit Vigorous. *Leaves* Heart-shaped. Shiny dark green, tinted purple-bronze in autumn.
• CULTIVATION Very useful for north walls, but not suitable for ground cover.
• OTHER NAMES
H. helix 'Deltoidea'.
• HEIGHT 5m (15ft).
• SPREAD 3m (10ft).

H. hibernica 'Deltoidea'

☀ ◊ ❄❄❄

H. HIBERNICA
Habit Very vigorous.
Leaves With 3–5 triangular lobes, middle lobe much larger, heart-shaped at the base. Glossy mid-green with paler grey-green veins.
• OTHER NAMES
H. helix subsp. *hibernica*, *H. helix* 'Hibernica'.
• HEIGHT 6m (20ft).
• SPREAD 6m (20ft).

H. hibernica

☀ ◊ ❋❋❋   ♈

H. HELIX 'Ivalace'
Habit Bushy, moderately vigorous.
Leaves Shallowly 5-lobed, curled, and crimped. Glossy dark green.
• CULTIVATION Good for ground cover and for growing up low walls.
• OTHER NAMES
H. helix 'Mini Green'.
• HEIGHT 1m (3ft).
• SPREAD 1.2m (4ft).

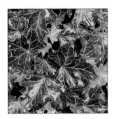

H. helix 'Ivalace'

☀ ◊ ❋❋❋   ♈

H. HELIX 'Pittsburgh'
Habit Bushy, weakly climbing. **Leaves** Neatly 5-lobed, middle lobe long and pointed. Glossy mid-green.
• CULTIVATION Suitable for low walls and for ground cover.
• OTHER NAMES
H. helix 'Hahn's Self-branching'.
• HEIGHT 1m (3ft).
• SPREAD 1.2m (4ft).

H. helix 'Pittsburgh'

☀ ◊ ❋❋❋

H. HIBERNICA 'Lobata Major'
Habit Vigorous.
Leaves Large, 3-lobed. Glossy dark green.
• OTHER NAMES
H. helix 'Lobata Major'.
• HEIGHT 5m (15ft).
• SPREAD 5m (15ft).

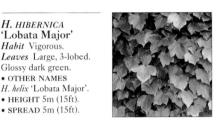

H. hibernica 'Lobata Major'

☀ ◊ ❋❋❋

H. HELIX 'Gracilis'
Habit Slender, open.
Leaves Sharply lobed. Dark green, tinted purple in winter.
• CULTIVATION Not suitable for ground cover.
• HEIGHT 5m (15ft).
• SPREAD 5m (15ft).

H. helix 'Gracilis'

☀ ◊ ❋❋❋

H. HELIX 'Sulphurea'
Habit Moderately vigorous.
Leaves Medium-sized, irregularly 3-5 lobed. Greyish-green, splashed and margined with pale sulphur yellow.
• CULTIVATION Good for walls and ground cover.
• OTHER NAMES
H. hibernica 'Sulphurea'.
• HEIGHT 3m (10ft).
• SPREAD 3m (10ft).

H. helix 'Sulphurea'

☀ ◊ ❋❋❋

H. HELIX 'Merion Beauty'
Habit Bushy, weakly climbing.
Leaves 5 neat, sharp lobes. Glossy mid-green.
• CULTIVATION Not suitable for ground cover.
• HEIGHT 1.2m (4ft).
• SPREAD 1m (3ft).

H. helix 'Merion Beauty'

☀ ◊ ❋❋

H. ALGERIENSIS 'Ravensholst'
Habit Vigorous, self-clinging.
Leaves Large, oval to triangular, unlobed. Glossy mid-green.
• CULTIVATION May be killed or damaged in hard winters.
• OTHER NAMES
H. canariensis 'Ravensholst'.
• HEIGHT To 6m (20ft).
• SPREAD 5m (15ft).

H. algeriensis 'Ravensholst'

☀ ◊ ❋   ♈

H. HELIX 'Parsley Crested'

Habit Branched, and trailing.
Leaves Undulate, with prominent veins, and crested margins. Bright green.
• CULTIVATION Unsuitable for ground cover.
• OTHER NAMES *H. helix* 'Cristata'.
• HEIGHT 2m (6ft).
• SPREAD 1.2m (4ft).

H. helix 'Parsley Crested'

☼ ◊ ❋❋

H. HIBERNICA 'Digitata'

Habit Vigorous.
Leaves Broad, divided into 5 finger-like lobes. Glossy dark green.
• CULTIVATION Very useful for north walls. Unsuitable for ground cover.
• HEIGHT 6m (20ft).
• SPREAD 6m (20ft).

H. hibernica 'Digitata'

☼ ◊ ❋❋❋

H. HELIX 'Nigra'

Habit Dense.
Leaves Small. Very dark green, turning purple-black in winter.
• CULTIVATION Good for low, north-facing walls.
• HEIGHT 1.2m (4ft).
• SPREAD 1.2m (4ft).

H. helix 'Nigra'

☼ ◊ ❋❋❋

H. HELIX 'Woerner'

Habit Vigorous.
Leaves Bluntly lobed. Grey-green, with paler veins, turning purple in winter.
• CULTIVATION Very useful for north- and east-facing walls.
• HEIGHT 4m (12ft).
• SPREAD 3m (10ft).

H. helix 'Woerner'

☼ ◊ ❋❋❋

H. HELIX 'Glymii'

Habit Slender, rather open.
Leaves Oval, pointed, sometimes curled or twisted in winter. Glossy dark green, turning purple in winter.
• CULTIVATION Not suitable for ground cover.
• OTHER NAMES *H. helix* 'Tortuosa'.
• HEIGHT 2.5m (8ft).
• SPREAD 2m (6ft).

H. helix 'Glymii'

☼ ◊ ❋❋❋

H. HELIX 'Atropurpurea'

Habit Vigorous.
Leaves 5-lobed. Dull deep green, turning purple in winter, when veins usually remain green; stem and leaf stalks purple.
• CULTIVATION Excellent for shady walls.
• OTHER NAMES *H. helix* 'Purpurea'.
• HEIGHT 4m (12ft).
• SPREAD 2.5m (8ft).

H. helix 'Atropurpurea'

☼ ◊ ❋❋❋ 🏆

H. HELIX 'Manda's Crested'

Habit Dense.
Leaves 5-lobes, pointed, wavy-edged. Mid-green, becoming copper-tinted in winter.
• CULTIVATION Good for ground cover.
• OTHER NAMES *H. helix* 'Curly Locks'.
• HEIGHT 2m (6ft).
• SPREAD 2m (6ft).

H. helix 'Manda's Crested'

☼ ◊ ❋❋ 🏆

H. HELIX 'Adam'

Habit Dense.
Leaves Small, shallowly 3-lobed. Light green, variegated pale creamy-yellow.
• CULTIVATION Frequently grown as a houseplant. If grown outdoors it may be damaged in winter, but it will usually recover.
• HEIGHT 1.2m (4ft).
• SPREAD 1m (3ft).

H. helix 'Adam'

☼ ◊ ❋

H. HELIX 'Heise'
Habit Dense.
Leaves Small. Grey-green with cream variegation.
• CULTIVATION Suitable for ground cover in sheltered and confined spaces.
• OTHER NAMES *H. helix* 'Mini Green'.
• HEIGHT 30cm (12in).
• SPREAD 60cm (24in).

H. helix 'Heise'

☼ ◊ ❀❀

H. HELIX 'Angularis Aurea'
Habit Moderately vigorous, open, irregular.
Leaves 3-lobed. Glossy light green, with bright yellow variegation.
• CULTIVATION Not suitable for ground cover.
• HEIGHT 4m (12ft).
• SPREAD 2.5m (8ft).

H. helix 'Angularis Aurea'

☼ ◊ ❀❀❀   ♈

H. HELIX 'Glacier'
Habit Slender-stemmed, but dense.
Leaves Silvery grey-green, with a narrow white margin.
• CULTIVATION Thrives in dappled shade. Suitable for ground cover.
• HEIGHT 3m (10ft).
• SPREAD 2m (6ft).

H. helix 'Glacier'

☼ ◊ ❀❀❀   ♈

H. HELIX 'Goldheart'
Habit Moderately vigorous. **Leaves** 5-lobed, with a long, pointed central lobe. Dark green, with yellow centre variegation.
• CULTIVATION May be slow to establish, but then grows rapidly. Not suitable for ground cover, but excellent for an east- or west-facing wall.
• HEIGHT 6m (20ft).
• SPREAD 6m (20ft).

H. helix 'Goldheart'

☼ ◊ ❀❀❀

H. HELIX 'Eva'
Habit Slender-stemmed, but dense.
Leaves Small. Grey-green with creamy variegations.
• CULTIVATION Frequently grown as a houseplant. If grown outdoors, may be damaged in winter, but will usually recover. Suitable for a warm wall.
• HEIGHT 1.2m (4ft).
• SPREAD 1m (3ft).

H. helix 'Eva'

☼ ◊ ❀❀   ♈

H. HELIX 'Buttercup'
Habit Moderately vigorous. **Leaves** Light green in shade, becoming yellow-green or bright yellow-green in sun.
• CULTIVATION Good for sunny walls.
• HEIGHT 2m (6ft).
• SPREAD 2.5m (8ft).

H. helix 'Buttercup'

☼ ◊ ❀❀   ♈

H. HIBERNICA 'Anne Marie'
Habit Dense.
Leaves Usually 6-lobed. Light greyish-green with creamy variegation, mostly at the margins.
• CULTIVATION Often grown as a houseplant. If grown outdoors, may be damaged in winter, but will usually recover. Suitable for a warm wall.
• HEIGHT 1.2m (4ft).
• SPREAD 1m (3ft).

H. hibernica 'Anne Marie'

☼ ◊ ❀❀

H. COLCHICA 'Sulphur Heart'
Habit Very vigorous, self-clinging or trailing.
Leaves Large, broadly, and irregularly oval. Dark green with a central yellow splash, becoming pale green and deep green at the margins.
• OTHER NAMES *H. colchica* 'Paddy's Pride'.
• HEIGHT 5m (15ft).
• SPREAD 3m (10ft).

H. colchica 'Sulphur Heart'

☼ ◊ ❀❀❀   ♈

ADDITIONAL SPECIES AND CULTIVARS

Numerous variants of plants exist that differ slightly from the normal form of species. Some of these variants exist in the wild and are termed subspecies (subsp.), varieties (var.), or forms (forma or f.). Others are known as cultivars – a contraction of *culti*vated *var*ieties – and they exist only in cultivation. The cultivar name is enclosed in inverted commas and follows the botanical name, for example *Ceanothus* 'Cascade'. Below are listed some additional shrubs and climbers to those described in the book. A cross-reference is given to the page number of the species or a close relative.

SHRUBS

❧ *Abutilon* x *suntense* 'Jermyns'. Similar to *A.* x *suntense* 'Violetta' (p.120), but with clear, deep mauve flowers.

❧ *Acer palmatum* 'Garnet'. A strongly growing cultivar with finely cut, deep garnet red leaves, similar to *A. palmatum* Dissectum Atropurpureum Group (p.196).

❧ *Berberis* x *frikartii* 'Amstelveen'. Small, dense, evergreen shrub, to 1m (3ft) tall, with arching branches, glossy, spiny, dark green leaves, and pale yellow flowers in spring, similar to ❧ *B. verruculosa* (p.77).

❧ *Berberis* x *frikartii* 'Telstar'. Similar to 'Amstelveen' (above), but larger, to 1.2m (4ft) tall, and more spreading in habit.

❧ *Berberis* x *media* 'Parkjuweel'. Low, dense, prickly shrub, to 1m (3ft) tall, with glossy, semi-evergreen, bright green leaves that colour brilliantly in autumn. Similar to *B. gagnepainii* (p.76).

❧ *Berberis thunbergii* 'Bagatelle'. A very compact, deciduous, dwarf shrub, to 30cm (1ft), similar to *B. thunbergii* f. *atropurpurea* (p.75), but much smaller, with dark purple leaves.

❧ *Buddleja davidii* 'Black Knight'. A fine cultivar with long trusses of fragrant, very dark violet flowers, similar to ❧ *B. davidii* 'Royal Red' (p.38).

❧ *Buddleja davidii* 'Dartmoor'. As above, but notable for the unusually compact, broad panicles of magenta flowers.

❧ *Buddleja davidii* 'Empire Blue'. As above, but with rich violet-blue flowers, each with an orange eye.

❧ *Caryopteris* x *clandonensis* 'Heavenly Blue'. Similar to *C.* x *clandonensis* 'Arthur Simmonds' (p.201), but more compact, and with flowers of a slightly darker shade of blue.

❧ *Ceanothus* 'Burkwoodii'. Dense, spreading, evergreen shrub, to 1.5m (5ft) tall, with glossy green leaves and rich deep blue flowers throughout summer and autumn. Similar to, but smaller than ❧ *C.* 'Autumnal Blue' (p. 136).

❧ *Ceanothus* 'Cascade'. Vigorous, evergreen shrub, to 4m (12ft), bearing long clusters of powder-blue flowers in late spring and early summer, similar to ❧ *C. thyrsiflorus* var. *repens* (p.200) but with an open, arching habit.

❧ *Ceanothus* x *delileanus* 'Topaz'. Deciduous shrub to 3m (10ft), with pale indigo-blue flowers produced throughout summer. Similar to *C.* 'Gloire de Versailles' (p.201).

❧ *Ceanothus* 'Puget Blue'. Dense, free-flowering, evergreen shrub, with deep blue flowers from spring to early summer, similar to *C. impressus* (p.122), but with longer, narrower leaves.

❧ *Chaenomeles* x *superba* 'Crimson and Gold'. Dense, thorny, deciduous shrub, to 1m (3ft) tall, similar to ❧ *C.* x *superba* 'Rowallane' (p.163), but with masses of dark red flowers with conspicuous golden anthers, followed by spherical yellow fruits.

❧ *Chaenomeles* x *superba* 'Knap Hill Scarlet'. As above, but with a profusion of large, brilliant orange-scarlet flowers, over long periods in spring and early summer.

❧ *Choisya* 'Aztec Pearl'. Small, aromatic, evergreen shrub with glossy, bright green leaves, similar to ❧ *C. ternata* (p.68), but with larger, pink-flushed flowers, in spring, and again in late summer.

❦ *Choisya ternata* 'Sundance'. As for the species ❦ *C. ternata* (p.68), but with bright yellow young leaves fading to lime green.

❦ *Cotinus coggygria* 'Royal Purple'. Similar to *C. coggygria* 'Notcutt's Variety' (p.40), but has dark red-purple leaves and plumes of deep pink flowers.

❦ *Cytisus* 'Burkwoodii'. Vigorous, arching, deciduous shrub, similar to ❦ *C. scoparius* f. *andreanus* (p.209), but bearing cerise flowers with crimson, yellow-margined wings.

❦ *Cytisus* 'Lena'. A compact, vigorous, free-flowering shrub, as above, but having dark red flowers with yellow-margined wings and a pale yellow keel.

❦ *Daphne bholua* 'Gurkha'. A very hardy, deciduous variant of the species (p.141), with very fragrant, purplish-pink and white flowers.

❦ *Daphne bholua* 'Jacqueline Postill'. As above but a very hardy, evergreen or semi-evergreen form, with much larger and more showy blooms.

❦ *Forsythia* × *intermedia* 'Lynwood'. Vigorous, free-flowering cultivar, similar to *F.* × *intermedia* 'Beatrix Farrand' (p.90), with a profusion of large, broad-petalled, rich yellow flowers.

❦ *Genista tinctoria* 'Flore Pleno'. A dwarf, semi-prostrate form, similar to the species (p.168), but more floriferous, and with double yellow flowers.

❦ *Hamamelis* × *intermedia* 'Jelena'. Similar to ❦ *H.* × *intermedia* 'Diane' (p.51), but with dense clusters of large, yellow flowers flushed with rich coppery-red tones.

❦ *Hebe* 'Red Edge'. Dwarf shrub, similar to ❦ *H. albicans* (p.180), with crowded, blue-grey leaves, margined red, and bearing pale lilac flowers in summer.

Hydrangea macrophylla 'Mariesii'. A 'lace-cap' cultivar which produces flat heads of rose-pink flowers. If grown on acid soils flower colour is a rich blue. Similar to *H. macrophylla* 'Lilacina' (p.132).

❦ *Hypericum* 'Rowallane'. Graceful, semi-evergreen shrub, to 2m (6ft), with bowl-shaped, rich golden

flowers, to 7cm (3in) across, from summer to autumn. Similar in effect to, but slightly more tender than ❦ *H.* 'Hidcote' (p.207).

❦ *Kalmia latifolia* 'Ostbo Red'. As for the species (p.110) but with large, showy clusters of deep pink flowers, opening in early summer from crimped, red buds.

❦ *Lavandula angustifolia* 'Twickel Purple'. Similar to ❦ *L. angustifolia* 'Hidcote' (p.199), but more compact, to 60cm (24in), and with broader leaves and lavender-blue flowers.

❦ *Lavandula* × *intermedia* Dutch Group. As above, but more robust. Grows to 1.2m (4ft), with broad leaves and long slender spikes of lavender-blue flowers.

❦ *Lavandula stoechas* subsp. *pedunculata*. As for the species (p.199), but with shorter spikes of dark purple flowers with red-tinted bracts, borne on longer stems.

❦ *Lavatera* 'Barnsley'. As for ❦ *L.* 'Rosea' (p.111), but flowers open white to palest pink, and have a marked red eye.

❦ *Ligustrum ovalifolium* 'Aureum'. Similar to the species (p.55). A vigorous evergreen or semi-evergreen shrub with mid-green leaves broadly margined with yellow.

❦ *Mahonia* × *media* 'Lionel Fortescue'. A free-flowering cultivar, similar to ❦ *M.* × *media* 'Buckland' (p.51), but with long, upright racemes of bright yellow flowers.

❦ *Mahonia* × *wagneri* 'Undulata'. Similar to *M. aquifolium* (p.166), but to 2m (6ft), and with lustrous leaves with wavy margins. Bears clusters of deep yellow flowers in spring.

❦ *Philadelphus* 'Sybille'. Arching, deciduous shrub, to 1.2m (4ft) tall, similar to ❦ *P.* 'Beauclerk' (p.91), bearing single white flowers with a purple-stained base, and intensely heady fragrance.

❦ *Photinia* × *fraseri* 'Red Robin'. Similar to *P.* × *fraseri* 'Birmingham' (p.24), a dense, upright evergreen shrub with glossy, sharply toothed leaves that are brilliant red on emergence.

♀ *Pieris* 'Flaming Silver'. Compact shrub, similar to, but smaller than the species *P. japonica* (p.19), with leaves that are bright red on emergence, later developing a pink margin that matures to striking silvery-white.

♀ *Pieris japonica* 'Debutante'. A dwarf form of *P. japonica* (p.19); very compact, forming a low mound of evergreen leaves with dense, upright panicles of white flowers.

♀ *Pieris japonica* 'Mountain Fire'. As for *P. japonica* (p.19), but the brilliant red young leaves turn a glossy chestnut brown.

♀ *Pieris japonica* 'Valley Valentine'. As for *P. japonica* (p.19), but with large, pendent clusters of crimson buds which open to produce dark, dusky, purple-red flowers.

♀ *Prunus tenella* 'Fire Hill'. Similar to the species (p.160). It grows to 2m (6ft) and has upright stems clothed in a profusion of small, single, almond-like deep rose-pink flowers, which appear from mid to late spring. Flowers are followed by small, almond-like fruits.

♀ *Ribes sanguineum* 'Tydeman's White'. Similar to ♀ *R. sanguineum* 'Pulborough Scarlet' (p.73), but with pure white flowers. This is the best white-flowered form.

♀ *Rosmarinus officinalis* 'Severn Sea'. Similar to the species, but with arching branches bearing bright blue flowers.

♀ *Salvia officinalis* Purpurascens Group. A bushy, evergreen or semi-evergreen shrub, with oblong grey-green leaves, tinted more or less purple. It can be used as a culinary herb. See also ♀ *S. officinalis* 'Icterina' (p.224).

♀ *Weigela* 'Mont Blanc'. A vigorous, deciduous shrub with large, fragrant, funnel-shaped, pure white flowers, pink-tinted with age, in late spring and early summer. See also ♀ *W. florida* 'Foliis Purpureis' (p.183).

♀ *Yucca flaccida* 'Golden Sword'. Similar to ♀ *Y. flaccida* 'Ivory' (p.178), but its leaves have a broad, creamy-yellow central band.

CLIMBERS

♀ *Cissus rhombifolia* 'Ellen Danica'. A vigorous, bushy cultivar, similar to the species (p.282), with large, glossy green, deeply cut and lobed leaves.

♀ *Jasminum officinale* 'Argenteovariegatum'. As for the species (p.246), but with grey-green leaves margined with silvery-white.

♀ *Jasminum* x *stephanense*. Hardy, vigorous climber to 7m (22ft) or more, similar to ♀ *J. officinale* (p.246), but with fragrant, pale pink flowers in mid-summer.

Lapageria rosea var. *albiflora*. As for ♀ *L. rosea* (p.250), but the large, fleshy, bell-shaped flowers are white.

♀ *Lapageria rosea* 'Nash Court'. Similar to ♀ *L. rosea* (p.250), but bears soft pink flowers marbled with darker pink.

♀ *Lonicera periclymenum* 'Belgica'. Similar to ♀ *L. periclymenum* 'Graham Thomas' (p.268), but the "Early Dutch honeysuckle" produces red-purple flowers, yellowish with age, in early summer, and again in late summer.

♀ *Lonicera periclymenum* 'Serotina'. As above; the "Late Dutch honeysuckle" bears rich red-purple flowers from mid- to late summer.

♀ *Passiflora caerulea* 'Constance Elliott'. Similar in size, habit and foliage to the species (p.258), but with exceptionally beautiful, creamy white flowers.

♀ *Vitis* 'Brant'. A vigorous, fully hardy vine to 9m (28ft), with bright green leaves, turning dark red and purple with yellow-green venation in autumn. Bears cylindrical bunches of sweet, edible, black grapes in autumn. See also *V. vinifera* 'Purpurea' (p.276).

Vitis vinifera 'Incana'. Similar to ♀ *V. vinifera* 'Purpurea' (p.276), but the leaves are grey-green with white veins and a cobweb-like covering of downy hair.

♀ *Wisteria floribunda* 'Rosea'. Similar to ♀ *W. floribunda* 'Alba' (p.244), but with long racemes of pale, rose-pink flowers, each tipped with purple.

GUIDE TO SHRUB AND CLIMBER CARE

IF SHRUBS AND CLIMBERS are to give of their ornamental best, it is essential to provide the best possible growing conditions to suit their needs. Yet few gardens are blessed with the ideal fertile, moisture-retentive, and well-drained loam. However, the drainage, aeration, and moisture-holding properties of most soil types can be improved by the addition of well-rotted organic matter. Very wet soils can be improved by the installation of drainage systems, and soil acidity or alkalinity can be modified to some degree by either liming acid soils or by adding well-rotted organic matter to alkaline soils. Such modifications are best regarded as short term, since the nature of the soil depends largely on the nature of the parent rock. Garden soils, however, will naturally tend to be moist or dry, heavy or light, acid or alkaline. Fortunately, a wide range of shrubs and climbers can be grown in most gardens, even where soils fall short of the ideal. Most shrubs tolerate a wide range of pH and soil types, although climbers, which are usually more vigorous and therefore more demanding of nutrients, will benefit from the addition of a balanced general purpose fertilizer.

When choosing shrubs and climbers, consider the rainfall, temperature, and humidity levels that prevail on the site. Check local factors, such as frost pockets and wind shelter, especially in coastal gardens where salt spray may cause problems, and ensure that light levels are appropriate. When planting climbers it is important to use supports that will accommodate the plant's eventual size, vigour, and climbing method.

SELECTING SHRUBS

CONTAINER-GROWN SHRUB
GOOD EXAMPLE

Vigorous, well-balanced top growth

ROOT-BALLED SHRUB
GOOD EXAMPLE

POOR EXAMPLE

Twiggy, sparse stems and little new growth

Pot-bound roots

RENOVATING POOR EXAMPLE

Tease out roots and cut back damaged or very long roots

Root ball should be firm

Root ball should be firm

Wrapping should be intact

Well-established fibrous root system

Selecting Climbers

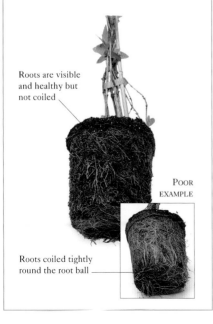

GOOD EXAMPLE

Vigorous,
healthy stems

Label

Healthy
buds

POOR
EXAMPLE

Spindly, weak
growth with
damaged buds

GOOD EXAMPLE

Roots are visible
and healthy but
not coiled

POOR
EXAMPLE

Roots coiled tightly
round the root ball

Soil Preparation and Planting

Shrubs and climbers offered for sale should be accurately labelled, healthy, undamaged, and free from pests and diseases. When buying, inspect the plants thoroughly and make sure that the shrubs have evenly distributed branches close to ground level. Standards should branch from a clear stem of the required height. Climbers should have a well-balanced framework of strong shoots with healthy, living buds. Reject any with signs of pests or disease or weak shoots.

Selecting plants
Shrubs and climbers are usually sold as container-grown plants. However, shrubs may have been field-grown and potted up in the season before sale. If possible, check that the root system is well-established, with healthy, white root tips. Do not buy pot-bound plants, which have roots coiled tightly around the pot or protruding from the bottom.

Deciduous plants are sometimes sold with bare roots in the dormant period. Check that these have an evenly developed, fibrous root system, with no signs of drying out. Evergreen shrubs and conifers are also offered as root-balled specimens, with the root system and its surrounding soil wrapped in netting or hessian. Check that the root ball is firm, and the wrapping intact.

When to plant
The dormant period is the time to plant bare-root and root-balled shrubs. During the late autumn to early winter the soil is still warm enough to allow good root establishment to enable the shrub to begin vigorous growth in spring.

Plant only in mild spells during winter; roots will not grow well in very cold soils, and may freeze or succumb more readily to soil-borne diseases. In theory, shrubs in containers can be planted at any time of year, but autumn

PLANTING A CONTAINER-GROWN SHRUB

1 *Water the potted shrub well. Dig a hole roughly twice the width of the shrub's root ball. Support the shrub and root ball and ease it gently out of the pot. Place into prepared planting hole.*

2 *Lay a cane across the top of the hole, to check that the soil level matches the shrub's existing soil level. Adjust the planting depth as necessary, by adding or removing topsoil beneath the root ball.*

3 *Backfill around the shrub in stages, firming gently as you proceed. Shake the plant carefully to avoid air pockets, and to ensure good contact between soil and roots. Water and mulch.*

4 *Prune out any diseased, damaged, inward-growing and crossing wood. Cut out very long, weak, or straggly stems, and any that mar the overall balance of the shrub's framework.*

is best only if plants are fully hardy. Spring-planted shrubs need more aftercare, especially with watering, as they may die or their growth badly checked if they are allowed to dry out. Container-grown climbers may be planted at any time of year, provided that the soil is not frozen, dry, or waterlogged. Evergreen and herbaceous climbers establish best if planted in spring when the soil warms up, but may also be autumn-planted in mild and protected situations. Shrubs and climbers that are not fully hardy should be planted in spring so that they are established before their first winter.

Soil preparation

The best seasons for soil preparation are late summer and autumn, and as large an area as is practicable should be cultivated. To do this, remove all weeds, especially perennial ones, and double dig the planting area, adding well-rotted organic matter in the lower trench. Alternatively, work large quantities of it into the top 30–45cm (12–18in) of soil. For climbers, also fork in a balanced slow-release granular fertilizer at 50–85g per sq m (2–3oz per sq yd).

How to plant

When planting container-grown or root-balled shrubs, dig a hole twice the width of the root mass, or up to three times the width on clay soils. Bare-rooted shrubs need a hole of sufficient size to spread their roots out fully. The depth must be sufficient to allow the final soil level to be the same as it was in the pot or nursery, as indicated by the soil mark on the stem. Plant wall shrubs about 22cm (9in) from the wall, so that the roots are not in its rain shadow, and lean the plant in towards the wall.

For climbers, the planting hole should be twice the diameter of the pot, but where this is impossible, for example, when planting beneath a host plant, make the hole large enough to accommodate the root ball comfortably. In most cases, the top of the root ball

should be level with the surrounding soil. Plant clematis so that the final soil level is about 5–6cm (2–2½in) deeper than it was in the pot (to supply new growth in case of clematis wilt). Grafted climbers should also be at this depth to cover the point of graft, so that the graft itself can root. Backfill with soil, and firm in gently. Insert canes at the base of the plant, taking care not to damage the roots, and secure them to the support. Fan out the main shoots and attach them firmly, but not too tightly, to the canes and to the support if they will reach it. Remove any dead, damaged or badly placed shoots. Twining or tendril climbers attach readily to their supports, but may need some initial guidance.

Water all newly planted shrubs and climbers thoroughly, and apply a 5–7cm (2–3in) layer of mulch to a radius of about 60cm (2ft) to aid moisture retention and suppress weeds.

PLANTING AGAINST A WALL

Dig a hole approximately 22cm (9in) from the wall base, leaning the plant towards the wall. Place plant in hole and fill in, firming back the soil. Tie the plant to the cane support. Attach the cane to the wire framework on the wall so that the sideshoots can be supported and tied in. Plants that have a twining growth habit may also need initial support.

ROUTINE CARE

Young shrubs and climbers need regular routine care to enable them to establish well in their first growing season. As well as tending to their feeding and watering needs, you should check plants regularly for signs of pests and diseases, and treat them as necessary. This initial care will pay good dividends in later seasons as the plants will produce healthy growth and flower abundantly.

Watering and Mulching
Particular attention should be paid to watering plants until they become well established. Apply water copiously to the base of the plant to ensure that the soil is well soaked. Do not water lightly and often, as this encourages roots to come to the surface, where they are more vulnerable to temperature fluctuations and drying out. Established shrubs and climbers need watering only in periods of prolonged drought. There may, however, be restrictions on irrigation at such times, so maintain a mulch over the root area to aid conservation of soil water during dry periods. Mulching with bulky well-rotted organic material is ideal as it also improves the soil. Mulching not only retains soil moisture but also moderates extremes of temperatures around the roots and helps suppress weeds. Bark or wood chips are useful mulches and are an attractive ground cover material.

Weeding
Weeds compete with shrubs and climbers for valuable soil nutrients, so the area around all newly planted shrubs an climbers should be kept weed-free until they are well established and have produced growth dense enough to suppress the weeds themselves. Apply about 5–10cm (2–4in) of mulch, avoiding the area immediately around the stem. For newly planted specimens, cover an area about 45cm (18in) wider in diameter than the root system. For established plants the mulch should extend to 15–30cm (6–12in) beyond the area of top growth. Do not apply mulch to dry soils or in cold weather.

CUTTING OUT DEAD WOOD

Dead wood is a potential food source for plant diseases, so remove as soon as possible. Cut out at the base or cut back to a healthy, well-placed bud. Cutting out dead wood enhances the shape of the plant and provides space for new growth.

DEADHEADING A RHODODENDRON

Remove flowerheads as soon as they fade, before new buds develop fully. Grip the end of the flowerhead firmly, twist and then snap off cleanly at the base of the stem (see inset), taking care not to damage young growth near the stem.

REMOVING SUCKERS

Rub out suckers between finger and thumb as soon as they are noticed. If they are too large to treat this way, cut or pull off suckers at their point of origin. If pulled off, pare over the wound with a sharp knife to ensure a clean cut.

CUTTING BACK CLIMBERS

*Using sharp secateurs, cut back climbers that have outgrown their allotted space or which are blocking gutters. Trim the stems irregularly to produce a natural effect. (*Hedera colchica *'Sulphur Heart' shown here)*

Feeding

Most shrubs benefit from the application of fertilizers, especially if they are pruned regularly. Slow-release fertilizers are best applied in early spring, following the manufacturer's recommended rate of application. The rapid boost to growth provided by quick-release fertilizers will be most effective if they are applied as growth begins in late spring. Liquid fertilizers act even more rapidly, and are best used when shrubs are in strong growth. Climbers need annual feeding to maintain vigorous, healthy growth so apply a dressing of balanced fertilizer in spring during the plant's first two seasons, and then use a slow-release fertilizer at the manufacturer's recommended rate.

Deadheading

Some shrubs and climbers benefit from deadheading so that energy is diverted into new growth rather than to the production of seed. When flowers fade, pinch them off with finger and thumb, taking care not to damage any new growth buds. Some climbers, including many clematis, produce ornamental fruits or seed heads, so only about one-quarter to one-third of the dead flowers should be removed. This is sufficient to induce a second flowering without compromising later displays of fruits or seed heads.

Removing suckers

Some grafted shrubs produce suckers from below the graft union on stems or roots, which, if allowed to develop, will spoil or compete with the top growth. Rub out the buds before the shoots emerge. If the shoots have grown, cut them off as close as possible to their point of origin (*see illustration above*).

Removing reverted shoots

Many variegated plants are propagated from mutations, or sports, of green-leaved forms, and they will occasionally revert to the green-leaved parent type. Reverted shoots are nearly always more vigorous and, if left, will outgrow their variegated counterparts. To control them, cut back any reverted shoots to a main stem as soon as they appear.

PRUNING AND TRAINING

Some shrubs, particularly evergreens of compact habit, need little pruning other than the routine removal of dead, crossing, damaged, or diseased wood. Many others, however, do require pruning, or a combination of pruning and training, for them to realize their full ornamental potential.

Pruning

The aims of pruning are to create a well-balanced branch framework, encourage new, healthy growth, and to maintain the quality of flowers, fruits, foliage, or stems. All shrubs and climbers should have any dead, diseased, or damaged wood pruned out regularly. Pruning may also be used to renovate old or overgrown specimens.

Pruning normally stimulates growth: the terminal bud of a stem contains chemicals which inhibit the growth of lower buds so its removal usually results in the more vigorous development of lower shoots. Hard pruning promotes more vigorous growth than light pruning,

FORMATIVE PRUNING

To establish a healthy, strong framework for a climbing plant begin pruning and training after planting in late winter or early spring. The plant shown here is Jasminum nudiflorum.

Remove any crossing or rubbing shoots with sharp secateurs. Make the cut just above a healthy bud.

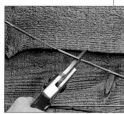

To encourage new, strong growth to form, cut back the sideshoots to a suitably placed bud.

Cut out any congested growth from the centre of the plant which may compete with new growth.

Tie in all the sideshoots securely to the support using soft twine.

so bear this in mind when pruning or correcting unbalanced growth. Prune weak growth hard to encourage the plant to produce vigorous growth, and only lightly prune plants which are already producing strong growth.

With climbers, pruning and training is usually necessary to create a strong framework of sturdy stems and to guide growth to cover the support. Thereafter, regular pruning aims to promote the production of flowering or fruiting wood, and to control growth so that it does not swamp less vigorous plants, or damage roofs, gutters, or masonry.

Sometimes, however, a plant that has been carefully pruned still does not flourish. In such cases a judgement needs to be made about whether to continue nurturing and encouraging the plant, or to replace it.

Where to cut
As with any other mechanical damage, pruning wounds form a potential entry point for disease. In order to reduce this risk it is vital to make neat cuts with clean, sharp tools.

Cut stems which have a whorled arrangement of buds (3 or more buds arising from different points around the stem) or an alternate arrangement of

buds just above a bud pointing in the desired direction of growth. Make an angled cut just above a healthy bud, slanting away from the bud, so that it finishes slightly above the bud's base. If the cut is too close, the bud may be damaged or killed; if too far away, the stem itself may die back.

Plants with buds in opposite pairs should be cut straight across the shoot, just above a pair of healthy buds (*see illustration below*).

Training climbers
During the first growing season after planting, train climbers to grow in the desired direction by tying in the strongest shoots to the support, aiming to produce a balanced framework of main stems to cover the support evenly. As growth proceeds, progressively guide soft twining stems and tendrils into the support while they are still flexible.

In late winter or early spring following initial planting, when danger of severe frost has passed, cut back each sideshoot to an appropriately placed bud near to the main stems, and tie in the pruned shoots. The following year, again cut back each stem to a bud that faces in the desired direction of growth. Tie in the new growth to extend the framework.

Opposite shoots
Prune stems with opposite shoots just above a strong pair of buds or shoots, making a clean straight cut.

Alternate shoots
Prune stems that have alternate shoots by making a clean, angled cut just above the shoot.

How to cut
Make an angled cut so that its lowest point is opposite the bud base, and the top just clears the bud.

Cut back any other shoots that do not form part of the branch framework to within two buds of the main stem.

Pruning established climbers

Some climbers flower on shoots produced in the current year or occasionally on shoots produced late in the growing season of the previous year. These are usually pruned in late winter or early spring, before the new buds begin to develop, and will flower later in the same season on new shoots. Other climbers flower on the previous season's ripened wood or on even older shoots. These are pruned immediately after flowering, to allow new shoots time to ripen before the winter. These are the shoots that will bear the following season's flowers. Some early flowering climbers will produce a second crop of flowers later in the season if pruned

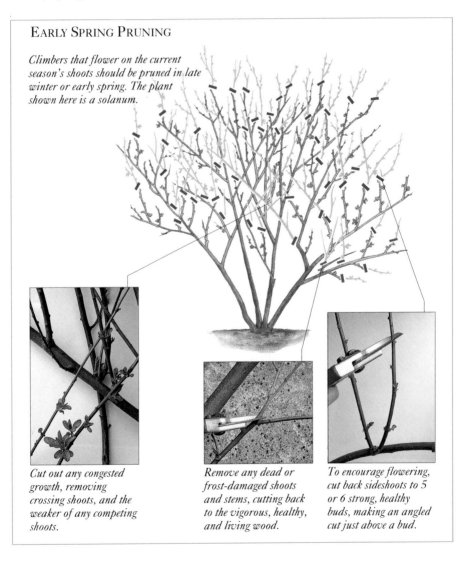

EARLY SPRING PRUNING

Climbers that flower on the current season's shoots should be pruned in late winter or early spring. The plant shown here is a solanum.

Cut out any congested growth, removing crossing shoots, and the weaker of any competing shoots.

Remove any dead or frost-damaged shoots and stems, cutting back to the vigorous, healthy, and living wood.

To encourage flowering, cut back sideshoots to 5 or 6 strong, healthy buds, making an angled cut just above a bud.

early enough. Distinguishing between first and second year wood is normally straightforward: first year wood is still pliable and usually green; second year wood is usually grey or brown. When pruning climbers, always remove all dead or damaged wood and any congested growth. Cut back stems that have outgrown their allotted space, both to maintain the shape of the climber and to control excessive growth.

Prune evergreen climbers in early spring, after the danger of severe frost has passed and as plants resume new growth. However, evergreen climbers that are grown for their flowers as well as foliage will produce flowers on the previous season's wood, so delay pruning these until after flowering. In both cases, remove any dead or damaged wood and trim stray shoots to keep the plant within bounds. Climbers that have

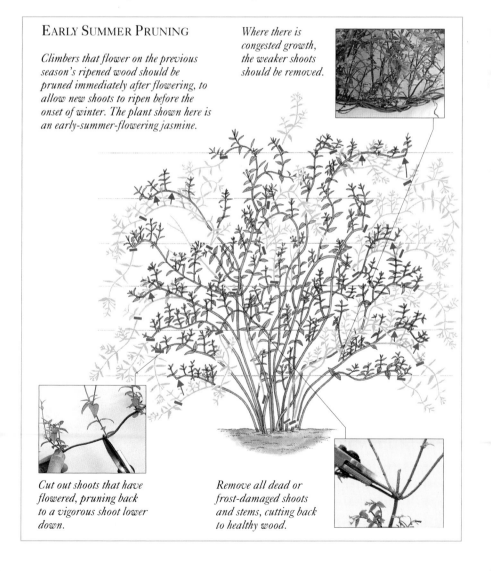

EARLY SUMMER PRUNING

Climbers that flower on the previous season's ripened wood should be pruned immediately after flowering, to allow new shoots to ripen before the onset of winter. The plant shown here is an early-summer-flowering jasmine.

Where there is congested growth, the weaker shoots should be removed.

Cut out shoots that have flowered, pruning back to a vigorous shoot lower down.

Remove all dead or frost-damaged shoots and stems, cutting back to healthy wood.

been pruned during the previous growing season may be pruned again when fully dormant in mid-winter to improve and tidy up their appearance. This is particularly important for deciduous species, whose framework is more clearly visible when leafless in winter. Do not remove ripened wood, which will bear the following season's flowers. Pruning should not be carried out in frosty weather.

Overgrown or neglected climbers may be pruned hard back to their main framework to rejuvenate them and they may then be retrained. One or two seasons' flowers may be lost after drastic pruning, but strong new growth is usually assured if the plants are fed, watered thoroughly, and mulched.

Climbers that attach themselves by aerial roots need very little training once established. All other climbers need

EARLY WINTER PRUNING

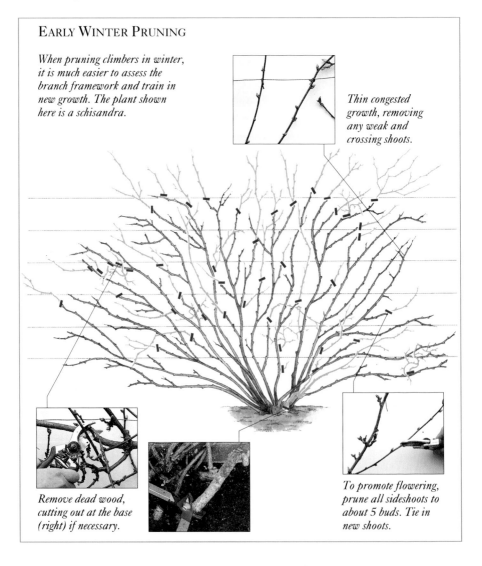

When pruning climbers in winter, it is much easier to assess the branch framework and train in new growth. The plant shown here is a schisandra.

Thin congested growth, removing any weak and crossing shoots.

Remove dead wood, cutting out at the base (right) if necessary.

To promote flowering, prune all sideshoots to about 5 buds. Tie in new shoots.

their new shoots trained in annually in order to maintain the desired shape. During the growing season each year, select the strongest stems and tie them in to extend or maintain the main framework. Tie in securely to the support at regular intervals. Check all ties periodically to ensure that they are not constricting the stems as they thicken with age, and loosen or re-tie, as and when necessary.

Pruning shrubs

Evergreen shrubs usually need little formative pruning but sometimes need shaping to ensure balanced growth. This is best done in mid-spring, after planting. Formative pruning of deciduous shrubs is carried out in the dormant season, between mid-autumn and mid-spring, at or after planting. The amount of pruning necessary depends on the type of shrub and the quality of the plant purchased.

PRUNING EVERGREEN SHRUBS

After flowering, prune evergreen shrubs by removing dead and damaged wood and cutting back flowered stems. Also cut back any that spoil the shrub's outline. The plant shown here is Prunus lusitanica.

Cut back flowered stems to a main stem. Remove any congested and crossing stems.

Cut back any badly placed stems to healthy, well-placed, outward-growing shoots.

Cut back any dead or damaged wood to healthy growth or, if necessary, to the base.

The aim of pruning is to create a shrub with a balanced framework of well-spaced branches. After planting, remove completely any dead, damaged, and weak stems. Cut back crossing and congested stems to an outward-facing bud, or cut out at the base to produce an open-centred framework.

If a particularly vigorous shoot distorts the balance, cut it back lightly. If, when purchased, the shrub does not have a strong branch framework, cut it back hard to promote vigorous growth. Exceptions to this procedure include very slow-growing shrubs, such as the Japanese maples (*Acer palmatum*), which need minimal pruning. The pruning of acers is best done in summer, as they will bleed sap if pruned in spring. Sometimes, well-formed shrubs make too much top growth in relation to their root system. To create a more stable

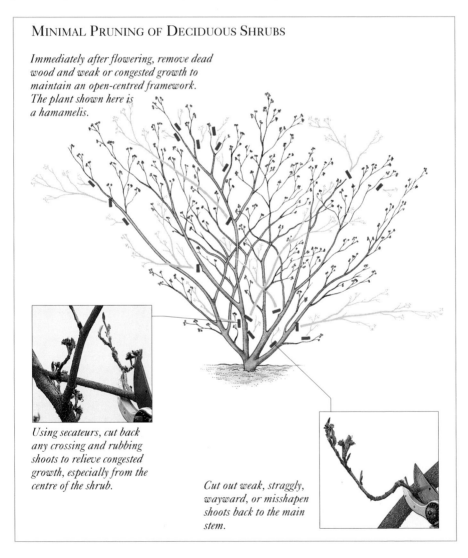

MINIMAL PRUNING OF DECIDUOUS SHRUBS

Immediately after flowering, remove dead wood and weak or congested growth to maintain an open-centred framework. The plant shown here is a hamamelis.

Using secateurs, cut back any crossing and rubbing shoots to relieve congested growth, especially from the centre of the shrub.

Cut out weak, straggly, wayward, or misshapen shoots back to the main stem.

plant, thin out about one-third of the stems and reduce the remainder by one-third of their length.

Maintenance pruning

For maintenance pruning, deciduous shrubs can be divided into four groups: those that require minimal pruning; those that are pruned in spring and usually flower later in the year on the current season's growth; those that usually flower on the previous season's wood and are pruned after flowering in summer; and those of a suckering habit.

Minimal pruning

Shrubs that do not regularly produce vigorous growth from the base or lower branches, such as *Amelanchier*, need little pruning. Their chief need is the removal of dead, diseased, and damaged wood in order to maintain a balanced framework and to promote healthy growth. Minimal pruning should be done after flowering.

Spring pruning

Cut back dead or damaged stems to healthy wood or, if necessary, back to the base. Remove weak, twiggy, or spindly growth at the base. To retain an open framework, thin the remaining growth by one-fifth to one-third, by taking out the oldest wood at the base. Finally, prune the stems of the previous year's growth to within 2–4 buds of the older wood to stimulate new growth.

Some large shrubs, such as deciduous *Ceanothus*, form a permanent woody framework. In the first spring, lightly prune the main stems. In the second spring, cut back the previous year's growth by half. During late winter to early spring of subsequent years, prune hard, leaving only 1–3 pairs of buds of the previous season's growth. When mature, remove some of the oldest wood annually to prevent congestion.

Summer pruning

Deciduous shrubs that flower in spring and early summer bloom directly on wood produced in the previous year, or on laterals that grow from the previous year's wood. Examples are *Cotoneaster* and *Syringa*. Cut out all weak or damaged wood at planting time and trim the main shoots back to a healthy bud or pair of buds to promote the development of a strong framework. If any flowers are produced in the first season, prune again immediately after flowering, cutting back flowered shoots to a strong bud and removing any spindly shoots. Mulch and fertilize after pruning. Repeat this procedure in subsequent years.

As plants mature, after their third year, thin out up to one-fifth of the oldest wood annually, cutting back to within 5–8cm (2–3in) of ground level. When pruning it is important to maintain a well-balanced shape, so be flexible when following these guidelines. Some shrubs in this group begin vigorous growth during flowering, so when removing flowered wood take care not to damage new shoots, as this will spoil the following year's blooms. Others, such as *Chaenomeles*, have a naturally twiggy habit and, when grown as free-standing specimens, need little pruning when mature.

Pruning suckering shrubs

Some shrubs, such as *Kerria*, flower on the previous year's wood, but make most of their new growth from ground level, as opposed to flowering on a permanent woody framework.

At planting time, prune these suckering species by cutting out the weak growth but retaining the strong shoots and their sideshoots. During the following year, immediately after the plant has flowered, remove any weak, dead, or damaged stems and cut the flowered stems back hard to a strong bud or pair of buds. In the third year and in subsequent years, cut back one-quarter to one-half of all flowered wood to within 5–8cm (2–3in) of ground level.

Prune the remaining flowered shoots to about half their length, cutting them back to vigorous replacement shoots. Mulch and fertilize after pruning.

PROPAGATION

Shrubs and climbers may be propagated by seed, cuttings, layering, division, or grafting. Propagation by seed is simple, but can be slow in producing plants of flowering size, and is unsuitable for hybrids and cultivars, as the offspring will be variable. It is, however, the only way of increasing annual climbers and the easiest way of propagating herbaceous climbers.

A number of different techniques are used to propagate plants by cuttings. Many of these are relatively simple and have the advantage that the plants produced are identical to the parent plant, and so can also be used to increase cultivars, hybrids, and sports.

Growing from seed

Seed may be purchased or collected directly from plants in the garden. However, with species that bear male and female flowers on separate plants, individuals of both sexes must be grown in proximity to produce seed. Some seed requires pre-treatment before sowing. Those with hard coats, such as tree peonies, need nicking or rubbing with sandpaper so that they can absorb the water necessary for germination. Other hard-coated seeds need soaking in cold water (e.g. *Camellia*, *Pittosporum*), or warm water (e.g. *Caragana*, *Coronilla*) for a few hours before sowing.

The seeds of many temperate plants need a cold period before they will germinate. This is achieved either by sowing in an open frame in autumn, or by mixing seed with damp vermiculite and storing in the refrigerator at 0.5–1°C (33–34°F). Chilling requirements vary, from 6–8 weeks for some deciduous species, to as little as 3 weeks for some conifers. Check regularly and sow immediately when signs of germination are seen. Seed of most hardy species should be sown in autumn, and those of tender species under glass in spring. If buying seed in packets, always follow the sowing and planting out instructions.

To grow from seed, fill seed pans or trays with seed compost and firm gently with a presser board. Sow seed thinly onto the surface and cover them to their own depth with sieved seed compost. Water from above using a fine rose

SOFTWOOD CUTTINGS

1 *In spring, take cuttings of non-flowering shoots with 3–5 pairs of leaves. Reduce to 8–10cm (3–4in), making a straight cut below a node (see inset).*

2 *Remove lower leaves. Insert the cuttings, as soon as possible, into prepared pots of cutting compost, spacing them to ensure that the leaves do not touch each other.*

nozzle on the can. Mix tiny seeds with fine, dry horticultural sand to permit thin, even sowing; no additional cover of compost is needed. For fine seed, stand the seed container in a tray of water so that the compost can take up water from below, as watering from above may disturb the seed.

Cover the seed with a thin layer of horticultural grit, or place a clear plastic film or glass over the top to prevent the compost from drying out. After sowing, place the container in a cold frame, greenhouse, or propagator. Temperate species will germinate at about 12–15°C (54–59°F), while warm temperate and tropical species prefer 21°C (70°F). Inspect regularly and water as necessary.

Once the seed has germinated, spray the seedlings with a suitable fungicide to reduce the risk of grey mould (*Botrytis*) and other fungal diseases. When they are large enough to handle, with at least two leaves, gently lift them out of their container and replant them into trays (pricking out) or pots of compost.

Keep the seedlings in good light but out of direct sun until they have become established. The young plants should be allowed to adjust gradually to outside

SOWING SEED IN CONTAINERS

Place the seed in the ridge of a folded piece of paper and gently tap them out so that they are evenly distributed onto the seed compost. Cover the seed to their own depth with sieved compost. Water, label and place in a cold frame or propagator, depending on their temperature requirements. Prick the seedlings out when they are large enough to handle, holding them only by their leaves. Transfer the seedlings to trays or individual pots of compost. Protect from direct sun until established.

3 *Water the cuttings with a fungicide solution, label them, and place them in a propagator. Maintain a temperature of 18–21°C (64–70°F).*

4 *When well-rooted, harden off gradually, separate the cuttings gently, and pot up into individual pots. Keep the cuttings in a shaded position until well established.*

Mallet cuttings
Remove a stem produced on the previous year's growth. Cut it above each sideshoot and about 2.5cm (1in) below. Reduce the sideshoot to 10–13cm (4–5in) and trim off lower leaves.

temperatures (hardening off) until they are large enough to plant outside. If the plant roots fill the pots before they are large enough to plant out, they should be potted up into larger containers.

Softwood cuttings
Softwood cuttings are suitable for raising many, mainly deciduous, shrubs and climbers. They are taken in spring from fast-growing shoot tips and they will root quickly – but they will also wilt and rot rapidly if the correct growing conditions are not provided.

In early morning, take cuttings of pliable, single-stemmed shoots, and seal in opaque plastic bags to conserve moisture. Prepare and plant up (*see pp. 304–5*). After planting, water in thoroughly and apply fungicide. Place pots into a mist unit or propagator, or spray them regularly with a hand sprayer to keep moist. Maintain high humidity, at about 18–21°C (64–70°F). Spray weekly with fungicide.

Once rooted, harden the cuttings off gradually by admitting more air into the propagator. Gently remove the rooted cuttings from the pot and carefully separate by teasing the roots apart. The cuttings can now be potted up individually into potting compost and kept in a shaded position until they become well established.

Greenwood cuttings
Nearly all plants that are propagated by softwood cuttings can also be increased by greenwood cuttings. These cuttings use slightly firmer stems taken from vigorous shoots in late spring when growth has slowed down. Treatment is the same as for softwood cuttings, but greenwood cuttings may also benefit by being dipped in rooting hormone before they are inserted into the cutting compost. If the cutting is longer than 8–10cm (3–4in), remove the soft tip and trim off the bottom leaves. Greenwood cuttings may also be taken with a heel (*see p. 310*), which should be trimmed neatly.

Semi-ripe cuttings
Many evergreen and some deciduous shrubs can be propagated by semi-ripe cuttings. These cuttings are taken in mid- to late summer, or sometimes in early autumn, from the current season's wood that is firm at the base, but still soft at the tip. They will offer slight resistance to bending when flexed gently between thumb and fingers.

Cut a stem from the parent plant just above a node (leaf joint). Remove the sideshoots from the main stem and trim each one to 10–15cm (4–6in) long. These are the cuttings. Trim off the soft tip of each shoot and remove the lowest

Semi-ripe cuttings
Wound one side of the base of a semi-ripe cutting to stimulate rooting: carefully remove a shallow sliver of bark about 2.5cm (1in) long from one side of the base (see inset).

pair of leaves, cutting flush with the stem. Stimulate rooting by wounding the cutting (*see p. 306*) and dipping the base into hormone rooting powder. Insert it into a seed tray or individual pots filled with cutting compost and place in a propagator or a cold frame. Once the cuttings are well rooted, pot them on into larger pots. Harden them off and grow them on in their pots until they are large enough to transplant outside.

Mallet cuttings

Mallet cuttings, taken in mid- to late summer, are a variation of semi-ripe cuttings, with a mallet-shaped plug of the previous year's growth at their base (*see illustration, page 306*). They are usually used for shrubs with hollow or pithy stems, as the older section of wood is less prone to rot.

Prepare pots, or a propagator equipped with basal heat, by filling with either cutting compost or fine grade bark, or an equal parts mix of peat and perlite or grit. Select healthy shoots from the parent plant. Insert the mallet cutting into the compost, ensuring that leaves of adjacent cuttings do not touch, as this can create ideal conditions for rot fungi. Firm them in and water thoroughly with fungicidal solution. Place in a cold frame, or in a propagator with basal heat at 21°C (70°F). Keep the

---

PROPAGATING BY HARDWOOD CUTTINGS

1 *Select strong, healthy, fully ripened wood of the current season's growth, of about pencil thickness (see inset, left). Avoid thin, weak stems (centre), and old wood (right).*

HEALTHY WEAK OLD

2 *Remove deciduous leaves and soft growth from the tip. Cut into 15cm (6in) lengths. Dip the bases into hormone rooting powder.*

3 *Insert the cuttings into prepared pots of cutting compost, leaving about 2.5–5cm (1–2in) of the cutting above the surface. Label, water, and place in a cold frame.*

compost just moist. Cuttings in a cold frame will need insulation against frost, provided by covering the frame with hessian matting or old carpet. With basal heat, cuttings should have rooted by the following spring. Without heat, the cuttings will take a further growing season before they are well rooted, and they are unlikely to become well established before the following autumn. Keep the frame closed, but open to provide ventilation during mild winter weather. In late spring and early summer gradually admit air into the frame to harden off the cuttings, and begin to liquid feed them every two weeks. The cuttings will need good light, but must be protected from direct sun. When well rooted, pot them up into individual containers or plant them in a line out in open ground until large enough to plant out in their final position.

SIMPLE LAYERING

1 *Bend a young, low-growing, flexible, shoot down to soil, marking position with a cane. Dig a shallow hole. Trim off any sideshoots and leaves from the stem.*

2 *On underside of stem, cut a shallow tongue of bark (see inset) at the point where it touches the ground. Dust wound with hormone rooting hormone.*

3 *Peg stem down into soil using bent wire, so the stem's cut surface is held in contact with the soil. Fill in planting hole with soil and lightly firm down.*

4 *Once the layered stem has rooted, gently lift the new plant and cut from the parent plant, severing close to new, young roots. Pot up layer or plant out.*

Hardwood cuttings

Hardwood cuttings are suitable for a number of evergreen and deciduous shrubs and climbers. These cuttings are taken during autumn and early winter, from woody, fully ripened shoots of the previous season's growth (*see illustration on page 307*). Remove a length of stem of about pencil thickness, cutting at the junction between the current and previous season's growth. Trim into 15cm (6in) lengths, making a horizontal top cut just above a bud or pair of buds, and a sloping bottom cut, just below a bud. For evergreens, make the top cut just above a leaf and the bottom cut below a leaf. Remove the leaves from the lowest two-thirds of the stem. If the remaining leaves are large, cut them in half. Dip the end in rooting hormone.

Hardwood cuttings may be rooted in trenches in the open. Insert, about 15cm (6in) apart, against the vertical side of a flat-backed trench that is approximately 12–15cm (5–6in) deep, with a layer of coarse sand in the bottom. Alternatively, insert into pots of cutting compost in the cold frame 10cm (4in) apart. Leave 2.5–5cm (1–2in) of the cutting above soil level. Firm and water in well.

Keep the cuttings weed-free and well watered, and check the condition of open-ground cuttings after frost. Re-firm if they have been lifted by frost. Cuttings in the cold frame should root by the following spring. Harden off before potting up or planting out. Cuttings in the open should be left until autumn and then transplanted to their final position.

Layering

Layering is a method of propagation whereby a stem is encouraged to root before severing it from the parent plant. There are a number of variations, of which simple and serpentine layering are the most straightforward. Many deciduous and evergreen shrubs, such as *Aucuba*, *Carpenteria* and *Corylopsis*, can be increased by simple layering, and many climbers will self-layer by rooting where they touch the ground.

In autumn or spring, about 12 months before layering, prune a low branch on the parent plant to encourage vigorous shoots. In the ensuing year, prepare the soil to receive the layer. Ensure that the soil is friable, and add grit and humus to heavy soils. Peg a selected shoot down (*see illustrations on page 308*). Keep the rooting zone moist during the following growing season. Rooting should occur by autumn, but leave the shoot in place until the following spring.

Check that there is a good root system on the shoot before severing from the parent plant and potting up or planting out. If the rooting is poor, leave the shoot in place for a further growing season to allow more time for the root system to become established.

SERPENTINE LAYERING

A number of climbers can be increased by using the technique of serpentine layering. To do this, carefully bend a trailing shoot down from the plant to the previously prepared soil. Trim off any leaves and sideshoots on the stem. Wound the stem close to the nodes, dust the cut with rooting hormone, and then peg down with wire (see inset). Separate the developed plantlets in autumn and then trim the old stem from the new plants before replanting and staking.

HEEL CUTTINGS

Heel cuttings, which may be taken from greenwood, semi-ripe or hardwood stems, have a 'heel' of older wood at the base. The heel contains higher concentrations of natural growth hormones which assist the plant with rooting. Pull away a healthy sideshoot of the current season's growth, taking with it a heel of older wood at the base. Neaten the base by trimming off the tail with a sharp knife and then insert into cutting compost.

Layering climbers

The method for layering climbers is similar to that used for shrubs, except that suitable, vigorous stems are often produced without preparatory pruning. Vigorous growers such as *Wisteria* will root without the need for rooting hormone.

Serpentine layering produces a number of new plants from the same stem (*see illustration, page 309*).

Root cuttings

Some shrubs, such as *Aesculus parviflora* and *Rhus* species, and climbers, such as *Solanum*, can be propagated by root cuttings. Young shrubs may be lifted when dormant and the soil teased from the roots, although this is impractical for larger shrubs and climbers. For the latter, carefully dig a hole about 30–60cm (12–24in) from the base of the plant to expose the roots. Select roots between 0.5–1cm (¼–½in) thick, and cut them off

close to the main stem (*see illustration, right*). Keep them in moist sacking or in a plastic bag until they can be prepared.

Wash off the surface soil and remove and discard the fibrous lateral roots. Make a horizontal cut at the top of the cutting, and a slanting cut at the bottom, to ensure that they are inserted the right way up. Cuttings should be 5–15cm (2–6in) long. The colder the rooting environment, and the thinner the root, the longer the cutting needs to be; cuttings rooted outdoors need to be at least 10cm (4in) in length. Dust the cuttings with fungicide and insert them into the compost in a pot with the horizontal cut uppermost. Shrubs that root readily can be inserted directly into friable soil in open ground. For climbers, and shrubs that root less easily, prepare pots of cutting compost or a mix of equal parts peat and sand. Insert the cuttings vertically, at about 5–7cm (2–3in) apart, with the cut end horizontally protruding slightly. Top with a 3mm (⅛in) layer of grit or coarse sand. Label, water, and allow to drain. This should supply sufficient moisture until the shoots develop; over-watering is likely to lead to rotting, especially in cool conditions.

Place pots in the cold frame, cool greenhouse or propagator. Cuttings will root within ten weeks outdoors, or eight weeks in a cold frame or greenhouse. In the propagator, with gentle bottom heat at 18–24°C (64–75°F), new shoots should appear within four to six weeks.

If the cuttings are growing rapidly, pot up in potting compost once they have formed a good root system. Slower growing cuttings can be left in place for up to twelve months, but should be fed fortnightly with a liquid feed.

Heel cuttings

Plants can also be propagated by taking heel cuttings from either greenwood, semi-ripe or hardwood stems. This method had the advantage of providing the cutting with higher concentrations of natural growth hormones which assist the plant to root (*see illustration, left*).

PROPAGATION FROM ROOT CUTTINGS

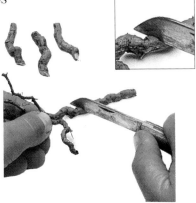

1 Dig a hole well away from the base of the plant to expose the roots. Select roots about 1cm (½in) thick and, using secateurs, cut off several sections measuring at least 10cm (4in) in length.

2 Wash off loose soil and remove and discard fibrous, lateral roots. Cut into sections about 5cm (2in) long, making a horizontal cut at the top end and an oblique cut at the base (see inset).

3 Insert each cutting vertically into prepared pots of cutting compost, so that the tips are just protruding from the surface of the compost. Top up the pot with a 1cm (½in) layer of sand. Water well, label them, and then place in a cold frame, greenhouse or propagator.

4 When well rooted, and plants have produced shoots about 2.5–5cm (1–2in) high, pot on into individual pots. Harden off and apply liquid feed during the growing season. Provide climbing plants with the support of canes. Plant out in autumn or spring.

GLOSSARY OF TERMS

Italicised words have their own entry.

ACID (of soil). With a pH value of less than 7, or lacking in lime; see also *alkaline* and *neutral*.

ADVENTITIOUS (of roots). Arising directly from a stem or leaf.

AERIAL ROOT. Plant root emerging from a stem above ground to provide anchorage.

ALKALINE (of soil). With a pH value of more than 7, or lime-rich; see also *acid* and *neutral*.

ANTHER. The part of a *stamen* that produces pollen.

AXIL. The angle between a leaf and stem where an axillary bud develops.

BLOOMED. Covered with a bluish-white deposit.

BRACT. A modified leaf at the base of a flower or flower cluster. It may resemble a normal leaf or be reduced and scale-like in appearance.

BUDDING. Bud-grafting, a form of grafting. See *Guide to Shrub and Climber Care*, pp.290–311.

CALYX. The outer part of a flower, usually small and green but sometimes showy and brightly coloured; it is formed from the sepals and encloses the petals in a bud.

CATKIN. A flower cluster, normally pendulous. Flowers lack petals, are often stalkless, surrounded by scale-like bracts, and are usually unisexual.

CLIMBER. A plant that climbs using other plants or objects as support: leaf-stalk climber by coiling its leaf stalks round supports; *root climber* by producing aerial supporting roots; self-clinging climber by means of suckering pads; *tendril climber* by coiling its tendrils round supports; twining climber by coiling its stems. *Scandent*, scrambling and trailing climbers produce long stems that grow over supports, attaching themselves loosely or not at all.

COROLLA. The part of a flower formed by the petals.

CORYMB. Flower cluster where inner flower stalks are shorter than the outer ones, giving a rounded or flat-topped head.

CUTTING. A section of a plant which is removed and used for propagation. For the various methods see *Guide to Shrub and Climber Care*, pp.290–311.

DECIDUOUS. Losing its leaves annually at the end of the growing season; semi-deciduous trees lose only some leaves.

DIVISION. A method of propagation by which a plant clump is divided into separate parts during dormancy. See *Guide to Shrub and Climber Care*, pp.290–311.

ELLIPTIC (of leaves). Broadening at the centre and narrowing towards each end.

EPIPHYTE. A plant which grows on another without being parasitic, obtaining nutrients and moisture from the atmosphere without rooting in soil.

EVERGREEN. Retaining its leaves all year round, although losing some older leaves regularly throughout the year. Semi-evergreen trees retain only some leaves or lose older leaves only when the new growth is produced.

FIREBLIGHT. A bacterial infection that attacks blossom first, then stems and foliage.

FISSURED. Bark that is split or cracked, due to age or weathering.

FLORET. A single flower in a head of many flowers.

FRIABLE. Soil of a crumbly texture, able to be worked easily.

GENUS (pl. genera). A category in plant classification, consisting of a group of related *species*.

GLOBOSE. Spherical.

GRAFTING. Method of propagation by which an artificial union is made between different parts of individual plants. The point of graft is the place on the grafted plant where this union has been made. See *Guide to Shrub and Climber Care*, pp.290–311.

HABIT. The characteristic growth or general appearance of a plant.

HEEL. The small portion of old wood that is retained at the base of a cutting when it is removed from the stem.

HERBACEOUS. Non-woody plant of which the upper parts die back to the rootstock at the end of the growing season. .

HERMAPHRODITE. Bisexual, having both male reproductive organ (*stamen*) and female (pistil) in the same flower.

HUMUS. The organic residue of decayed vegetable matter in soil. Also often used to describe partly decayed matter such as leafmould or compost.

HUSK. The rough outer layer of a fruit or seed.

HYBRID. The offspring of genetically different parents, usually produced accidentally or artificially in cultivation, but occasionally arising in the wild.

LATERAL. A side growth that emerges from a shoot or root.

LAYERING. A method of propagation by which a stem is induced to root by being pegged down to the soil while still attached to the parent plant. See *Guide to Shrub and Climber Care*, pp.290–311.

LEAFLET. A subdivision of a compound leaf.

LINEAR (of leaves). Very narrow with parallel sides.

LIME. Compounds of calcium; the amount of lime in soil determines whether it is *acid*, *neutral* or *alkaline*.

LOBE. A rounded projecting segment or part, forming part of a larger structure.

MICROCLIMATE. A small, local climate within a larger climate area, such as a greenhouse or a protected area of a garden.

MULCH. A layer of *organic* matter applied to the soil over or around a tree to conserve moisture, protect the roots from frost, reduce the growth of weeds, and enrich the soil.

NEUTRAL (of soil). With a pH value of 7, the point at which soil is neither acid nor alkaline.

ORGANIC. 1. Compounds containing carbon derived from decomposed plant or animal organisms. 2. Used loosely of mulches, composts, etc. derived from plant materials.

PALMATE (of leaves). Having four or more leaflets growing from a single point, as in horse chestnut (*Aesculus hippocastanum*).

PANICLE. A compound, branched raceme in which flowers develop on stalks (peduncles) arising from the main stem.

PERENNIAL. Living for at least three seasons; commonly used of *herbaceous* plants, and *woody* perennials, i.e. trees and shrubs.

PETAL. One portion of the often bright and coloured part of the *corolla*.

PETIOLE. The stalk of a leaf.

PHYLLODE. An expanded leaf stalk, which functions as, and resembles, a leaf blade.

PINCH OUT. Remove the growing tip of a plant, with finger and thumb, to induce the production of sideshoots or the formation of flower buds.

PINNATE (of leaves). A compound leaf in which the leaflets grow in two rows on each side of the midrib.

PROPAGATOR. A structure that provides a humid atmosphere for seedlings, cuttings, or other plants being propagated.

PROSTRATE. With stems growing along the ground. Also called procumbent.

RACEME. An unbranched flower cluster with several or many stalked flowers borne singly along a main axis, the youngest at the apex.

RECURVED. Of petals or leaves, curved backwards.

REVERT. To return to an original state, as when plain green leaves are produced on a variegated plant.

RHIZOME. Underground, creeping stem, that acts as a storage organ and produces leafy shoots.

ROOT. The part of a plant, normally underground, that functions as an anchorage and through which nutrients are absorbed. See also *aerial root*, *root climber*.

SCANDENT. Ascending or loosely climbing. See also *climber*.

SEPAL. Part of a *calyx*, usually green. They may be insignificant, but are sometimes showy.

SHRUB. A *woody*-stemmed plant, usually branching from or near the base.

SPATHE. One, or sometimes two, large *bracts*, that surround a flower cluster or individual bud.

SPECIES. A category in plant classification, the rank below *genus*, containing closely related, very similar individual plants.

SPORT. A mutation, caused by an induced or spontaneous genetic change, which may produce shoots with different characteristics, or flowers of a different colour from the parent plant.

STAMEN. The male floral organ, bearing an *anther* that produces pollen.

STIGMA. The area of the female part of the flower which receives pollen.

STRATIFICATION. The storage of seeds in warm or cold conditions to break dormancy and aid germination.

STYLE. The part of the flower on which the *stigma* is carried.

SUB-SHRUB. A plant that is *woody* at the base, but whose shoots die back in winter.

SUCCULENT. A plant with thick, fleshy stems and leaves, adapted to store water.

SUCKER. Shoot growing directly from a plant stem, or from below ground level, directly from the root.

TENDRIL. A modified leaf or stem, usually long and slender, able to attach itself to a support. See also *climber*.

TIP PRUNING. Cutting back the growing tip of a shoot to encourage sideshoots.

TRUSS. A compact cluster of fruits or flowers, often large and showy, e.g. rhododendrons.

TUBER. Thickened, usually underground, food storage organ, derived from a stem or root.

UMBEL. A usually flat-topped or rounded flower cluster, in which the individual flower stalks rise from a central point. In a compound umbel each primary stalk ends in an umbel.

VEGETATIVE GROWTH. Non-flowering, usually leafy growth.

VEGETATIVE PROPAGATION. The increase of plants other than by seed, normally producing genetically identical results.

WINGED (of seeds or fruits). Having a marginal flange or membrane.

WHORL. The arrangement where three or more organs, e.g. leaves, arise from the same point.

WOODY. With branches of hard, woody fibres, that persist, unlike soft-stemmed herbaceous plants. A semi-woody stem contains some softer tissue and may be only partially persistent.

Aristolochia
Evergreen or deciduous, twining and scrambling climbers with attractive foliage and flowers.
elegans see *A. littoralis*
littoralis (Calico flower) 254

Aronia (Chokeberry)
Deciduous shrubs, grown for their flowers, fruits, and autumn colour.
arbutifolia (Red chokeberry) 70
melanocarpa (Black chokeberry) 94

Artemisia
Evergreen, semi-evergreen, or deciduous shrubs and sub-shrubs, and also perennials, grown for their usually aromatic foliage.
abrotanum (Southernwood) 222
arborea see *A. arborescens*
arborescens 219
argentea of gardens see *A. arborescens*
Asarina erubescens see *Lophospermum erubescens*
Asiatic sweetleaf see *Symplocos paniculata*

Asparagus
Evergreen, semi-evergreen, or deciduous shrubs and climbers, grown for their attractive leaves. The genus includes perennials.
scandens 279

Asteranthera (Masterwort)
One species of evergreen climber with aerial roots.
ovata 255

Aucuba 309
Evergreen shrubs, grown for their foliage and fruits (produced only where plants of both sexes grow).
japonica 153
‘Crotonifolia’ 155
Australian bluebell see *Sollya heterophylla*
Australian rosemary see *Westringia fruticosa*

Azara
Evergreen shrubs and trees, with glossy leaves and yellow flowers, made up of a mass of stamens.
microphylla 53
serrata 90
Azores cherry laurel see *Prunus lusitanica* subsp. *azorica*

Azorina
Frost tender. One species of evergreen sub-shrub with attractive flowers in spring and summer.
vidalii 157

B

Bag flower see *Clerodendrum thomsoniae*
Balkan spurge see *Euphorbia characias* subsp. *wulfenii*
Balloon pea see *Sutherlandia frutescens*

Ballota
Evergreen or deciduous sub-shrubs, and perennials, grown for their flowers and leaves.
acetabulosa 220
Bamboo palm see *Rhapis excelsa*
Banana shrub see *Michelia figo*

Banksia
Frost tender. Evergreen shrubs and trees, grown for their flowers, foliage, and habit.
coccinea (Scarlet banksia) 74

Bauhinia
Frost tender. Evergreen, semi-evergreen, or deciduous shrubs and climbers with attractive flowers. The genus also includes trees.
galpinii (Orchid tree) 115
punctata see *B. galpinii*

Beaumontia
Frost tender. Evergreen, twining climbers with fragrant flowers and striking foliage.
grandiflora (Herald’s trumpet, Nepal trumpet flower) 236
Beauty bush see *Kolkwitzia amabilis*
Belgian evergreen see *Dracaena sanderiana*
Beloperone guttata see *Justicia brandegeeana*
Benjamin bush see *Lindera benzoin*

Berberidopsis
One species of evergreen, twining climber.
corallina (Coral plant) 254

Berberis (Barberry)
Deciduous, semi-evergreen, or evergreen spiny shrubs, grown for their usually yellow flowers, and for their fruits. Deciduous species have attractive autumn colour.
‘Barbarossa’ 136
darwinii (Darwin barberry) 25
empetrifolia 168
x *frikartii*
‘Amstelveen’ 287
‘Telstar’ 287
gagnepainii 76
julianae 77
linearifolia

‘Orange King’ 91
x *lologensis*
‘Stapehill’ 91
x *media*
‘Parkjuweel’ 287
‘Rubrostilla’ 212
x *stenophylla* 90
thunbergii
‘Bagatelle’ 287
f. *atropurpurea* 75
‘Aurea’ 206
‘Rose Glow’ 118
verruculosa 77

Bignonia
One species of evergreen, tendril climber; it may be deciduous in cool climates.
capreolata (Cross vine, Trumpet flower) 271
jasminoïdes see *Pandorea jasminoïdes*

Billardiera
Frost tender. Evergreen, twining climbers, grown for their fruits.
longiflora 277
Bine see *Humulus lupulus* ‘Aureus’
Bird-of-paradise see *Caesalpinia gilliesii*
Black broom see *Cytisus nigricans*
Black chokeberry see *Aronia melanocarpa*
Black-eyed Susan see *Thunbergia alata*
Black-gold philodendron see *Philodendron melanochrysum*
Blackthorn see *Prunus spinosa*
Bladder senna see *Colutea arborescens*
Bleeding heart vine see *Clerodendrum thomsoniae*
Bluebell creeper see *Sollya heterophylla*
Blue daisy see *Felicia amelloides* ‘Santa Anita’
Blue marguerite see *Felicia amelloides* ‘Santa Anita’
Blue passion flower see *Passiflora caerulea*
Blue potato bush see *Solanum* ‘Royal Robe’

Bomarea
Frost tender. Herbaceous or evergreen, scrambling climbers, grown for their tubular or bell-shaped flowers.
caldasii 271
kalbreyeri of gardens see *B. caldasii*

Boronia
Frost tender. Evergreen shrubs, grown for their flowers.
megastigma (Brown boronia,

Calycanthus
Deciduous shrubs. Purplish- or brownish-red flowers in summer with strap-shaped petals.
occidentalis (California allspice) 114

Camellia
Evergreen shrubs and trees, with attractive flowers in varying forms from late winter to spring.
'Cornish Snow' 61
'Dr Clifford Parks' 66
'Innovation' 65
'Inspiration' 64
japonica (Common camellia)
  'Adolphe Audusson' 67
  'Alba Simplex' 61
  'Alexander Hunter' 67
  'Althaeiflora' 67
  'Apollo' 67
  'Ave Maria' 62
  'Berenice Boddy' 62
  'Betty Sheffield Supreme' 63
  'Chandleri Elegans' see 'Elegans'
  'Contessa Lavinia Maggi' see 'Lavinia Maggi'
  'Elegans' 64
  'Elegans Supreme' 65
  'Gloire de Nantes' 65
  'Giulio Nuccio' 67
  'Janet Waterhouse' 61
  'Julia Drayton' 66
  'Jupiter' 65
  'Lady Vansittart' 61
  'Lavinia Maggi' 63
  'Margaret Davis Picotee' 63
  'Mathotiana' 67
  'Mrs D. W. Davis' 62
  'R. L. Wheeler' 67
  'Rubescens Major' 65
  'Sieboldii' see 'Tricolor'
  'Tomorrow's Dawn' 62
  'Tricolor' 63
'Leonard Messel' 65
reticulata
  'Butterfly Wings' see 'Houye Diechi'
  'Captain Rawes' 67
  'Early Crimson see 'Zaotaohong'
  'Early Peony' see 'Zaomudan'
  'Guixia see 'Captain Rawes'
  'Houye Diechi' 66
  'Moutancha' see 'Mudan Cha'
  'Mudan Cha' 64
  'Peony' see 'Mudan Cha'
  'Semi-plena see 'Captain Rawes'
  'William Hertrich' 66
  'Zaomudan' 66
  'Zaotaohong' 66
saluenensis 63
sasanqua
  'Narumigata' 61

'Shiro-wabisuke' 61
tsaii 61
x *williamsii*
  'Anticipation' 66
  'Bow Bells' 64
  'Brigadoon' 64
  'Caerhays' 66
  'Clarrie Fawcett' 62
  'Donation' 62
  'E. G. Waterhouse' 63
  'Francis Hanger' 61
  'George Blandford' 64
  'Golden Spangles' 65
  'J. C. Williams' 62
  'Joan Trehane' 63
  'Jury's Yellow' 62
  'Mary Christian' 64
  'Mary Larcom' 63
  'St Ewe' 64
  'Water Lily' 65
Campanula vidalii see *Azorina vidalii*

Campsis
Deciduous climbers with aerial roots, grown for their flowers.
x *tagliabuana*
  'Mme Galen' 274

Canarina
Frost tender. Herbaceous, scrambling climbers grown for flowers.
canariensis (Canary Island bell flower) 278
Canary-bird bush see *Crotalaria agatiflora*
Canary creeper see *Tropaeolum peregrinum*
Canary Island bellflower see *Canarina canariensis*
Candollea cuneiformis see *Hibbertia cuneiformis*

Cantua
Evergreen shrubs, grown for their showy spring flowers. Only *C. buxifolia* is generally cultivated.
buxifolia (Magic flower of the Incas) 162
dependens see *C. buxifolia*
Cape leadwort see *Plumbago auriculata*

Caragana
Deciduous shrubs, grown for their leaves and flowers.
arborescens (Siberian pea-tree)
  'Nana' (Dwarf Siberian pea-tree) 166

Carissa
Frost tender. Evergreen shrubs, grown for their flowers and habit. Spring–summer flowers.
grandiflora
  'Tuttlei' see *C. macrocarpa*

'Tuttlei'
macrocarpa (Natal plum)
  'Tuttlei' 91
spectabilis see *Acokanthera oblongifolia*

Carpenteria
One species of evergreen shrub with attractive flowers and leaves.
californica (Tree anemone) 99

Caryopteris
Deciduous sub-shrubs, grown for their foliage and blue flowers.
x *clandonensis*
  'Arthur Simmonds' 201
  'Heavenly Blue' 287
Cassia corymbosa see *Senna corymbosa*
Cassia didymobotrya see *Senna didymobotrya*

Cassinia
Evergreen shrubs, grown for their foliage and flowers.
leptophylla
  subsp. *vauvilliersii*
  var. *albida* 179

Catharanthus
Frost tender. Evergreen shrubs, grown for their flowers. Useful for summer bedding in cool climates.
roseus (Madagascar periwinkle, Rose periwinkle) 175

Cayratia
Evergreen and deciduous shrubs and tendril climbers, grown for their leaves.
thomsonii 276

Ceanothus (California lilac)
Evergreen and deciduous shrubs (sometimes tree-like), grown for their dense, mainly blue flowers.
'Autumnal Blue' 136
'Burkwoodii' 287
'Cascade' 287
x *delileanus*
  'Gloire de Versailles' 201
  'Topaz' 287
impressus (Santa Barbara ceanothus) 122
incanus (Coast whitethorn) 101
x *pallidus*
  'Perle Rose' 184
  'Puget Blue' 287
thyrsiflorus
  var. *repens* (Creeping blue blossom) 200

Ceratostigma
Deciduous, semi-evergreen, or evergreen shrubs, grown for their blue flowers and autumn colour.

ACKNOWLEDGMENTS

Key: l = left, r = right, t = top, c = centre, a = above, b = below

Photography by:

A. D. Schilling 78bl, 195br, 204br

A–Z Botanical Collection Ltd/Geoff Kidd 66cla, 67br; Mrs W. Monks 104tr, 143br; Rosemary Greenwood 187cla; Derek Gould 189bl; Frank Hough 192br

Gillian Beckett 33bl, 79br, 106br, 154bl, 157b, 163tl, 202tr, 208tr, 217tr, 253l, 254bl, 271tl, 278br, 280tr

Kenneth Beckett 241tl

Christopher Brickell 74tr, 75tl, 79bl, 82cra, 84br, 90tl, 115tr, 129tl, 135tl, 135tr, 185tr, 239tl

Pat Brindley 92br, 252tr

Brinsley Burbridge 249br

Neil Campbell-Sharp 42bl, 122tl, 257bl, 279tl

Eric Crichton 10bl, 11t, 47tl, 94tl, 168tr, 200br, 225tr, 257br, 271br

Raymond Evison 261tr, 261cra, 262cla, 264cla, 264clb, 264tr, 265cra, 266cla, 266crb

John Glover 74br, 171bl

Derek Gould 20br, 32tr, 87clb, 90br, 206tl, 207br, 245br, 261br, 274bl

Neil Holmes 121tr

Photos Horticultural 13t, 14t, 27tl, 28cla, 47r, 83tl, 85br, 144t, 187cra, 192tl, 230tl, 233tl, 255tl

RHS, Wisley/Mark Sleigh 145b

Peter Rose, Winkfield 285cra

Royal Botanic Gardens, Kew 117tr, 127

Harry Smith Collection 19tr, 21bl, 23, 24tl, 32br, 34br, 39br, 41tr, 42tr, 45tl, 47bl, 49bl, 51tr, 56bl, 58, 62br, 66br, 66cla, 71bl, 74l, 75bl, 78br, 79clb, 80tl, 80crb, 81tr, 81bl, 82tr, 84tl, 87tr, 88bl, 90bl, 109bl, 116br, 122r, 126tr, 128bl, 129bl, 131tl, 133l, 134bl, 136br, 137br, 149l, 159tl, 161tl, 161r, 172bl, 175br, 187br, 187tl, 188br, 191tr, 192cla, 198br, 199bl, 209tl, 212tr, 214tr, 214br, 215tr, 225tl, 238tl, 240tl, 241tr, 242r, 244br, 248tl, 249tl, 250tl, 251bl, 253br, 254tl, 254br, 256tl, 256tr, 256br, 262bl, 272l, 278tr, 278l, 282br

John Wright 186tl

Additional photography: Eric Crichton

Picture Research: Fiona Watson

Every effort has been made to trace the copyright holders. Dorling Kindersley apologizes for any unintentional omissions and would be pleased, in such cases, to add an acknowledgment in future editions.

Abbreviations			
C	centigrade	in	inch, inches
cm	centimetre	m	metre
cv.	cultivar	mm	millimetre
F	fahrenheit	oz	ounce
f.	forma	sp.	species
ft	foot, feet	subsp.	subspecies
g	gram	var.	variant